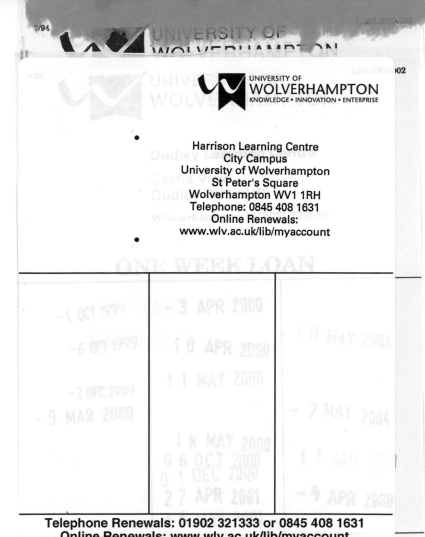

WOMEN
IN MASS
COMMUNICATION

Second Edition

PAMELA J. CREEDON
EDITOR

SAGE Publications
International Educational and Professional Publisher
Newbury Park   London   New Delhi

For information address:

SAGE Publications, Inc.
2455 Teller Road
Newbury Park, California 91320

SAGE Publications Ltd.
6 Bonhill Street
London EC2A 4PU
United Kingdom

SAGE Publications India Pvt. Ltd.
M-32 Market
Greater Kailash I
New Delhi 110 048 India

Printed in the United States of America

Library of Congress Cataloging-in-Publication Data

Main entry under title:

Women in mass communication / edited by Pamela J. Creedon — 2nd ed.
    p.   cm.
    Includes bibliographical references and index.
    ISBN 0-8039-5386-0. — ISBN 0-8039-5387-9 (pbk.)
    1. Mass media and women. 2. Mass media—Study and teaching
3. Women in the mass media industry. I. Creedon, Pamela J.
P94.W65W67   1993
302.23'082—dc20   93-20782

94 95 96 97 10 9 8 7 6 5 4 3 2

Sage Production Editor: Astrid Virding

Contents

Preface

This book has grown over the past four years. The contributors to this edition have changed and grown: A number are now tenured and promoted, several have changed jobs and/or universities, and there are some additional perspectives from new contributors.

Overall, the book has been a collective, cooperative effort from the start. The royalties from the first edition of the book, approximately $5,000 through April 1992, have been donated to the Commission on the Status of Women of the Association for Education in Journalism and Mass Communication to fund research and programming. It wasn't difficult to decide where the money could best be used—for the past five years authors in the book have chaired the Commission (Lana F. Rakow, H. Leslie Steeves, Jane Rhodes, myself, and Sue A. Lafky); another author, Maurine H. Beasley, has been elected president of the association for 1993-1994.

Royalties from the second edition will continue to fund activities of the Commission as it moves ahead on major challenges to the status quo in journalism and mass communication education. One of the projects supported by the Commission has been a much-needed survey of AEJMC membership to provide a basis from which to monitor the status of women and minorities in the organization. Some of the findings of this benchmark study are reported in Chapter 14.

The second edition is quite a bit different from the first: Several chapters have been added; chapters have been expanded and updated; a conscious effort has been made to be more inclusive; and the contents have been organized according to three primary themes.

The first section deals with broad research issues. It overviews the work that has been and is being done on incorporating feminist theory and feminist perspectives in mass communication, particularly in terms of race and culture.

The second section contains perspectives on sexism and economic equity in the mass communication industries. Studies in this section vary considerably in methodology, but tell the same story of the Sisyphean journey for women in mass communication practice. This section has been expanded to include the professional perspective of Marlene Sanders in

Chapter 10a and an overview of the literature on visual images of women in the media in Chapter 12.

The final section, which focuses on faculty and students in mass communication programs, has also been expanded. In addition to a new chapter on the construction of gender in textbooks, it has a new chapter that analyzes the status of women faculty in journalism and mass communication. The section also provides some specific recommendations for educators and students who wish to participate in challenging gender values.

New to this edition is an index. An index is a very important tool in making a book useful and accessible. Doing an index is much more than a clerical task because the choices made about what to include and what not to include reflect one's standpoint and understanding of the context of meaning within the chapters.

Some Very Important Acknowledgments

I thought the process of putting together a second edition of a book would be much easier than a first. I was wrong. It was much more invigorating, challenging, and frustrating than I suspected. However, once again, thanks to the support and assistance of many people, the book is a much better product for all of the effort.

I am indebted to a number of people. The second edition would not have been possible without the support of my professional leave by Pamela J. Shoemaker, director of The Ohio State University School of Journalism. Sophy Craze, who replaced Ann West as the book's editor at Sage Publications, gave me additional insight and support to make the book what it needed to be.

As in the first edition, a great deal of theoretical direction came from Lana Rakow and H. Leslie Steeves. Marilyn Crafton Smith and Sue Lafky also played vital roles in the second edition, helping me to explore new concepts and to find a way to fit it all together. Other authors performed way above the call of duty to complete their chapters or revisions, in spite of illness, technology traumas, and unreasonable deadlines.

Finally, I want to thank several other special people. Kelly Reid helped to keep me grounded when I needed it and let me theorize when I needed that too. My mother, Louise Creedon, is a source of constant support for every project that I ever attempt. My sister, Barb, and my brother, Jim, have supported me in being myself and have always provided help whenever I've asked for it. And thanks to my late father, James, for teaching me his strong sense of personal and professional ethics.

PART ONE

Perspectives on Re-Visioning Gender Values in Mass Communication

1 The Challenge of Re-Visioning Gender Values

PAMELA J. CREEDON

Have things gotten better or worse for women in mass communication since the first edition of this book in 1989? On the surface, things probably look better. We can point to a few more women—white and women of color—who are visible in media roles and content. In journalism and mass communication education today, more than two thirds of the students enrolled in print and broadcast news, photo and magazine journalism, and advertising and public relations are women.[1]

The quiet revolution in values that we expected to result from the gender switch, however, has not occurred. The potential of the gender switch to bring about a paradigmatic rupture in the basic assumptions of mass communication practice is as yet largely unrealized.

Why? There are many plausible explanations, principal among them are: Feminist theory has had little effect on mass communication research; the increased number of women in the field has had no significant effect on the practice; mass communication education has remained essentially unchanged. The remainder of this chapter will examine the viability of these three explanations and define a re-visioned approach to bringing about a transformation in gender values in mass communication education and practice.

The approach taken for this examination is called re-visioning. I first learned about the process of "re-vision" on reading Adrienne Rich's 1979 book titled, *On Lies, Secrets, and Silence*. As she explained it, "Re-vision—

AUTHOR'S NOTE: I would like to thank Lana F. Rakow, H. Leslie Steeves, Marilyn Crafton Smith, Ramona Rush, Susan Kaufman, Sue A. Lafky, Kelly Reid, and Patty Hickey for comments and conversations that have been helpful in developing this chapter.

the act of looking back, of seeing with fresh eyes, of entering an old text from a new critical direction—is for women more than a chapter in cultural history; it is an act of survival. Until we can understand the assumptions in which we are drenched we cannot know ourselves" (p. 35).

I have since found that re-visioning process expands one's ability to see how assumptions affect women and men, as well as various groups of people, differently. Broadly construed and applied, the re-visioning process also can expose hegemonic assumptions about race, class, sexual preference, ethnicity, and so forth.

One might expect that such careful scrutiny of assumptions, or re-vision, to be endemic to mass communication. Budding journalists are certainly taught to approach every story critically, but fairly, to be especially careful about making assumptions. But, for reasons that will become clear in the next few pages, assumptions about gender and gender values, which are in-stitutionalized within mass communication, are not easily seen and, when made visible, are assiduously defended as essential, natural.

Since 1977 the majority of students enrolled in journalism and mass communication education programs have been female, so I suggested in the first edition of this book that this lack of scrutiny of assumptions was an anomaly. I expected that as women entered the workforce, they would act as change agents forcing gender assumptions to be exposed.

In fact, the potential to bring about change in the dominant value system became the theme of the first edition of this book. We explored the potential of the gender switch to energize a widespread re-vision of values in the mass communication canon. We examined the potential effect that the en-trance of a critical mass of women into traditional mass communication jobs in newspapers, magazines, radio, television, public relations, and adver-tising would have. We concluded the volume with a future scenario in which communication media were available to and used for political and cultural participation by all members of society.

We have eliminated that picture of an idyllic future in this edition. In its place we have inserted a more pragmatic vision and a call to direct action at a more basic level—our curricula. We retained the re-visioning theme, however, because we still believe in the need to change mass communica-tion as we know it today—whether or not the impetus is provided by the gender switch.[2]

Developing a Shared Language About Gender

Understanding gender is at once very simple and very complex. The deeper one probes into scientific, political, economic, or other cultural assumptions about gender the more complex and more diverse the ranges of opinion prove to be.

Feminist theory has shown us that gender is not just the name of a person, place, or thing. Gender is a verb, the act of naming that person, place, or thing (Rakow, 1986). Gendering, the gerund, is the process that begins the moment that a baby takes its first breath of cultural pollution. Gender differences, then, are the "sets of attributes socially and culturally constructed on the basis of birth assignment as male or female" (Bleier, 1987, p. 111).

Feminist ontology, or the study of how we are, suggests that the gendering process is grounded in ideas from the "Enlightenment," a European philosophical movement dating from the 1700s, that coincided historically with the medical science belief that the male of the species carries a miniature baby in his sperm. During the "Enlightenment" period thinking was organized into dualisms—mind/body, public/private, nature/culture, reason/emotion, and so forth. The assumption underlying these pairs of supposed opposites was that one of them described a male characteristic and the other a female characteristic, leading us to the conclusion that male is the opposite of female. The result is that we now "live in a culture built on a particular set of gender assumptions and structured to amplify if not produce gender asymmetries and inequalities, and we come to view these differences as part of the natural world" (Bleier, 1987, p. 112).

Page duBois (1982) describes how male citizens in the fifth century B.C. knew themselves to be different from females through their Amazon myths and different from animals through their Centaur myths; then the philosophers of the fourth century B.C. told them *why* they were different "by describing a social order based on ideas of hierarchical difference, of the natural inferiority of women to men, of foreign slaves to citizens, of animals to slaves" (p. 150). In the Enlightenment, as discussed earlier, these differences were organized into dualisms.

Feminist scholarship has shown how assumptions about gender differences based on these dualisms have provided the framework for most of our knowledge about science, history, and so forth (Benderly, 1987; Eisler, 1987; Lenz & Myerhoff, 1985; Rakow, 1986). For example, in the mid-1800s empirical studies showed that women's brains were somewhat smaller than men's brains. This led scientists to the conclusion that women were less intelligent than men, rather than to the recognition that brain size was relative to the physical size of one's body. More recently, scientists have been looking for biological explanations of mathematical propensities. Based on empirical studies of male rats, they have conjectured that because testosterone apparently enhances the development of the right hemisphere in a *male rat's* brain—the side of the brain that purportedly controls visuospatial skills—*men* have naturally superior mathematical ability (Bleier, 1987).

Assumptions about gender influence news content, too. The prevailing meaning attached to the facts about the gender switch has been that a female majority in the field will cause decline in salaries and status for the field. "Velvet ghetto," for example, is the term that has been used to describe the impact of women in public relations, while the "pink-collar ghetto" label is attached to predominantly female reporting positions. Both terms certainly undercut a positive construction of the meaning of women entering the field.

Feminists have argued that attaching a negative meaning to the gender switch fits closely with George Gerbner's (1978) description of cultural resistance. According to Gerbner, when the dynamics of a social movement threaten or promise to overpower or restructure a particular set of social relations or values, the dynamics of cultural resistance come into play. He describes the three main tactics of resisting change as discrediting, isolating, and undercutting (p. 48).

Elisabeth A. van Zoonen (1992), who studied the role of the media in constructing a public identity for the women's movement in the Netherlands in the late 1960s and early 1970s, found clear evidence of cultural resistance in news stories she analyzed. She concluded that coverage of the movement was based upon three storylines: women's " 'emancipation' is legitimate, 'feminism' is deviant; movement activists are quite different from and not representative of 'ordinary' women; the movement is directed against men" (p. 453).

Without using storylines based on dualistic assumptions, a re-vision of the media coverage of feminism would include the various voices of the movement, without presenting one as superior to the other and without creating an image of weakness out of diversity. A re-vision of the storyline about the gender switch might feature its potential to revitalize an industry, which is losing touch with its audience and is plagued by job cutbacks, circulation declines, advertising revenue losses, and market fragmentation (Faludi, 1991).

Feminisms

To better identify and understand the feminist perspectives on change used throughout the book, a brief overview of feminist theory will be helpful. In an essay written in 1987 about feminist theories and media studies, H. Leslie Steeves distinguished feminisms by several broad organizing principles—biologistic, individualistic, social psychological or sociocultural, and economic. While Steeves suggested that all forms of feminism have a contribution to make, she suggested that socialist feminism—which comes to terms with the public-private dichotomy on which patriarchy depends and which addresses crucial contextual considerations of class and race—offered the greatest potential as a comprehensive framework for addressing women's oppression in mass communication (p. 95).

More recently, Kathryn Cirksena and Lisa Cuklanz (1992) have suggested five feminist frameworks for communication studies along with the basic dualisms that they address: liberal (reason and emotion); socialist (public and private); radical (nature and culture); psychoanalytic (subject and object); and cultural (mind and body). The central dualism in each of these frameworks can be reduced to its primary opposition or fundamental assumption of male versus female (e.g., nature/male, culture/female).

Cirksena and Cuklanz have further identified three approaches from feminist theory designed to challenge the fundamental gender values that structure the system: "integration; valorizing the female; and rejecting binarisms for more multifaceted ways of thinking about the world" (p. 37). Integration favors an acceptance and valuing of masculine and feminine components to achieve wholeness. Valorizing the female is a strategy that places more value on female-associated attributes. In their opinion the most compelling approach is found in the arguments of those who reject binarisms and suggest that human identity is a product of multiple intersections such as gender, race, ethnicity, and sexuality.

Activist strategies that derive from these theories largely fit into two overarching categories: liberal and radical. The liberal approach seeks reformation of the existing system; the radical approach seeks transformation through the establishment of some type of new order (e.g., valorizing the female or rejecting binarisms). "In practice, feminists at both ends of the spectrum [both radical and liberal], engaged in similar projects, [are] sometimes distinguishable only by their analysis of the forces leading to the need for the project" (Hansen & Philipson, 1990, p. 8, cited in Byerly & Warren, 1992).

The following three sections on feminist theory, mass communication practice, and pedagogy will examine why—in spite of the gender switch—a significant re-visioning of gender values in mass communication has yet to take place.

Feminist Theory and Mass Communication Research

As in the first edition, the content of this book is framed from a feminist perspective. This means that the various authors have approached their chapters using feminist epistemological premises to study the assumptions of how we know and apprehend meaning. Another characteristic of feminist research is its emphasis on action; its goal is to change the unequal status of women in the culture.

> This emancipatory impulse can be found in positions ranging from a radical insistence that the purpose of research is a total transformation of patriarchy and corresponding empowerment of women, to the more liberal insistence that specific attention be paid to the policy implications of the research on women. (Fonow & Cook, 1991, p. 6)

The strategies used to accomplish these two goals—transformation and reformation—change over time as contexts change. The result is that although the goals remain constant, it appears that what feminists want changes. However, it's just that the media focus shifts, and maybe our individual attention shifts depending on where we are ideologically. Radical feminism has always been alive, well, and maligned.

A good case study in reformist feminism is equal opportunity because it shows how changing contexts affect feminist strategies (see also Chapter 10a by Marlene Sanders). The first Conference on Equal Opportunity was held at the White House in 1965. Initially, equal opportunity seemed to signal good times ahead for women and minorities. So in the late 1960s and early 1970s, laden with unconscious baggage about proper roles and behavior, and convinced that rejecting "women's" values was necessary to gain respect and promotions, the first wave of "equal opportunity" baby boomers entered the job market. Feminists riding on the crest of this wave in mass communication aggressively confronted employment barriers through legal action at *Newsweek, Time, Fortune, Life, The New York Times, Detroit News, The Washington Post,* and the *Associated Press,* among others. However, soon it became apparent that a lawsuit could not address the fact that women only had been given "equal" opportunity to prove constantly they were "as good as" or better than men.

Shana Alexander (1988) compares the movement of the equal opportunity generation into the labor force with the re-opening of Pandora's box:

> When we decided to be equals, we meant, without thinking of it, equals in a man's world. We were still playing by their rules, or defining equality in their terms. We forgot that we are different from men; we are the other, we have different sensibilities. Today younger women across America are paying for our error. (p. 44)[3]

By the 1980s it was clear that this dress-alike, look-alike contest in the workplace had produced a double bind for women. Women were expected to perform "equally" in the workplace and at home. Susan Kaufman (1992) describes how the media coverage of lifestyle changes unwittingly helped to expose this double bind. Media messages told women they were liberated, while visual images showed them how miserable they were trying to be superwomen.

Aware of the implicit dualisms and unequal "rewards" of equal opportunity, women in the 1990s are voicing anger about their treatment in the public and private spheres. In mass communication practice, the activism has a new face: the aggressive legal challenges of the 1970s have given way to caucuses or support groups organizing for negotiated change (Byerly & Warren, 1992). This new face of feminist activism is portrayed as concern about "women's" issues by the media. Government and industry responses, for example, have ranged from the development of sexual harassment policies to "protect" women, to the addition of a "Mommy" track, which reinforces women's roles as primary caregivers.[4]

Though feminist challenges in the name of equal opportunity have brought new responses from government and industry, all in all they have brought about little substantive change because the basic issue—the gendered nature of the system—is never addressed.

Incorporating Feminist Theory in Mass Communication

Has the feminist call for a new paradigm—a new value system derived from a new gender order—affected mass communication research? According to Cirksena and Cuklanz, because "dualistic assumptions inform most communication studies, feminist criticisms should be central in developing alternative modes of structuring knowledge and practice in communication," (p. 40); however, they find that communication scholarship has been resistant to feminist critiques, particularly on the quantitative and interpretative fronts.

Feminists argue that quantitative techniques distort women's diverse experiences and silence women's voices by translating them into categories predefined by researchers. For example, in Chapter 2, Jane Rhodes points out how women of color are homogenized with white women in quantitative research looking at gender differences. In Chapter 18, Carolyn Stewart Dyer suggests that for women and other oppressed groups the "mainstream" interpretation of the First Amendment is hollow. She explains how freedom of speech is a negative freedom—*freedom from* government interference in speech, rather than a *right to* speak. Yet "mainstream" communication research largely continues to ignore these and other female-centered insights (e.g., Rakow, 1992; Rush & Allen, 1989).

Resistance can take many forms, particularly when scholarship pushes on the boundaries of established theory. Three primary resistance strategies appear in mass communication research: annihilation, accommodation, and appropriation.

In a research context, annihilation occurs when feminist theory, or the input of individual feminists, is ignored or considered to be of no importance, which, in effect, symbolically annihilates its value. Symbolic annihilation has been described by Gaye Tuchman (1978a) as the systematic portrayal of women in media content in stereotypical, demeaning, or trivializing ways. As Chapter 13 by John R. McClelland illustrates, sufficient studies of media content have been done to prove the existence of this strategy beyond an empirical doubt. Evidence of annihilation in a research context is difficult to prove, as Ramona Rush (1992) detailed in her initial laundry list of "Scholargate's Dirty Tricks." It can include not inviting qualified females to become members of a research team to administer a grant, recommending only particular instructors as thesis/doctoral committee chairs, and selectively excluding papers, awards, honors, offices, and so forth from administrative reports, grant applications, reviews, and other evaluations.

The accommodation response can involve acknowledging the existence of feminist scholarship in one's research, but not incorporating it in any substantive way in the construction of meaning. This approach is found in studies where the fact that social changes have occurred is acknowledged, but the interpretation of the study's findings is based on traditional, dominant values. Seen from another angle, accommodation also means cutting and splicing the feminist perspective so that it fits within the traditional research framework. Karen and Sonja Foss (1989) conducted an examination of the use of a feminist perspective in communication research over a 10-year period in articles appearing in five journals. They concluded that the publication process requires "adjustment to the expectations of the status quo" (p. 81).

When new strains of mass communication scholarship develop without conscious acknowledgment of their relationship with—or origins in—feminist scholarship, we have evidence of a third form of resistance: scholarly appropriation. For example, framing theory, which is gaining popularity in mass communication research, traces its development primarily through male theorists—e.g., Goffman (1974), Gitlin (1980), and Gamson (1989). Equally strong primary roots, it can be argued, could be developed from feminist film theory and critical cultural studies, particularly feminist Marxist analysis.[5]

Paradigm Paralysis

A paradigm is "the entire constellation of beliefs, values, techniques, and so on shared by the members of a given community" (Kuhn, 1962,

p. 175). The existing or old paradigm is derived from "Enlightenment" values discussed earlier. New paradigm scholarship, according to Karen and Sonja Foss (1989) is distinguished by five assumptions: (1) wholeness; (2) process; (3) interconnectedness of knowledge; (4) approximation (rather than absolute truth); and (5) cooperation.

Ignored, accommodated, or appropriated, feminist scholarship's potential to challenge assumptions and constructions of gender in the dominant paradigm in mass communication has been muted. Carolyn G. Heilbrun (1987) believes that feminist scholars in literary theory like herself have dropped a "bomb" on the dominant paradigm—not unlike that dropped by Darwin on the dependable, classical world of the scientific community in 1857—but are still waiting for its full impact to be felt.[6]

For several reasons, the "bomb" either hasn't dropped, or else it hasn't been noticed in mass communication. One explanation may be that the dearth of female full professors, deans, department chairs, and directors means that many feminist scholars in mass communication, particularly those who use radical epistemological premises, are assistant or associate professors. Challenges, therefore, when they occur, are easily resisted because they come from the bottom up—from the grassroots, rather than from the traditional hierarchical top-down pattern, in which only senior members of the profession, who are perceived as having the appropriate status, can challenge the dominant research paradigm.

Another explanation may be that the paralysis in mass communication is endemic. The field is a hybrid social science, a by-product of "parent" disciplines like sociology and psychology. If it is endemic paralysis, then the energy for transforming mass communication will need to come, not from grassroots feminism within mass communication, but through "trickle-down" feminism from outside the field, a paradigm change that flows from a "parent" to its "offspring."

Ultimately, however, the answer to the inertia may be more fundamental. Thinking about it brings to mind the ubiquitous scene of a lone woman in a meeting room filled with men: she makes a suggestion, only to be told by her boss, "That's interesting Ms. Jones, now would one of you men like to make it?" So why is it the least bit surprising that feminists, who insist that the hierarchically structured, dualistic assumptions that we inherited from the Greeks are inadequate, who insist it is time for another rupture in the paradigm, but who are speaking within a room filled with patriarchal theory, are not being heard?

The dilemma for feminists is "how to challenge and simultaneously gain visibility and legitimation" for a perspective that advocates a rupture in the content and form of the dominant paradigm (Foss & Foss, 1989, p. 73). Will there come a time, feminists ask, when a Ph.D. from an institution that fills its graduates with patriarchal theories and paradigms will be viewed as a disadvantage, rather than as a badge of courage?

Methodology

Two assumptions frame the following discussion: (1) All research has a political dimension, and (2) when the political dimension of research challenges the orthodoxy (dominant values), it creates controversy. The content of this book challenges many research assumptions so it is vital to acknowledge some of the anticipated controversy explicitly. First, the chapters in this book represent a rich blend of quantitative and qualitative research and a variety of approaches, including personal testimony—often considered a hallmark of feminist scholarship and openly rejected by some scholars. Further, this book's mixture of methodologies may trouble those who believe that there is one superior or preferred methodology and research orientation.

Feminist scholars are quick to remind us that *methodology* refers to the techniques and practices used in the research process, but *methodolatry* is quite a different story. "Methodolatry," as Mary Daly (1973) describes it, is:

> Tyranny [which] hinders new discoveries. It prevents us from raising questions never asked before and from being illuminated by ideas that do not fit into established boxes and forms. The worshippers of Method have an effective way of handling data that doesn't fit into the Respectable Categories of Questions and Answers. They simply classify it as non-data, thereby rendering it invisible. (p. 11)

This book purposely features alternative methodologies for approaching the study of gender. This sharing and acceptance of a variety of methodologies serves to support a variety of approaches to gender research by not modeling conformity to a dominant pattern.

Some feminist scholars are also cautioned to avoid reverse "methodolatry" when reading chapters in the book that use quantitative data from surveys to report on gender differences. Sandra Harding (1987) recommends that feminists practice "fruitful ambivalence" with regard to the scientific method in order to infuse it with feminist values and goals (p. 302). Authors of chapters using quantitative approaches in this book are keenly aware of the pitfalls of reductionist and linear thinking when analyzing for causation.

Some empiricists may find portions of the content of this book to be equally unacceptable because the empirical approach to knowing and knowledge does not allow one to draw conclusions based on impressions and experiences. The empirical approach requires clear evidence that the scholar approached the subject with an hypothesis that specifies an expected finding and then tested this hypothesis.

Another approach taken by chapter authors is to provide a qualitative review of literature and studies in a particular area. While qualitative research has its critics, it has champions in many disciplines. It is especially valuable where an existing body of knowledge has not been systematically examined and organized from a theoretical perspective. Scholars can then use these descriptive reviews as a springboard for analysis and recommendations.

The blend of these methodologies is part and parcel of changing the system and improving women's (and ultimately people's) position in it. "We need to begin seeing these disputes not as a process of naming issues to be resolved but instead as opportunities to come up with better problems than those with which we started" (Harding, 1987, p. 287). The diverse methodologies used throughout this book are designed to be a theoretical and practical example of the essence of re-visioning.

Feminism and Mass Communication Practice

As the chapters throughout Part II demonstrate, the progress of women and people of color in the mass communication workforce in the last four years has been slow at best, and there's evidence of slippage in some areas. By *progress* we mean the move toward an improved status for women, in terms of both workplace opportunities and environment.

Of course, we are able to "see" more women in news roles as news deliverers and makers. And we have continuing examples of what Carolyn Byerly and Catherine Warren (1992) call feminist interventions in newsmaking, "a collection of strategies and activities used to resist and overcome male hegemony in news organizations and content."[7]

Yet the process of gathering and defining the news has not changed fundamentally.[8] There are several possible explanations. First, mass communication is a profit-driven, advertising-supported business, and the entrance of women in the field has not offset the power of these relationships to determine news content (Gamson, 1984; Tuchman, 1978a). Second, females entering the news industry find that the news definers still are predominantly white males, and these editors and owners control the hiring and firing decisions. Third, workplace routines and norms force reporters to conform to dominant values, rather than act on empowering values.

Let's examine the third explanation for the lack of change in news values a little more closely. We can learn from sociological studies that entry-level employees adapt to workplace norms, reasoning, for example, that they must prove themselves, the job market is tight, or they are lucky to be employed. Over time they learn to internalize and rationalize the norms as fair and balanced, rather than to question the assumptions upon which they are based (Blaxall & Reagan, 1976; Davidson & Gordon, 1979).

These sociological findings can be applied to mass communication. Joann Byrd (1992), ombudsman [sic] for *The Washington Post,* recently wrote that "as long as journalists have no motives other than keeping the public informed, no personal or political axes to grind, news judgment is fair" (p. 106). Her comment reflects an internalized journalistic norm that, aside from external constraints such as space and time, fairness is based on the impartial or detached observation of a reporter.

From a feminist perspective, it is vital to re-vision assumptions about impartiality and detachment upon which the fairness norm is based. One premise of feminist epistemology is that impartial or detached observation is not necessarily a desirable goal because fully acknowledging our emotional responses to the world can serve as a source of insight and restore a lost dimension to current conceptions of rationality (Fonow & Cook, 1992).[9]

Another important concept from feminist theory is standpoint epistemology: knowledge and knowing are inescapably contextualized (Cirksena, 1987; Harding, 1986). News judgments are ways of knowing, and as such they are inescapably gendered.

Feminist standpoint epistemology seeks to replace "the Enlightenment vision captured by empiricism" by explaining scientific knowledge as useful in understanding the world as it exists, but that a feminist vision is more complete, less distorting of the relations between the natural and social worlds (Harding, 1987). Standpoint epistemology seeks to replace the "Enlightenment" vision that women were less capable of reason than men, with theories that suggest that "knowing" is a characteristic of social experience including gender, race, class, ethnicity, and sexual preference. Gorelick (1991) suggests:

> Women's oppression is a complex of many contradictions and requires a new standpoint-based methodology, created by researchers and participants of diverse race, class, and other oppressed groups, refocusing and re-visioning knowledge based on theory, action and experience. (p. 461)

Standpoint epistemology stands as a direct challenge to traditional newsgathering norms including objectivity.

The Objectivity Apologetic

An apologetic serves as defense against an accusation of fault, wrongdoing, or inappropriate behavior. Objectivity in a journalism context was defined by Walter Lippmann in 1922: "It means that he [sic] is ready to let things be what they may be, whether or not he wants them to be that way. It means that he has conquered his desire to have the world justify his prejudices" (p. 46).[10]

Objectivity is the journalistic apologetic that defends against the use or acknowledgment of affect or standpoint in the perception and construction of news stories. It is actually a relatively recent journalistic norm that evolved from controversies surrounding news coverage around the turn of the century, which demonstrated that facts flow from interpretation; they are neither absolutely true or accurate (Gamson, 1984).

Gaye Tuchman (1978b) describes the objectivity apologetic as a strategic ritual that protects journalists from charges of bias toward special or official interests. As yet no one has been able to define the ritual's parameters or procedures in order to guarantee that it is always a part of the news judging process. This ambiguity actually may be a tacit acknowledgment that journalists can't report facts objectively because news sources represent the dominant interests in society.

> Opinions that support existing arrangements of economic and political power are more easily treated as facts, while facts that are troublesome to the prevailing distribution of class power are likely to be dismissed as opinionated. And those who censor dissenting views see themselves as protectors of objectivity and keepers of heterodoxy when, in fact, they are the guardians of ideological conformity. (Parenti, 1986, p. 50)

In sum, objectivity is a normative ideal; in practice, objectivity *is* a standpoint —white and male.

Why haven't women changed the definition of news? Until journalists— women and men—are able to see the values embedded in the gendered, normative assumptions of journalism routines, the influx of women in journalism and mass communication can only affect the biological sex of the field.

Page duBois (1982) explains why re-visioning assumptions is so important in transforming values:

> The clearest of assumptions in an age are those which are unspoken, which buttress every argument, which form the background of every utterance. In a sense the study of the transformation of discourse about difference is a case of silence becoming speech, of a society finding a language in which to speak of things unsaid in the past. (p. 18)

It remains to be seen whether the challenge to transform will start from within the traditional media system or from without, using feminist channels of communication where content and leadership in the communication process is woman-centered (see Chapter 4 by Marilyn Crafton Smith). In fact, the development of more accessible computer communication technologies may enable feminist transformative efforts to be linked both across the United States and globally.

Feminism and Pedagogy in Mass Communication

Pedagogy involves all aspects of the professional functioning of a teacher, including textbooks, classroom instruction, advising, and curricula. It also involves aspects of the environment in which the teacher functions, such as collegiality, sexual harassment, power harassment, and mentoring.[11] What effect has feminism had on pedagogy in mass communication?

By tracing the general evolution of feminist scholarship, we can explore its impact on pedagogy. Brenda Dervin (1987) describes three stages in feminist scholarship: (1) a focus on sex differences; (2) a focus on improving society and making women more like men; (3) a focus on giving voice to women. Recent scholarship points to the existence of a fourth stage: a focus on woman-centered meaning, which moves beyond simply allowing women to voice their experiences within the existing system to a place where women create their own meaning and communication structure (e.g., Brown, 1990; Rakow, 1992).

It is fairly easy to find evidence of the impact of Stages 1 and 2 in mass communication pedagogy. For example, we now have historical documentation that women worked as printers during the colonial era, thanks to the work of Susan Henry cited in Chapter 19. Maurine H. Beasley, Marion Marzolf, Kay Mills, and numerous others have contributed additional research insights into the roles of women in other aspects of journalism history.

Linda Steiner suggests in Chapter 17 that journalism textbooks have reached Stage 2: making women more like men. By studying college textbooks published in the last century, she found that women had moved from invisibility to anomaly; then through an essentialist period when men and women were thought to have "natural" differences in reporting abilities; to the present generation of textbooks, which have seen fit to erase gender in the interest of objectivity. Using feminist standpoint theory, Steiner suggests that current textbooks ignore the fact that perceptions are always grounded in the material conditions of people's lives; erasing gender in them denies that people have different bodies and experiences.

The relatively facile incorporation of feminist scholarship from Stages 1 and 2 can be explained in terms of its "fit" within the dominant value system reflected in "mainstream" scholarship. According to Susan Henry in Chapter 19, the reason why feminist scholarship has been readily accepted in journalism history is: Journalism history research has not challenged fundamental assumptions about journalism history; the male-developed framework for history has been left largely intact.

However, as the chapters in Part III of the book demonstrate, Stages 3 or 4—giving voice to women or developing woman-centered meaning, are much more difficult to find. The success of the first edition of this book provides evidence that some efforts are underway to create courses that deal with the topics of gender and race in the media. Often these are isolated or discrete courses, however, rather than sweeping, inclusive, curriculum-wide efforts. Certainly, individual teachers also have moved in the direction of alternative meanings, but full incorporation of Stages 3 and 4 in "mainstream" pedagogy appears to be a long way off.

Because faculty have a significant role in the development and content of the curriculum, as well as relative freedom to decide what will be taught in an individual class, it is important to understand more precisely who is teaching tomorrow's communicators, what issues they face, what concerns they have, and how they perceive their roles.

In 1989, members of the Association in Journalism and Mass Communication (AEJMC) passed a resolution pledging to work toward 50% representation of women and minorities on faculties by the year 2000.[12] However, the results of a 1992 survey of AEJMC members reported in Chapter 14, show that only 28% of the association's members were women and only 8% were minorities—including women.[13] The combined total of women and minorities was 34%. As Larissa S. Grunig discusses in Chapter 16, the haste with which the percentages are increased takes on added significance with regard to concerns about advising, mentoring, and role modeling, particularly since females constitute more than 60% of the undergraduate students enrolled in journalism and mass communication education, and racial and ethnic minorities—including women—are about 19% of undergraduates (Kosicki & Becker, 1992).

Only about 13% (39) of the respondents to the survey were women with the rank of full professor, a figure well below the national average across disciplines of 17%, according to data from the National Science Foundation. This is not surprising, however, since the cohort analysis completed by K. Viswanath and Gerald M. Kosicki shows that 8 out of 10 women teaching in mass communication today entered within the past 12 years. Moreover, the dearth of female full professors sends a significant negative message to female students who see women in less powerful positions. Adding to the image of female powerlessness are the findings of Susan Kaufman (personal communication, January 29, 1993) that women deans,

directors, or department chairs lead only 11% (21) of the 188 programs at
schools that belonged to the Association of Schools of Journalism and Mass
Communication in 1992.[14]

The realities for women in journalism and mass communication education are also not encouraging. Textbooks and scholarship have not kept
pace with feminist theory. The number of female faculty members is
increasing, but women are likely to be young, untenured, outsiders. However, we can find a call to action in Chapter 20. A proposal for a new curriculum that is holistic and inclusive and that addresses some primary
pedagogical concerns is outlined by Lana F. Rakow. It's a model that is
operating successfully at the University of Wisconsin-Parkside, where, not
surprisingly, she is the associate vice chancellor.[15]

Let's return to the question raised in the introduction to this chapter:
Why is the potential of the gender switch in mass communication to bring
about changes in basic values in the field as yet unrealized? The answer,
which is given in various ways throughout this book, is threefold: Communication scholarship suffers from paradigm paralysis; women entering
the mass communication professions are constrained by gendered norms;
and communication pedagogy is moving too slowly on its avowed commitment to be more inclusive. These themes are developed in depth in the
remainder of the book: Part I. Perspectives on Re-Visioning Gender Values
in Mass Communication; Part II. Perspectives on the Status of Women in
the Mass Communication Industries; Part III. Perspectives on the Mass
Communication Classroom.

A Concluding Polemic on Book Editing and Standpoint

Many argue that language is a key ingredient in the consensus construction of meaning and reality. A living language is one that communicates
the consensus meaning of its culture and cultural norms. It is also structured and enforced by norms and rules based on the assumptions of those
who make the rules. Thus, if a word is not in the dictionary, if a sentence
is not in proper grammatical form, or if capitalization style is not followed,
it violates a rule and it's consequently considered to be wrong.

Feminists are making creative and controversial challenges to those who
enforce the rules of the English language. In *Amazons, Bluestockings and
Crones: A Feminist Dictionary,* Cheris Kramarae and Paula A. Treichler
(1992) discuss ways and words that feminists have used to break through
the gatekeeping, rule-enforcing mechanisms that preserve what Julia
Penelope (1990) calls PUD (Patriarchal Universe of Discourse).

To participate in the challenge, a conscious decision was made to violate several conventions of style in this book. Racism in the language is recognized by capitalizing *Black* when referring to race for two reasons. One is that *Black* or *African American* is often used to designate race or ethnicity and has replaced the term *Negro*.[16] Second is to recognize and draw attention to the political nature of issues involving race. Conversely, the term *white* is not capitalized in this book in order to symbolically deny equal political power to the term.

A second decision was made to honor the preference of Black feminist author bell hooks that her name appear without capital letters.[17] A request to break this capitalization rule was made, but rejected in the first edition of the book and her name was capitalized. The request to honor bell hook's preference is being made again, and whatever the outcome, this paragraph will remain as evidence of the change or lack thereof.

A third violation will be found in the reference lists at the conclusion of each chapter. The guidelines of the Publication Manual of the American Psychological Association (APA), third edition, have been modified. The modification is rather simple: Chapter reference sections include the first names of authors, rather than just initials as APA dictates. The meaning of the modification is that readers will most likely be able to tell if an author is male or female, which should provide them with at least a crude gender clue about an author's assumptions. It also slightly reduces the authority of a last name, which is almost always derived from men (husbands or fathers).

Finally, it is important to acknowledge that the authors in this book do not presume to speak for all women. bell hooks suggests that women's experiences of patriarchy differ by race, class, and culture (hooks, 1984). Although there are 28 contributors in this second edition, we are predominantly white, highly educated, and female. Although many of us do share aspects of similar cultural backgrounds, as feminists we have grown to understand that—like gender—race and class are also relationships of power, not simple variables that can be plugged into an equation to determine difference. Toward that end we have made a conscious effort to include research from other cultural perspectives in this edition of the book. However, the overall focus of the book is North American, particularly on the U.S. media system. Chapter 3 by H. Leslie Steeves is a notable exception, providing a look at the global context of gender and mass communication.

Much as this book intentionally does not advance one preferred research methodology or feminist theory, it should not be construed as an argument for a superior (female) value system. As Rakow says in Chapter 20, the concept of re-visioning gender values advances the need to value diversity— not any one particular set of values. Riane Eisler (1987) suggests that "if we free ourselves from the prevailing models of reality, it is evident that there is another logical alternative: there can be societies in which difference is not necessarily equated with inferiority or superiority" (p. xvii).

The power of a critical mass of women and people of color in journalism and mass communication will not come from numbers alone, but from the conscious commitment to start a chain reaction spreading in myriad directions that will challenge the values of the mass communication enterprise in which women—and men—must take responsibility for the meanings they create and for those they omit. From a feminist perspective, the unwillingness to acknowledge one's participation in the creation of meaning is a heinous political act.

Notes

1. The figures were provided by Lee B. Becker from the 1991 data set generated by the Census of Enrollment in Journalism and Mass Communication Project, portions of which are reported annually in *Journalism Educator* (Kosicki & Becker, 1992). Actual enrollment figures by major or sequence and gender are: news editorial—70% female; broadcast news—66% female; photojournalism—80% female; magazine—79% female; advertising—68% female; public relations—81% female. The only areas in which males outnumber females are broadcast production—54% male, and broadcast production and news combination—52% male.

2. Although I do not believe that women students are powerless to change professional norms and pedagogy, cultural conditioning and the nature of the academic system militate against such activism.

3. I do not construe this argument to be essentialist. Rather, I think it represents a recognition that culturally derived differences between men and women affect women's ability to participate equally in the workplace.

4. Some policies acknowledge a parent track, in which fathers and mothers have opportunities for extended leave or postponement of career decisions like tenure, for child rearing or family illness. However, this solution—Mommy or Parent Track—continues the devaluation of the private sphere and makes progress in the public sphere more arduous for women, possibly producing the outcome of earlier career burnout.

5. One could argue that, rather than from appropriation, this resistance stems from a lack of awareness of feminist theory. However, this argument would be indefensible if made in response to an obvious omission of the contribution of "mainstream" scholarship. It should be acknowledged that Gaye Tuchman (1978b) is often mentioned in the work of framing theorists. However, her work is mentioned in isolation and not related to later feminist scholarship in the area.

6. Carolyn Heilbrun decided not to wait any longer. She resigned from the English department faculty at Columbia University in 1992.

7. An example of feminist intervention used by Byerly and Warren (1992) is the 1991 protest by *The New York Times* employees over coverage of the William Kennedy Smith rape story. Anna Quindlen, 1992 Pulitzer prize winning columnist at *The New York Times*, summed up the tenor of the outrage: "Any woman reading the *Times* profile now knows that to accuse a well-connected man of rape will invite a thorough reading not only of her own past but of

her mother's, and that she had better be ready to see not only her name but her drinking habits in print" (Quindlen, 1991, p. E 17).

8. I have selected the news editorial field for this illustration; however, similar gendered norms are found in other areas of mass communication such as public relations and advertising.

9. Susan Henry (1990) provided an example of how she became aware of nearsightedness and blind spots in her work on the life of Doris Fleischman, a pioneer in public relations history, business partner, and wife of Edward L. Bernays. Henry found that she had ignored the last third of Fleischman's life, a time when Fleischman left the public limelight and wrote a book glorifying the role of a wife. "Simply put, she did not live the life that I wanted her to live, so I at first did not look carefully at it, and I wrote very little about it" (p. 20).

10. Clearly Lippmann wrote this from a subjective viewpoint, before controversies about the power of sexist language and generic pronouns in constructing reality had been articulated. The 3-year-old son of a colleague reinforced the importance of continuous feminist critiques of how language influences reasoning when he shared his early attempt at deductive thinking: "If Mary is the mother and Jesus is the son, then Joseph must be God because God *is* the father." He likely understands the rest of the message too: If Joseph is God, and Joseph is a man, then man *is* God.

11. Ramona Rush proposed the term *political power harassment* in a paper titled: *Old Issues—Unresolved: Women Educator's Status in the Academy*, which was presented at the AEJMC convention in Montreal, August, 1992.

12. The resolution, introduced by Ramona Rush, was passed at the 1989 AEJMC national convention. It states: "Therefore, be it resolved that the Association for Education in Journalism and Mass Communication (AEJMC) encourages its members and affiliates to have at least 50 percent of their faculties and administrations comprised of females and minorities by the year 2000." AEJMC also revised its Constitution in 1990 to reflect this commitment to diversity in gender and race and to pledge that it "will monitor the status of women and minorities on a regular basis, report its findings to the membership, and take affirmative steps to rectify problems" (AEJMC Constitution, Revised 1990, Section 5). The AEJMC membership survey reported on in Chapter 14 was conducted as part of this monitoring mandate.

13. It should be noted that not all individual faculty members at AEJMC member institutions are members of AEJMC. Approximately 3% of the survey respondents were African American, 2.8% Asian American, and less than 1% Hispanic. The number of minority respondents was 88, of whom only 22 were females. A more detailed report on the minority data from the survey was being prepared at this writing.

14. Susan Kaufman (1992) addressed the roadblocks encountered by women in their movement into administrative leadership positions in journalism and mass communication programs in her doctoral dissertation. She identified these roadblocks as (1) isolation, (2) denial by younger women that problems persist, (3) lack of administrative training, (4) lack of mentors and role models, (5) lack of a system by which to identify future leaders.

15. Responding to a comment that academic feminism has had little impact on the real world, a recent issue of *The Women's Review of Books* (February, 1993) contained a series of articles by feminists describing their attempts to incorporate theory into their classrooms. The disciplines covered included: theology, medicine, English, geography, law, women's studies, social work, architecture, and management.

16. H. Leslie Steeves has noted that the convention appears shifting to a strategy of alternating *Black* and *African American* in one's text.

17. This paragraph was written before I talked with the publisher about bell hooks. As suggested by Marilyn Crafton Smith, I am planning to bolster my request this time by asking: How do you handle e.e. cummings?

References

Alexander, Shana. (1988, September). A woman undone. *Ms., 17*(3), 40-45.

Benderly, Beryl Lief. (1987). *The myth of two minds: What gender means and what it doesn't mean.* Garden City, NY: Doubleday.

Blaxall, Martha, & Reagan, Barbara. (1976). *Women and the workplace.* Chicago: University of Chicago Press.

Bleier, Ruth. (1987). A polemic on sex differences in research. In Christie Farnham (Ed.), *The impact of feminist research in the academy* (pp. 111-130). Bloomington: Indiana University Press.

Brown, Mary Ellen. (Ed.). (1990). *Television and women's culture: The politics of the popular.* Newbury Park, CA: Sage.

Byrd, Joann. (1992). Fair's fair: Unless it isn't. *Media Studies Journal, 6*(4), 103-112.

Byerly, Carolyn M., & Warren, Catherine. (1992, May). *Toward an examination of feminist intervention in newsmaking.* Paper presented to the Feminist Scholarship Interest Group at the meeting of the International Communication Association, Miami.

Cirksena, Kathryn. (1987). Politics and difference: Radical feminist epistemological premises for communication studies. *Journal of Communication Inquiry, 11*(1), 19-28.

Cirksena, Kathryn, & Cuklanz, Lisa. (1992). Male is to female as _ is to _: A guided tour of five feminist frameworks for communication studies. In Lana F. Rakow (Ed.), Women *making meaning: New feminist directions in communication* (pp. 11-44). Norwood, NJ: Ablex.

Daly, Mary. (1973). *Beyond God the Father.* Boston: Beacon.

Davidson, Laurie, & Gordon, Laura Kramer. (1979). *The sociology of gender.* Chicago: Rand McNally.

Dervin, Brenda. (1987). The potential contribution of feminist scholarship to the field of communication. *Journal of Communication, 37,* 107-120.

duBois, Page. (1982). *Centaurs and Amazons: Women and the pre-history of the great chain of being.* Ann Arbor: University of Michigan Press.

Eisler, Riane. (1987). *The chalice and the blade.* San Francisco: Harper & Row.

Faludi, Susan. (1991). *Backlash: The undeclared war against American women.* New York: Crown Publishers.

Fonow, Mary Margaret, & Cook, Judith A. (Eds.). (1991). *Beyond methodology: Feminist scholarship as lived research.* Bloomington: Indiana University Press.

Foss, Karen A., & Foss, Sonja K. (1989). Incorporating the feminist perspective in communication scholarship: A research commentary. In Kathryn Carter & Carole Spitzack (Eds.), *Doing research on women's communication: Perspectives on theory and method* (pp. 65-91). Norwood, NJ: Ablex.

From theory to practice. (1993, February). *Women's Review of Books, 10*(5), p. 17.

Gamson, William A. (1984). *What's news: A game simulation of TV news.* New York: Free Press.

Gerbner, George. (1978). The dynamics of cultural resistance. In Gaye Tuchman, Arlene Kaplan Daniels, & James Benet (Eds.), *Hearth and home: Images of women in the mass media* (pp. 46-50). New York: Oxford University Press.

Gitlin, Todd. (1980). *The whole world is watching.* Berkeley: University of California Press.

Goffman, Erving. (1974). *Frame analysis: An essay on the organization of experience.* New York: Harper & Row.

Gorelick, Sherry. (1991). Contradictions of feminist methodology. *Gender & Society, 5*(4), 459-477.

Hansen, Karen V., & Philipson, Ilene J. (1990). Women, class and the feminist imagination. In Karen V. Hansen & Ilene J. Philipson (Eds.), *Women, class and the feminist imagination* (pp. 3-40). Philadelphia: Temple University Press.

Harding, Sandra. (1986). *The science question in feminism.* Ithaca, NY: Cornell University Press.

Harding, Sandra. (1987). The instability of the analytical categories of feminist theory. In Sandra Harding & Jean F. O'Barr (Eds.), *Sex and scientific inquiry* (pp. 283-302). Chicago: University of Chicago Press.

Heilbrun, Carolyn G. (1987). Women, men, theories and literature. In Christie Farnham (Ed.), *The impact of feminist research in the academy* (pp. 217-225). Bloomington: Indiana University Press.

Henry, Susan. (1990, October). *Near-sightedness and blind spots in studying the history of women in journalism.* Paper presented at the American Journalism Historians Conference, Coeur d'Alene, ID.

hooks, bell. (1984). *Feminist theory: From margin to center.* Boston: South End.

Kaufman, Susan J. (1992). *Developing administrative leadership among women in journalism and mass communication education programs: A conceptual model.* Unpublished doctoral dissertation, Indiana State University, Terre Haute.

Kosicki, Gerald M., & Becker, Lee B. (1992). Annual census and analysis of enrollment and graduation. *Journalism Educator, 47*(3), 61-70.

Kramarae, Cheris, & Treichler, Paula A. (1992). *Amazons, bluestockings and crones: A feminist dictionary.* London: Pandora Press.

Kuhn, Thomas S. (1962). *The structure of scientific revolutions.* Chicago: University of Chicago Press.

Lenz, Elinor, & Myerhoff, Barbara. (1985). *The feminization of America: How women's values are changing our public and private lives.* Los Angeles: Jeremy Tarcher.

Lippmann, Walter. (1922). *Public opinion.* New York: Free Press.

Okin, Susan Moller. (1989). *Justice, gender and the family.* New York: Basic Books.

Parenti, Michael. (1986). *Inventing reality: The politics of the mass media.* New York: St. Martin's.

Penelope, Julia. (1990). *Speaking freely: Unlearning the lies of the fathers' tongues.* Elmsford, NY: Pergamon.

Quindlen, Anna. (1991, April 21). A mistake. *The New York Times,* p. E 17.

Rakow, Lana F. (1986). Gender research in communication. *Journal of Communication, 36*(4), 11-26.

Rakow, Lana F. (Ed.). (1992). *Women making meaning: New feminist directions in communication.* New York: Routledge & Kegan Paul.

Rich, Adrienne. (1979). When we dead awaken: Writing as re-vision. In Adrienne Rich (Ed.), *On lies, secrets, and silence.* New York: Norton.

Rush, Ramona R. (1992, August). *Old issues—unresolved: Women educators' status in the academy.* Paper presented at the annual convention of the Association for Education in Journalism and Mass Communication, Montreal.

Rush, Ramona R., & Allen, Donna. (1989). *Communication at the crossroads: The gender gap connection.* Norwood, NJ: Ablex.

Steeves, H. Leslie. (1987). Feminist theories and media studies. *Critical Studies in Mass Communication, 4*(2), 95-135.

Tuchman, Gaye. (1978a). *Hearth and home: Images of women in the mass media.* New York: Oxford University Press.

Tuchman, Gaye. (1978b). *Making news.* New York: Free Press.

van Zoonen, Elisabeth A. (1992). The women's movement and the media: Constructing a public identity. *European Journal of Communication, 7,* 453-476.

2 "Falling Through the Cracks"
Studying Women of Color in Mass Communication

JANE RHODES

Women of color remain the most often ignored group in mass communication research despite the growing interest in gender as a category of analysis, and the development of feminist methodology. Even a cursory look at the literature in mass communication and journalism reveals that women of color continue to be marginalized as subjects of inquiry, or are absent altogether.

Questions of race, ethnicity, and gender are becoming increasingly popular topics of study in contemporary communication research; however, scholars tend to treat these categories as disparate variables. Thus studies that consider gender usually focus on white women, and assume that the results can be generalized to all women. Research that focuses on race emphasizes the experiences and perceptions among the men of a given group, and assumes that the results include women. Indeed, particularly in the social sciences, gender has no color, and race has no sex—the discrete and separate categories demanded by survey research, content analysis, experimental design, and many qualitative research methods, makes it difficult to recognize the intersections of race, gender, class, sexual orientation, and other social constructions.

Increasingly, feminist scholars are acknowledging that the applications of feminist theory to the study of communication has been centered around middle-class white women, and that progress in developing a broader and more inclusive theoretical framework has been halting, at best (Houston, 1992; Rakow, 1992). This dilemma is further compounded by how the politics of difference manifests itself in research. Scholars are suggesting that a preoccupation with the obvious traits of race, gender, or sexuality— or in the words of critical theorists, the fetishization of difference—has obscured the underlying meaning and political implications of these categories. In the process, women of color often fall through the cracks unless a deliberate effort is made to study them as subjects, audiences, and producers of mass communication.

An obstacle to this research agenda is the fact that much of the scholarship concerning women of color is interdisciplinary, requiring the researcher to increase their field of knowledge dramatically if they are to do justice to the task. This is a daunting process; one must know the literature on African American, Native American, Asian American women, and Latinas, or the vast categories of foreign-born women. And this material stretches beyond most traditional training in journalism, mass communication, and media studies.

One must also consider the political and career implications for conducting research on women of color. In an academic environment in which feminist scholarship is marginalized, at best, or condemned as political indoctrination, at worst, such projects can be a risky proposition for any scholar. White women and men are cautious about treading in an area in which they may not be familiar, and can be openly hostile to research they consider outside the mainstream. Women of color, who are in painfully small numbers in higher education, are often reluctant to jeopardize their fragile status in the academy by taking on controversial projects. Paula Matabane has noted that among African American women in mass communication, "only a tiny fraction has an interest in feminist theory or women's issues more broadly" (Matabane, 1989, p. 120). Today, the numbers of investigators studying women of color is reflected in the paucity of the research.

The present discussion will focus on African American women as an example of this scholarship, but it should not be taken as representative of all women of color. In the past decade, there has emerged a growing body of writing about African American women in the humanities and social sciences. For example literary scholars have traced the stereotyped roles of Black women in Anglo and Afro-American literature such as the mammy, the concubine, the tragic mulatto, and the matriarch, and suggests that Black women writers such as Paule Marshall, Toni Morrison, Gwendolyn Brooks, and Zora Neale Hurston have been instrumental in transforming these images.

Historical studies in the past 15 years have gathered the writings and documents of Black women since colonial times (Lerner, 1973), studied the emotional, physical, and sexual subjugation of female slaves (D. White, 1985), uncovered the stories of Black women as leaders in the antislavery, women's suffrage, and civil rights movements (Giddings, 1984), and analyzed the Black woman's resistance to slavery and sexual oppression (Davis, 1981), as well as numerous other accomplishments.

Social scientists, beginning with Ladner in 1971, have called for research that acknowledges the Black woman's experience as a legitimate area of study. One sociologist characterized Black women's experience as a dialectic in which the "dominant image of black women as 'beasts of burden' stands in direct contrast to American ideals of womanhood: fragile, white, and not too bright" (Dill, 1979, p. 555). More than a decade later increasing numbers of scholars have seized the opportunity to examine African American women's social, psychological, and political status and role in society.

But most mass communication research has done little more than document the absence of African American women in the media. For example, in the area of television studies, one group of investigators noted that Black women were "largely ignored and excluded from significant TV roles" (Hinton, Seggar et al., 1974, p. 423). Research on the images of women on television continued to echo this theme throughout the 1970s and early 1980s, with at least one scholar declaring that women of color were the most underrepresented group in television (Reinhard, 1980, pp. 169-246). In the next decade, another study suggested that the lack of representations of Black women in dramatic television programs "both reflects and functionally perpetuates their powerlessness" in American society (Rhodes, 1991, p. 33). Although theoretical and methodological approaches to such inquiry have become more sophisticated, the results have generally remained the same.

A review of four prominent journals in mass communication published in the last 3 years bears out this contention.[1] A recent issue of one journal, which was devoted to media representations of difference, spent only one paragraph out of seven articles discussing women of color. One empirical study of African American journalists argued that gender was not a factor in job satisfaction, while another study of racial differences in media did not use gender as a variable (see Bramlett-Solomon, 1992, and Becker, Kosicki, & Jones, 1992). One need not belabor the point. Regardless of methodology, women of color are generally rendered invisible by mass communication research, or their invisibility is simply reinforced.

One exception to this trend has been the work of media historians, many of whom have been active in resurrecting the stories of African American women communicators. Work in the past decade has revealed that there were several dozen Black women journalists working for the Black press at the end of the 19th Century, the most famous being Ida Wells-Barnett (Beasley & Gibbons, 1977, pp. 38-46); and women of color have gained an increasing (but still grossly underrepresented) presence in the nation's newsrooms in the past 15 years (Mills, 1988, pp. 174-195). Recent studies have uncovered little-known women who have made significant contributions to the mass media (see, e.g., Bramlett-Solomon, 1991; Diggs-Brown, 1992; Rhodes, 1992; Streitmatter, 1991).

There is little doubt that this exclusion of women of color in the research literature parallels their economic, social, and political status in society. It also reflects Black women's distance from feminism and the women's movement. bell hooks suggests that poor and non-white women were alienated from the early white feminist movement because it was frequently anti-male, it only "provided bourgeois white women with a public forum for expressing their anger," and did not offer potential solutions to minority women's problems (hooks, 1984, pp. 68, 70, 75). Black women activists and scholars frequently shunned issues about gender that they perceived to be irrelevant to their lives. Feminism was seen as a threat to the stability of the Black community, and Black women were, and still are, often faced with demands from white feminists and Black men to choose which form of oppression is most important.

Yet, out of this struggle a Black feminist movement has evolved that identifies the connections between racial and gender oppression. hooks has described this transformation: "for black women, our struggle has not been to emerge from silence into speech but to change the nature and direction of our speech, to make a speech that compels listeners, one that is heard" (hooks, 1989, pp. 5-6).

Black feminism developed from the juncture between anti-racist and anti-sexist struggles and has been most visibly manifest in the works of Black women writers (E. White, 1985, p. 7). In the 1980s a small group of Black women began to construct a theoretical base that focused on their status in society, and that theory has influenced much of the scholarly progress in other disciplines cited above. Some locate the beginning of contemporary Black feminism with the publication of the Combahee River Collective statement in 1977, which declared: "We believe that sexual politics under patriarchy is as pervasive in Black women's lives as are the politics of class and race. We also often find it difficult to separate race from class from sex oppression because in our lives they are most often experienced simultaneously" (Hull, Scott, & Smith, 1982, p. 16).

Since then Black feminists in literature, arts, and the academy have articulated a wide range of views, but generally share a commitment to focus attention on the distinct needs and experiences of Black women and to critique sexism in the Black community, while at the same time acknowledging a deep connection to and solidarity with Black men.

More recently, Patricia Hill-Collins identified several themes of Black feminism; among them are the quest to control negative representations of

Black women, and the need for group self-definition (Collins, 1990). She found a "recurring humanist vision" in Black women's intellectual thought that challenges the hierarchies of power in American society. For example, numerous cultural critics have identified the damaging stereotypes of African American women—that is, mammy or Black matriarch—that justify and reinforce their oppressed position. Collins credits Black feminists with being in the forefront of efforts to counteract these images, and create alternative and more realistic representations. A recent example is Julie Dash's film *Daughters of the Dust,* the first feature-length movie produced and directed by an African American woman. Said Dash about the film, "I wanted it to be healing, cleansing, and empowering" (Rule, 1992, p. B 3).

The themes articulated by Collins offer a range of possibilities for scholars interested in the media images of women of color, or in how women find a vehicle of expression through mass communication. A handful of studies have sought to apply the theoretical perspectives of Black feminism to studies of culture and communication. For example, Bobo (1988) examined the responses of African American women to the film *The Color Purple* and examined their positive readings of the film. She found that in contrast to whites, who engaged in an uncritical assessment, or African American men who offered an angry response, African American women were both critical of the movie's racist content and found the themes of Black women's independence and survival empowering.

Carby's study of Black women blues performers in the early days of the music recording industry considers how race, class, gender, and sexuality were articulated in a cultural product. Carby disputes the notion that Black women's blues reflected an ideology of despair and utter dependence on men. To the contrary, she suggests these performers expressed self-awareness, economic and social independence, and a wide range of sexual identities. In her comparison of the blues singer with the more middle-class Black woman writer of the period, Carby provides insights into how Black women sought to create and control their image through the means of communication at their disposal (Carby, 1986). Both Bobo and Carby locate their subjects' experiences with mediated communication as rooted in a distinct Black female tradition oriented around public expression and community life.

Such research can pave the way for new insights in this area, for there are numerous questions yet to be explored. For example, if mass media are a prime force in the transmission of culture and societal values and norms, why have Black women been systematically excluded from this process? What is the interplay between advertising, marketing, public relations, and media content that enables the communications industries to pay scant attention to Black women as a group? Have the mass media deliberately or unintentionally contributed to the political and economic forces in America that have perpetuated Black women's low status?

At this stage, there is little data or analysis available to begin answering these questions. As other contributors to this book have discovered, we frequently don't know how many Black women are in the media workforce, or in the audience. We don't know what their reactions to media content are, or how other consumers interpret media representations of Black women. We don't know the stories of many Black women "firsts" in journalism and the entertainment media. We know little about their education, training, and job preferences as mass communicators.

The first step toward filling these gaps is to create a baseline of data; studies investigating women or minorities must separate women of color and evaluate their responses as a distinct population. Research projects must be developed to produce detailed audience profiles of Black women and other women of color at all economic levels. Communication researchers must familiarize themselves with the information accumulated in the social sciences and humanities that have begun to address these and related questions. This research agenda must also be undertaken by researchers employing all methodologies; it is not enough for historians to study famous Black women, or for empirical analysts to count the numbers of Black women in a media market. Scholars in critical and cultural studies must begin to move beyond the analysis of class and gender and recognize that they too have ignored large segments of society.

A key to the success of this research agenda will be the cultivation and training of women of color as scholars, who number only a handful in communication studies today. The more we know about women of color and their relationship to the mass media, the better equipped we will be to press for changes in their images, to improve the industry's recognition of their presence as an audience, and to promote their hiring as professional communicators.

Note

1. *Journalism Quarterly, Journal of Communication, Journal of Broadcasting and Electronic Media,* and *Critical Studies in Mass Communication.*

References

Beasley, Maurine H., & Gibbons, Sheila. (1981). *Women in media: A documentary source book.* Washington, DC: Women's Institute for Freedom of the Press.

Becker, Lee B., Kosicki, Gerald M., & Jones, Felecia. (1992) Racial differences in evaluations of the mass media. *Journalism Quarterly, 69,* 124-134.

Bramlett-Solomon, Sharon. (1991). Civil rights vanguard in the deep south: Newspaper
portrayal of Fannie Lou Hamer, 1964-1977. *Journalism Quarterly, 68,* 515-521.

Bramlett-Solomon, Sharon. (1992). Predictors of job satisfaction among Black journalists.
Journalism Quarterly, 69, 703-712.

Bobo, Jacqueline. (1988). *The Color Purple:* Black women as cultural readers. In E. Deidre
Pribram (Ed.), *Female spectators: Looking at film and television* (pp. 90-108). London:
Verso.

Carby, Hazel. (1986). "It just be's dat way sometime": The sexual politics of women's blues.
Radical America, 20, 9-22.

Collins, Patricia Hill. (1990). *Black feminist thought: Knowledge, consciousness, and the
politics of empowerment.* New York: Routledge & Kegan Paul.

Davis, Angela. (1981). *Women, race and class.* New York: Random House.

Diggs-Brown, Barbara. (1992, August). *Phillipa Duke Schulyer: African-American woman
journalist.* Paper presented to the Association for Education in Journalism and Mass
Communication, Montreal.

Dill, Bonnie Thornton. (1979). The dialectic of Black womanhood. *Signs: Journal of Women
in Culture and Society, 4,* 543-555.

Giddings, Paula. (1984). *When and where I enter: The impact of Black women on race and
class in America.* New York: William Morrow.

Hinton, James L., Seggar, John L., et al. (1974). Tokenism and improving imagery of Blacks
in TV drama and comedy: 1973. *Journal of Broadcasting, 18*(4), 423-432.

hooks, bell. (1984). *Feminist theory: From margin to center.* Boston: South End.

hooks, bell. (1989). *Talking back: Thinking feminist—thinking Black.* Boston: South End.

Houston, Marsha. (1992). The politics of difference: Race, class, and women's communication. In Lana F. Rakow (Ed.), *Women making meaning: New feminist directions in
communication* (pp. 45-59). New York: Routledge & Kegan Paul.

Hull, Gloria T., Scott, Patricia Bell, & Smith, Barbara. (Eds.). (1982). *All the women are
white, all the Blacks are men, but some of us are brave: Black women's studies* (pp.
13-22). Old Westbury, NY: Feminist Press.

Ladner, Joyce A. (1971). *Tomorrow's tomorrow: The Black woman.* Garden City, NY:
Doubleday.

Lerner, Gerda. (Ed.). (1973). *Black women in white America: A documentary history.* Garden
City, NY: Anchor.

Matabane, Paula. (1989). Strategies for research on Black women and mass communication.
In Pamela J. Creedon (Ed.), *Women in mass communication: Challenging gender
values* (pp. 117-122). Newbury Park: Sage.

Mills, Kay. (1988). *From the women's pages to the front pages.* New York: Dodd, Mead.

Rakow, Lana F. (1992). The field reconsidered. In Lana F. Rakow (Ed.), *Women making
meaning: New feminist directions in communication* (pp. 3-17). New York: Routledge
& Kegan Paul.

Reinhard, J. C. (1980). The 52 percent minority. In B. Rubin (Ed.), *Small voices and great
trumpets: Minorities and the media* (pp. 169-246). New York: Praeger.

Rhodes, Jane. (1991). Television's "realist" portrayal of African American women: The case
of L. A. Law. *Women and Language, 14,* 29-33.

Rhodes, Jane. (1992). Mary Ann Shadd Cary and the legacy of African-American women
journalists. In Lana F. Rakow (Ed.), *Women making meaning: New feminist directions
in communication* (pp. 210-224). New York: Routledge & Kegan Paul.

Rule, Sheila. (1992, February 12). Director defies the odds, and wins. *The New York Times*, p. B 3.

Streitmatter, Rodger L. (1991). No taste for fluff: Ethel L. Payne, African-American journalist. *Journalism Quarterly, 68,* 528-540.

White, Deborah Gray. (1985). *Ar'nt I a woman? Female slaves in the plantation South.* New York: Norton.

White, E. Frances. (1985). Listening to the voices of Black feminism. *Radical America, 18,* pp. 2-3, 7-25.

3 Gender and Mass Communication in a Global Context

H. LESLIE STEEVES

This book is about gender[1] and mass communication in the United States. Yet we live in an age with almost unlimited possibilities for intercultural influence. American television programs—news and entertainment—are beamed (or cabled) into homes on every continent, and Western wire services such as AP and UPI dominate the world news. AT&T's term *global telecommunity* implies information transfer capabilities almost beyond imagination two decades ago. These and related developments are making it inappropriate to study mass communication—including gender inequities therein—without attention to the larger global context.

This chapter attempts to provide some of that context. However, it is not possible in limited space to describe the status of women in relation to mass communication in every other country in the world—even if detailed and up-to-date information were available from every country. In addition, it is inappropriate for me—as an American—to represent the rest of the world. Rather I will discuss global issues that I believe have implications for all women and that make a sensitivity to the rest of the world crucial in U.S. studies of gender and media.

Although I will present descriptive information as a part of this discussion, such information should *not* be assumed to provide an accurate picture of what is known about gender and media relations around the globe. Rather it is intended only to illustrate commonalties or differences that

AUTHOR'S NOTE: I would like to thank Pamela J. Creedon, Elli Lester-Massman, Marilyn Crafton Smith, and Nancy Worthington for their helpful suggestions on this chapter, and Rebecca Arbogast for our many conversations about these issues. I am also indebted to Margaret Gallagher's extensive work, on which this chapter relies heavily.

should concern us, and also to provide interested readers with a starting point for further study. Throughout this discussion I will note sources for readers, and I will argue that research and action can be enhanced by drawing on the works of women in other countries as well as by using media and information technologies to network globally.

Western Influences on Global Gender and Media Issues

One important reason for Americans to study gender and media issues elsewhere is to develop a sense of responsibility for the influences of the United States and other industrialized nations on the rest of the world's media and information systems. These influences include both Western patriarchy and Western feminism.

Cees Hamelink (1983, p. 1) points out that cultures evolve, in part, in response to the need to adapt to their unique environments. Cultures have influenced each other throughout history, providing new options that have been selectively incorporated or rejected. In recent centuries, however, the autonomy of many cultures to define their own destinies has been sharply curtailed. For example, European colonial powers engaged in systematic efforts to transform their colonized territories: They brought European languages, religion (primarily Christianity), styles of government, law, education, mass media, and, of course, European assumptions about gender roles. Although transformation by force or by coercion certainly still occurs in many parts of the world, the mass export of information and information hardware has radically altered the nature and pace of cultural influence, affecting industrialized as well as less developed countries.

> Never before has the synchronization with one particular cultural pattern been of such global dimensions and so comprehensive. Never before has the process of cultural influence proceeded so subtly, without any blood being shed and with the receiving culture thinking it had sought such cultural influence. It is remarkable that this process should happen exactly when technological development seems to facilitate optimal possibilities for mutual cultural exchange. (Hamelink, 1983, p. 4)

Cultural expansionism and imperialism (or "synchronization"[2]) have been the subject of much international debate in the past two decades. Opposing sides are often described as "free flow" advocates, who believe that the information market will regulate itself and that everyone should have access to existing information, versus advocates of a New World Information and Communication Order (NWICO), where Western expansionism is curbed. A major outcome of these debates was the publication of the 249-page "MacBride Report," *Many Voices, One World* (International Commission for the Study of Communication Problems, 1980).[3] The report paid only token attention to women's concerns. Although most of the problematic issues discussed in the MacBride Report (such as underrepresentation, distortion, and inequities in access to technologies and information) apply to many marginalized and oppressed groups, it has since been pointed out that women are disproportionately affected by these problems and by increased transnationalization. Women also have been most neglected in efforts to remedy the problems. Hence women's concerns require explicit analysis and action (e.g., UNESCO, 1985, p. 4; Roach, 1993, pp. 13, 16).

Given the importance of media and information issues for women globally, from which point(s) of view should these issues be addressed?"Women" are not one homogeneous group, as feminists are quick to acknowledge. Power relations among men and women, racial and ethnic groups, various classes, and men and women living in rural and urban areas may vary considerably from culture to culture. Western feminisms have at times neglected this immense variation. Because of this, Western feminists are frequently accused of meddling inappropriately in other cultures, particularly Third World[4] cultures. As Nicole-Claude Mathieu notes (1988, p. 5), "They are charged with ethnocentrism, imperialism, and even racism." At the least, Third World women often complain that Western women do not understand their unique circumstances[5] and their need to align with oppressed men. Neera Desai and Maithreyi Krishnaraj (1987, p. 18) note that issues such as sexual freedom and sexual preference may not be as relevant in developing countries as in the West, and that in conditions of general deprivation, behaviors of "aggressive individualism" may be dysfunctional.

I have argued elsewhere that a socialist feminist perspective may be useful in considering gender inequities in many global contexts (Steeves, 1987; Steeves & Arbogast, 1993). This is because one central reality facing most of the world's women is intractable poverty related, in part, to transnational power, class privilege, and greed. Socialist feminists have drawn on neo-Marxism to challenge the dualisms of the Enlightenment, especially the public-private dichotomy, and to emphasize capitalist class inequities that they assume contribute importantly to patriarchy (Barrett, 1980). Recognizing the reality of women's varied experiences of oppression, socialist feminists have struggled in the past decade to confront racial and ethnic oppression, as well as class oppression. Recognizing also that socialist experiments (most now failed) have not emancipated women, socialist feminists continue to examine women's varied experiences of the activities of capitalism, including increased privatization and technological expansionism.[6] I have argued that socialist feminist efforts to draw on neo-Marxism (Althusser, 1971) and Stuart Hall's (e.g., 1980a) and others' writings on ideology, alongside efforts to address a variety of inequities, make this perspective relevant to the study of women and communication in many contexts. However, socialist feminism is also a product of Western theory and politics. Where relevant, it must be applied critically and reflexively, and also collaboratively with local feminists.

Five Global Gender Issues

Given this introduction, I will next draw on literature associated with both the NWICO debates and feminist scholarship to discuss five interrelated global issues that I feel are relevant to Western scholars and to all women. First, I believe we need to recognize and critique a major factor in Western, patriarchal influence on media: the transnational corporations, which, with the support of national governments and international lending agencies, constitute the highest economic level of global decision making. Second, given this assumption, we need to understand how transnational goals are supported by marketing and advertising, which in turn influence editorial and entertainment content. Third, it is important to be aware of global commonalities in women's experiences in mass media, regardless of the ultimate sources or causes of these experiences. Fourth, it is useful to know how other women are resisting both indigenous and Western patriarchal influences. These responses can help us understand our commonalities and may offer models for research and action in our own country. Finally, the global linkages made possible by new information technologies may create opportunities to collaborate with women around the world— both to critique these technologies and to use them for our own purposes.

Gender and Transnational Corporations

Probably the most profound contemporary Western influences on gender and media inequities around the world are imposed by transnational corporations (TNCs),[7] which make international research, production, and distribution decisions. The significance of the values underlying these decisions and their inevitable effects on national media decisions, on local media organizations, and on media content therefore cannot be overlooked. This is an important emphasis of the MacBride Report (International Commission for the Study of Communication Problems, 1980, p. 108).

In addition, with regard to communication technology, the world is increasingly at the mercy of the largest corporations, which are based primarily in the United States, Western Europe, and Japan.[8] These corporations receive support and assistance from the governments of their home countries (e.g., via industrial policies) and from international banks and aid agencies, which target Third World and newly industrializing countries for sales (Melody, 1991; Sussman, 1991). In the past decade there have been several major mergers between TNCs in the communication/information sector. Gerald Sussman and John Lent (1991, p. 21) note that this convergence means fewer sources from which Third World countries can select technologies and capital assistance, and hence greater difficulty in resisting financial absorption. Melody (1991, pp. 35-37) points out ways in which the expansion and diversification of TNCs enables them simultaneously to decrease the share of risk they must assume, the bulk of which they pass on to others: their suppliers (e.g., via pressures for subsidies, tax concessions, the maintenance of low-wage labor, and exemptions from social controls), their home countries (by negotiating special privileges), and their customers (which succumb to global pressures to import the latest technologies).

It is not difficult to see that the creative and financial rewards in such a system go to those already at the top of the system. The fact that few women advance to the top of TNCs means that women seldom either contribute to or directly benefit from research and development, let alone distribution decisions. Further, in most developing countries, women constitute the majority of the urban and rural poor. Hence, it is these women who may ultimately suffer the most from TNC policies that provide the greatest benefits to the already rich. This may happen because new technologies are adopted that the poor cannot afford. Melody (1991, pp. 29, 39) points out that this is likely to be the case with the adoption of enhanced telecommunication technologies such as the integrated services digital network (ISDN). Such technologies may provide greater efficiency for the needs of the largest government and private organizations, but greatly increase the cost for small users whose only concern at present is basic telephone service. In addition, the acquisition of new and expensive technologies may reduce or eliminate finances available for less expensive technologies that already benefit the rural poor. The Kenya Broadcasting Corporation (radio and television), for instance, has taken on major debts to upgrade its technology. Repayment of these debts requires profitable services, which has resulted in a reduction of radio programming available to remote rural areas and to those speaking minority languages (Heath, 1992, p. 44).

Put simply, the market system relies on divisions of labor, power, knowledge, and wealth. The world market system is therefore consistent with the many dualistic assumptions of the Enlightenment —that hierarchical distinctions exist among people—certainly among the classes, and between the genders and the First and Third Worlds. Two issues that further illustrate these values are, first, the exploitive hiring practices of TNCs in electronics factories based in Third World countries, and second, the role of these corporations in military information research.

The invention of communication technologies in transnational corporations affects women directly through jobs in electronics factories based in Third World countries. Whereas women's participation in the labor force often declines with modern economic growth and the introduction of new technologies that are typically operated by men,[9] an exception is the expansion of labor-intensive electronics manufacturing for export that has created large numbers of factory jobs for women in the Third World (Lim, 1981; Srinivasan, 1981; Ward, 1986). In these plants, young women without children are the favored employees. Lim (1981, p. 184) quotes an investment brochure published by the Malaysian government that gives some of the reasons:

> The manual dexterity of the oriental female is famous the world over. Her hands are small and she works fast with extreme care. Who, therefore, could be better qualified by nature and inheritance, to contribute to the efficiency of a bench-assembly production line than the oriental girl?

Lim (p. 189) notes that these jobs do free young women from some very conservative norms of patriarchal societies and provide some financial and social independence. However, they subject the women to new forms of exploitation: The jobs are low-paying, unstable, and dead-end, and many of the jobs are highly stressful and have health risks.[10]

It is also noteworthy that much of the research carried out in the largest transnational corporations is funded by the Department of the Defense. Because communication and information technologies are crucial to weapons, intelligence, and propaganda systems, many communications technologies are initially developed for military and related purposes (Schiller, 1981, p. xiii). Of course, military systems around the world are almost universally male; and their technologies, according to many feminists, are not gender neutral. Elise Boulding, for example, points out that one major goal of technological research and development is the ability to control by force, and that men have been the leaders in this project: Men have always operated the "palace-temple-army-technology complex" and women have operated the "kitchen-garden-homecraft-childbearing complex" (Boulding, 1981, pp. 16-17). Military expenditures therefore contribute to other factors that subvert women's efforts to obtain more economic power. Although the feminist peace movement in the First World, including Israel and South Africa, has largely excluded the Third World (Leonardo, 1985), there are many examples of Third World women's courageous activism in confronting particular instances of military and political injustice (Sen & Grown, 1986, p. 73). Perhaps the end of the Cold War will one day bring a redirection of technological research and development—away from military purposes and more toward environmentally sensitive and sustainable purposes. At present, however, this is a global discussion theme and not a reality. The U.S. statements at the U.N. conference on Environment and Development (the "Earth Summit") in Rio de Janeiro in June 1992 indicated much less concern with the environment than with the protection of present economic interests.

Representations of Women in Global, Mainstream Media

Given the exclusion and oppression of women by TNCs, including those that make and sell communications-related products, the next area to examine is how this power is translated into media representations[11] and employment. To address these issues UNESCO commissioned two major reviews of the literature worldwide related to women and media (Gallagher, 1981; UNESCO, 1985). Later, UNESCO's International Program for the Development of Communication (IPDC) compiled the *World Communication Report* (UNESCO, 1989), a detailed volume on the status of communications globally, including a section on "Women in Communication." Many recent, edited collections on feminist scholarship, as well as several bibliographies, report research in international contexts. Margaret Gallagher lists and describes these collections and other resources in a recent issue of *Communication Research Trends* (Gallagher, 1992). John Lent's (1991) international annotated bibliography is especially noteworthy.[12] Newsletters such as *Media Report to Women,*[13] *WIN News,*[14] *Sex Roles Within Mass Media,*[15] and *Echo*[16] provide up-to-date information. The International Women's Tribune Centre, located in New York City, is another good resource.[17] In addition, conferences of organizations such as the International Association for Mass Communication Research, the International Communication Association, and the Association for Education in Journalism and Mass Communication have sessions for feminist scholarship, with papers frequently examining representations and roles in media.

Many studies of gender representations are grounded on the assumption that mass media contribute to systems of representation that make up ideological processes in society, an assumption consistent with socialist feminism. Some studies also examine links between representations and the transnational economy, consistent with a critical, political economic stance, as well as with feminism. Advertising is often singled out for analysis as a major factor in profits of the communication industry, and the key to the survival of most mass media (Gallagher, 1981; UNESCO, 1985, 1989). UNESCO (1989, p. 212) suggests that the media's need for advertising revenue is growing along with trends toward increased privatization and commercialization.

> With the advent of direct broadcasting by satellite (DBS), controls are weakening and foreign-generated advertising is now a feature of the media menu in countries which had previously operated non-commercial national broadcasting systems. Moreover, there is a move away from the short advertising "spots" which have typified traditional commercial broadcasting towards longer "informercials" and sponsored programmes. (p. 212)

Given the increased transnationalization and privatization of communications, and hence increased need for profitability via advertising, it is more important than ever for feminists to examine the origins, functions, and consequences of advertising in a global context.

Advertising. Most advertising space is bought by transnational advertising firms based in industrialized countries (Murdock & Janus, 1985). Because women in many cultures make the majority of private consumption decisions, they are an important target for these advertisers. One aspect of advertising that has gender implications is its persuasive, unidirectional nature. Advertising research has become highly sophisticated and can identify techniques that are most likely to increase the appeal of goods and encourage materialistic values. Because products often advertised are nonessential, luxury items, poor women's oppressed status is likely to be reinforced, as is their status as consumers. In fact, international studies of media advertising have consistently reported images of women that reflect the capitalist and consumerist orientation of the Western agencies that create most of the advertisements and of the transnational corporations that make the products (Gallagher, 1981; Lent, 1991; UNESCO, 1985).

An extreme example of the partnership between transnationals and advertising is the transnational magazine, which is produced in the West but is adapted to the language and culture of each country in which it is distributed. For example, several women's magazines (with varying levels of success) have been published in Paris, supported by major fashion and cosmetics advertisers, and distributed in Francophone Africa. Terez Doumbia and Niaina Hanitra (1989)—of Senegal and Madagascar, respectively—have observed some changes in women's representations in these magazines. Whereas the advertising of the 1970s encouraged an image modeled after the European woman, the 1980s have placed more of an emphasis on traditional African looks. Doumbia and Hanitra (p. 23) attribute these changes at least partially to a new interest in African styles on the part of European fashion designers, who are seeking inspiration in "modernized African costumes." At the same time, the equation between beauty and consumption remains as strong as ever.

> Women's magazines suggest that we admire the pictures of African beauties in gorgeous boubous made of expensive Western fabrics, posing in front of Volvos or Renaults. All this, however, is accessible only to those who can afford to buy a new car or fly to Paris for the weekend. In the final analysis, this is propaganda of a "black superwoman" image, of lifestyles very few African women can aspire to, of dreams only a handful can pay to make come true. (p. 25)

One area that has been inadequately studied is the process by which selected Western values and conventions of gender representation become incorporated into—or rejected by—the advertising of other cultures. Such research requires cross-cultural comparisons that are grounded in a thorough understanding of the different contexts involved.[18]

Another advertising issue is its impact on entertainment and editorial content. If accepted, advertising may have a profound effect on the content of locally produced media; and new developments in cable broadcasting do not appear to be reversing this phenomenon (Gallagher, 1987b, pp. 30-31). Advertising likewise exerts influence on Western media content that is then exported to other parts of the First and Third Worlds. Armand Mattelart and his co-authors (Mattelart, Delcourt, & Mattelart, 1984, p. 100) point out that popular U.S. series, like the advertisements embedded in them, negate inequities and contradictions in society. Many European and other countries have recently acquired more channels but do not have the resources to produce their own programming. It is far cheaper to buy U.S. series than to produce their own. These sophisticated series utilize numerous technical devices (e.g., image and camera angle changes) that are known to appeal to viewers. As they become more popular, they tend to suppress or marginalize other forms of demand. Mattelart et al. (1984, p. 89) question to what extent the United States should have the power to become the imagination for the rest of the world.

Entertainment and Editorial Content. The UNESCO literature reviews (Gallagher, 1981; UNESCO, 1985, 1989) and Lent's (1991) bibliography summarize what was known up to 1991 about representations of women in print and broadcast media in Latin America and the Caribbean, Western Europe, Central and Eastern Europe, the Middle East, Africa, Asia, Australia, and Canada, as well as in the United States. In general, many of the same observations are made internationally that are made in the United States. Gallagher (1981, p. 70) noted that her review "presents a picture remarkable only for its overall consistency when compared from one country to another." Later reviews note little change in this general picture and offer considerable evidence in support of their conclusions.

In mainstream media entertainment (whether film, print, radio, or television), studies around the world show that women are grossly underrepresented. Also much magazine content for women—including the popular *fotonovelas* of Latin America[19]—as well as broadcast content (e.g., soap operas), reinforce traditional ideologies of oppression and encourage escapism. Of course, much media content throughout the world consists of exports from the United States, some of which are critiqued in other chapters. There is evidence of contradictions between imported representations of women and indigenous values (e.g., Gallagher, 1981, p. 37). However, almost nothing is known about how these Western products are interpreted by women in other cultures. Even though it is likely that in most cases audiences "read" representations as they are intended, there are indications that—at least under certain conditions—Third World women may actively resist dominant messages (e.g., Mattelart, 1986, pp. 14-15).[20]

In media news, research indicates that women are mostly absent. In fact, according to Gallagher (1981, p. 77), no country with available data reported that more than 20% of the news was about women, and in most cases the figure was much lower. This has changed little since 1981. Most existing news about women is trivial—related to family status or appearance. Where important women's activities are covered, they are often simultaneously undermined or demeaned. U.S. news, of course, indicates a similar pattern, including its coverage of international women's activities. This coverage is important because of its impact on foreign news, which often relies on Western releases. It is worth noting that even U.S. coverage of the three U.N. Decade for Women Conferences—1975 (Mexico City), 1980 (Copenhagen), and 1985 (Nairobi)—was often marginalized (placed in lifestyle sections) and sensationalized (emphasizing conflict) (Cooper & Davenport, 1987).

Gallagher (1981, pp. 70-71) suggested that in countries with commitments to social change—such as the People's Republic of China and socialist states of Eastern Europe—images of women were "exceptionally positive." However, UNESCO (1985, pp. 86-89) cited studies in Cuba, the former Soviet Union, Vietnam, and the People's Republic of China indicating a tendency to incorporate patriarchal assumptions within revolutionary themes as well as increasing uses of advertising reflecting commercial interests of the West. Although it is important to realize that traditional and transnational ideologies of gender oppression did negatively affect women's roles and representations in socialist media, it is also clear that women were not oppressed in the same range of ways—or to the same degree —as in countries more affected by transnationalization and privatization. The radical changes that have taken place in most of the communist and socialist world in recent years, plus the media integration of European Community (EC) member states, are resulting in much concern and discussion about implications for women.[21] The 1990s will certainly bring more analysis and activism around gender and media issues in the European community.

One way in which media content may improve for women is as a consequence of efforts to use the media for development, though little research has addressed this question. Gallagher (1981, p. 71) speculated that although little evidence was available, images of women in some African countries might be benefiting from development projects. A few other scholars have made similar suggestions. For example, Michèle and Armand Mattelart (1982) describe Mozambique's emphasis on small-scale media at the community level. While women may still be at a disadvantage, they are more likely to participate in media decision making than where media are centralized in cities. This optimism is tempered by research on extension information efforts in developing countries—efforts often modeled after extension services in the United States. Kathleen Staudt (1985) and Mary Ngechu (1992) found that even though poor women grow 80% of the family food in East Africa, pertinent information on agricultural practices and technologies did not reach these women. Such information was much more likely to reach only the better-off women farmers and men. Likewise, Neera Desai and Maithreyi Krishnaraj (1987, p. 284) report that educational television and radio programs for women reinforced stereotypes and did not address women's real needs. Although women comprise 36% of agricultural workers in India, rural development programs were directed at men. At best, women might appear "as folk dancers or as health advisers for pregnant mothers" (Desai & Krishnaraj, p. 284).

Clearly this is a gloomy picture. However, it is important to point out that mass media are not just creators and reinforcers of patriarchal ideologies around the world; they also offer women and other disadvantaged groups a means of placing their issues on the international agenda. How might this be done? There are many possibilities. These include publishing research, such as studies cited in previous paragraphs, and carrying out and publicizing conferences and events. The most common strategy is to increase women working in mainstream media organizations.

Women's Roles in Mainstream Media Organizations

The UNESCO literature reviews indicate that throughout the world much more is known about images of women than about women's participation in media industries. There are many levels for discussion of women's participation. Certainly it is useful to know about women's success in obtaining media jobs. But it is also important to ask whether this will make a difference. In other words, will increased numbers of women change media content and policy? Or will women conform to the practices of existing structures?

Women's Jobs in Media. In general, employment data on women and media around the world are incomplete and unreliable (Gallagher, 1981; *Media Asia,* 1987; Seager & Olson, 1986; UNESCO, 1985, 1989). Joni Seager and Ann Olson (1986, chart 34) were able to report simple data on proportions of women in the media workforce from only 46 countries, and on both print and broadcast media from only 25. Their data indicate that women made up more than 30% of the total media workforce in Costa Rica, Chile, Taiwan, and Venezuela (35%), and in Cuba, Thailand, and the United States (40%). Women made up 5% or less of the media workforce in Bangladesh (1%), Peru and Japan (2%), and Haiti and Honduras (5%). Countries that reported only broadcast media data reported 30% or more women in the workforce in Sweden (30%), Singapore (38%), and Jamaica (50%); and less than 5% in Australia (0%), Austria (2%), Ghana (3%), and Norway (4%).

Perhaps more revealing than numbers of women in media is specific information about their jobs. Gallagher (1981, p. 86) found that data from Latin America, Africa, and Eastern Europe were almost nonexistent, and data from Asia and Western Europe were incomplete. The available data indicate major problems of vertical and horizontal segregation, as is also the case in the United States.[22] These similarities are not accidental, and may be significantly attributable, in many contexts, to the impact of first, colonial powers[23] and later, Western development agencies and multinational corporations. As previously noted, these various forces introduced not only media, but Western assumptions about their operation.

Gallagher found that throughout the world women were virtually absent from top executive positions, and at the lower levels, women were segregated into lower paying clerical occupations. The few women in news positions typically handled traditional "women's" features and less important assignments. Other problems discussed by Gallagher (1981, pp. 94-99) include: job conditions assuming male roles (e.g., the expectation of high performance in youth with no consideration for childbearing and child care), women's poor record of active union membership, protective legis-lation for media women (e.g., laws in some countries restricting overtime and night work for women), and inadequate training and education for women in media.

UNESCO (1985, 1989) notes a few new studies from several countries. However, none of this more recent information changes the general pat-terns reported earlier by Gallagher. UNESCO (1985, pp. 80-81) sum-marizes research by Gallagher (1984) on the progress of men and women television employees over a 10-year period (from the early 1970s to 1983) in Belgium, Denmark, France, The Federal Republic of Germany, Ireland, Italy, the Netherlands, and the United Kingdom.

> In absolute terms and across all of the organizations studied, the average woman was at a disadvantage compared to the average man right from the date of recruitment. She was appointed to a lower-level job, in a lower salary band. Over time, this difference was actually increased (in organizations in Belgium, Denmark, France, Germany and Italy). (UNESCO, 1985, p. 81)

Gallagher (1987b) also edited five case studies on professional women in broadcasting in five countries: Canada, Egypt, Ecuador, India, and Nigeria. Again, the similarities were more striking than the differences. In her introduction, Gallagher notes women's minority presence, women's absence from technical jobs and senior management, and women's segrega-tion into certain program-making areas such as educational and children's programs (p. 13).

Despite these pessimistic results, UNESCO (1989, pp. 211-212) shows that around the world the proportion of women journalism students greatly exceeds the proportion of women working in journalism. These statistics likely forecast a growing number of women in journalism professions globally, though these women will continue to face many discouraging obstacles. In addition, Anne Cooper (1988) reports finding that, at least in some ways, women may be making more progress in some Third World media than in the West. Her study of one week's television newscasts in Japan, the United States, Colombia, Jamaica, and Sri Lanka indicates that women have a more prominent role as reporters and anchors in the latter three countries. She did, however, observe a bias against women as foreign correspondents in all five countries as well as an apparent universal tendency to assign women to cover health stories. It is important to note that this type of research is rare. Gertrude Robinson (e.g., 1981, 1990) and Sue A. Lafky (e.g., 1990) are among the few other scholars who do comparative work on women in media professions. There is great need for more such feminist scholarship.

Relationships Between Media Jobs and Content. On the surface, it appears that research and political efforts to increase numbers of women employed in mass media, particularly at the higher levels, indicates a liberal feminist orientation. Many feminists would argue that such efforts ignore patriarchal structures that are unlikely to change with the simple addition of women. However, Zillah Eisenstein (1981) has argued persuasively that patriarchal structures and products can't help but change as increasing numbers of women participate in them and appeal to them for support. Empirically, very little media research has addressed the issue.[24]

In their reviews of the minuscule amount of international research on connections between media portrayals and the gender of employees, Gallagher (1981, pp. 108-112) and UNESCO (1985, pp. 64-67) found little evidence that images of women in media are improved when women are producing the images. Although there is some evidence that women approach their work differently from men,[25] it appears that traditional values usually prevail. For example, Cornelia Butler Flora (1980) found that a sexually explicit series of Venezuelan *fotonovelas* were written primarily by women. Sue Lafky (1990) analyzed survey data to compare the attitudes and values of journalists in the United States, Britain, and West Germany. She found that social learning from education, job experience, and elsewhere was a stronger predictor of attitudes toward journalistic roles or ethical dilemmas than gender.

Gallagher (1981, pp. 109-110) cites a British drama producer to point out a related problem: Women who do make it to the top may dissociate themselves from younger women, believing that others should have to sacrifice as much as they did. Yet another constraint involves traditional professional attitudes that contribute to the devaluing of women's concerns. UNESCO (1985, pp. 66-67) cites Angela Spindler-Brown (1984) to illustrate the extent of the problem via the experiences of an all-women collective working within the mainstream media. The collective, called *Broadside,* was hired by Channel 4 in the United Kingdom to produce a series of programs for airing in 1983. The group began with the intention of working in a nonhierarchical fashion, but was eventually forced into a traditional style by industrial and trade union pressures.

Even so, the relative lack of structure led to clashes with the Channel 4 management, whose administrative routines demanded individual leadership. Although the programmes—which applied a distinct women's perspective to current affairs issues—were a critical and popular success, *Broadside* was not commissioned to produce another current affairs series for Channel 4. (UN-ESCO, 1985, pp. 66-67)

Liesbet van Zoonen (1988) examined this issue in detail, pointing out its complexity and the variety of assumptions involved. She notes (pp. 42-43) that those who assume women will produce different content sometimes make mutually exclusive assumptions: Some assume that there will be less sex-stereotyped material as women share more equally in producing hard news, while others assume that a higher value will be associated with "soft," "feminine" news. Both points of view may result in the recruitment of more privileged women, who have little sensitivity for lower class and minority women.

In addition, it is important to examine the multifaceted macro-level constraints on the female or male gatekeeper (Gallagher, 1981; Spindler-Brown, 1984). Of course, substantial constraints are imposed by the transnational corporations that control the production and distribution of media and information equipment and software. Local roles for women in media are important, but cannot compensate for women's absence at the highest levels of corporate power. Patriarchal influences from other global sources (e.g., aid agencies) and indigenous sources (e.g., national governments) pose other obstacles. Two overt means of resisting patriarchy in mass communication are to develop national media policies that support women's concerns and to create alternative women's media.

Women's Resistance to the Global Media Oppression

National Media Policies. Feminist theory (e.g., Eisenstein, 1984) supports the value of efforts to change policy and law in order to thwart patriarchal influences—both from external and internal sources.[26] Few countries have as yet developed comprehensive national information policies, though there has been much discussion about the need for such policies in many national contexts. Discussions in developing countries have tended to focus primarily on issues of dependency in the world technology market and urban biases in local access. In the absence of comprehensive policies, some countries have taken some specific actions to limit the activities of transnational corporations (Mattelart et al., 1984, p. 65). These actions include: requiring the use of the national language in advertising; requiring advertising to be created within the country and to utilize local talent; limiting advertising activities in certain sectors such as pharmaceuticals and food; and fixing quotas on the importation of foreign films and publications. Mattelart et al. (p. 66) note that some such policies contain inconsistencies. For example, in Brazil, although there was tight control over the cinema industry, almost none of the restrictions applied to television. Margorie Ferguson (1986, pp. 65-66) points out that Britain imposed a 14% limit on foreign television programming; however, by far most feature films shown and videos rented in Britain originate from other countries, the largest proportion from the United States.

Mattelart et al. (1984, p. 107) suggest that most countries underestimate the power of the transnational market to thwart national efforts to develop autonomous policies. They also note (p. 11) that the New World Information and Communication Order's emphasis on quantitative information transfer has allowed many Third World governments to pass over embarrassing questions of power within their own societies and has therefore in fact limited the construction of a new order.[27] The same is true of some policies indicating an overemphasis on "cultural identity" or a denunciation of "evil others." For example, efforts to put quotas on imported films may merely serve as a mask for greater profits to sectional local interests, no doubt controlled by upper class males.[28]

All of these complications suggest that even if national information policies can provide some cultural protection from the transnational market, it is important to ask: Whose culture is being protected (see also Mathieu, 1988, p. 8)? To what degree are women, poor women, and minorities forgotten? Therefore in addition to policies addressing issues of national identity and cultural autonomy, each country must develop media policies to explicitly protect disadvantaged groups from indigenous forms of oppression as well—for example, policies on acceptable media representations of women and on women's employment in and ownership of media and information industries. In preparation for the 1985 U.N. Decade for Women Conference in Nairobi, Kenya, a questionnaire was distributed to all U.N. member states by the UN Centre for Social Development and Humanitarian Affairs (UNESCO, 1985, p. 30). The questionnaire included a section on media policies, including "policies and guidelines requiring media to promote the advancement of women" (p. 33). Questionnaire responses were received from 95 governments, though the completeness of their responses and interpretations of particular questions varied widely. Responses to this policy question addressed representations of women, women's employment, or both.

With regard to representations, only a few countries indicated they had policies on sex-role portrayals of women in media (e.g., Sweden and Denmark, UNESCO, 1985, p. 34), and it was generally unclear to what extent these policies were enforced. Several countries, however, indicated plans to develop regulatory codes on images of women or on antisexist language (pp. 34-36). Since the UNESCO data were collected, the Canadian Radio-Television and Telecommunications Commission (CRTC) adopted a detailed set of regulatory codes on representations of women in media. The adoption of these codes in 1986 followed extensive research to evaluate a 2-year trial period (1982-1984) of self-regulation.[29] The research indicated that self-regulation was only partially successful. Therefore the Commission decided that it would make broadcasters' license renewal contingent on following the guidelines developed in 1982. Additional research was carried out in 1988 (Canadian Radio-Television and Telecommunications Commission [CRTC], 1990), and the guidelines were strengthened and updated in 1990 and in 1992.[30]

In addition to information on policies addressing representations of women, the U.N. questionnaire obtained some information on policies related to women's employment in media. Although many countries appear to have laws or policies against unequal pay and sex discrimination, many of these laws are vaguely worded and, in most cases, it appears that their effectiveness has not been evaluated. Such policies appear to have little impact on deeply entrenched patterns of inequality, and numerous obstacles to the successful enforcement of policy were reported in the questionnaires:

> Patriarchal or paternalistic attitudes are frequently quoted (Dominican Republic, Greece, Tanzania, Venezuela), and Italy cites loss of interest in the feminist movement. El Salvador lists *"el machismo y el hombrismo"*. . . . Zimbabwe (along with Australia and Niger) mentions lack of funds; it also lists low awareness of the need to increase women's participation in the communication sector, and a lack of a clearly articulated government or private sector policy. Columbia notes "lack of political will." Australia mentions the "implicit feeling" in many organizations "that there exists no problem in this area." The United States notes resistance to change in a traditionally male field of employment. Other commonly cited obstacles are female illiteracy (e.g., Afghanistan), low out-reach of existing media (e.g. the Gambia), and male resistance to competition for jobs (e.g., the Philippines). (UNESCO, 1985, pp. 35-36)

The UNESCO report concluded that laws *against* discrimination were unlikely to be effective without strong accompanying policies of affirmative action. Only eight countries said they practiced affirmative action; however, only five (Australia, Denmark, Norway, the United States, and Sweden) understood the question to refer to efforts to recruit women for particular posts or grades deliberately (UNESCO, 1985, pp. 41-43). In recent years Canada has taken an especially progressive role in employment equity, as in gender representation. On September 1, 1992, the CRTC announced an employment equity policy that will be considered in decisions about granting and renewing licenses (CRTC, 1992). Groups included in this policy include women, aboriginal peoples, persons with disabilities, and visible minorities. New personnel, mechanisms, and procedures have been created to facilitate the policy.[31] One new national organization, Canadian Women in Radio and Television (CWRT), deserves mention. CWRT formed in 1991, dedicated to increasing the involvement and impact of women in radio, television, and related fields, such as music, film, cable, and telecommunications. This is done through activities such as training and development, a bilingual newsletter, monitoring and advising on managerial openings, and awards programs.[32]

Alternative Media. Another important means by which women can resist patriarchal and Western hegemonic influences is to establish their own media organizations. One such organization is the ISIS collective (Women's International Information and Communication Service), based in Santiago and Rome, which uses multiple formats to publish audiovisual material and other information for women around the world (e.g., see ISIS International, 1986; UNESCO, 1989, p. 217).

An excellent source of information on international media and media-related groups, organizations, and events for women is the *Directory of Women's Media,* published annually by the National Council for Research on Women.[33] This publication provides lists and brief descriptions in the categories of: periodicals, presses/publishers, news services, radio/television, film/video/cable, music, theater/dance/multimedia, art, crafts/cards/T-shirts, writers' groups, speakers' bureaus, distributors, media organizations, bookstores, libraries/archives/museums, and directories/catalogs.

The 1992 issue of this publication clearly reflects the degree to which North American and European women have organized to publicize women's points of view. For example, Table 3.1 summarizes information from this publication on women's periodicals.[34] No developing country lists more than 9 women's periodicals (except Argentina with 21), while the United States lists more than 600.[35] It is important to note that many of the publications based in the United States and other First World countries appear to have international circulations and some deal specifically with Third World women's issues.[36] However, their actual diversity of circulation and availability to women internationally is questionable without further research.

Data on other women's media and publication activities indicate a similar trend. The United States predominates by far, Canada, Australia, and Europe follow, and a few Third World countries show some limited activity. Again, however, some of the First World activity is international in nature. For example, the United States has six women's news services,

Table 3.1 Periodicals for Women

Number of Periodicals	Countries
>100	USA (609)
>50	England (51); Canada (59)
40-49	—
30-39	Germany (38)
20-29	Argentina, Australia (21)
10-19	Netherlands (17); France, Italy, Switzerland (11)
5-9	Belgium, Chile, Dominican Republic, Japan, Mexico, (9); Peru (8); India (7); Ireland, Philippines, Sweden (6); Austria, Brazil, New Zealand, Spain, Uruguay (5)
2-4	Ecuador, Israel (4); Columbia, Costa Rica, El Salvador, Greece, Kenya, Nicaragua, Norway, Pakistan, Senegal, South Africa, Sri Lanka, Venezuela (3); Barbados, Bolivia, Fiji, Finland, Iceland, Hong Kong, Malaysia, Puerto Rico, South Korea, Tanzania, Thailand, Zambia, Zimbabwe (2)
1	Belize, China, Denmark, Ghana, Jamaica, Lebanon, Nigeria, Panama, Papua New Guinea, Russia, Scotland, Singapore, Sudan, Trinidad & Tobago, Uganda, Vietnam

SOURCE: *1992 Directory of Women's Media* (National Council for Research on Women, 1992). The data include both indexed and unindexed women's periodicals listed in the Directory. Unindexed periodicals were those for which updated information was unavailable at the time of publication.

three of which are international. They include the U.S.-based WINGS (Women's International Newsgathering Services), which distributes its radio program via tape and satellite to stations around the world.

It is important to point out that without detailed examinations of each of the various periodicals, wire services, media productions, or media organizations listed in the *Directory of Women's Media,* it is impossible to know to what extent they were or are independent of Western-influenced advertising or of national, patriarchal structures and ideologies. For example, since 1979 the *Manushi* collective in New Delhi, India, has published a highly successful magazine that offers features and fiction confronting the oppression of women in Indian society (Kishwar & Vanita, 1984). Through hard work and with the help of subscriptions and donations, *Manushi* has not accepted advertising depicting women in oppressive roles—which rules out most advertising. However, the publication has faced much local resistance. On March 11, 1986, *Manushi* workers went so far as to stage a hunger strike at the New Delhi post office to protest "years of harassment by postal department staff."[37] The publication has managed to survive such resistance and retain its editorial policy. In contrast, Gallagher (1981, p. 138) describes efforts by the editorial staff of *Viva* magazine in Nairobi to print stories on issues such as "prostitution, birth control, female circumcision, polygamy and sex education." In 1980 the editor was told to drop such issues because of threats to withdraw advertisements. *Viva* survived through the 1980s, but with less space devoted to feminism than to advice on beauty, fashion, and decorating. *Viva* ceased publication in 1990.

In general much more descriptive and comparative research is needed on the histories, publication processes, and content of alternative women's periodicals throughout the world, including the impact of advertising on content and on audience interpretations. As advertising becomes necessary, the line between "alternative" and "mainstream" often becomes difficult to distinguish, and the outcome may not be positive for women.

New Technologies and Global Networking[38]

It is evident from the above discussion that most of the research on women and media can still be described within the traditional categories of broadcast and print media. However, as Margaret Gallagher (1987a, p. 22) points out, to think globally means to think in terms of an information economy where boundaries between traditional categories will become more blurred.

> In the new broadband telecommunications systems, the same "wire" can deliver via our television screens not just traditional television programming, but individualized subscriber programming (pay-TV), videotex news, consumer catalogue and reference information, as well as specialised services such as electronic mailing, electronic shopping, home banking, security alarm systems, and so on. In other words, the television screen is becoming the common delivery station around which a wide range of formerly separate business, information and communications enterprises are converging. (Gallagher, 1987a, p. 22)

It is crucial that feminists critique the economic and political processes that produce these new information technologies as well as their consequences for women. Evidence from the United States and Europe indicates that new satellite, cable, and VCR technologies are not democratizing women's and minorities' access to media. Rather they are opening up new opportunities for the exploitation of women via advertising and pornography (Gallagher, 1987a), opportunities that are increasing with the dismantling of socialism and communism in many parts of the world. Also these new communication technologies, like housework technologies, may increase women's isolation in their homes.[39]

In addition to critiquing new technologies, women can certainly invent their own technologies, as they have done throughout history (Stanley,

1983). Women also are finding ways to adapt new technologies to their own purposes. Both international networking and agenda-setting goals can be served via the creative use of computer technologies. PeaceNet is one well-known international computer network that encourages information-sharing among peace and social change individuals and groups, including women's groups.[40] Of course, computers can facilitate networking via newsletters such as those noted earlier.[41] But computers also make possible direct, inexpensive, two-way information transfers. Judy Smith and Ellen Balka (1988) argue that computer literacy is crucial for women's empowerment in a technological world. Of course, such empowerment means overcoming the computer "reticence" that afflicts many women (Turkle, 1988)—plus other obstacles to women's training and access, including discrimination in education and cost. Such obstacles will require much scrutiny in developing countries where compact disc libraries utilizing CD-ROM technology are currently being introduced and may include information especially useful to women.[42]

There are many other obstacles women face in efforts to participate in and perhaps subvert the communications revolution. The economic power of TNCs is among the most serious of these obstacles. An important way to confront economic power is by political organization, and at least in some countries it appears that political organization is paying off in new policies on sex-role portrayals in the media and in affirmative action hiring policies.

In most instances, however, women have played little or no role in media policy making. Achieving such participatory status will require a combination of strategies including information sharing and support through networking. Such networking could be enhanced and supported via collaborative, *feminist* research between women—or perhaps between women and men—of different cultures. Feminist research does not imply Western forms of feminism. It implies a common theoretical and political concern with women's oppression, and an understanding that women of each culture have the right and deserve the support to seek means of addressing their own problems of oppression.

Shared, Global Gender Concerns

In sum, there are many reasons to consider international perspectives in studies of gender and media inequities in the United States. First, we need to understand the power of the transnational economy and its often blatant support for women's oppression in relation to mass communication. Second, our efforts to study representations at home and their links to economic motives should take on added importance as we understand the extent to which these representations are exported abroad and also copied in local, foreign productions. Third, research on women's employment becomes more important as we see Western organizational values transferred via development projects. (Of course, much development aid merely strengthens media structures that were first set in place by colonial powers.) Fourth, we can all learn much by studying activities of resistance by women in other countries—resistance via research, policy making, and alternative feminist media. Finally, recent advances in telecommunication and information technologies make it imperative that women learn about these technologies—both in order to challenge them and to use them collaboratively for feminist purposes.

Notes

1. A note on terminology: I sometimes have difficulty selecting among the terms *woman/women, gender* (the social construction of sexual difference), or *feminism* (the theoretical and political stance that women—as a gender—are unjustly oppressed). However, this book and chapter are about *women, as a gender, from feminist perspective(s).* I use all three terms frequently, but always with this underlying assumption. So although I have tried to make contextually appropriate selections, the reader will notice instances where alternative terminology might also be appropriate.

2. Cees Hamelink prefers the term cultural *synchronization* over *imperialism.* Imperialism implies direct, aggressive acts by one culture to influence another. But world trends toward the desire for and adoption of Western ways are much more subtle than that. Hamelink points out many instances where cultural autonomy is being lost, but where acts of imperialism are not obvious.

3. A 16-member commission (headed by Sean MacBride of Ireland and including communication scholars and journalists from all major regions of the world) was established by UNESCO in December 1977 to carry out a comprehensive analysis of communication problems in society and make recommendations. The commission's report, popularly called "The MacBride Report," was submitted to the Director-General in February 1980 (International Commission for the Study of Communication Problems, 1980, pp. 295-297). I should note that the term *New World Information and Communication Order* was first used at the 1978 UNESCO General Conference, was also used in the MacBride Report, and appears to be the most popular current descriptor for the desired new order. However, other terms such as *New International Information Order* were used prior to 1978 and continue to be preferred by some (Hamelink, 1983, pp. 69-72).

4. The term *Third World* appears to be surviving the end of the Cold War. It is used here in the conventional sense to refer to countries that are characterized by less industrialization, less urbanization, greater poverty, and generally less economic development than "First World" countries. Of course, an emphasis on such economic distinctions appears to equate countries as diverse as Thailand, Kenya, the Philippines, and Ecuador, ignoring immense variation among them on other dimensions. I should also note that I use the terms *Third World, less developed,* and *developing countries* interchangeably in this chapter, though the latter two terms are also problematic: "less developed" because it also prioritizes economic

development, and "developing" because it implies that First World countries are fully developed. See Pletsch (1981) for an excellent discussion of the "three worlds" concept.

5. Such circumstances include "caste in India, predominance of export-oriented industries in South-East Asia, significance of multinationals in Singapore, Malaysia and South Korea, sex tourism in Thailand and migration pattern in Philippines" (Desai & Krishnaraj, 1987, p. 3).

6. For examples of socialist feminist efforts to address women's experiences of racism and of capitalist expansionism, in light of the failures of socialism, see numerous essays in the socialist feminist journal, *Feminist Review*. See also edited volumes on Third World women, for example, several essays in Mohanty, Russo, and Torres (1991).

7. According to Thomas Guback and Tapio Varis (1982, p. 6), a "transnational corporation" or TNC: "is a corporation that owns or controls production or service facilities outside the country in which it is based." They further note that "instead of TNCs, one could also speak of multinational, international, or global corporations, firms, enterprises, or companies" (Guback & Varis [1982, p. 6], summarizing United Nations [1974, p. 25]). Therefore in this chapter the term *transnational* is used to refer to large corporations with activities in other countries besides their home countries.

8. See the MacBride Report (International Commission for the Study of Communication Problems, 1980, p. 109) for a listing of the 15 transnational corporations that had the most control over communications operations at that time. Eleven of the 15 were based in the United States. Since then foreign, particularly Japanese-based, corporations have gained a much larger share of the transnational market, including the communications market. Newly industrializing countries such as South Korea and Singapore are also making major inroads. (See Kichen [1992] for current data on the largest U.S. and foreign transnationals, including those involved in communications-related businesses.)

9. There has been much research on the gender impact of new industries that has indicated that important market activities by women were often displaced by factories staffed by men (e.g., Cain, 1981; Desai & Krishnaraj, 1987). Gallagher (1987a, p. 23) cites evidence that women have lost out similarly in the production of new information technologies.

10. These health risks are portrayed strikingly in *The Global Assembly Line,* a film co-produced by Maria Patricia Fernandez Kelly and Loraine Gray and distributed by New Day Films.

11. Steeves and Arbogast (1993) provide a more theoretical discussion of issues related to media representations and women, particularly Third World women.

12. This extensive bibliography lists and describes literature in the following categories: global and comparative perspectives; Africa and the Middle East; Asia, Australia, and Oceania; Europe; Latin America and the Caribbean; and North America. An appendix lists organizations, periodicals, and other significant resources that focus on women and mass communication.

13. *Media Report to Women* is a bi-monthly newsletter with reports of research, conferences, and political and legal activity related to women and media around the world. For information write to Communication Research Associates, Inc., 10606 Mantz Road, Silver Spring, MD 20903-1228.

14. *WIN News* is published quarterly and includes information on women's activities worldwide with considerable emphasis on the Third World. Most issues have a section on "Women and Media," with information on recent publications and events. For information, write to Fran P. Hosken, 107 Grant St., Lexington, MA 02173.

15. *Sex-Roles Within Mass Media* is published once or twice a year in Stockholm, Sweden, and is financed by the Equality Group of the Swedish Television Company. Its purposes include maintaining an international mailing list of persons interested in gender and media, exchanging up-to-date information related to gender and media, and informing about upcoming

meetings and seminars. For information, write to Madeleine Kleberg, School of Journalism, University of Stockholm, Gjorwellsgatan 26, S-112 60, Stockholm, Sweden.

16. *Echo* is published quarterly by the Association of African Women for Research and Development (AAWORD), a pan-African, nongovernmental association based in Dakar, Senegal. AAWORD has organized various research working groups, including a working group on Women and the Mass Media in Africa. This working group is organizing a bibliography that will include English, French, and Arabic literature (see *Echo,* Vol. 1, Nos. 2-3, 1986, pp. 7-8). For information, write to AAWORD, B. P. 3304, Dakar, Senegal.

17. The International Women's Tribune Centre (IWTC) was founded following the 1975 U.N. Decade for Women conference in Mexico City. The Centre's resources include newsletters in English, Spanish, and French related to women in development issues, regional resource manuals with information and citations on women's organizations and projects, development training manuals, information bulletins, annotated bibliographies, and contact lists (International Women's Tribune Centre [IWTC], 1984, p. iii). For information, write to IWTC, 777 United Nations Plaza, New York, NY 10017.

18. Such cross-cultural comparisons of the United States and India have been undertaken by Michael Griffin, K. Viswanath, and Dona Schwartz (1992).

19. A *fotonovela* is a romance story in a comic book format with still pictures and captions. *Fotonovelas* are popular throughout much of the world including Latin America, Spain, Italy, and parts of Africa. However, most studies of this genre have referred to Latin America.

20. Hall's (1980b) suggestion that media messages may be read in a "dominant," "negotiated," or "resistant" fashion has been applied in efforts to identify circumstances under which dominant-hegemonic codes may be less effective for some women (e.g., Steiner, 1988). Also useful is Gramsci's theory of hegemony, which posits ideological institutions as a site for hegemonic cultural definition (e.g., Fiske, 1987, pp. 259-260).

21. For example, in October, 1990, the London-based World Association for Christian Communication formed the Network for Women in Communication (NETWIC), which aims to help women in media deal critically with mainstream media and form alternative media. A priority at present is to help the women of Eastern Europe, who are concerned with changes that follow the new political structures ("European Women," 1991). In November 1990 a conference entitled "Women and Men in Broadcasting: Equality in the '90s?" was jointly convened by the European Commission and the European Broadcasting Union. The conference examined both the status quo and prospects for equality in light of changing structures, new technologies, and increased privatization ("EC Tackles," 1991).

22. Vertical segregation refers to a concentration of women at lower organizational levels and horizontal segregation refers to their concentration in specific types of jobs. Both types of segregation characterize women's roles in U.S. media, despite the "feminization" phenomenon, discussed in chapters to follow.

23. Many studies of women in development have demonstrated that when cash economies were introduced, control of cash (via jobs) was primarily given to men. As in the West, women were assigned to the lower paying, lower status positions, or to unpaid labor at home—or both. (See, e.g., Robertson & Berger, 1986.)

24. This is true in the United States, as elsewhere, as indicated by Muriel Cantor's (1987) report to the Benton Foundation.

25. See UNESCO (1985, p. 65) and UNESCO (1989, p. 209). The UNESCO reports note studies in Denmark and the Netherlands suggesting that in some circumstances women carry out their work differently than men—for example, by seeking out female sources, by focusing on topics of likely interest to women, and by making connections between news topics and everyday life.

26. Steeves and Arbogast (1993) discuss the literature of development communication and feminist theory in relation to media law and policy in Third World contexts.

27. See Colleen Roach's (1990) comprehensive discussion of this and related issues.

28. Ferguson (1986, p. 62) points out another complication in devising national media policy in the face of transnational expansion: "Consumers buying their own dish aerials are beyond the reach of the receiving countries' regulations dealing with objective news reporting, advertising standards, questions of taste and decency or material suitable for children."

29. This research—on the portrayal of sex roles in Canadian television programming and advertising and radio programming and advertising—is presented in four volumes, all published in 1985 by the Canadian Radio-Television and Telecommunications Commission (CRTC).

30. Policy statements issued thus far by the CRTC are: "Sex-Role Stereotyping in the Broadcast Media: Policy Statement" (CRTC Public Notice 1986-351); "Industry Guidelines for Sex-Role Portrayal" (CRTC Public Notice 1990-99); and "1992 Policy on Gender Portrayal" (CRTC Public Notice 1992-58). Copies of these policy statements, as well as research reports, may be obtained by writing to the Canadian Radio-television and Telecommunications Commission, Ottawa, Ontario K1A 0N2.

31. The policy is entitled "Implementation of an Employment Equity Policy" (CRTC Public Notice 1992-59). It was announced in a news release issued by the CRTC on September 1, 1992, entitled "CRTC Announces Policies on Employment Equity Policy and Gender Portrayal for the Broadcasting and Cable TV Industries." Copies of the policy and news release are available from the Canadian Radio-Television and Telecommunications Commission, Ottawa, Ontario K1A 0N2.

32. For more information, write to CWRT, 350 Sparks Street, Suite 306, P.O. Box 627, Station "B," Ottawa, Ontario, K1P 562, Canada.

33. Information on this and related publications can be obtained by writing to National Council for Research on Women (NCRW), The Sara Delano Roosevelt Memorial House, 47-49 East 65th Street, New York, NY 10021. The Women's Institute for Freedom of the Press in Washington, D.C., began the publication in 1975 and published it until 1989. The publication was not updated until the NCRW published the 1992 edition. To compile the 1992 listings NCRW staff sent requests for information to those on the mailing list utilized by the Women's Institute for Freedom of the Press as well as to additional addresses obtained from other sources (conversation with NCRW office manager, September 23, 1992).

34. Some readers examining Table 3.1 in comparison to its counterpart in the 1989 edition of this book will note peculiar discrepancies—for example, the huge apparent increase in U.S. publications for women (from 373 to 609). Such discrepancies may reflect changes in data-gathering methods and the 2-year gap in the publication, as well as real changes in numbers of publications. It is likely that future editions of the Directory will provide increasingly accurate listings, especially of publications outside of the United States.

35. These periodicals vary considerably, as indicated in Marilyn Crafton Smith's chapter (Chapter 4) on alternative feminist media. Themes include: feminist legal issues, feminist political concerns, women's health, lesbian concerns, minority women, women's arts and literature, women and religion, women's sports, and feminist academic scholarship. Publications not listed are traditional, commercial women's magazines such as McCalls, Ladies Home Journal, and Family Circle. Outside of the United States, the most successful alternative feminist periodicals and their respective circulations in the mid 1980s were Emma in West Germany (300,000), Courage in West Germany (70,000), Spare Rib in the United Kingdom (30,000), Manushi in India (10,000), ISIS Women's World in Italy (5,000), and Broadsheet in New Zealand (4,000). In contrast, MS had a circulation of 463,000 (Seager & Olson, 1986, chart 34).

36. The 1992 Directory of Women's Media lists well over 50 U.S. publications that appear to have international content and circulations outside of the United States. Examples of these

publications are: *Media Report to Women* (previously noted), *Connexions: An International Women's Quarterly, Feminist Futures Network News, Women's International Network (WIN) News* (previously noted), *The Tribune,* publication of the previously noted International Women's Tribune Centre, *Seeds; African Women Rising; Let the Other Half Speak,* a publication of the Third World Women's Project of the Institute for Policy Studies in Washington, DC, *Worldwide News,* a publication of World Women in the Environment, and *Feminist Issues.*

37. "Sorting Out the Mail Sorting Division," *Manushi,* March 11, 1986, p. 40.

38. See Taylor, Kramarae, and Ebben's (1993) edited volume on *Women, Information Technology and Scholarship,* which includes an annotated bibliography as well as a number of essays.

39. The work of the Gender and New Information Technologies organization is significant along these lines. GRANITE, an international network of researchers, aims to encourage research related to gender and new information technologies. One of the major questions discussed at a November 1991 conference was the impact of new technologies on the private sphere. See Newsletter: *Gender & Mass Media,* No. 13, November, 1992, p. 16. See also Sparks and van Zoonen (1992).

40. PeaceNet users also have access to EcoNet (for users interested in environmental issues) and ConflictNet (for users working for social justice). For information, write to PeaceNet, 3228 Sacramento St., San Francisco, CA 94115. There are many other examples of such uses of technology. See examples in Penley and Ross (1991). See also Chapter 4 by Marilyn Crafton Smith in this volume.

41. These were *Media Report to Women; WIN News; Sex Roles Within Mass Media,* and *Echo.*

42. This was the topic of a presentation by Bettina Corke, U.S. Council for INSTRAW-Communication Task Force, New York, NY, at the Conference of the Association for Women in Development, November 22, 1991, Washington, DC.

References

Althusser, Louis. (1971). *Lenin and philosophy and other essays* (B. Brewster, Trans.). London: New Left Books.

Barrett, Michèle. (1980). *Women's oppression today.* London: Verso.

Boulding, Elise. (1981). Integration into what? Reflections on development planning for women. In Roslyn Dauber & Melinda Cain (Eds.), *Women and technological change in developing countries* (pp. 9-32). Boulder, CO: Westview.

Cain, Melinda. (1981). Java, Indonesia: The introduction of rice processing technology. In Roslyn Dauber & Melinda Cain (Eds.), *Women and technological change in developing countries* (pp. 193-204). Boulder, CO: Westview.

Canadian Radio-Television and Telecommunications Commission. (1990). *The portrayal of gender in Canadian broadcasting: Summary report 1984-1988.* Ottawa, Ontario: CRTC.

Cantor, Muriel G. (1987). *Women and diversity.* Unpublished report to the Benton Foundation.

Cooper, Anne M. (1988, July). *Television's invisible women: A five-nation study of anchors, reporters and correspondents.* Paper presented to the AEJMC, Portland, OR.

Cooper, Anne M., & Davenport, Lucinda D. (1987). Newspaper coverage of international women's decade: Feminism and conflict. *Journal of Communication Inquiry, 11*(1), 108-113.

Desai, Neera, & Krishnaraj, Maithreyi. (1987). *Women and society in India.* New Delhi: S. Narain & Sons.

Doumbia, Terez, & Hanitra, Niaina. (1989). What price dreams? *Democratic Journalist, 36*(7), 23-25.

EC tackles underrepresentation of women in mass media. (1991). *Media Report to Women, 19*(3), 4.

Eisenstein, Zillah. (1984). *Feminism and sexual inequality: Crisis in liberal America.* New York: Monthly Review Press.

Eisenstein, Zillah. (1981). *The radical future of liberal feminism.* New York: Longman.

European women launch media network under auspices of WACC. (1991). *Media Report to Women, 19*(2), 5.

Ferguson, Margorie. (1986). The challenge of neo-technological determinism for communication systems, industry and culture. In M. Ferguson (Ed.), *New communication technologies and the public interest* (pp. 52-71). London: Sage.

Fiske, John. (1987). British cultural studies and television. In Robert C. Allen (Ed.), *Channels of discourse* (pp. 254-289). Chapel Hill: University of North Carolina Press.

Flora, Cornelia Butler. (1980). Women in Latin American fotonovelas: From Cinderella to Mata Hari. *Women's Studies International Quarterly, 3*(1), 95-104.

Gallagher, Margaret. (1981). *Unequal opportunities: The case of women and the media.* Paris: UNESCO.

Gallagher, Margaret. (1984). *Employment and positive action for women in the television organizations of the EEC member states.* Brussels: Commission of the European Communities.

Gallagher, Margaret. (1987a). Redefining the communications revolution. In Helen Baehr & Gillian Dyer (Eds.), *Boxed in: Women & television* (pp. 19-37). New York: Pandora Press.

Gallagher, Margaret. (Ed). (1987b). *Women and media decision-making: The invisible barriers.* Paris: UNESCO.

Gallagher, Margaret. (1992). Women and men in the media. *Communication Research Trends, 12*(1), 1-36.

Griffin, Michael, Viswanath, K., & Schwartz, Dona. (1992). *Gender advertising in the U.S. and India: Exporting cultural stereotypes.* Unpublished paper. Minneapolis: University of Minnesota, School of Journalism and Mass Communication.

Guback, Thomas, & Varis, Tapio. (1982). Transnational communication and cultural industries. *Reports and Papers on Mass Communication,* No. 92. Paris: UNESCO.

Hall, Stuart. (1980a). Cultural studies and the centre: Some problematics and problems. In Stuart Hall, Dorothy Hobson, Andrew Lowe, & Paul Willis (Eds.), *Culture, media & language: Working papers in cultural studies, 1972-79* (pp. 15-47). London: Hutchinson.

Hall, Stuart. (1980b). Encoding/decoding. In Stuart Hall, Dorothy Hobson, Andrew Lowe, & Paul Willis (Eds.), *Culture, media & language: Working papers in cultural studies, 1972-79* (pp. 128-138). London: Hutchinson.

Hamelink, Cees. (1983). *Cultural autonomy in global communications.* New York: Longman.

Heath, Carla. (1992). Structural changes in Kenya's broadcasting system: A manifestation of presidential authoritarianism. *Gazette, 37,* 37-51.

International Commission for the Study of Communication Problems. (1980). *Many voices, one world* (MacBride report). Paris: UNESCO.

International Women's Tribune Centre. (1984). *Women using media for social change.* New York: IWTC.

ISIS International. (1986). *Powerful images: A woman's guide to audiovisual resources.* Rome: ISIS International.

Kichen, Steve. (Ed.). (1992, July 20). Special report on international business: The Forbes foreign rankings. *Forbes, 150*(2), 222-304.

Kishwar, Madhu, & Vanita, Ruth. (1984). (Eds.). *In search of answers: Indian women's voices from Manushi.* London: Zed Books.

Lafky, Sue A. (1990, August). *The role of gender in the professional values and orientation of journalists: A cross-cultural comparison.* Paper presented at the AEJMC, Minneapolis, MN.

Lent, John A. (1991). *Women and mass communications: An international annotated bibliography.* Westport, CT: Greenwood Press.

Leonardo, Micaela Di. (1985). Morals, mothers, and militarism: Anti-militarism and feminist theory. *Feminist Studies, 11*(3), 600-617.

Lim, Linda Y. C. (1981). Women's work in multinational electronics factories. In Roslyn Dauber & Melinda Cain (Eds.), *Women and technological change in developing countries* (pp. 181-191). Boulder, CO: Westview.

Mathieu, Nicole-Claude. (1988). "Woman" in ethnology: The other of the other, and the other of the self. *Feminist Studies, 14*(1), 3-14.

Mattelart, Armand, Delcourt, Xavier, & Mattelart, Michele. (1984). *International image markets* (David Buxton, Trans.). London: Comedia.

Mattelart, Michèle. (1986). *Women, media and crisis: Femininity and disorder.* London: Comedia.

Mattelart, Michèle, & Mattelart, Armand. (1982). "Small" technologies: The case of Mozambique. *Journal of Communication, 32*(2), 75-79.

Media Asia. (1987). 14(4), 181-242.

Melody, William H. (1991). The information society: The transnational economic context and its implications. In Gerald Sussman & John A. Lent (Eds.), *Transnational communications: Wiring the Third World* (pp. 27-41). Newbury Park: Sage.

Mohanty, Chandra, Russo, Ann, & Torres, Lourdes. (1991). (Eds.). *Third World women and the politics of feminism.* Bloomington: Indiana University Press.

Murdock, Graham, & Janus, Noreene. (1985). Mass communications and the advertising industry. *Reports and Papers on Mass Communication,* No. 97. Paris: UNESCO.

National Council for Research on Women. (1992). *1992 directory of women's media.* New York: National Council for Research on Women.

Ngechu, Mary. (1992). Gender sensitive communication research among male and female farmers. In S. T. K. Boafo & N. A. George (Eds.), *Communication research in Africa: Issues and perspectives* (pp. 53-68). Nairobi, Kenya: African Council for Communication Education.

Penley, Constance, & Ross, Andrew. (Eds.). (1991). *Technoculture.* Minneapolis: University of Minnesota Press.

Pletsch, Carl E. (1981). The three worlds, or the division of social science labor, circa 1950-1975. *Comparative Studies in Society and History, 23,* 565-590.

Roach, Colleen. (1990). The movement for a New World Information and Communication Order: A second wave? *Media, Culture & Society, 12*(3), 283-307.

Roach, Colleen. (1993). Report of the 4th MacBride Roundtable. *IAMCR/AIERI Newsletter, 3*(1), 12-16.

Robertson, Claire, & Berger, Iris. (Eds.). (1986). *Women and class in Africa.* New York: Africana Publishing.

Robinson, Gertrude J. (1981). *Female print journalists in Canada and the United States: A professional profile and comparison.* Working Papers in Communications, McGill University.

Robinson, Gertrude J. (1990, August). *Broadcast regulation and sex role stereotyping in Canada and the United States.* Paper presented at the Conference of the International Association for Mass Communication Research, Bled, Yugoslavia.

Schiller, Herbert I. (1981). *Who knows: Information in the age of the Fortune 500*. Norwood, NJ: Ablex.

Seager, Joni, & Olson, Ann. (1986). *Women in the world: An international atlas*. New York: Simon & Schuster.

Sen, Gita, & Grown, Caren. (1987). *Development, crises, and alternative visions: Third World women's perspectives*. New York: Monthly Review Press.

Smith, Judy, & Balka, Ellen. (1988). Chatting on a feminist computer network. In Cheris Kramarae (Ed.), *Technology and women's voices* (pp. 82-97). New York: Routledge & Kegan Paul.

Sparks, Colin, & van Zoonen, Liesbet. (Eds.). (1992). Gender and technology [Special issue]. *Media, Culture & Society, 14*(1).

Spindler-Brown, Angela. (1984, August). *Transforming television: Feminist experience in the U.K.* Paper presented at the 14th Conference of the International Association for Mass Communication Research, Prague, Czechoslovakia.

Srinivasan, Mangalam. (1981). Impact of selected industrial technologies on women in Mexico. In Roslyn Dauber & Melinda Cain (Eds.), *Women and technological change in developing countries* (pp. 89-108). Boulder, CO: Westview.

Stanley, Autumn. (1983). Women hold up two-thirds of the sky: Notes for a revised history of technology. In Joan Rothschild (Ed.), *Machina ex dea: Feminist perspectives on technology* (pp. 5-22). Elmsford, NY: Pergamon.

Staudt, Kathleen. (1985). *Agricultural policy implementation: A case study from Western Kenya*. West Hartford, CT: Kumarian Press.

Steeves, H. Leslie. (1987). Feminist theories and media studies. *Critical Studies in Mass Communication, 4,* 95-135.

Steeves, H. Leslie, & Arbogast, Rebecca A. (1993). Feminism and communication in development: Ideology, law, ethics, practice. In Brenda Dervin & Usha Hariharan (Eds.), *Progress in communication sciences* (Vol.XI, pp. 229-277). Norwood, NJ: Ablex.

Steiner, Linda. (1988). Oppositional decoding as an act of resistance. *Critical Studies in Mass Communication, 5,* 1-15.

Sussman, Gerald. (1991). Telecommunications for transnational integration: The World Bank in the Philippines. In Gerald Sussman & John A. Lent (Eds.), *Transnational communications: Wiring the Third World* (pp. 42-65). Newbury Park: Sage.

Sussman, Gerald, & Lent, John A. (1991). Introduction: Critical perspectives on communication and Third World development. In Gerald Sussman & John A. Lent (Eds.), *Transnational communications: Wiring the Third World* (pp. 1-26). Newbury Park: Sage.

Taylor, H. Jeanie, Kramarae, Cheris, & Ebben, Maureen. (1993). *Women, information technology, and scholarship*. Urbana, IL; Woman, Information Technology and Scholarship Colloquium, Center for Advaced Study, University of Illinois.

Turkle, Sherry. (1988). Computational reticence: Why women fear the intimate machine. In Cheris Kramarae (Ed.), *Technology and women's voices* (pp. 41-61). New York: Routledge & Kegan Paul.

UNESCO. (1985). *Communication in the service of women: A report on action and research programmes, 1980-1985*. Paris: UNESCO.

UNESCO. (1989). *World communication report*. Paris: UNESCO.

United Nations. (1974). *The impact of multinational corporations on development and international relations*. New York: United Nations.

van Zoonen, Liesbet. (1988). Rethinking women and the news. *European Journal of Communication, 3,* 35-53.

Ward, Kathryn B. (1986, July). *Women and transnational corporation employment: A world-system and feminist analysis*. Working Paper #120, Michigan State University.

4 Feminist Media and Cultural Politics

MARILYN CRAFTON SMITH

In the late 1960s media representing the second wave of feminism began to appear in the United States.[1] Destined to play an important role in the contemporary women's movement, these early media projects represented the means with which women could publicly challenge society and state their visions for the future. Producers of these media sought to create not only alternative forms of communication but also fundamental social change. For this reason, women's movement media offer us a means of understanding the subtleties, shifts, and currents of the movement over the past 25 to 30 years.

Although the women's movement is frequently referred to in its singular form, it actually comprises many ideologically diverse groups.[2] Rather than focus specifically on the ideological content of media representing any one of these feminist perspectives, this chapter will address feminist media conceived of as primarily alternative or independent, those that maintain either an ideological or structural distance from mainstream social relations and media institutions.

The first section reviews the context for the formation of women's movement media, the founding of which can be significantly attributed to the relations feminists had with the mass media. I will examine the ways in which feminist media, particularly print media, oppose the mass media to offer alternatives to women's movement supporters. The next section delineates organizational and operational practices which characterize

AUTHOR'S NOTE: I wish to thank both Nina Gregg and H. Leslie Steeves for their suggestions and discussions concerning the initial version of this chapter, and Pamela J. Creedon and Cheryl Claassen for their helpful editorial comments. The prior work on women's movement media by Mather (1974), Armstrong (1981), and Allen (1988/1989) has provided much of the initial legwork in accounts of the early feminist media projects.

feminist media: (1) their collectivist and collaborative processes; (2) the separatist impulse underlying media production; and (3) its reformulation by feminists of color. The third section briefly discusses networking activities of feminist media workers and media formats for print media, women's music, and computer networks for women. The final section reviews previous studies of feminist media, with primary emphasis on print media. Here, I focus on the need for more rigorous analyses of the feminist implications of women's media and offer directions for future research.

Political Precedents: The Formation of Women's Movement Media

In the mid-1960s there seemed to be little indication of widespread support for, or knowledge about, a social movement directed at women. Appellations such as the "women's movement," the "feminist movement," or even the more radical "women's liberation movement," had not yet been formulated. Often represented in today's mass media as the women's movement itself, the National Organization for Women (NOW), founded in 1966, was only in the beginning stages of establishing its chapter network. Moreover, little contact existed among women working for other causes such as the peace or civil rights movements. Working oftentimes in isolation from one another, groups of women engaged in various forms of political action, networking, theoretical development, and consciousness raising (C-R). Through this work they attempted to educate themselves and others about the inequities they experienced as women. Some sought to define women's oppression as a "class condition of women," using positions statements and other rhetorical strategies (The Feminists, 1973), while others wished to share their personal experiences of oppression, discrimination, and politics surrounding gender. Expressing this emerging consciousness became the basis for the founding of the women's movement media.

Jo Freeman (1973) and others have suggested that there were two distinct branches of the contemporary women's movement, the "reform" and "radical" components, or "women's rights" and "women's liberation" (Hole & Levine, 1971). These two styles defined to some extent not only the political strategies that each branch pursued but also the approach each took with the media it produced. Freeman contends that distinctions in structure and style more accurately differentiated the two originating branches than did ideology (Freeman, 1973, p. 795).

The style of organizational structure of the "reform" branch traditionally has been formal, with elected officers, boards of directors, and the use of by-laws. This top-down leadership structure may have caused the slow development of a mass base of support for the early national reform organizations (Freeman, 1973, p. 796). Trained in traditional forms of political action, the "reform" feminists pursued conventional avenues for social change through legislative means.

Periodicals or newsletters were published by the nationally organized groups as a service to their various memberships. NOW-affiliated groups at the state and local levels also published periodicals. Much like *The Woman's Journal,* which was the official publication of the National American Woman Suffrage Association,[3] these periodicals continue to be a significant record of the members' actions and of the directions taken by the groups working within the framework of organized institutional feminism.

In contrast, proponents of the second branch of feminist activism in the 1960s, the women's liberation branch, came to feminist politics with experiences gained in other liberation movements and groups associated with the Left, such as the radical student movement, the anti-Vietnam war/peace movement, and the civil rights movement. Increasingly dissatisfied with their status in Left organizations and with the sexism predominant there, these activists left to form their own political groups. The women's liberation branch had little organizational contact among the many small groups of which it was constituted. Its participants frequently condemned traditional organizational structures and avoided what they considered to be the patriarchal replication of top-down power structures. They instead adopted a style that often appeared spontaneous and leaderless.

Though the proponents of this branch had neither the resources nor the desire to form national organizations, their accumulated experience in local organizing enabled them to utilize the infrastructure of the radical community (Freeman, 1973, pp. 801-802). They transported their knowledge of grassroots organizing and underground media to the women's movement and the founding of its media. Their periodicals represent the more radical or "alternative" publications within 1960s feminism.

Although feminist media developed alongside the women's movement, additional factors contributed to the formation of feminist media projects. One factor was the reaction feminists had to the mass media's representation of women. Women and their concerns were rarely treated with any seriousness, given that their portrayals were either degrading or nonexistent. Traditional women's magazines also gave little attention to altering the status of women, as indicated by early research on media representations in these publications (Flora, 1971; Franzwa, 1974). Consequently, the mass media was a top priority for feminist criticism because of its blatantly oppressive representations of women. Throughout this period, feminist writings reflected an awareness of sex role ideology and the pervasive manner in which mass media representations contributed to this ideology (Friedan, 1963).

The reproduction of sexist ideology, however, was not the only reason for feminists in both branches to distrust mainstream media. Much of the their disillusionment derived from the mass media's coverage of the women's movement itself. In *The Politics of Women's Liberation,* Freeman (1975) shows how the media expressed antagonism, through the use of unflattering portrayals or the trivialization of feminists' political interests by focusing on marital status or mode of dress in interviews. The mass media rendered the political messages inaccurate, distorted, or trivialized (pp. 112-113).

The founding members of the larger institutionalized feminist organizations, such as NOW, had prior experience in working with the mainstream media and were able to gain the publicity they needed to increase their memberships. Their organizations also represented the type of complex, legitimated institutions with which the news media were willing to collaborate (Tuchman, 1978, p. 134). In the late 1960s and early 1970s, when the national news media simultaneously began to cover the women's movement, their professional news conventions mandated that reporters seek hard news "events" and people who could act as spokeswomen for the movement (Tuchman, 1978). Such practices ensured the omission of coverage of the symbolic, issue-oriented problems that were central to the radical movement's development. In addition, the selection of certain "media-nominated leaders" (such as Gloria Steinem and Betty Friedan) limited the public voice of the movement to those who met the news media's criteria for spokespersons, a practice contrary to the prevailing feminist belief that no one feminist could speak for all others (Tuchman, 1978, pp. 139-140).

Feminist hostility toward the mass media was expressed in the founding issue of *off our backs,* a feminist monthly newspaper, in 1970. The editors stated, "The women's movement can no longer afford to be naive about the nature and function of the mass media in this society. . . . We no longer need to use the mass media to tell people we exist." Further, they called for a "halt to all dealings with the mass media—no more interviews, no more documentaries, no more special coverage. We don't need them and we don't want them" (Ferro, Holcolm, & Saltzman-Webb, 1977, pp. 117-118). Indeed, many feminist periodicals allocated editorial space in each issue for analysis of the mass media (Allen, 1988/1989, p. 62).

Feminist objections to sexist portrayals of women in advertising were evidenced by the more than 8,000 letters on advertising that *Ms.* magazine received after its first issue (Mather, 1974, p. 155). Sexist attitudes and practices were prevalent among 1960s alternative presses as well. Practices such as the "selling of sex" to finance these publications caused feminists to form their own alternative media (Armstrong, 1981, pp. 54-55). Responding to the sexist representations found in the male-dominated mass media and alternative presses, many feminist editorial groups developed advertising policies opposing sexist advertising (Mather, 1974, p. 157).

A primary condition for the successful launching of a social movement is the ability to communicate with potential adherents. The media outlets developed by the women's movement activists became central organizing tools, with their capacity to relay information about political actions, to create a space for discussion about their concerns, and to offer support to and seek input from their readers. In these ways, feminists' overtly political media contrast with traditional mass media offerings. Features of organizational style and operating practices that characterize feminist media projects are examined more closely below.

Organizational and Operational Practices

Collectivity as Organizational Style

Women's movement media grew out of a specific historical period characterized not only by the richness of its protest and dissent, but also by its desire for alternative ways of living and working: an estimated 5,000 alternative grassroots cooperative businesses were reported as of 1976 (Gardner, 1976, cited in Rothschild-Whitt, 1979). The formation of these businesses was particularly prolific in fields requiring low capital needs (Rothschild-Whitt, 1979, p. 510). The development of low-cost offset printing, plus the use of typewriters and transfer lettering, made a publishing venture highly feasible to feminist groups with little capital.

Many early feminist publishing groups were collectively owned and operated. Activists chose the medium of print to produce newspapers, newsletters, magazines, and journals. Although most of the periodicals were published initially in the newsletter format, more than 132 other newspapers, magazines, and journals were in existence by 1973 (Mather, 1974, p. 2). The newsletter format is still a popular format for women's publications today.[4]

Many feminist media workers viewed the publishing collective as an extension of their own developing political awareness. The principle of equal participation became an operating goal. As in the C-R groups and other collectivist organizations, feminist collectives favored a consensual process over majority rule, and collective formulation and resolution of problems. Loosely structured staffing characterized the feminist media as it had the alternative media that preceded them (Allen, 1988/1989, pp. 55-56, 121; Mather, 1974, p. 145).

Rothschild-Whitt (1979, pp. 511-512) shows that collectivity entails an alternative view of authority. Whereas bureaucratic organizations tend to locate authority with individuals, either through incumbency or expertise, in collectively run organizations authority resides explicitly in the collective as a whole.

Three levels of incentives sustain potential members of cooperative work organizations. In contrast to bureaucratic incentives that are remunerative in nature, collectives' incentives include the fulfillment of values, solidarity (friendship), and material gain (Rothschild-Whitt, 1979, p. 515). The primary reason, however, is purposive. People join collectives to gain substantial control over their work, which enables them to structure both the product and the work process in accordance with their values and political goals. These findings were substantiated by both Mather (1974, p. 199) and Allen (1988/1989, p. 122) in their studies of women's movement media workers and by Armstrong's (1981) study of alternative media (pp. 22, 231). Indeed, staff members of many early feminist periodicals indicated that primary among their reasons for joining a collective were the opportunity to work with other women in a positive atmosphere and the need for women to develop their own media as a "forum" or vehicle for exchange of ideas (Mather, 1974, p. 199).

Although collaboration has been central to feminist media projects at the operational level, it also underlies the mutual sharing that goes on in the communication process itself. Feminist communication requires that women not only gain access to the communication tools, but that they actively participate in the communication process (Freeman & Jones, 1976, p. 5). A primary role of feminist periodicals has been the establishment of a space where members of the editorial collective and readers are able to exchange views.

The avenue for exchange may be manifested in extended space for editorials collectively written by staff members, for letters or other materials submitted to the editor, or for interviews of feminists. In particular, feminist publications emphasize reader participation that allows readers to speak for themselves. Mather (1974) has shown that an average of 6% of each issue of early feminist periodicals in her study was devoted to pages written by readers in letters to the editors (p. 200). She contrasts this figure with the percentages taken 6 years earlier of five traditional women's magazines in which no magazine exceeded 1%.[5] In contrast, *Ms.* allocated 5% of its pages to its readers' letters.[6] The "No Comment" section of *Ms.* (no longer part of the current *Ms.*) that reprinted items about women that were submitted by *Ms.* readers, provided readers an opportunity to express their discontent about mass media portrayals of women. In submitting materials taken from other advertising contexts as evidence of sexist representations of women, *Ms.* readers were able to engage in an oppositional decoding of the mass media (Steiner, 1988). Finally, the use of interviews permits individual women to speak for themselves. The inclusion of regular interview sections by feminist periodicals such as *off our backs* counters the mass media's use of movement spokeswomen and its treatment of movement issues (Allen, 1988/1989, p. 79).

Feminist periodicals are also distinguished by their inclusion of content not commonly found in the mainstream media (Allen, 1988/1989, p. 82). Attention to issues such as the politics of abortion, sexuality, women's health, violence against women, pornography, race, and class analyses, all of which are frequently ignored in the mass media press, commonly appear in feminist publications. In addition, these publications have included in their pages news of other publications and the formation of new feminist media, news of the women's movement, and occasionally collaboratively shared editorial content from other publishers (Allen, 1988/1989, pp. 124-128). In this respect feminist publishing has represented a collectivist effort on the part of many media producers within the movement.

Separatism as Politics

Reappropriating the knowledge and meaning of women's life experiences and advancing new ways of visioning the world lie at the heart of feminist media production. For some feminists, their goals may specify simply the daily dissemination of information that is deemed vital for a particular legislative action; for others the entire production process itself becomes a political act, a process whereby questions can be raised regarding the ethics and goals of publishing. Such a reclamation, however, has a subversive component in its allegiance to separatism, as feminists have attempted to control the production of their periodicals.

Separatism has been a prominent and constant component within feminism. One view of separatism that is often associated with radical feminism implicitly assumes a position outside patriarchal institutions, a separation from "institutions, relationships, roles and activities which are male-defined, male-dominated and operating for the benefit of males and the maintenance of male privilege" (Frye, 1983, p. 96). This separation is one that has been initiated by women.

Frye (1983) argues that total power is manifested in the unconditional access that men have historically had to women. As women choose to separate themselves from men, through the establishment of women-only projects or activities, they deny access to men and thus claim the assumption of power. Frye contends that, as women assume control over "what is said and sayable," over the nature of information imparted and to whom, they also assume the power to define. By controlling both faces of power, access and definition, women are "doubly insubordinate" (1983, pp. 105-107).

Through its power to give women control over their own ideas and words, a separatist dimension is inherently a part of women's movement media. The majority of media projects undertaken by contemporary feminists have primarily been women-only endeavors, established and operated by women for women.

The exclusivity of women-owned and -run media projects is unique to the contemporary women's movement. In her study of women's communications networks developed between 1963 and 1983, Allen (1988/1989) found that contemporary women's media projects are rarely subsidized by or operated with males, as were two feminist publications from the turn of the century: Susan B. Anthony's paper, the *Revolution,* funded by George Francis Train, and *The Woman's Journal,* established by a group of reformers that included Lucy Stone and her husband Henry Blackwell.

The strain over finances also raises the controversial question of whether to do business with mainstream media (primarily, but not solely, publishers), who are considered by some feminists to be the patriarchal press. Doing business with mainstream publishers, for example, through the sale of subsidiary rights, may enhance the financial status of a particular feminist press and ensure the possibility of producing more feminist works in the future. However, some feminist publishers may view this collaboration as a betrayal, as was the case with the editors of Persephone Press, a lesbian publishing house (now defunct). A clause was included in its publishing contracts that explicitly stated that the publishers would not sell rights to male publishing houses (Rich, Greenfield, McGloin, & Snow, 1980, p. 83). By including this clause, the publishers attempted to validate feminist publishing in its own right, by precluding women authors from perceiving their press "as an elementary experience before the real thing" (p. 83). More importantly, initiating business collaborations with a patriarchal press was seen as equivalent to relinquishing the goal of establishing an autonomous lesbian network in publishing.

Beyond Separatism: Publications by Women of Color

Initially white women were the majority of participants in the reform ("rights") and radical ("liberation") branches of the women's movement and in the media these branches spawned.[7] One explanation for the lack of participation by women of color is that the women's movement developed during a period of organized struggle for civil rights for Blacks, thus, support for the liberation of women could be construed as a threat against gains made for Blacks (hooks, 1981, pp. 176). In addition, many women of color supported the basic goals of feminism (advocacy of social equality for all women) but were hesitant to embrace a women's movement dominated by middle- and upper class white women whose concerns entailed fulfilling individualist aspirations for career success while "gaining entrance into the capitalist and patriarchal power structure" (hooks, 1981, p. 188). The liberal feminist assumption that work liberates women had little appeal to poor, nonwhite, and lower class women.

The view of separatism described above is problematic to women of color in that it privileges sexual difference as the single axis for feminist identity. From the perspective of women of color and lower class women, women's identity is not given solely in opposition to men or to male-defined institutions and structures. In cultures where " 'asymmetric race and class relations are a central organizing principle of society,' one may also 'become a woman' in opposition to other women" (Alarcón, 1992, p. 360, quoting Macdonell, 1986, p. 62). Thus, separatism for Black women may involve a separation from whites, the dominant group in race relations, rather than a separation from Black men who also are, and historically have been, oppressed by whites (Combahee River Collective, 1983, p. 275).[8] The insufficient attention given to the interconnected issues of racism, sexism, and classism by "Black liberation politics, the feminist movement, and class-based Marxist and socialist organizations" (Caraway, 1991, p. 52, referencing King, 1988, p. 52) undoubtedly has been a motivating force behind the formation of alternative media by women of color.

Although fewer in number, media projects developed by and about women of color voice the perspectives of Black, Native American, Asian, Hispanic, Chicana, and Third World women. In her 1990 study of periodicals by and about women of color, Kimberlie Kranich indicates that alternative periodicals by women of color were in existence as early as 1971, for example, *Asian Women* (1971) in Berkeley, *Comision Femenil Mexicana Report* (1971-1973) in Los Angeles, and *Triple Jeopardy* (1971-1975) in New York City. Kranich identifies 50 publications in 1990 that have a primary focus on women of color and that fall into diverse racial/ethnic categories: Asian (11), Black (22), Hispanic (6), Native American (3), and Women of Color (8), a category in which more than one race or ethnic group is represented.[9] In addition, 46 periodicals that are no longer publishing are listed from the period 1971-1988, and are identified as Asian (4), Black (14), Hispanic (8), Native American (7), and Women of Color (13).

Although Black women's periodicals began to appear in the early 1970s, the majority were established in the 1980s. Martha Allen (personal communication, September 10, 1988) reports that many of the early Black women's periodicals produced only one issue that would not be followed by subsequent issues until 1 or 2 years later. An example is *Up Front,* a Washington, DC, newspaper that, after several issues in 1984, resumed publication in 1988 (Kranich, personal communication, September 10, 1988).

Many periodicals by women of color, like those published by white feminists, are newsletters. Some are associated with women's organizations, for example, *Truth* (Association for Black Women Historians), *Pan Asian News* (Organization of Pan Asian American Women) and the *Sisterhood of Black Single Mothers Newsletter,* published by the organization of the same name (Kranich, 1990), or represent research centers as does *Center News* (the Center for Research on Women at Memphis State University). Scholarly journals, too, reflect the research being done about women of color, such as *Sage: A Scholarly Journal About Black Women,* or *Third Woman,* a forum for creative works of Latinas and other Third World women. Book publishers emphasizing women of color and multicultural issues have also gained prominence in the world of feminist publishing since the early 1980s; Kitchen Table: Women of Color Press (founded 1981) and the Aunt Lute Books Foundation are two notable examples.

Feminist Media Networking

Feminist publishers organized in a national network have become identified with the women-in-print subculture, or what is called the "women-in-print movement." Charlotte Bunch attributes the organization of the first Women in Print conference, held in Omaha, NE, in 1976, to the efforts of June Arnold (Doughty & Bunch, 1980, p. 72). Arnold wanted to bring together women involved in all aspects of feminist publishing, for example, presses, journals, newspapers, bookstores, and distributors. The conference attracted representatives from about 80 publications, presses, bookstores, and distributors ("200 Women's Media," 1982, p. 1). Although only "130 white feminists" were reported in attendance, this first conference was an extremely important event for dispelling the isolation felt by so many feminist publishers. Bunch noted that, as in the early periods of the women's liberation movement when young feminists discovered each other, this conference generated similar excitement (Doughty & Bunch, 1980, p. 72). It also encouraged the development of lines of communication among the different branches of the women-in-print movement. Subsequent women-in-print trade conferences have been held in 1981 (Washington, D.C.) and 1985 (Berkeley), but in more recent years feminist bookstore owners and publishers (women-only) have met prior to the annual meeting of the American Booksellers Association for 1- to

2-day conferences. International feminist book fairs have been held biannually since 1984 in London, Oslo, Montreal, Barcelona, and Amsterdam with future fairs scheduled for Australia (1994) and Brazil (1996) (Carol Seajay, personal communication, January 5, 1993).

There are numerous reasons why feminist authors might select a feminist publisher over one in the mainstream media (Jay, 1986, pp. 5-6). Feminist writers turn to feminist publishers specifically because feminist publishers are likely to share political goals. In addition, unlike a corporate firm that may promote only a small amount of the books it actually publishes (one out of six, according to Jay), feminist publishers tend to put more effort into promotion and distribution and to backlist the books, thereby keeping them in print indefinitely.

A network similar to the one that developed around women's publications and presses also coalesced around women's music and related broadcast media to promote women's music as well as messages of feminism (see Tilchen, 1984). This network has spawned numerous national and regional music festivals, the most prominent of which are the National Women's Music Festival and the Michigan Womyn's Music Festival. Feminist recording companies provide political and professional support to women musicians much like feminist publishers do to their authors. Women's music production and activities are reported in *Hot Wire,* a publication aligned with the women's music movement.[10]

In recent years a rapidly developing medium for communication among women is the electronic computer network, which has led to the formation of multi-participant e-mail lists, discussion groups, or electronic bulletin boards. Although these types of networks have existed for some time, there seems to have been a "positive explosion" in electronic media for women during the past 1- to 2-year period (Karla Tonella, personal communication, December 16, 1992). Because they function by way of institutional facilities or under the auspices of on-line computer services, the networks are not characteristically owned or operated by women. However, the networks explicitly address issues of interest to women and in many cases utilize moderators who direct the discussions toward feminist concerns.

Many e-mail "lists" or networks exists that focus on women's concerns.[11] Two examples of these networks are a newsgroup, SOC. FEMINISM, and a women's studies list, WMST-L. Cindy Tittle Moore, a moderator for the SOC. FEMINISM bulletin board, estimates that "several thousand people" read through that list although only about 50 of them comprise a core of regular contributors. A condensed version of material appearing on SOC. FEMINISM, which began in late 1989, has been available since April 1991 as FEMINISM-DIGEST and has approximately 69 subscribers (Moore, personal communication, December 18, 1992). WMST-L, a list moderated by

Joan Korenman, is a major source for information and discussion concerning women's studies. As of December 11, 1992, this list claims 1,436 subscribers from 27 countries (Korenman, personal communication, December 17, 1992). Founded in late 1991, WMST-L became available in digest form, WMST-L DIGEST, in January 1992.

Electronic computer networks are available to persons who work for or are associated with "organizations with investments in computers and their promises" (Cheris Kramarae & Jeanie Taylor, 1992). Potentially, the networks promise a democratization of information exchange, providing equal access to increasing numbers of users who may communicate at low or no cost across "barriers of space, time, and social categories" (Kramarae & Taylor, 1992). According to Lee Sproull and Sara Kiesler (1991, cited in Kramarae & Taylor, 1992), people who are marginalized in organization hierarchies are not so positioned in the "nets" because differences based on race, age, ableism, and physical appearance disappear. Sex, most commonly denoted by the name of the writer, is the one indicator of difference that remains for women on the networks (Kramarae & Taylor, 1992).

Many of the problems women experience on the networks are not dissimilar to ones women faced in the 1960s and 1970s when, prior to starting their own media, they attempted to work with men on alternative media projects. Similarly, several of the problems women experience in conversation are reproduced on the networks (Kramarae & Taylor, 1992). First, in networks that are "open" to both men and women, men tend to monopolize the discussions that occur. Kramarae and Taylor (1992) cite as an example a network called SOC. WOMEN whose messages, on some days, were entirely posted by men. Comserve's GENDER hot line became a moderated list in 1989 after it, too, had been over-run by male users (Tonella, personal communication, December 16, 1992). Thus, even in the case of networks whose topics are women's issues, discussion activities may be dominated by men.

Second, there is increased evidence of sexual harassment of women by men on the networks, with actions ranging from sexist jokes and limericks to hostile comments about women (Kramarae & Taylor, 1992). Kramarae and Taylor note that women who seek respect as scholars may be hesitant to point out sexist behavior on the networks publicly, a form of silencing that in effect limits women's participation. Third, men exhibit more assertive behavior on the networks as they send more messages, introduce more topics, and tend to disagree more frequently with others ("flaming," or the sending of "hot-tempered" messages). A related incidence reportedly occurred on the SAPPHO list, a women-only forum and support group for gay and bisexual women, when a user named "Julie" always appeared to be in disagreement with others on the list. Julie consequently absorbed all kinds of abuse for her stances, after which it was conjectured by other members that "Julie" might actually be a man (Tonella, personal communication, December 12, 1992). By questioning the identity of the user, the issue of deception (and the existence of imposters) on the networks is raised. An additional concern noted by Kramarae and Taylor (1992) is the transmission of pornographic material over the networks. Incidences of the transmissions of unsolicited "sexually explicit drawings and photographs" have been reported (Kramarae & Taylor, 1992).

Access to electronic networks is not available to all who wish to participate in discussions concerning women's issues or to all who wish to utilize the material for research purposes.[12] Most of the users of the networks are men, both inside and outside the university (Kramarae & Taylor, 1992), and most of the users (whether women or men) are privileged in their access, either through employment status in organizations (thus the availability of computers and networks), or through economic status whereby they can afford to pay on-line service charges and to purchase their own computer technology. Consequently, world-wide sex and class hierarchies are reproduced on the nets (Kramarae & Taylor, 1992). One way to resolve inequitable access is to follow the example of the San Francisco NET (SFNET), a collection of 11 San Francisco coffeehouses that have installed specially designed computer/modem tables. Coffeehouse patrons purchase a code for $1.00 from an employee, after which they decide on a topic to access, through events, travel, music, love, or chat hot lines. Among these hot lines, the most popular are the chat hot lines that link the coffeehouses for real-time debates (San Francisco NET, 1992). Such a system could be appropriated by feminists whereby the use of computers in public spaces would combine the already established network of women's coffeehouses and bars with on-line communication systems for women.

Researching Cultural Politics

As early as 1973, Anne Dudley Mather stated three reasons for researching feminist periodicals: the dearth of research in this area, the importance of women's media as a resource for research on the women's movement, and the need for research that makes more rigorous distinctions between media produced by "feminists" and those produced by "women." These concerns are still valid today.

Mather's study (1974) of early feminist publications was the first of its kind to review comprehensively the earliest publications of the current women's movement, those published between the years 1968 and 1973. This study also included a survey of suffrage publications and a brief analysis of *Ms.* magazine in its first year (1972) in comparison with other feminist publications of that year.

At the time of her research, Mather (1974) noted that there had been no significant work on the feminist press. Indeed, the omission of feminist media has been characteristic of much of the literature of the "press of protest."[13] *The Dissident Press* by Lauren Kessler (1984), however, does include a chapter that surveys briefly the historical context of feminist publishing from the suffrage periodicals of the 1840s to the variety of publications of the 1980s. Nevertheless, this work is limited by the brevity of the analysis of the publications and by its scope because it does not consider the plethora of periodicals associated with the recent women's movement. Additionally problematic is the unexamined assumption that magazines such as *Savvy; Working Woman,* and *Working Mother,* although directed at women, are equally representative of feminism.

In contrast, David Armstrong's study, *A Trumpet to Arms: Alternative Media in America* (1981), includes a chapter on "Sexual Politics" that is distinguished by its separate discussions of media aimed at disparate radical groups: women's liberation activists, lesbian-feminists, and gay men. In addition, he recognizes significant links between the underground press and the feminist media that succeeded it.

Martha Allen (1988/1989) examines media that have been produced by and for women from 1963 to 1983. In her study, Allen, the former editor of the *Directory of Women's Media,*[14] identifies eight characterizing features of women's communication networks, while focusing primarily on the many multi-issue, single-issue, and special-identity women's periodicals of the period.[15] A section on nonprint formats also includes discussion of music, film, video, and radio. Allen's study is rich with anecdotes and personal interviews with founders of women's media projects.

The two studies by Mather (1974) and Allen (1988/1989) represent the only comprehensive research available that together span 20 years of feminist media, with primary emphases on print media. Individual case studies have been undertaken of media projects such as those of Redwood Records[16] (Lont, 1984/1985), the Pittsburgh *Network News* (Downie, 1989), and the WIFP/WINS project (Women's Institute for Freedom of the Press/Women's International News Service) for the U.N. World Conference of Women in Nairobi (Kassell & Kaufman, 1989). Although outside the purview of this chapter, further research could examine feminists' use of related media formats such as video/film, music, radio, art, theater, graphic design, presses, printers, and news services.[17]

Particularly in need of future research are alternative media focusing on women of color. The formation of media projects by and about women of color during the second wave of feminism and the historically specific contexts out of which they have evolved need to be addressed to understand fully how these media developed independent of those linked to the reform and radical branches of the women's movement.[18] In addition to a consideration of their historical context, the media of women of color could be assessed in relation to mainstream media, to other minority media (see Wilson & Gutiérrez, 1985), and in relation to the politics and media of reformist or women's liberationist feminists.[19]

Because many publications are short lived, it is imperative, as Mather argued, that feminist media history be recorded. Although some feminist periodicals have endured, for example, 10 years or more, and although many new periodicals emerge to replace those that cease to exist, the problems of burnout, financial strain, internal disagreements, or changes remain and contribute to the short life cycle and ultimate demise of many of the media projects. These media products and their history are invaluable sources for future research on the feminist movement and yet many groups and their media often come in to and out of existence before they are appropriately archived or recorded. The dynamics of the formation process for a media project need to be recorded as well as reasons for a project's demise.[20]

Many archives group feminist periodicals, as well as other feminist media, with those that are categorized as "women's media." Mather's call for research that distinguishes feminist media from other alternative media, particularly those designated as being "by women," points to a still unresolved area within feminism. In addressing this distinction in relation to feminist novels (Coward, 1980) and feminist art (Barrett, 1982), both Rosalind Coward and Michelle Barrett caution against the confusion of women's experience with women's politics. Coward notes, in reference to women's novels, that although such media products may have recognizable roots in the women's movement, "their relation to feminism is not the necessary outcome of taking women's experience as central" (p. 58). She argues further that

> feminism can never be the product of the identity of women's experience and interests—there is no such unity. Feminism must always be the alignment of women in a political movement with particular political aims and objectives. It is a grouping unified by its political interests, not its common experience. (Coward, 1980, p. 63)

Making such a distinction does not imply that there is nothing progressive about "women's media" (Coward, 1980, p. 61). The reclamation of women's history and experience can contribute to a sense of unity for the producers and consumers of women's media, and we have seen how women's media producers have challenged the traditions and conventions of the mass media with alternative organizational structures, practices, and content. However, the conflation of feminist periodicals and women's periodicals into a single category of the "dissident press," when uncritically addressed, does little to illuminate our understanding of the radical texts of the women's movement. In her appeal for us to move beyond women's experience, Coward argues for us to "discover its 'representativeness' which would show the workings of ideology and its relation to objective, material structures of oppression" (p. 63).

Media researchers suggests that alternative media, which are aligned with the women's movement, play a key role in raising issues of concern to women that the mass media may then pick up and carry to a larger audience (Allen, 1987, p. 20; Kessler, 1984). Donna Allen (1987) states that although "the mass media may not tell it our way—that articulation is still our job," they "open up the questions for consideration by the public" (p. 20). Yet the mass media themselves represent a "field of allowable images" (Jaddou & Williams, 1981, p. 121), a field that comprises a core of traditional images and those newly incorporated or on their way to incorporation. The process of incorporation is one of dilution, whereby images of feminist struggle that are taken in by the mass media are made to conform to dominant values and representations. As Jaddou and Williams (1981) point out, images on their way to incorporation do not come out of thin air, but rather arise within the field of the unallowable, those marginalized representations that are directly suppressed, either economically (through limited exhibition, production, and distribution) or by the state (p. 121). Thus, although the mass media may provide a location for feminist issues to be raised for larger audiences, the degree to which the issues and their representations in the mass media conform to the feminist struggle distinguishes them from their oppositional treatment in feminist media. For example, as the mass media frames the collectivist feminist struggle in terms of the individual, the reductionist tendencies in the incorporation process are at work. In question here is the degree to which the feminist struggle is represented, whether it is redefined as individual struggle, or, similarly, embraced as "women's experience" by alternative women's media.

As feminists continue to evaluate what it means to be activists in relation to the goals of the women's movement, this evaluation must also include an accounting for the women's movement media themselves. Responding to a panel at the second International Feminist Book Fair in Oslo in 1986, K. Kaufman questioned the relationship of feminist politics to women's media and women's culture. She asked if we, as feminist media producers, authors, image makers, readers, and/or viewers, are being contained through our own participation/complicity. "Has the consumption of feminist culture—particularly in its avant-garde, alternative or progressive forms—become a passive and pacifying substitution for action toward substantive, structural change in women's status?" (Kaufman, 1986, p. 13).

The question is crucial because it highlights the need for an ongoing, thorough evaluation of women's activities and projects in order to assess their efficacy for social change. Feminism is founded upon the assumption that women are an historically oppressed group, and that through a variety of means, both ideological and structural, we must bring about fundamental changes in society to eradicate this oppression. Feminist media were founded upon the assumption that, to facilitate social change, women must establish various media formats through which they communicate their own words and images, their own expressions of what feminist politics means. Knowledge and its production are fundamentally linked to the conferrence of power. Recognizing this, feminist media workers have provided vehicles for the production and dissemination of knowledge about their own and other women's lives (see Kaufman, 1986, p. 13).

In order to be consistent with the politics of the feminist movement, to make explicit the structures and processes of women's subordination, feminist media will have to account for radical structural changes that feminism requires. Research into this media must consider the political impulses (and their limits) underlying feminist media production and consumption, including the impulses that motivate the formation of such media projects in the first place. Considering political impulses clarifies the role that women's media play in defining the politics and struggles of our feminism(s). As feminism has become increasingly involved in cultural politics, the use of more rigorous theoretical distinctions are required to ensure that the question be raised of how media representations, including those of feminist media, work to effect social change. Such an approach would continue to address the political utility of women's media projects and also serve the diverse groups within feminism.

Notes

1. Here I distinguish the second wave of the women's movement, which began in the 1960s, from the first wave, which was associated predominantly with the struggle for women's suffrage.

2. Feminist writers have attempted to categorize various perspectives in feminist thought, for example: liberal, radical, or socialist feminisms (Jaggar, 1983); psychoanalytic feminism (Donovan, 1985, pp. 91-116); post-structuralist and post-modernist feminisms (see Weedon, 1987, and Tong, 1989, respectively); or those feminisms identified with women of color or Third World women (Anzaldúa, 1990; Caraway, 1991; Collins, 1991; hooks, 1981; King, 1988).

3. *The Women's Journal* was first published from 1870 to 1890 by the American Woman Suffrage Association until this organization merged with the National American Woman Suffrage Association (NAWSA). From 1890 to 1917 this journal was the public voice of the mainstream suffrage movement and NAWSA. Between 1917 and 1931, it was published as *The Woman Citizen* by the Woman Citizen Corporation as a result of a bequest from Mrs. Frank Leslie to Carrie Chapman Catt, President of NAWSA.

4. The *1992 Directory of Women's Media* (The National Council for Research on Women, 1992), shows that 200 of the 609 publication entries include *newsletter* either in their titles or in the descriptions provided by the publications.

5. The percentages of pages devoted to letters to the editor were: *Good Housekeeping*, .7%; *Harper's Bazaar*, 0%; *Ladies Home Journal*, 1.0%; *McCalls*, 0.8%; *Vogue*, 0%. These percentages were taken from a study by Rita Mookerji (cited in Mather, 1974, p. 199).

6. *Ms.* reported, for example, that in 1979 the monthly averages of reader contributions were 300 Letters to the Editors, 600 unsolicited manuscripts, 750 poetry submissions, 400 article suggestions, 200 submissions for the "Gazette" (a section covering news of the women's movement), 1,600 submissions to "No Comment," and several hundred letters to specific authors or editors in response to their work. The *Ms.* letters to the editor are archived at the Schlesinger Library on the History of Women, Radcliffe College, Cambridge, MA.

7. A 1973 survey of staffs of 60 feminist periodicals revealed that only 9% of staff members were minority women (Mather, 1974, p. 199).

8. I wish to thank Nina Gregg for reminding me of this point in our discussion of separatism.

9. Kranich categorized the periodicals according to descriptions provided by the periodicals themselves.

10. The National Women's Music Festival was first held in the summer of 1974 at Champaign-Urbana, IL. In 1982, this annual festival moved to Bloomington, IN, where it has continued to be held (Tilchen, 1984, p. 294). In 1976, the Michigan Womyn's Music Festival, produced by the We Want the Music Collective, was begun by a group of women who rented land on which to hold the event. Since the first festival, which attracted 2,500 attendants, attendance has increased. This festival is an annual event where women live for 4-5 days in a women-only environment, surrounded by women's culture. Other large regional festivals include Sisterfire, produced by Roadwork in Washington, DC; a West Coast Women's Music and Comedy Festival; and more recently, the Southern Women's Music and Comedy Festival, of the latter produced by Robin Tyler Productions.

Several independent women's record labels promote the work of 1-2 artists and are listed in the *Directory of Women's Media* (Allen, 1989; National Council for Research on Women, 1992). Redwood Records and Olivia Records, Inc., two of the larger recording companies, represent a greater number of artists. Several independent companies produce specific types of music, for example, Musica Femina and Leonardo (classical) and Rosetta Records (lost blues and jazz recordings).

Independent news production companies gather and report on women's news, acting as a news service for alternative radio programming. Since 1986 the Women's International News Gathering Service (WINGS) has produced and distributed 29 minutes of news a month, headlining major news stories about women that are ignored by the mass media ("WINGS Radio Service," 1987, p. 6). In addition to WINGS, 10 other women's news services are indexed in the *1989 Directory of Women's Media* (Allen, 1989), 5 from the United States and 5 from other countries. The *1992 Directory of Women's Media* (National Council for Research on Women) lists 17 radio shows or radio production groups who produce music and public affairs programming for women.

11. Examples of the "lists" include: Comserve's GENDER (communication and gender); EDUCOM-W (technology and education issues of concern to women); SYSTERS (women in computer science); FEMINIST (the Feminist Task Force of the American Library Association); FEMECON (for women/feminist economists), FEMREL-L (women in religion, feminist theology), SWIP-L (feminist philosophy), SAPPHO and BIFEM (lesbians/bisexual women); WON (Women's Online Network, women and politics) and LIS (Lesbians in Science). Among the array of newsgroups found in Usenet/VNEWS are SOC. FEMINISM (a moderated newsgroup) and SOC. GENDER-ISSUES. *The Women's Studies and Gender Studies E-mail User's Guide to Networks for Women,* compiled by Karla Tonella, moderator of Comserve's GENDER hot line, is available from that hot line. WMST-L, the Women's Studies list, also retains an updated file of e-mail lists for women.

12. The content of online discussions and other public announcements are usually archived by each list and, therefore, retrievable as research data.

13. Mather (1974) notes two studies that examined the development of the alternative and underground press of the 1960s: Robert J. Glessing's *The Underground Press in America* (1970) and Laurence Leamer's *The Paper Revolutionaries* (1972). Although both provide a rich and important background to the period that spawned the women's movement, neither of these studies was sensitive to the struggle over gender politics that was emerging at the time.

John Downing's 1984 study, *Radical Media: The Political Experience of Alternative Communication,* examines a collection of alternative media organizations as case studies, emphasizing selected collectives in the United States, Portugal and Italy, and Eastern Europe. In the case study of Third World Newsreel, an alternative film collective, Downing alludes minimally to the "women's struggle" within the organization as well to the struggles that surfaced over the inclusion of Black films. Of the eight case studies from the United States, however, none is representative of the feminist political struggle of the past 25 or so years.

14. This directory was published annually between 1975 and 1989 by the Women's Institute for Freedom of the Press, Washington, DC 20008. As of the 1992 edition, it is published by the National Council for Research on Women, located at The Sara Delano Roosevelt Memorial House, 47-49 East 65th Street, New York, NY 10021.

15. Allen proposed eight characteristics that define the various components of the women's communication networks: (1) women speaking for themselves; (2) collective structures; (3) sharing, non-competitive; (4) critical assessment of mass media's role toward women and women's media; (5) a non-attack approach toward others in their reporting; (6) emphasis on the "open forum"; (7) inclusion of information not found in the mainstream media; and (8) an activist orientation (1988/1989, p. 50).

16. In her case study of Redwood Records, Cynthia Lont (1984/1985) examined the women's music industry from a variety of perspectives (a recording collective, producers, critics, retailers, etc.) that enabled her to capture a more comprehensive picture of this cultural venture. In Maida Tilchen's (1984) overview of the first 10 years of women's music aligned with contemporary feminism, she identifies four major trends in content that she categorizes as separatism, innovative, political, and women-produced.

Case studies can be useful in preserving a record of a publication's content and of the women who produced it. For example, *Lavendar Woman* by Michal Brody (1985) is about a Chicago newspaper that Brody helped found. Her study serves as a chronological record of the 26 issues published between 1971 and 1976, and includes 50 written pieces from the paper and interviews with seven former *Lavendar Woman* collective members. Individual publications also may be analyzed textually, as Rose Weitz (1984) does in her analysis of the *Ladder.* The first significant lesbian periodical in the United States, the *Ladder* was published between 1956 and 1972 by the Daughters of Bilitis (DOB), the first lesbian organization in this country.

Weitz traces the development of lesbian identity through the definitions of lesbianism found in the *Ladder* over the 16-year period.

17. Since the 1970s feminist scholarship has had a significant influence on film theory —see, for example, Kuhn (1982) and Brunsdon (1986). Numerous studies about feminist art and criticism exist, among them Pollock (1988), Robinson (1988), and Parker and Pollock (1987). An excellent source for material on multicultural artists is Lippard's (1990) *Mixed Blessings*.

18. Though she focuses on an earlier period, that of the early 1800s to post-reconstruction, Jane Rhodes (1992) examines the historical context in which Black women contributed as writers, editors, and publishers. Rhodes shows that African American women contributed to both the white-owned abolitionist newspapers and to Black-owned newspapers during the antebellum years, to the hundreds of publications established during the reconstruction period (1865 to the turn of the century), and later to the first periodicals targeting female audiences that were introduced in the post-reconstruction period (1992, pp. 213-219). A precedent for a Black women's alternative press is one of the best known Black women's magazines of the late 19th century, the *Woman's Era* (1894-1897), founded by Josephine St. Pierre Ruffin in Boston. Linked to the Black women's club movement of the late 19th century, the *Woman's Era* became the official publication of the National Federation of Afro-American Women when the organization was founded in 1896 (Rhodes, 1992, p. 219).

19. A case in point is the *Women of Color Newsletter,* whose history is closely aligned with that of its mother organization, the National Women of Color Association (NWOCA). The majority of the NWOCA's founding members were previously members of the Women of Color Caucus of the National Women's Studies Association (NWSA). Outraged by the firing by NWSA of Ruby Sales, the only woman of color ever to work in the NWSA national office, and by their endurance of "racism and insensitivity in the 14-year-old NWSA," the women of color at the 1990 NWSA conference in Akron, OH, walked out and later founded the National Women of Color Association. *The Women of Color Newsletter* is a product of that organization ("The 'Minority' Majority," 1991, p. 1).

20. Reports of new media projects are commonly featured in women's movement periodicals (see examples included in chapter 2 of Humphreys, 1989). The degree to which the formation or cessation process is examined may vary greatly, and thus the utility of these accounts will vary as well. *Feminist Collections, a Quarterly of Women's Studies Resources,* published by the Women's Studies Librarian, University of Wisconsin-Madison, and *The Feminist Bookstore News* (San Francisco) routinely report the formations and cessations of feminist media projects.

References

Alarcón, Norma. (1990). The theoretical subject(s) of This Bridge Called My Back and Anglo-American feminism. In Gloria Anzaldúa (Ed.), *Making face, making soul/haciendo caras: Creative and critical perspectives by women of color* (pp. 356-369). San Francisco: Aunt Lute Foundation Books.

Allen, Donna. (1987, January-February/March-April). Yes, we still have pioneers—They're working for women's equal media outreach to the public. *Media Report to Women,* p. 20.

Allen, Martha Leslie. (1989). *The development of communications networks among women, 1963-1983* (Doctoral dissertation, Howard University, 1988). *Dissertation Abstracts International, 49,* 2843-A.

Allen, Martha Leslie. (Ed.). (1989). *1989 directory of women's media.* Washington, DC: Women's Institute for Freedom of the Press.

Anzaldúa, Gloria. (1990). *Making face, making soul/haciendo caras: Creative and critical perspectives by women of color.* San Francisco: Aunt Lute Foundation Books.

Armstrong, David. (1981). *A trumpet to arms: Alternative media in America.* Boston: South End.

Barrett, Michelle. (1982). Feminism and the definition of cultural politics. In Rosalind Brunt & Caroline Rowan (Eds.), *Feminism, culture and politics* (pp. 37-58). London: Lawrence & Whishart.

Brody, Michal. (1985). *Are we there yet? A continuing history of Lavendar Woman, a Chicago lesbian newspaper, 1971-1976.* Iowa City: Aunt Lute Book Company.

Brunsdon, Charlotte. (Ed.). (1986). *Films for women.* London: British Film Institute.

Caraway, Nancie. (1991). *Segregated sisterhood: Racism and the politics of American feminism.* Knoxville: University of Tennessee Press.

Collins, Patricia Hill. (1990). *Black feminist thought: Knowledge, consciousness, and the politics of empowerment.* New York: Routledge & Kegan Paul.

Combahee River Collective. (1982). The Combahee River collective statement. In Barbara Smith (Ed.), *Home girls: A Black feminist anthology* (pp. 272-282). New York: Kitchen Table: Women of Color Press.

Coward, Rosalind. (1980). "This novel changes lives": Are women's novels feminist novels? A response to Rebecca O'Rourke's article "Summer reading." *Feminist Review, 5,* 53-64.

Donovan, Josephine. (1985). *Feminist theory: The intellectual traditions of American feminism.* New York: Frederick Ungar.

Doughty, Frances, & Bunch, Charlotte. (1980). Frances Doughty talks to Charlotte Bunch about women's publishing. *Sinister Wisdom, 13,* 71-77.

Downie, Susanne. (1989). A community-based medium: The story of the Pittsburgh feminist *Network News.* In Ramona R. Rush & Donna Allen (Eds.), *Communications at the crossroads: The gender gap connection* (pp. 193-201). Norwood, NJ: Ablex.

Downing, John. (1984). *Radical media: The political experience of alternative communication.* Boston: South End.

The Feminists. (1973). The feminists: A political organization to annihilate sex roles. In Anne Koedt, Ellen Levine, & Anita Rapone (Eds.), *Radical feminism* (pp. 368-378). New York: Quadrangle Books/The New York Times Book Co.

Ferro, Nancy, Holcolm, Coletta Reid, & Saltzman-Webb, Marilyn. (1977). Statement of purpose, *off our backs.* In Maurine H. Beasley & Sheila Silver (Eds.), *Women in media: A documentary source book* (pp. 117-118). Washington, DC: Women's Institute for Freedom of the Press.

Flora, Cornelia Butler. (1971). The passive female: Her comparative image by class and culture in women's magazine fiction. *Journal of Marriage and the Family, 33,* 435-444.

Franzwa, Helen. (1974). Working women in fact and fiction. *Journal of Communication, 24,* 104-109.

Freeman, Alexa, & Jones, Valle. (1976). Creating feminist communications. *Quest, 3,* 3-12.

Freeman, Jo. (1973). The origins of the women's liberation movement. *American Journal of Sociology, 78,* 792-811.

Freeman, Jo. (1975). *The politics of women's liberation.* New York: Longman.

Friedan, Betty. (1963). *The feminine mystique.* New York: Norton.

Frye, Marilyn. (1983). Some reflections on separatism and power. *The politics of reality: Essays in feminist theory* (pp. 96-109). Trumansburg, NY: The Crossing Press.

Gardner, Richard. (1976). *Alternative America.* Privately published.

Glessing, Robert J. (1970). *The underground press in America.* Bloomington: Indiana University Press.

Hole, Judith, & Levine, Ellen. (1971). *Rebirth of feminism.* New York: Quadrangle Books.

hooks, bell. (1981). *Ain't I a woman: Black women and feminism.* Boston: South End.

Humphreys, Nancy K. (1989). *American women's magazines: An annotated historical guide.* New York: Garland Publishing.

Jaddou, Liliane, & Williams, Jon. (1981). A theoretical contribution to the struggle against the dominant representations of women. *Media, Culture and Society, 3,* 105-124.

Jaggar, Allison. (1983). *Feminist politics and human nature.* Totowa, NJ: Rowman & Allanheld.

Jay, Karla. (1986, November). Power to the author. *Women's Review of Books, 4,* pp. 5-6.

Kassell, Paula, & Kaufman, Susan J. (1989). Planning an international communications system for women. In Ramona R. Rush & Donna Allen (Eds.), *Communications at the crossroads: The gender gap connection* (pp. 222-237). Norwood, NJ: Ablex.

Kaufman, K. (1986, October). A world of writers. *Women's Review of Books, 4,* pp. 13-14.

Kessler, Lauren. (1984). *The dissident press: Alternative journalism in American history.* Beverly Hills, CA: Sage.

King, Deborah. (1988). Multiple jeopardy, multiple consciousness: The context of a Black feminist ideology. *Signs: Journal of Women in Culture and Society, 14*(1), 42-72.

Kramarae, Cheris, & Taylor, Jeanie. (1992, March). Electronic networks: Safe for women? [Machine-readable file]. Portland, OR: Lewis & Clark College, Electronic Salon: Feminism meets Infotech, in connection with the 11th Annual Gender Studies Symposium (Producer). Portland, OR: Lewis & Clark College (Distributor).

Kranich, Kimberlie. (1990). A bibliography of periodicals by and about women of color. *Feminist Teacher, 5*(1), 26-41.

Kuhn, Annette. (1982). *Women's pictures: Feminism and cinema.* Boston: Routledge & Kegan Paul.

Leamer, Laurence. (1972). *The paper revolutionaries: The rise of the underground press.* New York: Simon & Schuster.

Lippard, Lucy R. (1990). *Mixed blessings: New art in a multicultural America.* New York: Pantheon.

Lont, Cynthia. (1985). Between rock and a hard place: A model of subcultural persistence and women's music (Doctoral dissertation, University of Iowa, 1984). *Dissertation Abstracts International, 45,* 2684-A.

Macdonell, Diane. (1986). *Theories of discourse: An introduction.* New York: Basil Blackwell.

Mather, Anne Dudley. (1974). A history and analysis of feminist periodicals. *Master's Abstracts, XII*(1), 41. (University Microfilms No. M-5203)

The "minority" majority form own national organization. (1991, March). *Women of Color Newsletter, 1*(1), pp. 1-2.

Mookerji, Rita. (1967). *A content analysis of five selected American women's magazines in the last twenty years.* Unpublished master's thesis, University of Georgia, Athens.

The National Council for Research on Women. (1992). *DWM: A directory of women's media.* New York: National Council for Research on Women.

Parker, Rozsika, & Pollock, Griselda. (1987). *Framing feminism: Art and the women's movement, 1970-1985.* London: Pandora Press.

Pollock, Griselda. (1988). *Vision & difference: Femininity, feminism, and the histories of art.* New York: Routledge, Chapman & Hall.

Rhodes, Jane. (1992). Mary Ann Shadd Cary and the legacy of African-American women journalists. In Lana F. Rakow (Ed.), *Women making meaning: New feminist directions in communication* (pp. 210-222). New York: Routledge & Kegan Paul.

Rich, Cynthia, Greenfield, Gloria, McGloin, Pat, & Snow, Deborah. (1980). Persephone Press. *Sinister Wisdom, 13,* 81-85.

Robinson, Hilary. (1988). *Visibly female: Feminism and art today: An anthology.* New York: Universe Books.

Rothschild-Whitt, Joyce. (1979). The collectivist organization: An alternative to rational-bureaucratic models. *American Sociological Review, 44,* 509-527.

San Francisco NET. (1992). *Leonardo, 25*(1), 5-7.

Sproull, Lee, & Kiesler, Sara. (1991). *Connections: New ways of working in the networked organization.* Cambridge: MIT Press.

Steiner, Linda. (1988). Oppositional decoding as an act of resistance. *Critical Studies in Mass Communication, 5*(1), 1-15.

Tilchen, Maida. (1984). Lesbians and women's music. In Trudy Darty & Sandee Potter (Eds.), *Women-identified women* (pp. 287-303). Palo Alto, CA: Mayfield.

Tong, Rosemarie. (1989). *Feminist thought: A comprehensive introduction.* Boulder, CO: Westview.

200 women's media plan cooperation at national "Women in Print" conference. (1982, January 1). *Media Report to Women,* pp. 1, 6-7 (as reported in *off our backs,* December, 1981).

Tuchman, Gaye. (1978). *Making news: A study in the construction of reality.* New York: Free Press/Macmillan.

Weedon, Christine. (1987). *Feminist practice and poststructuralist theory.* Oxford: Basil Blackwell.

Weitz, Rose. (1984). From accommodation to rebellion: The politicization of lesbianism. In Trudy Darty & Sandee Potter (Eds.), *Women-identified women* (pp. 233-248). Palo Alto, CA: Mayfield.

Wilson, Clint C., II, & Gutiérrez, Félix. (1985). *Minorities and media: Diversity and the end of mass communication.* Beverly Hills, CA: Sage.

WINGS radio service prepares for regular operation. (1987, January-February/March-April). *Media Report to Women,* p. 6.

PART TWO

Perspectives on the Status of Women in the Mass Communication Industries

5 The Progress of Women and People of Color in the U.S. Journalistic Workforce
A Long, Slow Journey

SUE A. LAFKY

Ever since the passage of the Equal Employment Opportunity Act of 1972, a piece of federal legislation enacted under intense lobbying efforts by the National Organization for Women, employers have been prohibited from discriminating on the basis of sex or race. For too many women and people of color, however, real equal employment opportunity remains confined to a slogan that sometimes appears at the bottom of a job advertisement.

This chapter, which focuses on the journalistic workforce, discusses the reasons why the ability of women and people of color to achieve equal footing with white men in the workforce depends on numerous equal opportunities, including those that

- allow them to gain the education and training needed to have the skills for the workforce.
- allow them to be treated equally with white men in promotion as well as hiring decisions.
- allow them to expand upon their training through networking on the job and through outside professional organizations.
- allow them to pursue careers without shouldering an inordinate amount of the burden for child care or other work at home.
- allow them to work in an environment free of racism and sexism.

For women and people of color, the stakes are high if equal opportunity cannot be achieved. As French feminist Simone de Beauvoir (1949/1961) observed in the late 1940s, opportunities through employment are central to women achieving equality with men.

It is through gainful employment that woman has traversed most of the
distance that separated her from the male, and nothing else can guarantee her
liberty in practice. (1949/1961, p. 639)

This chapter documents the status of women and people of color in the
journalistic workforce during the past three decades, and compares the
treatment of men and women journalists on a number of factors, including
education, income—and the opportunities mentioned above—that are vital
for success in the field.

In discussing these opportunities, it is important to understand the multi-
tude of social influences that lead to differential treatment in the workforce, and to distinguish between two kinds of discrimination that women
and people of color experience, one being labor market discrimination and
the other being pre-labor market—or societal—discrimination.

Labor market discrimination occurs when two equally qualified persons
are treated differently in the workforce on the basis of their gender, race,
age, sexual orientation, disability, or some other factor. Societal discrimination
includes the differences in roles in the workforce and in the home as well
as the sex role socialization that leads males and females to believe that
some work is appropriate for males and not females. Societal discrimination adversely affects the economic status of women by producing differences in workforce status or economic outcomes that cannot be accounted for
by differences in productivity-related characteristics or the qualifications
of the individual, such as education or experience (Blau & Ferber, 1986,
p. 229).

This chapter argues that the progress of women journalists and journalists of color has been hampered by both kinds of discrimination. Data
used in this chapter are taken from the U.S. Census Bureau as well as from
telephone surveys of U.S. journalists conducted in 1971, 1982-1983, and
1992 (Johnstone, Slawski, & Bowman, 1976; Weaver & Wilhoit, 1986,
1992). These three studies of journalists were confined to those working
for mainstream news organizations—daily newspapers, weekly newspapers,
news magazines, news services, television stations, and radio stations.
Such a definition of *journalist* is more narrow than the definition used by
the U.S. Census Bureau, which combines all editors and reporters working
for print and broadcast organizations into one category (Lafky, 1990), and
does not include women who have created their own media (see Marilyn
Crafton Smith's chapter in this volume).

In the U.S. workforce as a whole, white women have recently made
significant progress in their journey toward equality with white men (Nasar,
1992). Yet, true equality remains elusive, both in the area of outcome as

well as in opportunity. Though equality of outcome is not something that most Americans, with their faith in the power of individual initiative and talents, support, many are committed to equal opportunity in the labor force and in educational institutions. As Mickelson and Smith (1992) observed:

> The distinction between equality of opportunity and equality of outcome is important. Through this country's history, equality has most typically been understood in the former way. Rather than a call for the equal distribution of money, property, or many other social goods, the concern over equality has been with equal opportunity in pursuit of these goods. (1992, p. 360)

Background

The massive entry of women into the paid workforce is one of the most significant trends during the past few decades. In 1960 there were about 23 million working women who made up a little more than 30% of the nation's workforce. By the mid-1980s, there were nearly 50 million women —about 45% of all workers—holding jobs in the United States. More than 13.5 million women entered the labor force between 1972 and 1981, compared with fewer than 8 million men joining the labor force during that same period (Berger, 1986, p. 2). Meanwhile, the labor force participation of women grew from 52% in 1980 to 58% in 1990 (Waldrop & Exter, 1991, p. 36).

When Johnstone, Slawski, and Bowman conducted their study in 1971, they found that women made up about one fifth of the journalistic workforce. In the early 1980s, a survey of U.S. journalists commissioned by David H. Weaver and G. Cleveland Wilhoit of Indiana University suggested that the gap between men and women in the journalistic workforce was closely rapidly.

Women made up 33.8% of the journalistic workforce in 1982-1983, up from 20.3% in 1971. Yet a decade later, another survey of U.S. journalists by Weaver and Wilhoit found that women had only gained two tenths of a percentage point in representation, an increase that might very well be explained by sampling error.

Thus this most recent study of U.S. newsworkers found that the "typical" U.S. journalist continues to be a white male Protestant. However, the 1992 survey also found that among those journalists with less than 5 years of experience, women made up 45% of the journalistic workforce. Weaver and Wilhoit noted that the participation of women was higher among those with 5 to 9 years of experience (about 42%). However, they added that because the growth rate in American journalism has been so small during the past decade, and because there are far fewer women than men with 15 years or more experience, these increased percentages of women hired during the past decade have not changed the overall percentage of women in American journalism from 1982-83. (Weaver & Wilhoit, 1992, p. 4)

Despite the lack of improvement in the overall percentage of women in the journalistic workforce, there is some evidence of progress for women within their organizations. In 1992, 42% of both women and men said that they have some supervisory responsibility for news-editorial staff (Weaver & Wilhoit, 1992, p. 5), compared to 39.3% of the women and 51% of the men from the decade before (Lafky, 1991, p. 173). Things have not dramatically changed since University of Missouri researcher Jean Gaddy Wilson (1986) found in 1985 that only 6% of the top newspaper jobs and 25% of the middle management newspaper jobs were held by women. Meanwhile, only 17% of television news directors were women in 1992, according to a study by Vernon Stone of the University of Missouri (Kreimer, 1992, p. 10).

The representation of women in the journalistic workforce varied dramatically by medium in 1992, going from 24.8% for television newsrooms to 45.9% for news magazines. The most recent survey by Weaver and Wilhoit estimated that women make up 29% of the labor force in radio journalism, 24.8% in television journalism, 33.9% in daily newspaper journalism, and 44.1% in weekly newspaper journalism (Weaver & Wilhoit, 1992, p. 3).

After the results of the 1992 survey of U.S. print and broadcast journalists were released in late November at a session at the Freedom Forum headquarters in Arlington, VA, news organizations such as *The New York Times* and *Chicago Tribune* devoted less space to the slow progress of women in newsrooms than they did to the finding that more journalists identified themselves as Democrats in the 1990s than they did 20 years ago, and were 50 to 10 percentage points more likely than the U.S. population as a whole to say they are Democrats (Weaver & Wilhoit, 1992, p. 6).

Part of that difference stems from the fact that working women are more likely than men to be registered as Democrats (Faludi, 1991, p. 272). In fact, Weaver and Wilhoit found that 58% of women journalists identified themselves as Democrats, compared with 38% of the men. This same trend holds true for journalists of color, with 70% of the Black, 63% of the Asian, and 59% of the Hispanic journalists identifying themselves as Democrats (1992, p. 7).

Nevertheless, differences that exist between the political affiliations of journalists compared to the U.S. population as a whole are less likely to bias news coverage in any significant way compared to the biases that come from having a journalistic workforce that remains 92% white and 66% male.

The Slow Growth of the Workforce

The reasons why women made such slow progress in the journalistic workforce during the past decade stem in part from the slow expansion of that workforce during the 1980s. Weaver and Wilhoit estimated that only about 10,000 more full-time journalists were working for mainstream news organizations in 1992 than there were in 1982, a growth rate of just under 9%. In contrast, between 1971 and 1982 an estimated 42,572 full-time journalists entered the mainstream journalistic workforce—a 61% increase (Weaver & Wilhoit, 1992, p. 3).

But while women journalists did not make inroads in overall representation during the decade, there was some progress for people of color, going from 3.9% in 1982-1983 to 8.2% in 1992 (Weaver & Wilhoit, 1992, p. 5).

The greatest gains in the journalistic workforce for women and people of color take place at times when media organizations are expanding their staffs and are actively pursuing affirmative action hiring practices. The decade between the 1971 study by Johnstone and his colleagues and the 1982-1983 study, for example, was one in which women's rights activists took advantage of Federal Communications Commission regulations and federal equal opportunity legislation to challenge the hiring and promotion practices of news organizations. In 1971, the FCC added women to its equal opportunity rule that originally applied only to racial and ethnic minorities. This order prohibited discrimination against women and required television stations to file with the FCC affirmative action programs outlining their efforts at implementation of equal opportunity.

FCC regulations that mandated affirmative action only affected broadcast news organizations, and it was the broadcast sector of the journalistic labor force that showed the greatest gains in newsroom employees between the 1970s and 1980s. African Americans and other people of color did not make as many gains in broadcast organizations during the 1980s—years that coincided with a decreased interest in matters of equal opportunity and affirmative action on the part of the Federal Communications Commission (Stone, 1988, p. 293). In fact, during the Reagan presidency, there was a move toward government deregulation of a number of industries, including the broadcast industry. And during Mark Fowler's tenure as FCC commissioner, the FCC dramatically reduced the amount of information it collected on women and minority employees. One outcome of this reduced interest in collecting data about women and people of color, noted Susan Faludi in her best-selling book *Backlash,* was that it became "virtually impossible" to document discrimination in class-action lawsuits (1991, p. 372).

Race and Gender

The proportion of women who are journalists varies greatly by race, and among Asians and Blacks, women make up more than half the journalistic workforce. Weaver and Wilhoit noted in the preliminary report of their 1992 survey that "this suggests that increased emphasis on hiring minority journalists is likely to increase the representation of women at the same time" (p. 5).

The 1992 survey found that the proportion of women journalists was greater in all minority groups than it was for the white majority. In fact, while 33.3% of the white journalists were women in 1992, the same figure for Asian American journalists was 52.5%; for African American journalists, 53.2%; for Hispanic/Latino journalists, 48.1%; and for Native American journalists, 42.9%.

Although women make up significantly higher percentages among journalists of color than those of European descent, journalism remains an overwhelmingly white occupation. At an estimated 8.2% of the journalistic workforce, people of color are still lagging behind their estimated 24% representation in the U.S. population as a whole (Weaver & Wilhoit, 1992, p. 5).

But that 8.2% still amounts to an increase over the 3.9% of the workforce that was found to be people of color in the 1982-1983—a figure lower than the 5% recorded in the 1971 study by Johnstone et al. (Weaver & Wilhoit, 1992, p. 5). Although there are major gaps between the representations of whites and people of color in the journalistic workforce, there is evidence that affirmative action efforts have been somewhat successful, particularly among younger journalists. In fact, noted Weaver and Wilhoit:

> if only those journalists hired during the past decade are considered, the overall percentage of minorities is considerably higher than 8.2%, suggesting that there have been increased efforts, and some success, in minority hiring during the 1980s. But the percentage drops off sharply for those journalists with 10 or more years of experience, probably because of less emphasis on minority hiring during the 1960s and 70s, and possibly because more minorities are leaving journalism after 10 years on the job. (1992, p. 5)

There is no evidence that affirmative action has led to the hiring of unqualified journalists in the past two decades. In fact, the quantitative evidence suggests that journalists of color are held to even higher standards than their white counterparts. For example, every woman of color interviewed in the 1982-1983 survey of U.S. journalists was a college graduate, compared with 80% of the men of color, 71.2% of the white women, and 73.9% of the white men (Lafky, 1991, p. 165).

The Educational Gap Closes

In 1916, a young woman wrote to *The New York Sun* to ask where she could go to school to learn how to be "a woman reporter." In replying to the aspiring newswoman, a journalist identified only as Miss Gilbert informed the young woman that "the School of Journalism, Columbia University and at New York University, is open to women as well as to men." Gilbert cautioned the aspiring reporter, however, that before she spent time and money on a journalism education, she should make sure she had the right combination of talents to succeed, including "native resourcefulness . . . a certain amount of facility in writing," and "abounding good health." Gilbert saw journalism as a calling that demanded a special type of person. "You can never 'learn' to be a woman reporter as you could learn dressmaking or stenography, because reporting is a type of work requiring exceptional abilities," she wrote ("Learning to be a Reporter," 1916, p. 22).

What Miss Gilbert did not tell the young seeker of career counseling was that the Columbia University Graduate School of Journalism limited its enrollment of women to 10% of the class—a quota that stayed in place until the late 1960s (Beasley & Theus, 1988, p. 39). The classroom climate in college and university journalism programs has often been a chilly one for women—particularly before the 1975 regulations that put some teeth into Title IX, the primary federal law prohibiting sex discrimination in education. That law states, "No person in the United States shall, on the basis of sex, be excluded from participation in, be denied benefit of, or be subjected to discrimination under any program or activity receiving Federal financial assistance" (Mickelson & Smith, 1992, pp. 365-366).

Women accounted for 44% of the bachelor's degrees in journalism awarded in 1971 at U.S. colleges and universities (Hooper, 1971). Between 1980 and 1990, enrollment in journalism programs hovered consistently at about 60% female and 40% male (Becker, 1991; Peterson, 1988). Women first outnumbered men in college and university journalism programs in 1977, after a 60:40 ratio had favored men for four decades (Peterson, 1979).

One of the major changes charted in the studies of journalists done in the early 1970s and the early 1980s was the closing of the gender gap in educational preparation. As of 1982-1983, women in journalism were just as likely as men in the field to have completed a college education and majored in journalism. Johnstone and his colleagues found in 1971 that 60% of the men and 50.8% of the women had at least a bachelor's degree. By 1982-1983, 74% of the men and 73.6% of the women held at least a bachelor's degree (Lafky, 1991, p. 165-166).

In fact, other studies suggest that women journalists are often more educated than men in the field. Indiana University scholar Christine L. Ogan, for example, found in her 1982-1983 study of men and women newspaper managers that female managers were more likely than male managers to have a college education. Meanwhile, a 1988 study of daily newspaper journalists by the American Society of Newspaper Editors found that women had more education and better academic records than men (Stinnett & Henry, 1989).

Part of this difference stems from the fact that younger journalists are more likely than older journalists to have earned a college degree, and women journalists tend to be younger than men journalists. Nevertheless, the empirical evidence does not suggest that women are less prepared than men for careers in journalism—in fact, the opposite is the case.

Given that only 44.8% of journalists with less than 5 years of experience in mainstream print and programs are women (Weaver & Wilhoit, 1992, p. 5), it seems likely that many of those who make up the new female majority in journalism and mass communication classes are not concentrating on obtaining news editorial skills, although more research needs to be done in this area. A 1989 study by Carolyn Garrett Cline, for example, found that women make up 80% of those in student public relations organizations and classes (see Chapter 11, this volume).

It seems certain that the increased enrollment of women in journalism programs is related to their increased participation in the journalistic workforce. For the U.S. labor force as a whole, the higher educational achievements of women have been associated with their increased participation in the workforce. Between 1980 and 1990, for example, the proportion of the U.S. population aged 25 and older with 4 or more years of college climbed from 13% to 18% for women, and from 20% to 24% for men (Waldrop & Exter, 1991, p. 36). Mary Frank Fox (1989) found in 1988 that among women who had completed high school, 59% were employed. That employment rate was 72% among women with 4 years of college and 79% with 5 or more years of college.

The Gender Gap in Experience

Overall, women since the early 1980s have tended to be younger and have less professional journalism experience than men, a change from the previous decade when women tended to be older and less experienced than men in the field (Johnstone et al., 1976).

Women made up only 24.2% of the journalists with 20 or more years of experience in 1992, and the figures improve steadily as the number of years of experience decreases. Women made up 29.5% of the journalistic work-force for those with 15-19 years of experience, 34.1% of those with 10-14 years; 41.7% of those with 5-9 years, and 44.8% of those with less than 5 years (Weaver & Wilhoit, 1992, pp. 4-5).

The Income Gap

Like their counterparts in other fields, women in journalism continue to make less money than men in their chosen occupation. However, the wage gap between men and women journalists has narrowed in recent years—following another trend that is reflected in the U.S. workforce as a whole. Economists identify three periods in the past 200 years during which women made giant strides toward pay equality.

One was during the Industrial Revolution, in the mid-19th century, when farm girls streamed into factories. The second was during the rise of the corporation and the white-collar workforce in the first few decades of this century, when young, unmarried, middle-class women headed for offices. The third is happening now. (Nasar, 1992, p. 3:1; used by permission)

Between 1979 and 1989, after accounting for inflation, the median earnings of men who work full time year-round in the United States declined 3.8%, to $27,430. But at the same time, women's earnings increased by 10.4%, to $18,788 (Waldrop & Exter, 1991, 36).

When Johnstone and his colleagues conducted their study of U.S. journalists in 1971, they found that women in journalism made an average of 64 cents for each dollar earned by the average man in the field (Johnstone et al., 1976, pp. 82-83). By 1981, that disparity had lessened considerably, with women earning an average of 71% of what men made in journalism (Lafky, 1991, p. 167).

By 1992, the medium income for women journalists was $27,669 a year—81% of the medium income of $34,167 for men journalists (Weaver & Wilhoit, 1992, pp. 8-9). This increase is in keeping with a trend in the

U.S. workforce as a whole for higher pay for those with college educations. Among women aged 25 and older with 4 or more years of college, median income between 1979 and 1989 grew by 30%, to $21,659 (after accounting for inflation). But for women who did not complete high school, income grew by only 2%. In contrast, college-educated men gained only 4.5% in real income during the 1980s (to $37,553 in 1989), and men with only high school diplomas experienced a 16% drop in median income, to $21,650 (Waldrop & Exter, 1991, p. 37).

Weaver and Wilhoit noted that when years of experience are taken into account, the gender gap in income becomes even more narrow. In fact, they note:

> when a variety of predictors of income are controlled statistically (such as professional age, type of medium, size of news organization, managerial responsibilities, race, ownership of news organization, presence of a union for journalists, region of the country, and education level), gender predicts less than 1% of the variation in pay. (Weaver & Wilhoit, 1992, p. 10)

Although such findings may alleviate the responsibilities of individual news organizations for some of these disparities in income, they should not be interpreted as meaning that discrimination leading to gender-based income does not exist. Discrimination is one reason why women do not have managerial responsibilities and the same amount of experience as men.

Mary Gray, a professor of mathematics and statistics at The American University, has argued, for example, that it may not be accurate to use rank or managerial as a control variable when accounting for male and female differences in pay because "the assignment of initial rank and the promotion process are usually subject to the same possibilities for discrimination as the salary process itself" (Gray, n.d.).

Professional Affiliations

Professional organizations such as the Society of Professional Journalists and the National Press Club have long served as important sources for career enhancement and networking for news people. Such groups not only have served as the source for discussions about issues facing journalism professionals, but also are places where these professionals gain access to important news sources and information about career opportunities. For many years, however, women did not have equal access with men to these organizations.

Women responded to the closed doors of the most prestigious of the journalistic fraternities, Sigma Delta Chi (now known as the Society of Professional Journalists), in 1909 by founding their own journalistic sorority, Theta Sigma Phi, which eventually became the organization now known as Women in Communications, Inc. (Fitzgerald, 1987, p. 9). In Washington, D.C., women founded the Women's National Press Club in 1920 at a time when the men of the National Press Club refused to accept women in their organization. In fact, women could only cover news stories with the national and world leaders who often addressed the prestigious organization if the women sat in a tiny balcony that overlooked the male members and their male guests as they ate four-course meals in the ballroom (Mills, 1988, pp. 93-109).

It was not until 1969 that members of Sigma Delta Chi (now known as the Society of Professional Journalists) voted at their national convention in San Diego to admit women to membership (Huston, 1969, p. 13)—60 years after Sigma Delta Chi was founded as a journalistic Fraternity at DePauw University in Greencastle, IN. An account of that 1969 convention noted that the struggle for women to gain equality with men in one of the most prestigious organizations had not come easily.

"Proposals to admit women, originating with campus chapters, had been voted down at several previous conventions," noted Luther A. Huston in an article for *Editor & Publisher* (1969, p. 13).

> The idea that realism required recognition of the fact that women have proliferated in the news rooms in recent years to the extent that they are no longer just society reporters but cover general news assignments, work on copy desks, write columns and do most of the things men do on newspapers, has been slowly building up and this year the professional members joined, with few dissents, in supporting a pet project of the campus members.

Others at the convention, however, saw the admittance of women as more than simply a way to fulfill a "pet project" of collegians.

One delegate to the San Diego convention noted that Sigma Delta Chi was only half professional until it admitted all members of the profession. And other professionals, according to Huston, "expressed the fear that admission of women signed the death warrant of Theta Sigma Phi, the women's journalistic sorority." This, he added, was "based on the belief that women students in schools of journalism would not join a strictly female group when membership in a 'co-educational' society was open to them" (1969, p. 13).

The Women's National Press Club voted to admit men as members in 1971 and changed its name to the Washington Press Club. The National

Press Club agreed to accept women members the same year. However, the two groups did not merge until 1985.

Media observer James E. Roper, in an article for *Editor and Publisher,* noted that the delay came about because leaders of the Washington Press Club still resented that the men's club for so many years had kept women guests even out of its bar, and relegated women reporters to its balcony if they were to cover National Press Club luncheon speakers (Roper, 1985, p. 12).

The delegating of women to the balcony—and their eventual victories in gaining access to the networking and stories that were happening on the ground floor—is part of the lore veteran women journalists share in books such as *A Place in the News*—an exceptionally readable and informative account of the indignities suffered by women in the newspaper business as well as their struggles and accomplishments (Mills, 1988), as well as books such as *Waiting for Prime Time: The Women of Television News* (Sanders & Rock, 1988); and *The Girls in the Balcony: Women, Men and The New York Times* (Robertson, 1992).

Children and Family

One of the continuing challenges for women in journalism—like their counterparts in other fields—is the difficulty of combining career and family. A number of studies of women in journalism have found that they are less likely than men in the field to be married or to have children (Beasley & Theus, 1988; Goodrick, 1989; Lafky, 1991; Ogan, Brown, & Weaver, 1979).

"You can have it all—if you don't need too much sleep," noted the title of an article in a publication of the American Society of Newspaper Editors (Brand, 1986, p. 17). The "all" referred to taking care of a career as well as a spouse and children, which amounts to at least two full-time jobs for many women.

In 1982-1983, women journalists were more likely than men journalists to be married (42% vs. 62%), and were also less likely than men to be parents. Meanwhile, 75.5% of the men who had ever been married had children, a situation true for only 64.6% of the women. Among journalists as a whole, 57% of the women had children, compared with 70% of the men.

But times are changing. One reason why the gap is growing smaller between men's and women's income is that fewer women are dropping out of the labor force and most are taking less time to raise children than women in previous generations. By the 1990s, only 7% of working women in the United States were dropping out of the workforce in any given year, down from 12% in the mid-1970s (Nasar, 1992, p. 3:10).

A recent survey of U.S. women found that women are becoming more adamant about wanting more equal division of the household responsibilities. Next to money, "how much my mate helps around the house" is the single biggest cause of resentment among women who are married or living with a man, with 52% citing this as an issue. In fact, improvement in this area is one of the first things women mention when they talk about what would make their lives better (Townsend & O'Neil, 1990, p. 28).

Progress in this area, as well as in the area of affordable child care, is central to the progress of women in the workforce. As one study wryly observed, "The way to the top is still much clearer for women who, in terms of family responsibilities, travel light" (Fogarty, Allen, Allen, & Walters, 1982, p. 10, quoted in Delamont, 1989, p. 238).

Sexual Harassment

Unfortunately, as the discussion of marriage and family demonstrates, the battle for equality is not won when women are given the education that was previously reserved for men, join the organizations that were previously the domain of men, and given a chance to do work that was previously done by men. Perhaps there is no more dramatic example of this than the case of sexual harassment.

There is no way to measure the toll that sexual harassment has taken on the lives and careers of women in the journalistic workforce. However, there is ample evidence that this manifestation of sexism is just as prevalent in U.S. newsrooms as it is in society as a whole.

The U.S. Equal Employment Opportunity Commission, in its interpretation of the 1964 Civil Rights Act, defines sexual harassment as including unwelcome sexual advances, requests for sexual favors, and verbal or physical conduct of a sexual nature that creates an intimidating, hostile, or offensive workplace environment. Feminist scholars have noted that "sexual harassment is not primarily about sex, or physical attraction, or about boys' and men's attempts to be 'nice' to girls or women." Instead, it is about efforts to maintain difference and dominance—an "expression and enforcement of power and a binary gender hierarchy" (Kramarae, 1992, pp. 100-101).

In surveys taken after the Clarence Thomas confirmation hearings, and after Anita Hill's interrogation by an all-white, all-male Senate Judiciary Committee raised the consciousness of many about the ubiquitous nature of the problem, about half of women journalists reported being sexually harassed at some time during their career (Weaver, 1992, p. 24). Nationally, between 42% and 85% of women have reported being sexually harassed in the workplace ("Resources and Action Plans," 1992, p. 6). And in a 1992 poll of New York area executives, sexual harassment was the third most important employment issue after benefits and job security ("Four Interesting Facts," 1992, p. 5).

Although it is true that men do sometimes experience sexual harassment, studies find that men experience sexual harassment less severely, and with fewer negative psychological and physical effects (Strauss, 1990, quoted in Kramarae, 1992, p. 105). In fact, one study found that approximately 95% of all reports involved men harassing females (Truax, 1989, quoted in Kramarae, 1992, p. 105).

Lisa Olson, a former sportswriter for the *Boston Herald,* learned the hard way what can happen if you enter an all-male bastion such as the locker room. In fact, she left the United States for Australia because of the pressure she faced after settling a sexual harassment lawsuit against three New England Patriot football players and the management of the National Football League team (Reuters, 1992). There are similar incidents of women who have left their jobs after incidents of harassment, and other lawsuits as well. But many of these lawsuits are settled in secret, often with an agreement that none of the parties will discuss the case. Writer Carolyn Weaver (1992), in examining eight threatened or filed sexual harassment lawsuits against media organizations settled since 1985, found that only two were not settled confidentially (p. 25).

Conclusion

The progress of women and people of color in the journalistic workforce is tied to their progress in society as a whole, and that progress hinges on structural changes that will allow equal opportunity for all people regardless of gender or race. As Mickelson and Smith (1992) note, using a current metaphor: "If life is a game, the playing field must be level; if life is a race, the starting line must be in the same place for everyone" (p. 360).

The metaphor of life as a game or a race should not be carried too far. Nevertheless, the metaphor is a useful one if it isn't taken too literally, for it is true that only if sexism, racism, and other forms of discrimination are eliminated will all women and men have true equal opportunity in the labor force.

Meanwhile, the progress of women and people of color in the journalistic workforce during the past two decades can be linked to a combination of labor market conditions and equal opportunity legislation. The degree of progress in years to come depends on the continuance of these conditions as well as a commitment to antidiscrimination policies on the federal and state levels, changes in family structures that give men equal responsibility for housework and child care, and a commitment on the part of employers to allow men and women to accommodate the dual demands of career and family responsibilities.

Finally, the advancement of women and people of color also depends on the activism of those who have a direct stake in the attainment of equal opportunity. Those who seek social and economic justice in the workforce would do well to remember the words of Dr. Martin Luther King, Jr. (1963, p. 5), in his famous civil rights treatise, the letter from the Birmingham Jail: "We know through painful experience that freedom is never voluntarily given by the oppressor; it must be demanded by the oppressed."

References

Becker, Lee B. (1991). Annual enrollment census: Comparisons and projections. *Journalism Educator, 46*(3), 50-60.

Beasley, Maurine H., & Theus, Kathryn T. (1988). *The new majority: A look at what the preponderance of women in journalism education means to the schools and to the professions.* Lanham, MD: University Press of America.

Beauvoir, Simone de. (1961). *The second sex* (H. M. Parshley, Trans.). New York: Bantam Books. (Original work published in French, 1949.)

Berger, Gilda. (1986). *Women, work and wages.* New York: Franklin Watts.

Blau, Francine D., & Ferber, Marianne A. (1984). *The economics of women, men, and work.* Englewood Cliffs, NJ: Prentice Hall.

Brand, Janet. (1986, January). You can have it all—if you don't need too much sleep. *ASNE Bulletin,* p. 17.

Delamont, Sara. (1989). *Knowledgeable women: Structuralism and the reproduction of elites.* London and New York: Routledge & Kegan Paul.

Faludi, Susan. (1991). *Backlash: The undeclared war against American women.* New York: Crown Publishers.

Fitzgerald, Mark. (1987, October 17). Many women leaving newspapers. *Editor & Publisher,* p. 9.

Fogarty, M., Allen, A. J., Allen, I., & Walters, P. (1982). *Women in top jobs, 1968-1970.* London: Heinemann.

Four interesting facts about sexual harassment. (1992, Spring). *Perspectives: A Newsletter For and About Women Lawyers,* p. 5.

Fox, Mary Frank. (1989). Women and higher education: Gender differences in the status of students and scholars. In Jo Freeman (Ed.), *Women: A feminist perspective* (4th ed.) (pp. 217-235). Mountain View, CA: Mayfield.

Goodrick, Evelyn Trapp. (1989, August). *A comparison of women and men on editorial page staffs.* Paper presented at the annual convention of the Association for Education in Journalism and Mass Communication, Washington, D.C.

Gray, Mary W. (n.d.). *Achieving pay equity on campus.* Unpublished paper, The American University, Washington, D.C.

Hooper, Mary Evans. (1971). *Earned degrees conferred: 1970-71* (p. 14). Washington, DC: Government Printing Office.

Huston, Luther A. (1969, November 22). Sigma Delta Chi welcomes women to full membership. *Editor & Publisher,* pp. 13, 50.

Johnstone, John W. C., Slawski, Edward J., & Bowman, William W. (1976). *The news people: A sociological portrait of American journalists and their work.* Urbana: University of Illinois Press.

King, Martin Luther, Jr. (1963, June 24). Letter from Birmingham City Jail. *The New Leader,* pp. 3-11.

Kramarae, Cheris. (1992). Harassment and everyday life. In Lana F. Rakow (Ed.), *Women making meaning: New feminist directions in communication* (pp. 100-120). New York and London: Routledge & Kegan Paul.

Kreimer, Susan. (1992, Fall). Researcher finds progress by women in television news. *Iowa Journalist,* p. 10.

Lafky, Sue A. (1990). *The women of American journalism.* Unpublished doctoral dissertation, Indiana University, Bloomington.

Lafky, Sue A. (1991). Women journalists. In David H. Weaver & G. Cleveland Wilhoit (Eds.), *The American journalist: A portrait of U.S. news people and their work* (2nd ed.) (pp. 160-181). Bloomington: Indiana University Press.

Learning to be a reporter. (1916, July 22). *The Editor & Publisher,* p. 22.

Mickelson, Roslyn Arlin, & Smith, Stephen Samuel. (1992). Education and the struggle against race, class, and gender inequality. In Margaret L. Andersen & Patricia Hill Collins (Eds.), *Race, class, and gender: An anthology* (pp. 359-384). Belmont, CA: Wadsworth.

Mills, Kay. (1988). *A place in the news: From the women's pages to the front page.* New York: Dodd, Mead.

Nasar, Sylvia. (1992, October 18). Women's progress stalled? Just not so. *The New York Times,* pp. 3:1, 10.

Ogan, Christine L. (1983, May). *Life at the top for men and women newspaper managers: A five-year update of their characteristics.* A report for the Center for New Communications, Indiana University.

Ogan, Christine L., Brown, Charlene J., & Weaver, David H. (1979). Characteristics of managers of selected U.S. daily newspapers. *Journalism Quarterly, 56*(4), 803-809.

Peterson, Paul V. (1979). Enrollment surges again, increases 7 per cent to 70,601. *Journalism Educator, 33*(4), 3-8.

Peterson, Paul V. (1988). Journalism and mass comm enrollment leveled off in '87. *Journalism Educator, 43*(1), 4-10.

Resources and action plans on sexual harassment. (1992, Spring). *Perspectives: A Newsletter For and About Women Lawyers,* p. 6.

Reuters. (1992, February 25). U.S. woman sports writer settles sex harassment suit.

Robertson, Nan. (1992). *The girls in the balcony: Women, men and* The New York Times. New York: Random House.

Roper, James E. (1985, June 22). Press clubs merge: National Press Club and the Washington Press Club unite to end a rivalry that began 65 years ago over the status of women journalists. *Editor & Publisher,* pp. 12-13.

Sanders, Marlene, & Rock, Marcia. (1988). *Waiting for prime time: The women of television news.* Urbana: University of Illinois Press.

Stinnett, Linda Cunningham, & Henry, Barbara A. (1989). *The changing face of the newsroom.* Washington, DC: American Society of Newspaper Editors.

Stone, Vernon. (1988). Trends in the status of minorities and women in broadcast news. *Journalism Quarterly, 65*(2), 288-293.

Strauss, Marcy. (1990). Sexist speech in the workplace. *Harvard Civil Rights Civil Liberties Law Review, 25*(1), 1-51.

Townsend, Bickley, & O'Neil, Kathleen. (1990, August). Women get mad. *American Demographics,* pp. 26-32.

Truax, Anne. (1989). Sexual harassment in higher education: What we've learned. *Thought & Action: The NEA Higher Education Journal, 4*(1), 25-38.

Waldrop, Judith, & Exter, Thomas. (1991, March). The legacy of the 1980s. *American Demographics,* pp. 33-38.

Weaver, Carolyn. (1992, September). A secret no more. *Washington Journalism Review,* pp. 23-27.

Weaver, David H., & Wilhoit, G. Cleveland. (1986). *The American journalist: A portrait of U.S. news people and their work.* Bloomington: Indiana University Press.

Weaver, David H., & Wilhoit, G. Cleveland. (1992). *The American journalist in the 1990s: A preliminary report of key findings from a 1992 national survey of U.S. journalists.* Arlington, VA: Freedom Forum.

Wilson, Jean Gaddy. (1986, October). Women in the newspaper business. *Presstime,* pp. 31-37.

6 Through the Looking Glass
Diversity and Reflected Appraisals of the Self in Mass Media

MARILYN E. GIST

Discerning the secret of flight from a bird was a bit like learning the secret of magic from a magician. Once you know what to look for, you see things that you didn't see when you didn't know what to look for.

Orville Wright, quotation from Boeing Museum of Flight

The subtlest and most pervasive of influences are those which create and maintain the repertory of stereotypes. We are told about the world before we see it. We imagine most things before we experience them. And those preoccupations, unless education has made us acutely aware, govern deeply the whole process of perception.

Walter Lippmann, in *Leadership for America*

Recent news events challenged long cherished notions of the United States as a land of equal opportunity. Believing civil rights had been mastered in the 1960s, the national conscience was jolted in the 1990s by inexplicable events and judgments pertaining to Rodney King and Anita Hill. Despite the public outcomes of those dramas, and the hiccups of surprise in newsrooms and the judicial-political machinery, many private citizens echoed hollow satisfactions of "I told you so": civil rights and justice are not well served by nonrepresentative power structures.

AUTHOR'S NOTE: Some portions of this article appeared in: "Minorities in Media Imagery: A Social Cognitive Perspective on Journalistic Bias," by Marilyn Gist, 1990, *Newspaper Research Journal, 11*, 52-63. (Used by permission.)

Roughly 30 years after the Civil Rights Act, the lack of diversity in most professional and managerial occupations provides some support for this notion. For example, although ethnic minorities constitute 25% of the nation's population,[1] only 8% of newsroom employees are minorities and 54% of dailies employ no persons of color in their news or editorial departments (American Society of Newspaper Editors [ASNE], 1990). Women comprise 51% of the population, yet only 34% of the journalistic workforce (Weaver & Wilhoit, 1991). Further, the lack of diversity in managerial positions is cause for dismay. Minorities comprise less than 5% of all journalistic management positions and fewer than 1% of top management (ASNE, 1990). As indicated in other chapters in this book, women were represented in about a quarter of middle management jobs, but held very few top management positions through the 1980s.

Until recently, concerns with equal employment opportunity (EEO) have focused largely on such employment statistics. However, attention is shifting to the *qualitative* impact of *under*representation on decisions, products, and services that are provided by organizations. For example, some media organizations have examined the effects of underrepresentation on the product they disseminate. Among problems recognized are: (1) racial and gender bias in news coverage, (2) failure to cover issues of significance to the community, and (3) a potentially harmful impact on reader attitudes and tolerance within the circulation area.

This chapter explores the reality behind the numbers. It summarizes the experience of three media organizations that scrutinized their product closely. Their findings are considered within the framework of psychological theory to highlight the impact of journalistic practices on society at large and on those members of society for whom power and access have been marginalized.

Effects on News Coverage

Three newsrooms participated in an exploratory study of the effects of staffing representation on news coverage.[2] One newsroom was a network television house, and the second was a radio station; in each, 6% to 7% of the employees were ethnic minorities. The third newsroom was a metropolitan daily paper with 13% minority representation. Each newsroom produced multiple editions of the daily news. Retrospective data were collected by sampling of the news content from the 6-month period prior to the study. Dates from this period were chosen at random to yield at least 30-days coverage for each newsroom. Data used for analyses consisted of all photographic and verbal coverage disseminated to the public during each day sampled.

Proprietary analyses were conducted on the gender and racial content of photographic coverage and news copy that was produced by these newsrooms. Results of these analyses were consistent, revealing, and disturbing. As a group, women were rarely shown in photographic coverage unless they were in the background of the scene. Their representation as lead subjects in the copy was noticeably absent from headline stories, and was elsewhere confined to more "traditional" stories, such as those in lifestyle sections.

Further, the newsrooms in these studies were located in major urban centers where the minority populations ranged between 23% and 26%; each center reflected wide ethnic diversity. However, photographic coverage of minorities was limited almost exclusively to African Americans (who were not the largest racial minority group in their communities). In the copy as in the graphic content, news coverage frequently focused on controversial issues concerning minorities, with a tendency to portray them in a negative context (e.g., stories about crime, drugs, gangs, low achievement, poverty, broken homes, and teen-age pregnancy). In both photographs and text, when minorities were featured in a positive light, the context was most often athletics or entertainment. Another pattern distinguishing the presentation of minorities from nonminorities in the news was that of positive examples out of a negative context (e.g., African American youth breaks away from street gangs, or white volunteers provide academic tutoring for ghetto minority youth).

Many stories about nonminorities also could be categorized this way, but a significantly greater tendency was shown in each newsroom to present a more balanced picture of nonminority subjects: more positive or neutral stories from positive or neutral contexts, such as weddings, home purchases, political and community activities, for instance. In other words, unlike coverage of minorities in these samples, presentation of whites was not restricted to negative examples or sports/entertainment, but portrayed them in an extensive variety of mainstream activities.

In these samples, little evidence was found of "mainstreaming" diversity in the news on any of several fronts. First, women and minorities were underrepresented as quoted sources in news stories, as indicated by a low frequency of female first names, and Asian, Native American, or Latino surnames used in quoting sources. Further, reporters in the studies commented frequently that they either did not have or did not use source networks from minority communities in their coverage areas. When minority sources were used, there was heavy reliance on a very few individuals, such as church leaders, activists, a few political figures, and so forth. Although minorities are no more monolithic in opinion than whites, this was not reflected in the range of opinion sought by reporters.

Second, in neutral stories, ranging from politics to weather to housing or school issues, it was rare that professional or working class minorities were mainstreamed into the coverage in the way nonminorities are. In other words, minorities tended to make the news in negative stories or in stereotypically positive ones, but not in the many kinds of neutral or positive stories in which whites were typically featured. Women were somewhat more likely than minorities to be interviewed as bystanders who witnessed news events, although women were less likely than men to receive foreground photographic coverage.

Finally, because of the underrepresentation of diversity in the news product in these samples, there was minimal coverage of issues considered important to diverse members of the communities. Issues occurring in the coverage areas that many minorities felt were important, but that were limited or lacking in coverage, included: increasing real estate speculation by white developers in minority neighborhoods and the attendant displacement of minority families; an exodus of whites from a public school system; the disproportionately high police scrutiny of minority communities for drug use compared to lower scrutiny of white communities for major drug dealers; and the results of a university study validating that discrimination in one state's judicial system contributed to higher rates of detention and incarceration, and longer sentences, for African Americans as compared to whites with similar cases. Even though some issues concerning women, such as an impending vote on abortion rights, received more coverage than was typical of minority "issues," many women in the service area felt that other issues and concerns of women (e.g., reduction in aid to families with dependent children, increases in sexual assaults, women's health care issues) failed to receive the coverage deserved.

In sum, the content analyses of the news coverage of these three organizations reflected significant differences in the manner in which minorities and nonminorities, and men and women, were portrayed. They also showed an *under*representation in news coverage—in terms of quantity and diversity—of the populations in the areas served. Although these organizations may not reflect the journalistic practices of all other newsrooms, managers and staff in each organization expressed surprise at the extent of bias uncovered upon close scrutiny of their products.

The Product as a Reflection of Staff

A question that is frequently raised over these findings is why news coverage appears biased, given a staff of educated professionals who view themselves as enlightened, aware, and even liberal. Typical first reactions reflect a widely held journalistic philosophy: news is something that happens on its own and should not be "engineered"; rather, it must be reported with dispassionate objectivity. Subscribers to this philosophy suggest that the "bias" described above may actually reflect the "fact" that minorities and women are not *doing* much that is newsworthy. After all, these philosophers assert, most politicians and heads of major corporations are white males, so if a story breaks, photographic and written coverage will reflect that.

However, when a quarter of the nation's population is nonwhite and more than half the population is female, this justification skirts some important issues. When a weather disaster occurs in an area with population diversity (e.g., an earthquake in San Francisco, a hurricane in Florida), the event itself is racially neutral. But if journalistic *coverage* of those affected by the neutral event focuses principally on whites whose upscale homes are destroyed, or on whites whose loved ones are missing, it can be termed biased. Also, political elections can appear gender neutral (i.e., two males running on slates without "hot" gender issues). Yet coverage that fails to inquire about candidates' views toward ongoing women's concerns that are pending in the legislature, or coverage that solicits men's reactions to the candidates far more than women's on *non*-gender issues, can be termed biased. Similarly, many feature stories, as well as routine photographic coverage of festivals, malls, or neighborhood scenes, that repeatedly fail to reflect the ethnic and gender diversity of the population in a service area may be considered biased by those who are neglected. These charges of bias are justifiable to the extent that the coverage fails its goal of journalistic objectivity: the goal of reporting what's *there* (in demographic and public interest terms), as opposed to reporting selectively.

Unfortunately, evidence of such bias abounds, not only in dailies and broadcast journalism, but in advertising, in news and business magazines, in general broadcast programming, and in the film industry. Minorities and women are disproportionately excluded from, or are presented in negative or marginal ways, in mainstream coverage (cf. Dates & Barlow, 1990; Faludi, 1991). Despite the evidence, and repeated calls for change, progress has been slow.

Recall the premise that equality and justice (i.e., fairness) are not well served by nonrepresentative power structures. Judgment bias in other contexts suggests that news content closely parallels the demographic composition of a newsroom staff, particularly its managers. As an example,

Abbie Hoffman's death a few years ago received significant front page and front section space in a metropolitan daily that participated in this study. Extensive coverage of this "event" lasted over a week. However, conversations with newsroom employees who were under 30 or over 55 indicated that they failed to appreciate the significance of the "event"—failed to understand why it deserved so much space. Without diminishing the importance of Hoffman's life, it is useful to realize that, to a large segment of the population, he was truly *un*important. Yet the managers at this newspaper averaged 40 to 45 years old and, to them, Hoffman was an important figure—he was *news*. The question can be raised as to whether this story would have received such prominent or extensive coverage if the newsroom management were of a different generation. Similarly, if most news managers were African American, would Thurgood Marshall's life and death have received far more coverage than it did in many urban dailies and weekly newsmagazines? Or if most newsroom managers were female, would the occasional front page sports story be considered such important news? Would greater attention likely be given to the dramatic growth in successful women owned businesses? Would female managers judge as newsworthy more investigative journalism on issues pertinent to the marginalized status of women (e.g., the nation's extremely high rates of sexual assault and physical abuse of wives and children by men, the lack of research on women's health issues, the feminization of poverty—yet the limited attention given by society to these problems)?

These questions highlight a serious flaw in the dominant philosophy of journalism. Whether the issue is race, cultural diversity, gender, age, sexual orientation, economic class, or religion, the *determination* of what is news is highly subjective. Thus news judgment inevitably reflects the perceptual biases and interests of those making the judgment. Unfortunately, because women and people of color have grown accustomed to nonrepresentative coverage as the norm, and because they too are schooled with illustrative news examples deemed "objective," even they sometimes internalize the biases of the largely white male media establishment.

Given the photo and content analyses above, one can infer that the group that dominates newsrooms and managerial positions (i.e., a largely white male group) also dominates news *judgments*. Also, the cultural anchors of this group can be understood by reviewing both its historic and present practices with respect to diverse members of society (cf. Hacker, 1992; Morrison, 1992). Until very recently, this group viewed this country as mono-cultural—a great melting pot of Euro-American, male dominant tradition. Women and ethnic minorities have been marginalized economically, as well as in the national consciousness and popular history. However, the recent achievement of a more critical mass of diversity in the population and/or the workplace is challenging this marginal status.

Attention to one's culture, values, and perspectives is less necessary when there is little contact with those who may be different. As we shift to a more culturally pluralistic society, contrasts increase, along with a growing awareness that Euro-American males are as culturally unique in their views as are female and minority groups. The dominant group has its own values, assumptions, and perspective on events—often an exclusionary perspective—and these cultural anchors influence its judgments. That is why the well-educated and well-intentioned newsroom staffs produced the biased products described above. When the vast majority of those who make the decisions are nonminority, upwardly mobile males, the product will likely reflect their values and perspectives more than it will those of the more diverse area the newsroom seeks to serve. In sum, no medium is likely to achieve "objectivity" in its product without broad representation in its staffing and among its decision makers.

Impact on Psychological Development

These findings are disturbing on the ground of journalistic philosophy alone, but there are deeper issues of psychology and ethics worth considering. The most widely accepted psychological model of human interaction with the environment is social cognitive theory (Bandura, 1986). One aspect of this theory addresses the influence of the environment on individuals and their behavioral choices. A principal mechanism through which the environment exerts this influence is *self-efficacy,* which refers to one's belief in one's capability to perform a task—specifically, one's capacity to mobilize the cognitive and other resources required to execute a given course of action successfully (cf. Bandura, 1986; Gist, 1987; Gist & Mitchell, 1992). Self-efficacy has been demonstrated to predict performance in a number of clinical, health, athletic, career, and job task settings (cf. Bandura & Wood, 1989; Hackett & Betz, 1981; Stumpf, Brief, & Hartman, 1987; Taylor, Locke, Lee, & Gist, 1984). In other words, strong and positive self-beliefs predict successful performance, while weak and negative self-beliefs tend to predict failure.

The environment influences self-efficacy through personal experience, modeling, and persuasion. American media—both print and broadcast—exert significant modeling influence on society. Thus, not only does media coverage reflect the views and cultural biases of its dominant group, these views—the dominant tendencies in media modeling—become reflected appraisals that significantly influence the beliefs of *mass audiences.* One need only examine the psychology of advertising to recognize that many goods are sold because they are modeled in favorable circumstances. We buy a given product because, subconsciously, we hope to acquire some of the sophistication, youth, sex appeal, or sense of freedom with which it is associated in the advertisements. In other words, we identify in some way with the models in the ads, and make behavioral choices accordingly.

Recent research in the organizational sciences has demonstrated clearly the influence of various forms of modeling on self-efficacy and subsequent performance (cf. Gist, 1989; Gist, Schwoerer, & Rosen, 1989). Participants who were exposed to strong, positive modeling experiences developed stronger self-beliefs and subsequently outperformed those who did not benefit from positive modeling experiences. Importantly, the more similar to oneself the model is—in age, race, gender, and so forth—the more powerful the modeled effects (Bandura, 1977).

Extending these findings from the area of social cognitive theory to the issue of bias in media presentation of minorities, several important questions can be raised. To what extent does journalistic bias influence the developing self-image of female and minority youth? Although many youngsters do have strong, positive role models in their homes and communities, those who do not must rely to a greater extent on the secondary messages and images modeled in the mass media. To the extent that it is a common practice to portray African Americans most frequently in a negative light—criminals, drug addicts, and so forth—or as positive examples from a negative context, strong signals are being sent to developing African American youth about what they can become. Similarly, to the frequent extent that media neglect women, portray them as marginally powerful, or objectify them sexually, these signals become internalized by many women as low self-esteem or an obsession with physical attractiveness (cf. Steinem, 1992; Wolf, 1991). If a youngster wishes a broader or more positive path, which models provide data? Again, for most women and minority subgroups, there are few successful and positive role models in the media; for African Americans, sports and entertainment are the dominant fare. Might this explain the heightened enthusiasm among Black male youth for music and basketball?

While further, rigorous research is needed on the influence of media modeling, it is clear that Euro-American male youth are exposed to far more extensive media coverage of individuals similar to themselves in a variety of powerful and positive roles. And through their comparatively limited and negative portrayal of adult female and minority roles, the media do reflect strong (and biased) appraisals of what society expects or will permit from similar youth. It is probable that these models influence self-efficacy and the choices that each youth believes are viable for the future.

The potential for psychological destructiveness of biased reporting practices may be morally, as well as journalistically, abhorrent, and its impact extends beyond female or minority youth. For example, reporting, programming, and advertising practices maintain and further existing stereotypes that *whites* hold of minorities as well. When many choices of housing, schools, and recreational activities still remain separate (Hacker, 1992), where does a white child learn what to expect of minorities, how to think about them? Again, the media present powerful images, and often quite biased ones.

Nor are the children the only ones influenced by these messages. Many adults, who have never known or cared to see the balanced picture, find reinforcement of their beliefs in the daily media. To what extent do biased journalistic practices contribute to police practices in the war on drugs or against gangs? These police policies have been criticized as predatory by many minorities, who claim their communities and their people are scrutinized unduly and treated more abusively when compared to whites. To what extent are higher rates of incarceration among African Americans, and lower rates of conviction among whites (e.g., with Rodney King), a function of subtle racism among judges and juries—racism that is perpetuated by media bias? As they try to advance in organizations, to what extent are minorities (particularly African Americans and Latinos) and women faced with glass ceilings that are related less to objective qualifications than to subjective perceptions of nonqualification? To what extent do women continue to experience subtle but consistent *under*valuation of their worth in work-related settings (cf. Faludi, 1991; Stroh, Brett, & Reilly, 1992) and inattention by society to their concerns (e.g., Anita Hill) as a result of chronic media invisibility or sexual objectification? Indeed, to what extent do women disagree on women's rights or fail to recognize their inequitable treatment and power as a result of internalizing media messages that they are less important than men? To what extent are these perceptions continually reinforced by and for the advantage of the dominant group? And finally, how long can these practices continue given that more than 57% of working age women are already in the workforce (thus no longer in traditional nonworking roles), and given projections that Caucasian Americans will constitute 49% of the population by the year 2056 (Henry, 1990)?

The issues deserving increased attention are not just the extent of biased coverage but the *effects* on society of these tendencies. Although it is certainly true that problems exist within minority communities, they also exist among whites. Many minorities assert that bias remains; many feel branded as "hypersensitive" for mentioning it.

Blacks will always have as their primary defense "racism," that generic, omnipresent miasma they alone can feel. And the frustration is compounded by the difficulty of persuading those who do not feel that it even exists. As impossible as it seemed to earn the right to sit anywhere on a bus, it will be far more difficult to prove that the person next to you has a sign blocking his mind. (McClain, 1986, p. 42)

Increasingly, minorities in communications are speaking up, and not only in print. A recent conference at the Poynter Institute for Media Studies, "Broken Ladders/Revolving Doors: Retaining Minority Journalists,"[3] provided a forum for discussions on why minorities leave the field. Frequent among the reasons minority journalists cited for exodus from the business were: (1) feelings of not being listened to, (2) a growing disrespect for the biased journalism they witnessed and felt pressured to perpetuate in the name of good news judgment, and (3) subtle barriers to the kind of advancement that would allow them to make a difference. Barriers to advancement were clearly traced to management's expectations that the minority journalist adopt the kind of news judgment held by those in the power structure—the very *type* of judgment that many minorities feel reflects an ethnically biased journalistic perspective, but one common among white editors and newsroom managers. Failing to adopt the same pattern of judgment, minorities were considered unqualified for developmental opportunities and given little access to positions of judgmental responsibility.

Statistical and anecdotal evidence suggests that advancement for women and minorities is stymied unless the diversity they represent is suppressed—unless their perspective aligns with that of the dominant culture. In practice, what many organizations manifest in their search for "qualified" minorities and women for management positions is that they want people who differ in terms of EEO statistics, but who *think* and *act* in concert with the dominant culture's perspective. Thus the cycle continues of judgments being made by those with one perspective—even though that perspective may blatantly neglect or misrepresent large segments of a diverse community.

Diversity and Product Quality

All this suggests that more than solely journalistic desirability, there are psychological, social, and ethical reasons to recognize and change reporting bias. Toward that end, we must recognize the bias inherent in each of our perspectives, bias that comes from growing up in a specific culture.

Being culturally anchored is not wrong, but without diversity in positions of influence, those anchors tend to degenerate from prejudice into racism or sexism. Prejudice is characterized by conscious or subconscious assumptions of superiority over those who are different. However, although most people hold some prejudice, the *impact* of those views is not uniform. Because *-isms* arise when prejudice combines with power, systemic gains are typically achieved for the group *in* power at the expense or mistreatment of those with *less* power. Such practices exert subtle but insidious influences on the lives of marginalized members. For example, as reflected by the media establishment, society holds subtle negative views of minorities and women. These reflected appraisals of their marginalized value most likely harm self-image, thus becoming an internal barrier to personal development and career preparation of minorities and women. For those who do enter mass communications, these subtle negative views are manifest in glass ceilings to advancement, which, in turn, prevent minorities and women from having much decision-making influence. In the absence of a different voice, the "system" of American media continues to perpetuate many biased views, views that provide disturbing evidence of racism and sexism. Far from dispassionate, journalistic objectivity, much of mass communications can be likened to a fun-house mirror: a looking glass through which we see distorted images of ourselves and others.

Many organizations have focused on EEO efforts primarily as a responsibility. Certainly, there are legal requirements to be met, but these should not obscure these deeper issues behind the numbers. Diversity should be viewed as an asset, not a liability. It is necessary at *all* levels of the organization to ensure that cultural bias is mitigated in journalism. However, a statistically diverse workforce alone may not accomplish that goal; there must be heterogeneity of *perspective* (i.e., women and minorities whose views challenge the status quo). Also, there must be a commitment within the management ranks to reflect fully the culture of the nation, or of a local community, not just that of one of its segments, and to support the career advancement of diverse people by supporting their differing judgments about what is news. To become objective, journalistic judgment must acknowledge the faces and voices of difference in a community and not screen them out simply because they fall outside the current comfort zone.

Expanding the journalistic comfort zone can be facilitated by recognizing that minority news and minorities in the news are of interest not only to the minority community. The same is true of women's issues. Both groups are large and vital proportions of the population; issues, opinions, and events affecting either women or minorities also are important beyond those groups. Thus "minority news" or "women's news" is *everybody's* news.

To *assume* that it is not—that women's and minorities' issues and events are trivial, that only stereotypically interesting things occur among these groups, or that most women and minorities simply are not involved in mainstream activities—is to assume the superiority of white male culture for making and holding opinions about news. Any evidence of that assumption is a blight on journalistic objectivity.

As indicated by the case studies cited above, and from other, similar studies of how the media marginalize groups,[4] there is more evidence of that dangerous assumption than we tend to acknowledge. Yet as Frederick Douglass said,

> The whole history of the progress of human liberty shows that all concessions yet made to her . . . claims, have been born of earnest struggle. . . . If there is no struggle, there is no progress. . . . This struggle may be a moral one, or it may be a physical one, and it may be both moral and physical, but it must be a struggle. Power concedes nothing without a demand. It never did and it never will.[5]

Achieving unbiased media is far more than an objective rooted in journalistic philosophy; it is a moral imperative. It is the responsibility of each individual engaged in mass communications to evaluate not only one's comfort with the products produced, or whether they sell, but recognize the sweeping effects these products have on all members of society. The implications of biased mass communications for the development and lifelong success of minorities and women are far reaching; Douglass's words underscore the work to be done.

Notes

1. Data on current U.S. population is drawn from the *Statistical Abstract of the U.S.*, 1992, U.S. Bureau of the Census.

2. The studies cited were commissioned by news operations, which asked to remain anonymous, of their own product and were conducted by the author.

3. Broken Ladders/Revolving Doors: Retaining Minority Journalists Conference, The Poynter Institute for Media Studies, St. Petersburg, FL, January 1990.

4. See for example: Thom Lieb, "Protest at the *Post*: Coverage of Blacks in the *Washington Post Magazine*," *Mass Comm Review*, 15(2/3), 65-66 (1988); Carolyn Martindale, "Coverage of Black Americans in Four Major Newspapers, 1950-1989," *Newspaper Research Journal*, 11(3), 96-112 (Summer 1990); Carolyn Martindale, "Changes in Newspaper Images of Black Americans," *Newspaper Research Journal*, 11(1), 40-50 (Winter 1990); Carolyn Martindale, "Coverage of Black Americans in Five Newspapers Since 1950," *Journalism Quarterly*, 62(2), 324-325 (Summer 1985); Edward C. Pease, "Kerner Plus 20: Minority News Coverage in the Columbus *Dispatch*, *Newspaper Research Journal*, 10(3), 17-37 (Spring 1989); Don Sneed,

Dan Riffe, & Roger Van Ommeren, *Press Coverage of Blacks and the Black Community: The Minority Legislators' Perspective,* paper presented at the Association for Education in Journalism and Mass Communication (AEJMC) annual convention, Portland, OR, July 1988; Don Sneed, Dan Riffe, & Roger Van Ommeren, *Black Legislators Describe Their Relationship With the Local Press: A Preliminary Report,* paper presented at the AEJMC annual convention, Portland, OR, July 1988.

5. Frederick Douglass, "Speech Before the West Indian Emancipation Society (Aug. 4, 1857)," in Philip S. Foner, *The Life and Writings of Frederick Douglass 437* (1950).

References

American Society of Newspaper Editors Minorities Committee. (1990). *1989 employment survey.* Reston, VA: American Society of Newspapers Editors.

Bandura, Albert. (1977). *Social learning theory.* Englewood Cliffs, NJ: Prentice Hall.

Bandura, Albert. (1986). *Social foundations of thought and action.* Englewood Cliffs, NJ: Prentice Hall.

Bandura, Albert, & Wood, Robert. (1989). Effect of perceived controllability and performance standards on self-regulation in complex decision-making. *Journal of Personality and Social Psychology, 56,* 805-814.

Dates, Jannette L., & Barlow, William. (1990). *Split images: African Americans in the mass media.* Washington, DC: Howard University Press.

Faludi, Susan. (1991). *Backlash: The undeclared war against American women.* New York: Crown Publishers.

Gist, Marilyn E. (1987). Self-efficacy: Implications for organizational behavior and human resource management. *Academy of Management Review, 12,* 472-485.

Gist, Marilyn E. (1989). The influence of training method on self-efficacy and idea generation among managers. *Personnel Psychology, 42,* 787-805.

Gist, Marilyn E., & Mitchell, Terence R. (1992). Self-efficacy: A theoretical analysis of its determinants and malleability. *Academy of Management Review, 17,* 183-211.

Gist, Marilyn E., Schwoerer, Catherine, & Rosen, Benson. (1989). Effects of alternative training methods on self-efficacy and performance in computer software training. *Journal of Applied Psychology, 74,* 884-891.

Hacker, Andrew. (1992). *Two nations: Black and white, separate, hostile, and unequal.* New York: Scribner.

Hackett, Gail, & Betz, Nancy E. (1981). A self-efficacy approach to the career development of women. *Journal of Vocational Behavior, 18,* 326-329.

Henry, William A., III. (1990, March 23). Beyond the melting pot. *Time,* pp. 28-31.

McClain, Leanita. (1986). *A foot in each world.* Evanston, IL: Northwestern University Press.

Morrison, Toni. (1992). *Race-ing justice. en-gender-ing power.* New York: Pantheon.

Steinem, Gloria. (1992). *Revolution from within: A book of self-esteem.* Boston: Little, Brown.

Stroh, Linda K., Brett, Jeanne M., & Reilly, Anne H. (1992). All the right stuff: A comparison of female and male managers' career progression. *Journal of Applied Psychology, 77,* 251-260.

Stumpf, Stephen A., Brief, Arthur P., & Hartman, Karen. (1987). Self efficacy expectations and coping with career-related events. *Journal of Vocational Behavior, 31,* 91-108.

Taylor, M. Susan, Locke, Edwin A., Lee, Cynthia, & Gist, Marilyn E. (1984). Type A behavior and faculty research productivity: What are the mechanisms? *Organizational Behavior and Human Performance, 34,* 402-418.

Weaver, David H., & Wilhoit, G. Cleveland. (1991). *The American journalist: A portrait of U.S. news people and their work* (2nd ed.). Bloomington: Indiana University Press.

Wolf, Naomi. (1991). *The beauty myth.* New York: William Morrow.

7 Newspapers
Is There a New Majority Defining the News?

MAURINE H. BEASLEY

In 1985 the University of Maryland College of Journalism released pre-liminary findings of a study that called attention to the "new majority" in schools of journalism and mass communication. This referred to the growing influx of young women that had tilted journalism school enroll-ment from predominantly male to predominantly female in less than a decade. At that time journalism enrollment was about 60% female. In 1991, two thirds of all graduates were women (Kosicki & Becker, 1991, p. 68).

The Maryland report was designed to call attention to discrimination faced by women as they moved from college into employment. It pointed out how the career paths of the "new majority" differed from those of the men who had preceded it, with women less drawn to newspaper work than to other forms of communications. It concluded that women were making an impact on the male-dominated field of journalism but that they en-countered far more obstacles than men in advancing to the top. The entire study, titled *The New Majority: A Look at What the Preponderance of Women in Journalism Education Means to the Schools and to the Professions,* was published in 1988 (Beasley & Theus, 1988).

The Maryland research stopped short of answering the question of whether a new majority is defining the news. This chapter addresses that issue, reviewing the findings of the report and describing the remarkable uproar that it generated, chiefly from women newspaper editors. As direc-tor of the Maryland research, I contend that the report was misunderstood by journalists who clung to outworn news concepts in covering the stories.

First, a look at the research itself. Funded by a $34,000 grant from the Gannett Foundation, the study consists of four main segments: A summary of the historical discrimination faced by women journalism students attempting to break into the job market; a case study of the experiences of Maryland graduates, both male and female; two roundtable discussions, one by prominent women in the field and another by recent graduates and students, focusing on problems confronting women; and finally four recommendations to journalism educators to assist women students in overcoming discrimination.

The historical overview traces the enrollment of women in journalism schools from the beginning of these institutions in pre-World War I days to the mid-1980s. By drawing on histories of journalism education, memoirs, biographies, and other data, the study traces how women were forced to settle for secondary status for decades within the journalism schools as well as the newspaper business to which journalism schools were oriented.

Anecdotal evidence on women's status cited in the study highlights this finding and includes the following examples.

■ Carl W. Ackerman, a member of the first class at the Columbia University School of Journalism and later its dean, noted initial opposition to admitting women in 1912 by quoting a professor asked for advice on the subject: "His classic reply was that no teacher could teach mathematics to a boy if there was a girl in the room and that if a boy could learn mathematics with a girl in the room he would never grow up to be a man" (Ackerman, 1949). (Columbia allowed women to enroll only under a rigid quota system that remained in effect until the late 1960s.)

■ Florence R. Boys, woman's page editor of the *Plymouth* (IN) *Pilot,* who successfully syndicated her material, advised women students at the University of Missouri School of Journalism in 1924: "My woman's page was begun for my husband's paper. . . . It would probably be difficult, if not impossible, for a woman to make a good living on it alone. It is a good sideline for the wife or daughter of an editor" (*Women and the Newspaper,* 1924, p. 13).

■ A woman journalism graduate who responded to a survey on women's status in journalism published in 1938 summed up the experiences of women attempting to obtain employment on daily newspapers: "With all the managing editors I have met, education and writing ability are not the essential they seek in a woman reporter. In the very few women they do take on (for flashy feature work), what they look for is the bold front and the 'gift of the gab' " (Logie, 1938, p. 27).

The Maryland study refers to articles in *The Matrix,* the magazine of Theta Sigma Phi, an honorary journalism sorority, that showed World War II temporarily opened newspapers' doors to women, although they swung shut again after the war ended. The following are cited.

■ .A report in October, 1940, on pre-war prejudice against women expressed at a symposium for women journalism students at Ohio State University: "There seemed to be a general agreement among the members of the employers' symposium that women don't have any more chance for jobs on newspapers than Jews have of surviving in Germany" ("Employers' Symposium," 1940).

■ A 1941 description by Abbie A. Amrine, a journalism graduate employed by a Kansas newspaper, on how the approach of war provided a long-sought opportunity to move from women's pages to general reporting: "Now taking the place of a man who has been drafted, I am working with the more drastic complications of deaths, accidents, rains, and community speakers. My conclusion is that the men have been impressing us with a false importance of their jobs" (Amrine, 1941).

■ Exclamations by Betty Hinckle Dunn, national secretary of Theta Sigma Phi, in 1942: "Jobs, jobs, jobs! And no one to fill them. Odd, isn't it, how the job picture has changed in war months. Flippantly I tell my friends, 'The war means more opportunities for women and Negroes' " (Dunn, 1942).

The Matrix was used as a barometer of attitudes toward women graduates because it circulated widely in schools of journalism, many of which had chapters of Theta Sigma Phi. Barred from joining Sigma Delta Chi, the male journalism fraternity, women, who constituted only a small fraction of journalism students, found professional support in their Theta Sigma Phi affiliation.

When women were urged to leave newspaper jobs at the end of World War II, *The Matrix* reported on the surge of domesticity that restricted women's roles. These examples are given in the Maryland study:

■ A panel of established career women in Los Angeles told young journalism graduates to make marriage their primary aim, according to *The Matrix* of October, 1951: "If you're playing with the idea of becoming a part-time mother—that is, combining your household with your pre-marital career—don't do it" (Sherwood, 1951).

■ Betty Angelo, a reporter who resigned her job on the *Detroit News,* urged women journalism graduates in 1953 to seek jobs on metropolitan newspapers to hunt husbands: "I worked for a big city newspaper five

years and met, among numerous other marriageable males, my husband—
a newspaper editor on a rival paper. I could have saved myself a year
and a half [spent working on a small-town newspaper] if I'd only come
to the big city sooner" (Angelo, 1953).

Against this background of different expectations for men and women,
journalism education remained almost totally male-dominated in the 1960s
and early 1970s, although the proportion of women students increased.
Women faculty, however, were grossly underrepresented in the teaching
ranks, making up only 8% of the total in 1971-1972. The Maryland research
quoted from a survey of the status of women journalism educators at 60
colleges and universities presented at the Association for Education in
Journalism convention in 1973. It concluded: "If you teach journalism in
a college or university which has a sequence accredited by the American
Council on Education in Journalism and you are a woman, you tend to be
ranked lower, promoted more slowly and paid less than your colleagues
who are male" (Marzolf, 1977, pp. 261-262).

In 1977, when journalism enrollment nationally reached a record 64,000,
the proportion of women students reached more than 50% but little notice
was taken of this development. Since then the percentage has continued to
climb. The number has escalated with a total of 151,740 undergraduate
students enrolled in journalism and mass communications programs in the
United States in 1991 (Kosicki & Becker, 1991, p. 68). The Maryland
study was the first one to draw national attention to the influx of women
into journalism schools and to point out the impact of this development on
the employment market.

The study drew on figures gathered at Ohio State University, where
major journalism enrollment surveys are done annually. The Ohio surveys
made it plain that the journalism students were turning away from the
news-editorial programs that traditionally occupied a pre-eminent position
in the curriculum. In 1980 Paul V. Peterson, a professor at Ohio State,
observed, "When sequences are analyzed, there is a clear indication that a
growing percentage of students are enrolling in the advertising and public
relations sequences while the number in news-editorial is declining. The
first two sequences are more heavily female populated as well" (Peterson,
1980, p. 3).

Changing enrollment patterns cannot be attributed to any single cause.
The closings of metropolitan newspapers, mushrooming communications
industries, new forms of technology, low starting salaries, and declining
patterns of readership all play a part in making news-editorial sequences
less attractive to the majority of journalism students than previously. Still

the influx of women students itself cannot be overlooked in the relative fall of news-editorial enrollments.

Peterson concluded the statistics clearly revealed "more females [than males] looking at non-traditional forms of journalism for careers." He also saw in the statistics a reflection of past discrimination. "I still think they [young women] see the newsroom as an all-male bastion" (personal communication, March 26, 1984).

Indeed, women graduates appeared to experience somewhat more difficulty than male graduates in finding journalism-related jobs, including those on daily newspapers, in the mid-1980s, the Maryland study reported. It uses these figures from the Dow Jones Newspaper Fund/Gallup Survey of 1983 journalism graduates:

- Although women represented 64.1%, or 11,326 of the total of 17,670 graduates surveyed, they were less likely than male graduates to locate news-editorial jobs. While 14.6% of the graduates as a whole found jobs in news-editorial areas, only 11.8% of the women did so.
- Although 9.4% of the graduates found jobs on daily newspapers, women were less likely than men to be in this category, with only 6.9% of the women reporting jobs on daily papers.
- A higher percentage of women graduates were unemployed than the graduates as a whole, with 14.2% of the women continuing to seek media-related work 6 months after graduating compared to 11.8% for the total group.

The figures suggest that journalism schools were turning out an increasing number of graduates who would encounter sexual bias in their careers. Were they being properly prepared to recognize sexism and to overcome it? Would the predominance of women graduates mean that journalism education would be perceived as a second-rate educational program (because occupational programs predominantly for women like nursing and elementary education long have lacked the status of programs for men)?

These were questions the Maryland researchers attempted to address through the second major portion of their project—a survey of Maryland journalism alumni and students as well as their employers. In common with those of other large state universities, Maryland's journalism program expanded greatly in the late 1970s and early 1980s. In 1968 there were only 120 majors, 80% of whom were men, but by 1984-1985 there were more than 1,000 undergraduate majors, of whom 69% were women. In advertising and public relations sequences, women represented about 80% of the enrollment.

Headed by Kathryn T. Theus, associate director of the study, investigators sent out 642 questionnaires to a sample of male and female graduates beginning with the class of 1981 and including graduates of other classes at 3-year intervals back to 1951. Of these, 356 were returned, yielding a 55% response rate. In addition, the researchers surveyed all potential graduates of the class of 1984, as well as an employer sample drawn from newspapers, agencies, or corporations where Maryland graduates were employed. There was a 60% response rate to the student survey of 280 persons and a 57% response rate from the 251 employers contacted.

Highlights of the alumni survey include the following:

- Males were more satisfied with their jobs, incomes, and chances for advancement than females.
- Women were 13 times more likely than men to have had career interruptions due to family responsibilities and seemed to suffer substantial income loss as a consequence. Women were out of jobs slightly longer than men and were twice as likely to change jobs as men.
- Alumni agreed that salaries of women doing journalism-related work were lower than those of men doing comparable work, and that men were promoted more quickly.
- Only 41% to 43% would encourage their sons or daughters to study journalism.
- In general, men were more likely to have married and to have larger families than women (Beasley & Theus, 1988, pp. 55-57).

The student survey did not show widespread variances between males and females in their attitudes toward their education, their careers, or sexual bias in the classroom and workplace. Almost one-third reported they had witnessed discrimination in the classroom based on sex. Curiously, in assessing their overall journalism experience, about 83% considered it very or extremely good, and 90% said they would major in journalism again. Yet less than half said they would encourage their children to study it and of those more would encourage their daughters than their sons (Beasley & Theus, 1988, pp. 57-58).

Women students perceived greater potential for discrimination in the workplace than men, although all recognized the presence of discrimination on the basis of sex. Women agreed more strongly than men with a statement on the questionnaire that women doing journalism-related work were lower paid than men doing comparable work. They also agreed more strongly with a statement that a man would be hired over an equally capable woman (Beasley & Theus, 1988, pp. 57-58).

The employer survey showed that only slightly more than one-third cited journalism as the most important undergraduate major for communication-related jobs. Males and females were evaluated rather evenly on job skills, although males were usually evaluated a percentage point or two better than females. Women employers, however, evaluated women employees significantly higher than did male employers in several areas including reporting and photography (Beasley & Theus, 1988, pp. 58-59).

Women employers more than men employers tended to agree with the statement that women doing journalism-related work were generally paid lower salaries than men doing comparable work. Employers were split on whether women were hired as a result of affirmative action policies. Slightly fewer than half of the employers reported they would encourage their sons to study journalism, but half would encourage their daughters to do so (Beasley & Theus, 1988, pp. 58-59).

To serve as a "reality check" on the statistical study, the Maryland researchers held two roundtable discussions in 1984. The first was of women who had achieved substantial successes in journalism careers. The second was of students and recent graduates.

Among participants in the first roundtable were six women representing newspapers: Marcia Slacum Greene, a reporter for *The Washington Post;* Claudia Townsend, city editor on leave from *The Post;* Nancy Monaghan, national editor, *USA Today;* Sharon Dickman, assistant metro editor, *Baltimore Evening Sun;* Mary Lou Forbes, associate editor, *Washington Times;* and Tonnie Katz, managing editor, *Baltimore News American.*

Comments included references to the competing demands of jobs and family life. Katz said, "I find at my office, which is very informal, that while I'm glad to have anyone go at any time to take a child here or there . . . I . . . don't do that. I wait until 10 p.m. till I get home for dinner . . . women still put that pressure on themselves" (Beasley & Theus, 1988, p. 90).

Townsend explained, "I had sort of anticipated being pushed off into the corner . . . as somebody who had a baby. . . . And they [*Washington Post* editors] crossed me up by offering me a promotion. . . . I sit and think about whether I'm going to let the baby stay home (with a sitter) . . . and is that going to drive me crazy" (Beasley & Theus, 1988, p. 90).

Monaghan pointed out that women appear to be trying harder than men to succeed in newspaper jobs: "They're trying to prove that they can do the job that men think they can automatically do." Therefore, the panelists agreed, women sometimes were willing to settle for less than men (Beasley & Theus, 1988, p. 93).

Dickman and Greene spoke of the difficulties women have in getting hired and moving up the newspaper career ladder. Dickman said, "[We at the *Baltimore Sun*] have more women applicants than men for jobs, but recently we had some openings, and we made three hires, one white woman, one white man and one Black woman. And that's generally how our hires go. . . . In companies like ours where there's a small number of women, it is the pioneering days" (Beasley & Theus, 1988, p. 97).

"The 1983 survey from the ASNE [American Society of Newspaper Editors] shows that of the major newspapers in the country in terms of editors there are 93 women and 1,027 men. . . . And the bottom line is there're 89.4 percent men compared to 10.6 percent of women in top management. I don't think that's going to change overnight," Greene pointed out (Beasley & Theus, 1988, p. 102).

Forbes urged women to develop their skills to compete successfully: "They [editors] cannot deny [you] if you're good and you constantly turn out a good product. You write the best obituaries in the office; you come up with a scoop out of police court every day. This is a great business for women because if you're good they can't deny it" (Beasley & Theus, 1988, p. 95).

The roundtable of students and recent graduates included two recent graduates employed by daily newspapers, Cristal Williams, *Easton* (MD) *Star-Democrat,* and Chris Harvey, *Prince George's Journal.* Both spoke of problems that they foresaw in combining careers with children.

As Williams put it, "One of the things I have thought about more since I have been working is, I guess, to postpone getting married" (Beasley & Theus, 1988, p. 113).

"I just couldn't picture myself in the job that I'm doing now and having children because you just work 50 to 60 hours a week, you work at night, you work on weekends," Harvey said. "To have little kids around, I would just have to take an easier job" (Beasley & Theus, 1988, p. 112).

Harvey also referred to pay scales in the field: "The thing that bothers me is the salary. I think maybe it's more noticeable on the littler papers especially because . . . there seem to be a lot more women. . . . Young women and people who are married and have come back to the field" (Beasley & Theus, 1988, p. 114).

From the roundtable discussions the Maryland researchers identified four areas for amplification in the study. These pointed to the need for women journalism students to (1) acquire strong basic writing skills, (2) have suitable role models, (3) learn how to persuade employers of their worth so they would not be forced to settle for less than men, and (4) plan how to combine family responsibilities successfully with their careers.

The question of women defining the news arose in connection with the issue of acquiring basic writing skills. The study cited work by Catherine S. Covert, a journalism professor at Syracuse University, who theorized that journalism is written in terms of winning and losing, conflict and controversy. Quoting examples from a journalism history textbook—"the press wins a beach-head," "the rise of the fourth estate," "the race for news,"—Covert held this was the language of male "winners," not that of women, a submerged group who have been conditioned to develop alternative values based on "concord, harmony, affiliation and community" (Covert, 1981, p. 4).

In Covert's opinion the old newsroom sobriquet "sob sister" conveyed women's position in relation to male journalists, revealing the fact that women reporters and their human-interest stories were "only marginally relevant to the rational [male] business of the newsroom day." According to this line of thought, the preference of women journalism students for sequences other than news-editorial may reflect the social conditioning of many women and their avoidance of male-designed news formulas. The Maryland report contended that if women students are less conflict-oriented than men, they are likely to choose media fields outside the mainstreams of journalism (Covert, 1981, p. 4).

Consequently the Maryland report recommended that journalism educators emphasize the blending of news and feature-writing that has occurred in recent years. To a degree this represents a blurring of the sharp lines that used to denote "hard news" (the front-page news stories denoting action) and "soft news" (the feature stories appealing to the emotions). Calling attention to the blatant sexual overtones of these terms, the Maryland study urged that journalism schools not perpetuate old stereotypes by assigning women students feature stories, for example, while grooming males to be campus editors or by giving male instructors general reporting courses and women instructors feature-writing classes.

The male orientation of the newspaper industry was apparent from studies cited in the report. One, conducted by Dorothy Jurney for the ASNE, showed that fewer than 12% of editors were women in 1985. Another, done in 1983, reported top women newspaper managers earned about 60.1% of men's salaries for comparable jobs, with the actual dollar gap given as $18,147 annually.[1]

A 1982 study of 200 recent journalism graduates of the University of North Carolina with newspaper experience also was noted. It showed the average salary classification for women on a 1-to-6 scale was 1.98, whereas the average category for men was 2.34. At the same time the men had more job experience than the women, indicating that the women had dropped out and returned or moved more often than the men (McAdams, 1984, pp. 10-12).

In addition, the Maryland report mentioned a "New Directions for News" study distributed by ASNE. It analyzed coverage by 10 leading newspapers of alimony and child support questions, enforcement of Title IX (the law prohibiting discrimination in education), the Equal Rights Amendment campaign, the 1977 National Women's Conference in Houston, pay equity, and the World Conference of the United Nations Decade for Women. The conclusion: News articles in some papers on these subjects were inadequate, unfair, or lacking in recognition of the issues (*New Directions for News,* 1983, pp. 3-4).

In light of this material, the Maryland study speculated that the nature of news itself might change, at least somewhat, if women become the majority in the newsroom—unless they are restricted to the prevailing male model to advance professionally. The report, however, chiefly concentrated on economic issues, noting it is possible that journalism and related fields may become "pink-collar ghettos" on the lower levels, with salaries and status there less than those of other major professions. It urged journalism educators to fight against discrimination and warned, "If salary and status in journalism-related fields decline relatively and those fields become less competitive, some of the most important work of a democratic society will become less attractive to students gifted in intellect, resourcefulness and general ability" (Beasley & Theus, 1988, p. 140).

The preliminary version of the Maryland report made headlines in October, 1985, following a press conference at the National Press Club in Washington to unveil a 5-year plan for upgrading the University of Maryland College of Journalism. A group of faculty members presented various research findings at the press conference. Media attention, however, focused on the "new majority" study instead of either the college's plan for development or research described by male faculty members. (These topics included examinations of science writing and findings that the public gains news primarily from print not television.)

To aid reporters in covering the event, the University of Maryland prepared press packets including press releases. The release on the "new majority" study was not written by the women associated with the research. It began, "Journalism and related professional fields are becoming principally female, with a danger that they will be 'pink-collar ghettos' offering lower salaries and status than they would as largely male fields, a new University of Maryland study says." The release said that "female-dominated fields such as teaching, social work, nursing and librarianship traditionally have been lower-income professions." It continued, "Although salaries in journalism-related fields (some of which already are noted for low pay) may not decline, there should be concern that they will not rise as they might if these fields remained predominantly male." It also pointed out that women are filling the ranks but are not yet well represented in management.

Some reporters at the press conference used the release as the basis for stories that sensationalized the issue. United Press International sent out a story beginning, "Women are quickly dominating the ranks of the news profession and their emergence threatens to keep both the money and the status of the industry low," a 2-year study by the University of Maryland says. The story said that women constituted about 40% of the daily news force. It led to headlines like the following: The *St. Louis Post-Dispatch*— "Study: Women May Devalue Journalism"; the *Easton* (MD) *Star-Democrat* —"News Women Creating 'Pink Collar Ghetto' "; *Deseret News* (Salt Lake City)—"Women Are Taking Over Journalism;" *Miami News*—"Journalism Seen Turning 'Pink-Collar.' "

Other newspapers handled the story more responsibly. *The Washington Post,* for example, headlined the story "Women Predominate in J-Schools" and used a comprehensive lead: "Women now make up 60 percent of all journalism students in the country and may soon outnumber men in communications, according to a University of Maryland study whose authors expressed fears that the shift will lower pay and the prestige of the field in comparison to male-dominated fields" (Arocha, 1985).

With a headline of "Women the 'New Majority' in Journalism Schools," the story received balanced coverage in the *Evening Sun* of Baltimore. Sharon Dickman reported, "Women have taken over the classrooms of journalism and mass communications schools around the country, but they still face discrimination when they graduate and look for work, a new University of Maryland study shows" (Dickman, 1985).

Some of the news coverage of the press conference drew an inflamed response. In a column in the *Trenton* (NJ) *Times,* reprinted in part in *Editor & Publisher,* Linda Cunningham, executive editor of the Trenton paper, declared, "Not since conservative Patrick Buchanan's column, which said it was a woman's fault if she were raped, has anything in the newspapers raised my dander so much." She quoted a statement attributed to this author at the press conference and carried in the UPI report: "If journalism joins other devalued professions dominated by women, such as nursing and teaching, the watchdog role of the news media might become trivialized" (quoted in Miller, 1985, p. 52).

"Hogwash," Cunningham wrote. "Spend 15 minutes in this newsroom [*Trenton Times*] and then tell me the women around there are less demanding or more inclined to believe unquestionably what their sources tell them. Ask my bosses if I demure daintily when thwarted or sit quietly in a corner." Reacting to the suggestion in the study that the nature of news might change if women predominate in the field, Cunningham retorted, "I'm often asked whether women editors approach the news differently from their male counterparts. My answer is, invariably, no. News is news; it has no sex" (quoted in Miller, 1985, p. 52).

Excerpts from Cunningham's attack and other criticism of the Maryland study appeared in a column in *Editor & Publisher* by Susan H. Miller, director of editorial development for Scripps Howard Newspapers. She quoted from a letter by Judith Clabes, editor of the *Covington* (KY) *Post:*

"A seething anger is growing to a crescendo of outrage over the disservice the Maryland 'research' has done to a whole group of professional, hard-working and dedicated women journalists." In common with Cunningham and Clabes, Miller apparently viewed the study personally. She asserted it "adopted unwarranted and unsubstantiated assertions about the professional performance of women" (Miller, 1985, pp. 32-33).

In a reply to Miller, also published in *Editor & Publisher,* I blamed initial media coverage—as well as the emotional response from a few token women editors—for obscuring the point. It was that women were clustered in relatively low-paid, low-prestige journalistic positions, not because they wanted to be, but due to societal factors that historically undervalued them economically. "The community press, where large segments of women increasingly are concentrated at low salaries, may not be in an economic position to embrace the watchdog function," I stated in my reply. And I concluded, "Let's see 'seething anger' and 'a crescendo of outrage' over discrimination in general and over low salaries in particular—whether men or women are being victimized" (Beasley, 1985, pp. 44, 33).

Defending the report's conclusions, Chuck Stone, writing in the *Philadelphia Daily News* in 1986, pointed out that women writers and journalists historically have not fared well at the hands of white males in terms of Pulitzer prizes and other professional recognition. Calling attention to criticism of the Maryland research by Linda Cunningham, Stone commented, "But let the word go forth to Cunningham, women journalists . . . and women writers everywhere. Maybe you have come a long way, baby. But in 1986, male America is still dumping on you." Stone, who is Black, said the issue translated into power for white males and weakness for "everybody else" (Stone, 1986).

The Maryland research did not directly take up the question of minority employment on newspapers although minority representatives participated in the roundtable discussions. Yet it should be emphasized that minority hiring—whether of men or women—remains at a relatively low level. In 1988 newsrooms were 7.02% minority compared to 6.56% a year before, an increase of only 0.46%, according to the American Society of Newspaper Editors. Since then modest improvement has occurred. According to a 1992 survey by the Newspaper Association of America, 11% of newspaper reporters/writers now are classified as minorities.[2] Yet a study released by ASNE in 1991 found no minorities were employed as journalists at 51% of U.S. daily newspapers, mostly in smaller markets.

Today there is little reason to think that the nature of news is changing dramatically. The coverage of the Maryland report itself speaks to that point. As the examples given in this chapter show, much of the coverage was biased and superficial. It conformed to the conventional male model of conflict, controversy and "spicy" headlines. Those women in decision-making roles who criticized the report appeared determined to prove that they had absorbed the same news values as their male predecessors. At the same time they displayed a "sob sister" response, attacking what they construed as personal aspersions on them instead of logically considering the issues. Although a new majority may be moving into newsrooms, it appears it is continuing to encounter roughly the same old definitions of news even though there are occasional efforts to broaden coverage.

At this point 7 years have elapsed since the release of the Maryland report. Is there reason to think the concerns that prompted the report no longer exist? Are women making a relatively smooth transition from journalism school into newspapers? Has the pay risen substantially? Are women moving rapidly up the newspaper ladder? Has the perception of discrimination been eliminated?

Unhappily the answer to all these questions is "no." For example, women represented 69.7% of a national sample of 1991 journalism graduates, but the percentage of all graduates that year specializing in the news-editorial field had declined from 21.8% in 1986 to 17.1%, according to the sample (Becker & Kosicki, 1992, p. 12). Those who actually looked for full-time employment with a newspaper declined, with newspapers and wire services hiring only 7.9% of the journalism graduates (Becker & Kosicki, 1992, p. 15). This was a sharp drop from 15.5% in 1986. Women students were much more likely to select advertising and public relations sequences than news-editorial (Becker & Engleman, 1988, pp. 4-5, 16).

Median weekly pay for new graduates at daily newspapers stayed at $350, about the same as in 1990. On nondaily newspapers it was even less—$289, a drop from $300 in 1990. By contrast, starting pay in public relations was higher. The median weekly salary in public relations went up from $295 in 1986 to $385 in 1991. The median in advertising, however, fell from $351 to $348 in 1991 (Becker & Kosicki, 1992, p. 17).

Once hired on newspapers, women can look forward to a slow climb upward, although women now constitute 38% of reporters/writers.[3] According to Jean Gaddy Wilson of the University of Missouri School of Journalism, "Women are creeping ever so slowly toward the year 2055 when projections indicate they will attain levels in newspaper editorships on a par with their level in the population (53 percent)." Wilson based her projections on a report compiled from the *Editor & Publisher Yearbook* that showed less than 1% increase in directing editorships for women—from 12.4% in 1986 to 13.03% in 1987 (Wilson, 1988, p. 1).

Even today women receive relatively little attention in newspaper content. A 1990 survey by the Media Watch project of Betty Friedan at the

University of Southern California and the American Society of Newspaper Editors took note of coverage about and by women in terms of photographs, bylines, and story sources on the front pages of 20 U.S. newspapers. It found females averaged only 14% as sources in stories and had only 28% of the bylines. *The Washington Post* ranked first in the number of women featured in front-page photographs (42% of those pictured in the *Post* were women compared to 41% of those shown in *USA Today*) (*About and by Women,* 1990, pp. 2, 7).

The *Post's* executive editor, Ben Bradlee, took no pleasure in the survey results, responding, "I am damned if I can see what conclusions should be drawn from your findings" (*About and by Women,* p. 7). The *Post's* feminist columnist, Judy Mann, contended on the other hand that the pictures told a story of a newspaper trying to be "relevant to [its] entire audience" (Mann, 1990). If newspapers do not succeed in becoming more relevant, their future looks doubtful. Newspapers are losing readers of both sexes, but women at a faster rate than men (male readership dropped from 63% in 1982 to 53% in 1987, while female readership dropped from 61% to 45%) (Miller, 1989, p. 12). The "new majority" is vitally necessary to redefining the news, but at the upper echelons it has little opportunity to wield influence.

Notes

1. A variety of studies in recent years has addressed the problem of women's slow progress into management. See Dorothy Jurney, "Percentage of Women Editors Creeps Upward to 11.7—But Other fields Continue to Progress Faster," *ASNE Bulletin,* January 1986, pp. 8-9. See also Christine L. Ogan, Charlene J. Brown, and David H. Weaver, "Characteristics of Managers of Selected U.S. Daily Newspapers," *Journalism Quarterly* 56 (Winter 1979), pp. 803-809, and Ogan, "Life at the Top for Men and Women Newspaper Mangers: A Five-Year Update on Their Characteristics," a working paper, Indiana University, 1983.

2. Information from a telephone interview by the author with John Blodger, vice president for labor relations, Newspaper Association of America, November 16, 1992.

3. Information from Blodger interview.

References

About and by Women. (1990). Reston, VA: Human Resources Committee, American Society of Newspaper Editors.

Ackerman, Carl W. (1949, June 6). *The inside of a newspaper should be like the inside of a home.* Speech given at the American Press Institute, New York (Box 164, Carl W. Ackerman papers, Library of Congress).

Amrine, Abbie A. (1941, October). This is our day. *The Matrix, 27,* 15, 19.

Angelo, Betty. (1953, October/November). Career: Metropolitan vs. community newspaper. *The Matrix, 39,* 14.
Arocha, Zita. (1985, October 15). Women predominate in j-schools. *The Washington Post,* pp. B1, 7.
Beasley, Maurine H. (1985, December 14). In defense of the "women in journalism" study. *Editor & Publisher,* pp. 44, 33.
Beasley, Maurine H., & Theus, Kathryn T. (1988). *The new majority: A look at what the preponderance of women in journalism education means to the schools and to the professions.* Lanham, MD: University Press of America.
Becker, Lee B., & Engleman, Thomas E. (1988, April). *1987 journalism and mass communications graduate survey.* Unpublished report. Columbus: Dow Jones Newspaper Fund/Ohio State University School of Journalism.
Becker, Lee B., & Kosicki, Gerald. (1992, July). *Survey of journalism and mass communications graduates 1991.* Unpublished report. Columbus: Ohio State University School of Journalism.
Covert, Catherine L. (1981). Journalism history and women's experience: A problem in conceptual change. *Journalism History, 8,* 2-6.
Dickman, Sharon. (1985, October 15). Women the "new majority" in journalism schools. *The* [Baltimore] *Evening Sun,* p. D2.
Dow Jones Newspaper Fund/Gallup Survey. (1984, January). *Final tabulation of 1983 journalism graduates.* Princeton, NJ: Author.
Dunn, Betty Hinckle. (1942, December). Matrix final. *The Matrix, 28,* 3.
Employers' symposium. (1940, October). *The Matrix, 26,* 7-8.
Kosicki, Gerald M., & Becker, Lee B. (1991). Annual census and analysis of enrollment and graduation. *Journalism Educator, 47*(Fall), 61-70.
Logie, Iona Robertson. (1938). *Careers for women in journalism: A composite picture of 881 salaried women writers at work in journalism, advertising, publicity and promotion.* Scranton, PA: International Textbook.
Mann, Judy. (1990, April 4). A touch of relevance. *The Washington Post,* p. D3.
Marzolf, Marion. (1977). *Up from the footnote: A history of women journalists.* New York: Hastings House.
McAdams, Katherine C. (1984, June). [Draft of untitled paper on comparison of work patterns and starting salaries between men and women journalism graduates of the University of North Carolina.] Unpublished manuscript.
Miller, Susan H. (1985, November 23). Was "pink collar" ghetto study deliberate sensationalism? *Editor & Publisher,* pp. 52, 32-33.
Miller, Susan H. (1989, Spring). Women's lifestyles: A special report. *Scripps-Howard Editors Newsletter,* p. 12.
New directions for news. (1983). Washington, DC: George Washington University, Women's Studies Program and Policy Center.
Ogan, Christine L. (1983). *Life at the top for men and women newspaper managers: A five-year update on their characteristics.* Working paper, Indiana University.
Ogan, Christine L., Brown, Charlene J., & Weaver, David H. (1979). Characteristics of managers of selected U.S. daily newspapers. *Journalism Quarterly, 56,* 803-809.
Peterson, Paul V. (1980, January). J-school enrollments reach record 71,594. *Journalism Educator, 34,* 3-9.
Sherwood, Midge Winters. (1951, October). No such thing as part-time mother. *The Matrix, 37,* 9-10.
Stone, Chuck. (1986, January 22). Women are still being dumped on. *Philadelphia Daily News,* p. 36.

Wilson, Jean Gaddy. (1988, January). Only 68 years to go. *Press Women, 51*, 1-3.
Women and the newspaper. (1924). (Journalism Series No. 30). Columbia: University of Missouri.

8 Magazines
Women's Employment and Status in the Magazine Industry

SAMMYE JOHNSON

There is no way of knowing how many magazines celebrated the industry's 250th anniversary in 1991, because no one knows for certain how many different magazines exist in the United States.

It has never been easy to define magazines, or to assign definitive figures to the industry. Even Frank Luther Mott's (1939) Pulitzer Prize-winning five-volume history of American magazines from 1741 through 1930 dealt only with certain important magazines, for "exact figures are impossible to obtain" (p. 341).

One key historical fact is that the first magazines were published in America within 3 days of each other in 1741: Andrew Bradford's *American Magazine, or A Monthly View of the Political State of the British Colonies* and Benjamin Franklin's *General Magazine, and Historical Chronicle, for All the British Plantations in America* (Mott, 1939, p. 24). Thereafter, magazine scholars and researchers are on their own. It is impossible to know how many magazines—even if there were agreement on what a magazine is—have been published since 1741.

Women have been active in the magazine industry as publishers, editors, writers, and readers since its beginnings. As early as 1787, letters from women were published in magazines, articles had feminine authors, and women were being wooed as readers. Noah Webster said in his December 1787 issue of *American Magazine,* "*Fair* readers may be assured that no inconsiderable pains will be taken to furnish *them* with entertainment" (Mott, 1939, p. 65). One of the earliest great magazine editors was a woman— Sarah Josepha Hale, who founded *Ladies' Magazine* in 1828. She merged her publication with Louis Godey's *Godey's Lady's Book* in 1837, and served as editor for 50 years, during which the magazine became famous for its elegant essays and hand-colored fashion plates (Mott, 1939, pp. 582-583).

Through the decades, magazine mastheads list women in top editorial positions. Women have always been recognized as important readers and subscribers, for magazines dedicated to women uniformly appear in the top 10 magazines by total circulation year after year, according to the Audit Bureau of Circulations (ABC) (1992).

In addition, the 87.3 million women who read an average of 10 different magazines a month constitute the majority of the nation's magazine readers (89% of the U.S. population, 18 years of age and older, or 164 million adults, make up the magazine industry's audience) (*The Magazine Handbook,* 1992, p. 37). Indeed, women are involved as readers and editors across the spectrum of magazine types. They have always played important roles in this medium.

However, there is mystery surrounding the magazine industry, in terms of people involved, numbers of titles, and kinds of publications. Regardless of the time frame, the magazine universe is so complex and so changing that it shifts constantly, being impossible to freeze into a quantifiable mass. So it should come as no surprise that the roles women play today— whether as magazine editors or advertising directors or circulation managers or writers—are as shrouded in swirls of mist as any romantic thriller.

Unfortunately, finding out about the heroine is hampered by the environment in which she lives and works.

The Magazine Environment

Look at any current magazine study or mass media textbook and the problem becomes evident. There is no agreement on how to categorize magazines, much less how to determine the exact dimensions of the industry. Donald N. Wood (1983) points out:

> Derived from the French word *magasin,* meaning "warehouse" or "storehouse," the modern magazine almost defies explicit description. About the only generalizations one dares to toss out are that the magazine is *usually* bound or stapled (unlike most newspapers) and is *normally* published on a regular schedule (unlike most books). The one characteristic common to the magazine industry is that, with a few notable exceptions, magazines are aimed at specialized audiences. (pp. 83-84)

One result is that some textbooks divide magazines, also referred to as periodicals, into general consumer, special interest consumer, business, association, farm, and public relations (Click & Baird, 1990, p. 6). Others never attempt to categorize magazines, but instead list types—news, city and regional, religious, women's, controlled circulation, and so forth. There simply is no consensus.

However, researchers who specialize in magazines (of whom there are very few) seem to be moving toward a three-part division: consumer magazines (publications of general or specialized interest sold to the public); specialized business magazines (which cover various aspects of particular industries or professions and which may be sold or given away free); and public relations magazines (published by corporations for specific internal or external audiences and that are almost always free). Unfortunately, some publications, like farm and religious magazines, cross divisions, making classification difficult.

Numbers present a daunting situation. Because there is no standard magazine classification, the range becomes awesome. Depending on what reference you choose, you can make a case for just about any set of magazine numbers.

The *Standard Periodical Directory 1992* provides data on more than 75,000 periodicals in the United States and Canada (Oxbridge Communications, 1992). To be included, a magazine need only be published at least once every 2 years.

The *Gale Directory of Publications and Broadcast Media,* often cited in magazine research and mass communication texts, lists 11,863 periodicals for 1993 (Gale Research, 1993).

The numbers become more manageable when you turn to the main source of information for advertisers. Standard Rate and Data Service, Inc. (SRDS) publishes data on consumer, farm, and business publications. For 1992, SRDS lists 2,055 consumer magazines and 263 farm magazines in *Consumer Magazine and Agri-Media Rates and Data* (Standard Rate and Data Service, 1992b); 5,656 specialized business magazines are classified in *Business Publication Rates and Data* (Standard Rate and Data Service, 1992a).

The Magazine Publishers of America (MPA)[1] has 308 member publishers representing 1,200 U.S. magazines in 1992, while the American Business Press (ABP)[2] has 121 member companies publishing more than 700 magazines. Both groups point out there are still many consumer and specialized business magazines that exist, but are not audited, surveyed, or even listed anywhere.

The Society of National Association Publications (SNAP)[3] numbers 320 publication members for 1992, although the *Encyclopedia of Associations* lists more than 22,000 nonprofit associations in America; many of them have some sort of publication (Gale Research, 1991, p. ix). A survey by the American Society of Association Executives (1992), which has more than 20,000 members, revealed that 95% of the respondents issued periodical publications (p. 112). These groups point out there are still many consumer and specialized business magazines that exist, but are not audited, surveyed, or even listed anywhere.

The problem intensifies when you turn to the largest and hardest to identify category: public relations magazines. No census has ever been taken, so estimates range from 10,000 (Click & Baird, 1990, p. 8) to 100,000 (Paine & Paine, 1987, p. 15).

New magazines are started every day. Samir Husni (1992), head of the Magazine Service Journalism Program at the University of Mississippi, reports that from 1985 through 1991 the number of new magazines started per year averaged 471 (p. 8). Based on past performance, it is estimated that only 20% of these new titles will continue to be published after 4 years (*The Magazine Handbook,* 1992, p. 6). The mortality rate for new magazines is high. Start-up figures and cessation rates for specialized business magazines and public relations magazines are not available.

Government data do not clarify the magazine industry, either. Bureau of Labor Statistics data are based on the printing and publishing industry as a whole, and include newspapers and books as well as printing establishments. Periodical figures are not always specified, nor is the term defined; the editor/reporter occupation classification is not limited to magazines.

For July 1992, the Bureau of Labor Statistics listed 123,600 employees at periodicals (U.S. Department of Labor, September 1992, p. 51). In the "printing, publishing, and allied industries, except newspapers" category (a segment that encompasses more than just magazines), women were 42.6% of the total employed; Blacks were 7.0%, and Hispanics were 6.4% in 1991 (U.S. Department of Labor, January 1992a, p. 197). In 1991, women were 51.1% of the editors/reporters employment category, with Blacks at 4.5%, and Hispanics at 2.8% (U.S. Department of Labor, January 1992b, p. 186).

Thus the magazine industry cannot be considered feminized, or racially balanced, and it does not appear to be moving in either of those directions. Interviews with women in the consumer magazine field support the concept of gender balance in the industry, which is documented by Bureau of Labor Statistics data. Most women do not believe the magazine industry is flooded with females, and many can remember times when they were the only woman reporter or editor in the room. Although women say men traditionally have held the top positions or have been better established in the corporate magazine hierarchy, they point out that the field is balanced "at least fifty-fifty" (Valys, 1992). Jobs are there for women at all levels, but pay equity is not.

Women at Consumer Magazines

Although numerous studies have been made of magazine content, advertising, and readers, there is a paucity of institutional research on the structure and roles of those employed at consumer magazines. One reason for this is that the magazine industry is very volatile, and numbers of magazines fluctuate, as do the numbers of jobs and people employed. There is no consistency in job title and position description, making salary surveys difficult. An editor at one magazine may have the responsibilities of an associate editor at another; a circulation manager at one company may be a circulation marketing director at another. Though all magazines need four kinds of personnel—editorial, advertising sales, circulation, and production—this does not mean that every magazine has four departments, or even four employees (Wright, 1987, pp. 480-481).

The earliest consumer magazine studies counted names on mastheads to determine positions held by men and women. While studies of editorial mastheads in 1970 revealed that men held more top positions than women, other research showed great variations among individual magazines (Butler & Paisley, 1980, p. 195). For example, a 1974 analysis of 18 well-known magazines found 70% of the editors at *Redbook* were women, while just 25% of the top editors at *Ladies' Home Journal* were women (Butler & Paisley, 1980, p. 195).

A study of magazine editors listed in *The Working Press of the Nation* in 1973 found

> that 11% are women, while 74% have men's first names, 13% give initials in lieu of a first name, and 2% have names used for both sexes. Women were most likely to edit technical magazines that have small circulations. Men edit the well-known women's and news magazines. Only 1 of the 25 listed news magazines was edited by a woman. (Butler & Paisley, 1980, p. 196)

Research conducted at Stanford University in 1977 examined the numbers of women and men on the editorial staffs of business, news, analytic, women's, and popular magazines; across all magazine types, 73% of the key editorships were held by men (Butler & Paisley, 1980, pp. 197-198). Yet other research has found 100% of the articles in a single issue were written by women (Butler & Paisley, 1980, p. 224).

More recent data are not available, for a systematic analysis of those employed at consumer magazines—male or female—has not been made. Except for David H. Weaver and G. Cleveland Wilhoit's inclusion of newsmagazine writers and editors in their major study of American journalists, there has not been a complete look at who works at consumer magazines. Weaver and Wilhoit (1986) estimate that newsmagazine journalists make up only 1.1% of the full-time editorial workforce in U.S. news media (p. 13).

Weaver and Wilhoit (1986) make the following comments about newsmagazine journalists: Women make up 31.7% of newsmagazine staffs, up a tad from the 30.4% reported by Johnstone et al. in 1971 (p. 21); minorities are less likely to be attracted to newsmagazines than to broadcast media or daily newspaper positions (p. 22); the newsmagazine journalist is, like the rest of the editorial workforce surveyed by Weaver and Wilhoit, a white Protestant male (p. 12); but the newsmagazine journalist has a much higher median income than the "typical" journalist, at $34,750 compared to $19,000 (p. 84); and newsmagazine journalists, who are the most highly paid group in the news media, also have higher job satisfaction (p. 103).

Folio: The Magazine for Magazine Management has conducted salary surveys of top managerial positions in editorial, production, circulation, and advertising sales, since 1985. However, there does not appear to be any continuous survey of lower echelon editorial staff such as assistant editors, editorial assistants, or staff writers. Salary surveys conducted by the Magazine Publishers of America are confidential, and are available only to members.

Folio's 1985 survey asked editors to report anonymously on their salaries and titles. The 1985 findings are based on responses from 484 people (53% response rate) in six positions: editorial management, editors, managing/executive editors, senior/associate editors, copy editors, and art directors. *Folio* breaks out salary averages by nine variables: region, type of magazine, average editorial pages produced annually, number of editors on staff, frequency, circulation, gender, number of magazines responsible for, and years of experience (Love & Angelo, 1985, p. 73).

Folio summarizes the results: "Wide variations in salaries for people with same title; lower pay for women; general dissatisfaction with editorial compensation" (Love & Angelo, 1985, p. 69). For example, when the average consumer magazine salary for editorial management (editorial director, vice-president-editorial, editor in chief, and editor-publisher) is indicated by gender, women's pay is 68% that of men's ($35,800 versus $52,350). And the same pattern of less money paid to women exists among editors, managing editors, senior/associate editors, copy editors, and art directors, although the discrepancy is not as great (Love & Angelo, 1985, p. 74).

In that 1985 survey, several women comment on differences in salary: "I'm still waiting for equal pay for equal work," and "Men make about 25 percent more, even if they work on less prestigious and smaller circulation magazines" (Love & Angelo, 1985, p. 71). *Folio* cautions readers about using the numbers: "It should be noted that the data here have been presented in the form of simple totals (only one variable was studied at a time). The interaction that may exist between the totals has not been examined" (Love & Angelo, 1985, p. 72).

Folio's 1986 editorial survey, with 518 editors responding (representing 45.6% of those surveyed), shows women still receiving less money than men in every level except copy editor. Male editors earned $14,204 more than females ($57,000 to $42,796), the greatest difference in the categories (Angelo, 1986, p. 80). Comments from women are revealing: "I have on five occasions been paid less than male predecessors, peers or replacements in jobs where I was praised as 'The star,' or 'The best ever,' " wrote a woman editor in the Northeast with almost 25 years of experience who earned a salary in the mid-$80,000s (Angelo, 1986, p. 82).

Folio changed its universe studied for this 1986 survey; no comparisons could be made to the salaries published the year before (Angelo, 1986, p. 90). Unfortunately, *Folio* changed its universe sample every time a salary survey was done.

In 1987, *Folio* has a 49% response rate, with 556 returns. Although the same nine factors are presented, *Folio* broadened its sample base, eliminating previous requirements. Therefore the survey could not be compared to any past ones (Zelkowitz, 1987, p. 94). Salary range closes in 1987 in all but two editor categories, with women earning between 96% and 100% of what men earn. However, the picture changes dramatically when consumer magazine editor and art director salaries are studied in terms of gender. A female editor makes just 78% of her male peer's salary, $35,620 versus $45,736. A female art director earns only 70% of the salary of a male director, $32,136 to $45,627 (Zelkowitz, 1987, pp. 97, 103).

Folio's 1988 survey, of 559 editorial professionals (53% response rate), reports that women continue to earn less than their male peers, from a low of 74% of men's salaries for consumer magazine editorial management to a high of 99% for managing editors (Steed, 1988, p. 103). In editorial management slots, women earn $43,747 to men's $59,200; in the editor category, women take in $37,568 to their male peers' $45,320 (Steed, 1988, pp. 106-107).

For 1989, *Folio* surveys 646 editorial professionals (47% response rate) and finds that "salaries of women in this sample are frequently much closer to those of their male counterparts than they were last year. . . . This is perhaps another indication that, on a long-term basis, the pay disparity between men and women is gradually eroding" (Steed, 1989, p. 122). Beginning with the 1989 survey, *Folio* uses a different set of variables: region, sex, years of editorial experience, eligibility for bonus/incentive, number of magazines responsible for, number of editorial employees supervised, circulation, frequency, average number of editorial pages, and range of average total compensation. Consequently, comparisons to previous years cannot be made.

Gender pay disparity increases during *Folio's* 1990 survey. There is a smaller response rate for 1990, with 545 surveys returned (39%), and editors cite budget concerns as their biggest editorial challenge. So it may not be surprising that salaries of females in consumer magazine editorial management average just 82% of male's salaries, $48,428 to $58,740 (Steed, 1990, p. 112). For editor slots, women earn $35,269, or 73% of men's $48,294 (Steed, 1990. p. 113). Only in the position of managing editor are salaries close, with women edging out men $37,130 to $36,563 (Steed, 1990, p. 114).

Folio argues that women are "continuing the slow but steady progress toward equal pay seen in earlier surveys" in discussing data from the 1991 editorial salary survey based on 582 responses (41% response rate) (Steed, 1991, p. 63). However, a close study of the figures reveals that the gap is greater in the top consumer magazine positions (editor in chief, publisher, and editor) than in mid-management positions (managing editor, senior/associate editor, and art director). For example, women editors earn just $38,681 while their male counterparts take home $49,280; this puts women's salaries at 78% of men's (Steed, 1991, p. 66). But in the managing editor and senior/associate editor jobs, women earn 91% and 97%, respectively, of men's salaries (Steed, 1991, pp. 68-69).

The 1992 *Folio* editorial salary survey, with 542 respondents (41% response rate), has a category change; only senior editors are surveyed rather than senior/associate editors because "this provides a sharper picture of senior editors' salaries, since combining the two titles had tended to make both sets of data less accurate" (Zelkowitz, 1992, p. 39). Salaries still show sharp gender differences for all consumer magazine categories except for senior editor, where women are earning $40,433, or 99% of men's $40,955 salary (Zelkowitz, 1992, p. 43), and managing editor, where females are earning 94% of what their male peers receive, $39,549 to $42,000 (Zelkowitz, 1992, p. 42). In the top editorial management jobs, women are paid $48,417 to men's $68,625, or 70.5% (Zelkowitz, 1992, p. 40). Female editors receive 73% of male editors' salaries, or $34,305 versus $47,158 (Zelkowitz, 1992, p. 41). Female art directors average $37,213, while males with the same title average $49,222, for 76% of male salaries (Zelkowitz, 1992, p. 44).

Folio also has surveyed consumer magazine professionals in circulation, advertising sales, and production. Each year, and in each category, men are more highly paid than women, reflecting the same gaps found in editorial. However, as mentioned above, a major problem with *Folio* surveys is that of changing samples; no consistency exists in the variables or the universe from year to year for comparison or longitudinal analysis.

Other salary data can be found in sources such as *Media Industry Newsletter, The Gallagher Report, The American Almanac of Jobs and Salaries,* and *Magazine Week.* The information, however, is not gender-specific, and varies considerably. But job categories not surveyed by *Folio* can be found there, such as assistant editor, executive assistant, editorial assistant, and staff writer. None of these sources indicates race, another variable that should be considered in studying magazine industry employment patterns.

Comments from women about salary discrepancy or discrimination are not included in *Folio* surveys after 1986. Recent interviews with women in the consumer magazine field reveal that most believe there has not been overt discrimination against them, and that in general, women are paid about the same as men in similar posts.

A woman in the magazine field for 10 years as a copy editor, associate editor, and managing editor at four publications, and whose salary peaked in the $20,000-$29,999 bracket, said:

> I could not advance because the only position I could advance to was a man's —and I was propping him up. One reason I got out of magazine management is because they need mothers. They need somebody who will make a personal investment in the quality and integrity of the publication that's well beyond the call of duty. I felt overly burdened by that.

This woman is now a freelance writer (Valys, 1992).

Another 15-year veteran who has been a staff writer, associate editor, business editor, editor, and senior editor at five different consumer magazines, said, "Most of the power has been in the hands of men. I think a lot of women end up doing detail things like editing or fact checking. In general, I had the same title and the responsibilities as a man." She is now with a trade magazine as a writer, where she is making as much as she made at a glitzy consumer magazine as senior editor (Valys, 1992).

Women at Specialized Business/Trade Magazines

In all its salary surveys, *Folio* examined the pay scales of those working on specialized business magazines as well as consumer magazines, generally surveying equal numbers of business and consumer magazine professionals. At business magazines in 1985, women earn less than their male peers, except in the copy editor category, with an even greater gap in salaries by gender than is found at consumer magazines. For example, in the senior/associate editor category, female business editors earn just 74% of what male business editors make, while women in this position at consumer magazines earn 95% of men's salaries (Love & Angelo, 1985, p. 78).

The 1986 *Folio* report still shows female business editors making less money than males in all categories except copy editor, where women earn about $3,000 more. However, men earn as much as $22,000 more than women in other positions (Angelo, 1986, p. 82).

A 10-year veteran woman editor in the Midwest, who received $35,000 a year, wrote, "My peers are all about my same age, and have my same amount of experience. They are also all male. They all make more than I do" (Angelo, 1986, p. 82).

In 1987, *Folio* reports, "Although the difference in salaries between the two types of magazines is small for men—with business magazine men outearning their consumer colleagues by 9.6%—women managers on consumer magazines, at an average salary of $75,633, make 61.2% more than their sisters on business magazines" (Zelkowitz, 1987, p. 91).

The 1988 *Folio* survey reveals that "women continue to earn less than their male counterparts—from a low of 66% of men's salaries for editorial management to a high of 88% for managing editors. And in every category, the difference in pay is larger on business magazines than on consumer magazines" (Steed, 1988, p. 103).

Folio's 1989 survey of editorial salaries puts the average consumer magazine payment for all female respondents ahead of that for business publications in all categories except for editor. The sharpest gender difference between business and consumer magazines is in the category of editorial manager. "On business magazines, male editorial managers earn 18% more than women, whereas on consumer magazines, women are 17% ahead (Steed, 1989, p. 124).

The 1990 look at business magazines by *Folio* has women earning less than men, by about the same amounts as at consumer magazines. For example, women who are in editorial management at business magazines earn 85% of men's earnings, $56,938 to $67,116; for consumer magazines, the differential is 82% (Steed, 1990, p. 112).

Studying the 1991 *Folio* data for business magazines' editors reveal the same kinds of patterns: Women earn less than men in the same editorial positions across the board, in varying amounts. For example, in the editor category, women make just 70% of their male peers, $39,494 to $56,147 (Steed, 1991, p. 66).

Results of the 1992 *Folio* survey show women ahead of men in two business magazine categories: managing editor, where women earn a smidgen more, $40,968, than men's $40,897 (Zelkowitz, 1992, p.42); and art director, where women are paid $42,464 to men's $41,861 (Zelkowitz, 1992, p. 44). But there's no reason to rejoice, because gender discrepancies are still great in the other categories.

The same patterns hold true for business magazine professionals in circulation, advertising sales, and production, according to *Folio* data. There's no attempt to compare business magazines within particular areas, either vertically or horizontally.

The 1987 Society of National Association Publications salary survey reinforced some of *Folio's* findings, although limited to association publications only. From a random list of 1,034 association publication executives, 485 questionnaires were used—a 50% response rate (SNAP, 1987, p. 3). Two findings were especially relevant. The first was that "the majority of positions held in association publications are held by women, although there are a majority of males in the positions of publisher, editor-in-chief, and advertising salesperson" (p. 6). The second was an analysis of average salary by sex and age. Not surprisingly, males made more money than females in almost every job category. No analysis was made of race (pp. 34-39). The Society of National Association Publications would not release information from its most recent survey of publication executives, done in 1989.

Additional data can be found in papers presented by journalism and mass communication professors at annual conventions of the Association for Education in Journalism and Mass Communication (AEJMC). For example, Dennis W. Jeffers, in his 1987 paper, *A Descriptive Study of Perceived Impact of Gender on Employment Status, Type of Work, Industry Relationships, Working Environment and Job Satisfaction in Livestock Industry Magazines,* points out that gender concerns had not, to date, been investigated in trade or business magazines (p. 3). Jeffers, a professor at Central Michigan University, distributed questionnaires to 69 livestock magazine staffers attending an annual meeting in 1986 in Fort Worth, TX. Although nearly 60% of the respondents were female, "women are under-represented in editorial positions and about equal in other positions on the magazines scrutinized." Those other positions included advertising, design, and production (p. 8).

Jeffers's data, which were consistent with the findings of other gender studies, showed that "in spite of the influx of women in the field . . . men are the managers and women are the technicians at livestock magazines" (p. 8). Jeffers does not analyze salary, but nevertheless, his research adds reliability to results of other gender-related studies in mass communication.

Jeffers's research focused on a very narrow part of the trade magazine category. Kathleen L. Endres, an associate professor at the University of Akron, broke ground on the category as a whole with *The Business Press Journalists: Who They Are, What They Do and How They View Their Craft,* presented at the 1988 AEJMC Convention. Pointing out that surprisingly little is known about the specialized business press or its journalists, Endres (1988) provides what is probably the most thorough demographic profile of business press editorial personnel to date, along with information about work patterns and perceptions of the field. Since no comprehensive list of full-time business magazine journalists exists, Endres drew her sample from SRDS's *Business Publication Rates and Data.* Her 374 questionnaires (45% response rate)

represent a cross section of journalists in the business press. They cover a number of different industries, live in different parts of the country and work for periodicals that span the circulation range of free to paid, the frequency rate of weekly to quarterly and the formats varied from magazine to newspaper. (p. 3)

Endres finds "the typical business press reporter or editor is a microcosm of U.S. journalists in general. Business journalists are likely to be white males in their mid-30s with bachelor's degrees" (p. 5). This supports Weaver and Wilhoit's (1986) research. However, Endres goes a long way toward providing needed information about women in this area of the magazine industry.

Although men made up 54% of those responding to Endres's survey, females outnumbered males in periodicals covering the retail and service industries, two areas where women dominate in the general labor force. In magazines covering the professions, building trades, industry, business/management, and transportation, men outnumber women (p. 6). Endres says men and women working on business magazines differ in several key respects, in areas corresponding to research done in public relations and that validate *Folio* salary surveys. Women are less likely to hold the jobs of editor or senior editor than men. Only in the managing editor position is there parity. Endres says:

Two explanations are possible for such a disparity. First, the relative inexperience of the women compared to the men. According to those responding to this questionnaire, women have about half the professional experience of men. The other explanation may deal with tradition. While none of the women reported discrimination as a weakness in the business press field, the small numbers of women employed in the top editorial positions seems to suggest that there may be more to this situation than mere inexperience. (p. 9)

Endres finds that women earn substantially less than men, with an average income of $25,658 versus $39,559 for men, a disparity that could be found across all editorial jobs on specialized business magazines. Differences in salaries tend to be smaller in the entry-level jobs. Yet even the female assistant/associate editor, the most common job for women at business magazines, receives less pay than her male peer, $21,956 to $24,714. The smallest differential is found in the reporter slot, where men receive $27,500 and women $27,000 (pp. 9-10).

Endres's study also provides racial information, something that rarely has been covered in magazine studies. The overwhelming majority of business press professionals are Caucasian, 98% of those answering the questionnaire. Only eight members of minority groups are identified: three Blacks, one Oriental, and four Hispanics (2%). Endres says the minorities are split between men and women, but, more disturbing, "That ethnic breakdown means that minority groups are more greatly underrepresented in the business press than the journalism field in general or the U.S. population" (p. 12).

Endres included other demographic information, such as birthplace, education, college major, marital status, memberships in professional organizations, as well as information about work patterns (job title, duties, job training, use of sources, relationship with sources and readers). She also asked respondents to evaluate the strengths and weaknesses of the field and to provide ways of improvement. According to Endres, "There were no comments from women about salary or occupational discrimination—not a one mentioned this. There was an open-ended question about job weaknesses where this could have been addressed. But it wasn't" (Kathleen Endres, personal communication, July 1988).

Women at Public Relations Magazines

This, the largest category of magazines in the United States, is also the hardest to study. So it is not surprising that there has been very little research specifically dealing with house organs. The International Association of Business Communicators[4] with about 8,800 members in the United States, does not identify how many of its members manage, edit, or produce either an internal or external magazine, nor are tabs kept on how many companies might be producing magazines. There is information about titles, with editor being listed 15% of the time (International Association of Business Communicators, 1987, p. 6). However, as with titles at consumer and business magazines, titles in corporate communications or public relations areas are not consistent. A manager or director is just as likely to produce or edit a magazine as an editor, coordinator, or specialist.

Interviews with women who have worked in this magazine field for several years provide some information as to their status as professionals. Said one who has spent 12 years as editor or senior editor at three different public relations publications:

> Women get to be editors—which people on the outside think is a top slot. But the reality is that public relations magazines are likely to be headed by a president and board of directors. And these slots are typically held by men. So the problems for women at public relations publications are not magazine industry issues, but corporate structure issues. As senior editor, I probably do what an editorial assistant would do at a consumer magazine. I am not autonomous; I have to clear things through management. Yet I'm not experiencing salary discrimination because I know a man would be paid the same because of this company's grade structure. Whoever has this job is essentially a technician.

This woman's current salary is in the $40,000-$45,000 range (Johnson, 1992).

Another woman who has been senior editor for 11 years on an external high-tech corporate magazine says:

> I think women can get the top slot and have influence. I believe that management is more concerned about talent than gender. Employers are looking for people who can do the job regardless of sex. However, the women I know who work in editorial jobs have—categorically—worked harder than the men. It seems like there's an unspoken rule that we must overachieve to stay on top.

Earning between $40,000 and $45,000, she adds, "The editor is a mystery person in the corporation. Top management has a hard time assessing the individual's worth as a writer/editor because it's hard to quantify words, layouts and designs" (Johnson, 1992).

Public relations research has not addressed the area of internal or external magazines put out by corporations. However, it is likely that much of the material in Chapter 11 of this book applies to this aspect of the magazine industry.

Magazine Research

Research about magazines, whether involving magazine journalism or the magazine publishing industry, has been scanty. Work on the demographics, attitudes, and beliefs of magazine professionals has also been neglected.

Scholarly magazine research simply has lagged far behind the work being done on other aspects of the mass media by mass communication researchers.

David Abrahamson, an associate professor at New York University, points out that despite the pivotal role of gender in editorial positions and advertising prospects for magazines in general, gender has been the object of little scholarly attention.

In his paper, *A Quantitative Analysis of U.S. Consumer Magazines: Baseline Study and Gender Determinates,* presented to AEJMC in 1992, Abrahamson says,

> Most studies have been the work of journalism historians, and their principal focus has been on 19th-century developments. Indeed, it can be argued that magazines as a subject for academic research have typically drawn less consideration than either television or newspapers. As a result, no clear normative view of consumer magazines as whole exists in the research literature. (p. 2)

Peter Gerlach (1987) has documented the infrequency of magazine research in publications on journalism and mass communication. Studying the years from 1964 through 1983 in *Journalism Quarterly,* a key refereed journal in the field, Gerlach found that only 6% of the articles published dealt with magazines. About half of these articles consisted of content analysis, followed by historical and economic topics. Others dealt with effect analysis, readership, communication analysis, and education (p. 179).

Gerlach also surveyed 40 AEJMC members who had published one or more articles about magazine research in *Journalism Quarterly,* asking their opinion of American magazine research, among other questions (p. 178). With 32 surveys returned (80% response rate), Gerlach found, "All in all, 68.7 percent of the respondents thought that magazine research has been unsatisfactory in one respect or another" (p. 181). Pointing out that descriptive content analysis and not studies of processes and effects have dominated magazine research, Gerlach's respondents also report that magazine research is not a well-funded area (p. 181).

Compounding the lack of magazine research has been a neglect of gender roles. Writing in *Journalism Quarterly* with my colleague William G. Christ, I have pointed out the lack of research on how women newsmakers are presented in magazines (Johnson & Christ, 1988, p. 889). We analyzed the representation of women on the cover of *Time* from its first issue in 1923 through 1987 because *Time* has argued "that history is made by men and women, no matter how strong the forces and movements that carry them along" (p. 890). Because of this, *Time* tends to feature personalities on its covers, as opposed to events, ideas, or themes. We use this characteristic to look at gender and analyze which women newsmakers have been covered. Out of 3,386 covers published in the 64-year period studied, only 482 covers show images of women on them, or about 14% (p. 892).

Only one woman is represented from the field of science and medicine, Dr. Virginia Johnson from the Masters and Johnson research sex therapy team in 1970, and only three women are categorized as CEOs or business executives: Helen Reid, vice president of the *New York Herald Tribune* (1934); Elizabeth Arden, founder and CEO of Elizabeth Arden cosmetics (1946); and Dorothy Chandler, vice president of the *Los Angeles Times* (1964) (p. 897). Despite the fact that women have entered the workforce in record numbers during the past two decades, no women have been presented on *Time's* covers in a business role since 1964 (p. 897).

There is a lack of coverage of women in other professional areas during the period from 1923-1987. Out of the total number of covers devoted to women, only 8% are political leaders; religious leaders make up 1%, government administrators 2%, activists 2%, and sports figures 5% (p. 895). The majority of women featured on *Time's* covers are artist/entertainers (37%); spouse or other relationship to a man like mother, daughter, or divorcee (22%); and socialites, royalty, and nobility (8%) (p. 895).

There are even several years where women are represented only on one cover, while in others, only one identifiable woman is featured. For example, 1925 has only one woman featured out of 52 covers, poet Amy Lowell, while 1982's only identifiable woman (some covers have women as "window dressing" or as part of a "mob scene") is actress Jaclyn Smith (p. 896). This is a bit unnerving.

Suggestions for the Future

Four areas need to be addressed before magazine publishing can be studied adequately: (1) articulation of what the field involves, (2) definitions that tackle methodological as well as structural and theoretical problems inherent in the magazine industry, (3) linkages among researchers in the field, and (4) analysis of the demographic and social order of magazine professionals.

To address the first area, Marcia Prior-Miller, an associate professor at Iowa State University, is developing a typology, or theory of magazines, for "without an adequate typology, designing quality comparative studies of magazines and magazine organizations and the professionals working in them is not possible" (personal communication, August 6, 1988).

Prior-Miller, who presented her preliminary analysis of magazine types at the 1992 AEJMC conference, says,

> The model suggests a framework, not only for testing against a wide variety of communication questions, but also for evaluating existing research on magazines—however limited that body of literature may be—to establish with a higher level of certainty than was previously possible, the theoretical links between a proposed research and already completed research. (1992, p. 32)

Regarding the second area, as can be discerned from reading this chapter, there are major difficulties in identifying the universe of magazine titles from which to draw samples for cross-sectional study. Prior-Miller points out that

> directories both duplicate the listings of other directories and omit large numbers of publications. Descriptions of the criteria for the inclusion or exclusion of titles is often less than adequate from the scientific perspective. Thus, any effort to design a careful sample immediately is confronted with this weakness in the sampling frame. (personal communication, August 6, 1988)

Prior-Miller's (1992) typology identifies magazines based on primary intended audience information function and primary intended audience structure, and results in four categories: lifestyle, occupation, scholarly, and organization (pp. 21-22).

Third, those interested in magazine research have difficulty building upon prior studies. There is a great deal of fragmented research, or as Prior-Miller puts it,

> Existing studies tend to be discrete and atheoretical. New generations of scholars tend to be overwhelmed by the lack of a coherent body of research on the history of the development of the field, the on-going social order, and the problems of communications within the medium. Given the dominant model of research on other media and the intellectual and financial support for continuing to work within that dominant model, young scholars understandably turn their interests in those directions. (personal communication, August 6, 1988)

Finally, until these methodological and structural concerns are met with functioning definitions and terminologies, professionals working in the magazine industry cannot be studied systemically. There is no agreement on job titles, nor has there been an attempt to break down staff responsibilities, reflecting size or type of magazine. What is needed is a project along the lines of Weaver and Wilhoit's (1986) study of American news journalists. Then, and only then, can issues relating to women and minorities clearly be addressed.

Notes

1. Information from a telephone interview of The Magazine Publishers of America, New York City, in November 1992.

2. Information from a telephone interview of the American Business Press, New York City, in November 1992.

3. Information from a telephone interview of The Society of National Association Publications, Washington, D.C., in November 1992.

4. Information from a telephone interview of The International Association of Business Communicators, San Francisco, in November 1992.

References

Abrahamson, David. (1992, August). *A quantitative analysis of U.S. consumer magazines: Baseline study and gender determinants.* Paper presented to the Magazine Division at the annual meeting of the Association for Education in Journalism and Mass Communication, Montreal, Canada.

American Society of Association Executives. (1992). *1992 policies and procedures in association management.* Washington, DC: Author.

Angelo, Jean. (1986, May). Editors' average salary: $52,240. *Folio: The Magazine for Magazine Management,* pp. 76-90.

Audit Bureau of Circulations. (1992, August 17). Consumer magazine paid circulation. *Advertising Age,* p. 39.

Butler, Matilda, & Paisley, William. (1980). *Women and the mass media: Sourcebook for research and action.* New York: Human Sciences Press.

Click, J. William, & Baird, Russell N. (1990). *Magazine editing and production* (5th ed.). Dubuque, IA: William C. Brown.

Endres, Kathleen L. (1988, July). *The business press journalists: Who they are, what they do and how they view their craft.* Paper presented to the Magazine Division at the annual meeting of the Association for Education in Journalism and Mass Communication, Portland, OR.

Gale Research. (1991). *Encyclopedia of associations 1992* (26th ed). Detroit: Author.

Gale Research. (1993). *Gale directory of publications and broadcast media 1993* (125th ed.). Detroit: Author.

Gerlach, Peter. (1987). Research about magazines appearing in *Journalism Quarterly. Journalism Quarterly, 64*(1), 178-182.

Husni, Samir. (1992). *Samir Husni's guide to new consumer magazines* (Vol. 7, 1992). Stamford, CT: Folio.

International Association of Business Communicators. (1987). *IABC Profile '87.* San Francisco: Author.

Jeffers, Dennis W. (1987, August). *A descriptive study of perceived impact of gender on employment status, type of work, industry relationships, working environment and job satisfaction in livestock industry magazines.* Paper presented to the Magazine Division at the annual meeting of the Association for Education in Journalism and Mass Communication, San Antonio, TX.

Johnson, Sammye. (1992, July-August). [Interviews with women working at public relations magazines]. Unpublished.

Johnson, Sammye, & Christ, William G. (1988). Women through *Time:* Who gets covered? *Journalism Quarterly, 65*(4), 889-897.

Love, Barbara, & Angelo, Jean. (1985, July). Editors' average salary: $34,623. *Folio: The Magazine for Magazine Management,* pp. 69-84.

Magazine Publishers of America. (1992). *The magazine handbook 1992-1993.* New York: Author.

Mott, Frank Luther. (1939). *A history of American magazines: Volume 1. 1741-1850.* Cambridge, MA: Harvard University Press.

Oxbridge Communications. (1992). *Standard periodical directory 1992* (15th ed.). New York: Author.

Paine, Fred K., & Paine, Nancy E. (1987). *Magazines: A bibliography for their analysis with annotations and study guide.* Metuchen, NJ: Scarecrow.

Prior-Miller, Marcia. (1992, August). *An analysis of "magazine type": Toward an empirically based typology of magazines and non-newspaper periodicals.* Paper presented to the Magazine Division, Association for Education in Journalism and Mass Communication annual meeting, Montreal.

SNAP (Society of National Association Publications). (1987, October). *Society of National Association Publications salary and benefits survey.* Washington, DC: Author.

Standard Rate and Data Service. (1992a, April). *Business publication rates and data.* Wilmette, IL: Author.

Standard Rate and Data Service. (1992b, April). *Consumer magazine and agri-media rates and data.* Wilmette, IL: Author.

Steed, Robert M. (1988, August). Editorial salary survey. *Folio: The Magazine for Magazine Management,* pp. 103-121.

Steed, Robert M. (1989, June). Editorial salary survey. *Folio: The Magazine for Magazine Management,* pp. 121-132.

Steed, Robert M. (1990, June). 1990 editorial salary survey. *Folio: The Magazine for Magazine Management,* pp. 110-120.

Steed, Robert M. (1991, June). *Folio's* 1991 editorial salary survey. *Folio: The Magazine for Magazine Management,* pp. 63-71.

U.S. Department of Labor, Bureau of Labor Statistics. (1992a, January). *Employment and earnings: Employed civilians by detailed industry, sex, race and Hispanic origin.* Washington, DC: Government Printing Office.

U.S. Department of Labor, Bureau of Labor Statistics. (1992b, January). *Employment and earnings: Employed civilians by detailed occupation, sex, race, and Hispanic origin.* Washington, DC: Government Printing Office.

U.S. Department of Labor, Bureau of Labor Statistics. (1992, September). *Employment and earnings: Employees on nonfarm payrolls by detailed industry.* Washington, DC: Government Printing Office.

Valys, Susan. (1992, August). [Interviews with women working at consumer magazines]. Unpublished.

Weaver, David H., & Wilhoit, G. Cleveland. (1986). *The American journalist: A portrait of U.S. news people and their work.* Bloomington: Indiana University Press.

Wood, Donald N. (1983). *Mass media and the individual.* St. Paul, MN: West.

Wright, John W. (1987). *The American almanac of jobs and salaries.* New York: Avon.

Zelkowitz, Suzanne. (1987, June). Editorial salary survey. *Folio: The Magazine for Magazine Management,* pp. 91-104.

Zelkowitz, Suzanne. (1992, August). Editorial salary survey. *Folio: The Magazine for Magazine Management,* pp. 39-44.

9 Radio
A Woman's Place
Is On the Air

JUDITH A. CRAMER

A woman's place in early radio was in singing, acting, and giving household hints. It was also in research, off-air interviewing, and writing. It was not, however, in announcing and reading the news, nor was it in managing or owning a radio station. World War II, affirmative action, and the women's movement of the 1970s combined to open those doors of opportunity.

Women in radio in the 1920s described their field as an excellent one—one where there was less sex discrimination than in other fields, and one in which the opportunities for moving into positions of greater creativity and responsibility were good (Marzolf, 1977). Bertha Brainard, assistant broadcasting manager of New York City's WJZ in 1928, seemed to support this assessment when she said, "The pioneering state of radio gives men and women equal opportunities and equal pay for equal work" (Marzolf, 1977, p. 124).

Opportunities for women in early radio were a logical extension of their roles in the home. For example, Ruth Crane pioneered the "Homemaker" program concept as host of "Mrs. Page's Home Economics," which aired 6 days a week on WJR in Detroit from 1929 until 1944. From there, Crane moved to Washington, D.C., to host WMAL's "Modern Woman" program (Beasley & Silver, 1977). Prior to World War II, most stations employed one female air personality, usually as host of the "Homemaker" program that aired anywhere from 15 minutes to an hour (Beasley & Silver, 1977).

An accomplished magazine and newspaper journalist, Mary Margaret McBride expanded the "Homemaker" program concept when she began her radio career on New York's WOR in 1934. She not only offered household tips and recipes on her "Martha Deane Program," but conducted human interest interviews as well. Unlike other hosts of "Homemaker" programs, she did not use a script, which played an important role in the creation of the talk radio show concept.

In 1933, the first radio news team was assembled at CBS. Paul White put together the team, which included one woman—*New York Journal-American* reporter Florence Conley (Marzolf, 1977, p. 129). Conley reported on what today we term "lifestyle" news.

The broadcasting industry employed its first woman news commentator, Kathryn Craven, in 1936, despite the belief by many in radio that a woman's voice was neither low nor authoritative enough to be giving the news (Hosley & Yamada, 1987, p. 22). Craven's 5-minute program, "News Through a Woman's Eyes," aired on CBS radio until 1938, when the program was dropped.

World War II increased the opportunities for women in all areas of radio because there was a wartime shortage of men. Radio station management was forced to open the doors to women as news reporters, announcers, and radio managers. Marion Taylor, among others, signaled a turning of the tide when she took over the "Martha Deane" show in 1941 (Marzolf, 1977, p. 132). According to Marzolf (1977), Taylor chose not to focus on the "women's angle," because she believed good and bad stories were not gender-related (p. 132). In 1936, CBS radio, according to its then-Director of Talks Helen Sioussat, relaxed its corporate policy to include hiring women as assistant directors and producers (Marzolf, 1977, p. 135). In addition, more and more women were working as news reporters.

During the 1940s, women also entered the announcing ranks in larger numbers. Although more women were employed in radio because of a shortage of men, men continued to receive top billing. Much of the women's programming was aired on weekends, and reports by female war correspondents were usually last in the network newscast or were relegated to the weekend when the male correspondents had time off.

By 1946, women comprised 28% of the people in broadcasting (Marzolf, 1977, p. 143). According to Marzolf (1977), a year later the *Labor Department Round-Up* predicted there would be many more opportunities in broadcasting for men and women with the conclusion of the war years, but this proved not to be the case for women (p. 143). When the men returned from war, they assumed many of the positions women had held.

Predictions were made that radio had reached its peak in growth and popularity during the World War II years, that with the advent of television and the ensuing competition between it and radio, women would have fewer radio career opportunities. After all, announcing positions were still almost nonexistent. The vast majority of radio's decision makers, Marzolf says (1977), were male and still held to the belief that women's voices were "poor," and that radio announcing meant irregular hours and equipment that was difficult to operate (p. 145).

In the 1950s, women slowly moved into other areas of radio. They found employment as "script girl," a position called "production assistant" when a man held it. Although women also became the interviewers and coordinators of radio programs like "Nightline" and NBC's weekend program "Monitor," it was routine procedure to rub the woman's voice off the tape so that an on-mike male announcer could ask the questions (Marzolf, 1977). In addition, the late 1950s saw a few women move into music programming as coordinators of disc jockey shows, although women were poorly paid and were expected to maintain high levels of energy and resourcefulness (Marzolf, 1977).

Less attention was given to researching radio trends with the inception of television in the 1950s. Studies do show, however, that women constituted 20% of all university and college broadcasting course graduates in the 1960s (Marzolf, 1977, p. 149). Yet, according to Marzolf (1977), radio only hired 60 to 80 of those graduates a year (p. 149).

In 1960, Smith and Harwood conducted the very first survey of men and women in broadcasting for the Association for Professional Broadcasting Education and the National Association of Broadcasters. The results, based on the responses of 156 women (72 in television, 84 in radio) and 1,573 men in radio and television, found that about 85% (140) of the women surveyed, regardless of education, were employed as clerks or secretaries in such areas as the traffic department (where the scheduling of commercials is done), and earned much smaller paychecks than men (p. 340).[1] In fact, Smith and Harwood (1966) reported that in weekly salaries ranging from $38 to $288 or more, 90% of the women in radio, compared to only 27% of the men, earned less than $96, and 7 out of 10 women in radio earned less than $77 a week (p. 340). Surprisingly, however, only about one fourth of the women in radio expressed dissatisfaction with their salaries. Certain benefits derived from their jobs, such as contact with other professionals, might have compensated for their low salaries (Smith & Harwood, 1966, p. 354).

According to the Smith and Harwood study, women 28 years ago entered radio by "chance" and worked in the medium an average of 3 to 4 years (p. 343). Men, on the other hand, trained for the radio profession and worked in the field for 10 to 14 years (p. 343). More than a fourth of the women and 47% of the men surveyed cited money and career advancement as reasons for leaving their last positions (p. 343). Interestingly, only a quarter of the women cited family and personal considerations as reasons for leaving their last positions.

The 1960s were a time of societal change, but a bias against women in radio newsrooms still existed and was reflected in the fact that women comprised just 4.7% of the radio and television newsroom staffs (Marzolf, 1977, p. 149). Responses to a survey conducted in 1977 of broadcast news directors offered the same old reasons for that bias: Men sounded more authoritative; women let personal problems affect their job performance; and women could not handle assignments (Marzolf, 1977, p. 149).

The 1970s signaled a turning point for women in radio. A 1971 survey of American Women in Radio and Television (AWRT) members found women were moving into larger radio markets, receiving better salaries, and attaining more responsible and audible positions. According to the survey results, women were more satisfied with their jobs but had become more conscious of discrimination, which they blamed on sex stereotyping. The AWRT members, however, believed the status of women in radio would improve, but thought it was up to the individual to improve it (Marzolf, 1977, p. 150).[2]

Women and Commercial Radio

A 1974 study of station managers revealed that prospects for women were bleak (Isber & Cantor, 1975). More than half of the managers still thought people did not like the sound of women on the air, even though earlier research refuted this stereotypical view (Marzolf, 1977, p. 150). Despite the dim outlook and some continuing large disparities in numbers and positions, women, nevertheless, made strides between 1972 and 1976.

In 1976, Stone surveyed 330 commercial radio stations and found that the number of stations where newswomen were on the air had more than tripled from 15% in 1972 to 49% in 1976 (p. 7). Even though radio was not making full use of women, it was becoming commonplace for radio news staffs to have women on the air.

In terms of pure numbers, positions, and salaries, women in the 1980s did not continue to make the same kinds of large gains in radio as they made in the 1970s. Parity between men and women in the radio newsroom did not come about at either the commercial network or local level. The least impressive gains were at the radio networks. As noted in the March 4, 1987, issue of *Variety* ("Women in Broadcasting," 1987), the number of women managers increased a maximum of just three percentage points between 1983 and 1986 (p. 110). According to *Variety*, CBS was the only radio network to employ women as general managers in 1983 and 1985; in 1987, however, no woman held that position at CBS (p. 110).

Table 9.1 Women and Minorities: Percentage of Workforce in Radio News Markets

| | 1986 | | 1991 | |
Markets	Women	Minorities	Women	Minorities
All Radio	32%	9%	29.4%	11.6%
Major	37%	16%	36.5%	18.3%
Large	35%	13%	35.9%	15.2%
Medium	29%	6%	21.5%	9.8%
Small	31%	5%	27.2%	4.7%

NOTE: The data in columns 1 and 2 are from "Women Gain, Black Men Lose Ground in Newsrooms," by V. A. Stone, 1987, *RTNDA Communicator*, p. 9. Copyright 1987 by RTNDA. Adapted by permission. The data in Columns 3 and 4 are from "Little Change for Minorities and Women," by V. A. Stone, 1992, *RTNDA Communicator*, p. 26. Copyright 1992 by RTNDA. Adapted by permission.

At the local level, improvement was gradual. For example, women comprised 29% (5,929) of the news anchors in 1986, a 9% increase over a 14-year period (Stone, 1987, p. 11). Overall, the number of women employed by local commercial radio station news departments (6,358) grew by 30% during this period (Stone & Dell, 1972, p. 4). Most of this growth took place in locally owned stations in large markets where, presumably because the size of the news staff is larger, they were more likely to hire a woman.

As of mid-1991, women constituted 29% of the commercial radio work force, a decrease of 3% from 1986 (see Table 9.1). Minorities now comprise 12% of the radio news workforce, up from 9% in 1986 but down from 13% in 1972 (Stone, 1988b, p. 11) (see Table 9.1).[3]

From 1990 to mid-1991, 250 radio newsrooms ceased operation, leaving about 5,800 working radio newsrooms (Stone, 1992, p. 26). This, in addition to the streamlining of news operations, caused a loss of 2,100 radio news jobs (p. 26). The number of women in radio news dropped from about 6,800 in the mid-1980s to 6,200 in 1990 to 5,000 in mid-1991 (Stone, 1992, p. 26). Some of this decrease is likely the result of a drop in the number of radio news operations.

Women in Radio News Management

The number of women news directors has grown steadily. The greatest gain, however, took place between the mid-1970s and mid-1980s, slowing considerably in the 1990s (see Table 9.2).

According to Stone (in press), female news directors have surpassed their male counterparts in yearly salaries, this despite the fact that the men have been employed in their current positions a year longer than the women

Table 9.2 Profiles of Male and Female Radio News Directors

	1976		1986		1991	
	Male	*Female*	*Male*	*Female*	*Male*	*Female*
% of ND Workforce	92%	8%	76%	24%	71%	29%
Median Age	30	35	33.8	27.5	34.9	28.9
Median # yrs. as ND here	3	3	2.2	1.5	2.5	1.5
Median Annual Salary	$7,200	$6,960	$15,600	$13,728	$17,600	$19,000

NOTE: The data in columns 1 and 2 are from "Surveys Show Younger Women Becoming News Directors," by V. A. Stone, 1976, *RTNDA Communicator,* pp. 10-11. Copyright 1976 by RTNDA. Adapted by permission. The data in columns 3 and 4 are from "Women Gaining as News Directors" by V. A. Stone, 1988c, *RTNDA Communicator*, p. 21. Copyright 1988 by RTNDA. Adapted by permission.
The data in columns 5 and 6 are from "Women Overtake Men in Radio News Director Pay" by V. A. Stone, in press, *RTNDA Communicator*. Adapted by permission.

(Stone, in press) (see Table 9.2). The women may have been hired in their current positions at higher salaries than the male news directors are currently earning, thus accounting for the difference.

Women and Public Radio

The introduction of National Public Radio in 1971 brought with it increased opportunities for male and female radio broadcasters. These new opportunities in radio emerged simultaneously with the second wave of the women's movement, thus offering the hope that public radio would open more career doors for women. In 1972, a survey of public radio stations found that women were employed at 103 public radio stations, with women comprising 14% of the management and 16% of all on-air positions (Butler & Paisley, 1980, p. 194). Two years later, women held 26% (3,452) of all public radio jobs (Butler & Paisley, 1980, p. 194).

In 1974, Caroline Isber and Muriel Cantor conducted a survey of 245 public television and 159 public radio stations on behalf of the Corporation for Public Broadcasting. Three hundred six men and 120 women in public radio responded to the survey. According to the "Task Force on Women in Public Broadcasting" report, 25% of National Public Radio's 16-member Board of Directors were women, while women constituted just 16% (234) of the membership on local boards of directors (Isber & Cantor, 1975, p. 141). Isber and Cantor reported that the number of women holding radio station manager positions was even less—12% (p. 141). The number of women in public radio management was especially disappointing because 80% of the public radio stations in 1974 had affirmative action plans and more than 70% of the stations were licensed to universities with affirmative action policies (Butler & Paisley, 1980, p. 194).

The Task Force Report also noted large disparities in the salaries, promotions, and assignments of women and men in public radio. The men made more money, but part of the explanation for this is that they had been in their present jobs longer than the women (Isber & Cantor, 1975). In the area of career advancement, a greater percentage of men than women in public radio received requested and unrequested promotions (Isber & Cantor, 1975).

The Task Force looked at 13 different kinds of adult public radio programs and found that 80% (375) of them had male narrators/moderators, 10% (49) had female narrators/moderators, and 10% (45) had male and female narrators/moderators (Isber & Cantor, 1975, p. 83). The men were much more likely to narrate/moderate discussions of business, economics, law, and government, with the women most often appearing in general human interest discussions (Isber & Cantor, 1975).

In the only survey since 1974 of public radio employment trends, Stone (1988a) found that the female share of the general news workforce (39%) tripled from 13 years earlier (13%) (p. 31). The survey showed that small and medium market salaries for reporters and news directors in public radio exceeded those of their commercial radio counterparts (p. 32). Stone (1988a) surveyed more than half of all public radio stations with working addresses (605) and found that although only one quarter (159) of the public radio news directors were women, they were just a little less likely than men to hold public radio news managerial positions or to work as newscasters/anchors (p. 32).

For minority newswomen, the news was good and bad. They comprised just 7% of the public radio news staffs and 12% of the public radio news directors in 1987 (Stone, 1988a, p. 31). Minority newswomen, however, were just as likely as minority newsmen and white newswomen to work as news directors (Stone, 1988a).

What Now, What Next?

In raw numbers, at least, women have made few gains in radio since World War II. As an example, today women comprise about 1% more of the overall radio news workforce than in 1946. An explosion of media, all competing for the same advertising dollar, has in the last few years propelled an increasing number of radio stations to carry satellite programming, automate fully, or change to greater revenue-producing, more cost-

effective formats that frequently result in streamlined newsroom operations or no local news commitment at all. This trend in radio economics
has meant that overall, there are fewer radio employment opportunities for
the men and women entering the radio industry.

The fact that not many more women are working in radio news today
than in 1946 does not reflect the strides women have made in securing
positions as reporters, announcers, and news anchors. The contemporary
women's movement, together with affirmative action, has helped open the
doors of opportunity for those women interested in radio careers. Today more
and more women are training for and working in on-air positions. These
advances, however, have not occurred with anywhere near the same speed
and magnitude of the 1970s.

Salaries

Although women radio news directors have exceeded the men in yearly
salary, that may not be the case in other radio news positions. Sally Wagner
has worked in radio news for 15 years. During the past 10 years she has
been a reporter and has shared the morning news anchor duties with her
news director at WTVN in Columbus, OH. According to Wagner, her salary
has more than doubled in that time (along with her responsibilities), but
she still feels that men with similar experience and responsibilities receive
greater compensation (personal communication, December 2, 1992).

Cynthia Smith, a producer at Black-owned and -operated WLIB in New
York City, does not believe that African American men and women earn
similar salaries for comparable work. She says "African American women
are paid less than African American men. Men get what they ask for. When
an African American woman walks in, it's more what you will settle for"
(personal communication, November 16, 1992).

According to Susan McInnis, a producer/host at public stations KUAC-
FM-TV in Fairbanks, AK, there is little or no salary disparity at university-
licensed public radio stations (personal communication, November 17, 1992).
Most often salaries coincide with job classifications, and within job classifications, experience.

Radio Management

Although there are fewer overall employment opportunities, women in
the 1990s don't seem to be experiencing the difficulties they had gaining
entrance into the radio workforce in prior years. Women are now immersed
in the next employment phase: finding work in the managerial ranks.

There has been continued growth for women in radio news management
in the 1990s. There also are more and more women holding radio sales

manager positions, but the station and general manager chairs remain occupied primarily by men. KUAC-FM-TV's Susan McInnis says there are no women managers at the public stations where she is employed. McInnis believes a "fear of diversity" is the reason for the dearth of women in management positions at KUAC (personal communication, November 17, 1992).

Forty-six-year-old Debbie Buglisi is the station manager of Liberty Broadcasting-owned WBAB and WGBB, and WHFM with which Liberty Broadcasting has a lease marketing agreement. In a telephone interview, Buglisi said that even though they still are few in number, many more women hold positions like hers because of the "crazy station acquisitions" of the late 1980s. Buglisi elaborated:

> The only way a company could make sure things continued running smoothly after they bought a station was to remove the general manager or general manager/owner. They would then promote the number two person to the top position. That meant that women would find themselves in the position of running the newly-acquired station. (personal communication, November 19, 1992)

According to Buglisi, it is not at all uncommon for women to make it to the number two position of station manager in the Liberty Broadcasting chain. Those holding the position of sales manager are most often promoted to station manager because they have experienced the business side of radio that news directors or music directors have not (personal communication, November 19, 1992).

As the former vice president of CBS AM stations and now the president and director of Women Broadcasters Incorporated (a group of three women awarded a radio station license in Montauk, NY, in 1990), Gail Barker has more than 20 years of broadcast management experience. Barker observes that women have worked their way up the ladder much more quickly in radio than in television because of radio's smaller profit margin. According to Barker, "the women who've become station or general managers have come up mostly through sales. The business has always been driven by sales. To be a general manager you have to be well-rounded, you have to be a lot of things and that includes understanding the business side of radio" (personal communication, November 18, 1992). For that reason, news directors rarely move into station or general manager positions. It is the sales managers (who are increasingly women) and program directors (too few of whom are women) who are most likely to ascend the ladder to station or general manager.

While some white women are slowly but surely filling the radio station managerial ranks as news directors, sales managers and station managers, minority women, particularly African American women, are not. And WLIB's Smith doesn't know why. Smith says she knows of just two African American women general managers, but knows there are a lot of African American women working in sales (personal communication, November 16, 1992). Because white women have found it easier to move into top management positions through sales, it may just be a matter of time before African American women begin to move into the top management ranks in greater numbers as well. If the number of African American women entering the radio industry does not significantly improve, however, then the outlook is dismal for African American women in radio station management.

Station Ownership

In 1987 Jane Evans, vice president and general manager of WBTH/WXCC in Williamson, WV, said in an interview in *RadioActive* that she believed women were considering station ownership more seriously because it was easier and more profitable, a quicker way of getting to where they want to be ("Women in Management," 1987, p. 14). In 1992, there is a rather different outlook for women in radio ownership.

In a telephone interview, Barker, the licensee of a radio station slated to broadcast from Montauk, NY, said the road to station ownership for women has become much bumpier.

> There isn't the preference to give licenses to women like there was in the late 1980s. Most of the women who want to go into ownership don't have the money and can't get the money from the banks, either because the banks traditionally have considered women bad risks or because they just don't have the money to lend. (personal communication, November 18, 1992)

According to Barker, even if a woman has the necessary money, being a station owner is extremely difficult these days because single, small stations can't compete with those that are owned by chains. As a result, single owners sell their stations to the chains so that they can make a profit on their investment (personal communication, November 18, 1992).

There are no figures of the number of women radio station licensees. According to the National Association of Broadcasters, the Federal Communications Commission does, however, keep statistics on the number of minorities, including men and women, who hold radio licenses. Minorities constitute 5.4% of all radio station licensees (NAB, personal communication, December 3, 1992).

Family Issues

Women have had their difficulties making inroads into radio station management and ownership, and family issues not traditionally faced by men have compounded these difficulties at least in some instances. WGBB, WHFM, and WBAB Station Manager Buglisi has two children. She says there are sacrifices:

> I get here as early as I can. I don't stay here until 10 p.m. With social engagements I ask "Is it something that's going to enhance my job?" Women are forced to make a distinction between activities that help business and those that don't because they have a lot of other responsibilities (home) that men don't have. (personal communication, November 19, 1992)

The mother of an 8-year-old daughter, 36-year-old News Director at WALK in Patchogue, NY, Susan Murphy believes it is very hard to work and raise a family. According to Murphy, the radio business, in some ways, can make it easier to have a child. Murphy, who anchors the morning drive news, says that even though she isn't able to wake up with her daughter or see her off to school (someone else does that), she *is* home when her daughter returns from school and is able to spend a good deal of time with her before each goes to bed. "Having a child gives you a different perspective, it influences the way you write or choose stories" (personal communication, August 26, 1992).

Stereotypes

The stereotype that having too many women on the air diminished the credibility of a radio news operation was alive and well in the 1980s. So too was the stereotype that women's voices are not low enough and thus not authoritative enough (Halper, 1987). For example, Kathy Lehr was the only woman news anchor at WLW in Cincinnati and was told by her program director that she was going to be taken off the air because her voice wasn't low or controlled enough. Fortunately for Lehr, the program director left the station before he could remove her from her on-air position (personal communication, June, 1988).

In 1992, these stereotypes have all but disappeared. WALK News Director Murphy is surrounded by four women anchors and just one male anchor. She says, "Talent and availability are what get you a job now. There's not so much a male-female quota . . . women aren't minority commodities anymore" (personal communication, August 26, 1992). WLIB's Smith says "there are just too many women in radio for women's voices to be an issue anymore" (personal communication, November 30, 1992). KUAC-FM-TV Producer/Host McInnis echoes that view. In a telephone interview the 45-year-old McInnis said, "There are no problems anymore with women's voices being too high. There are standards for both men and women" (personal communication, November 17, 1992).

Future Research

Contemporary research on radio and on women in radio is becoming even more scarce than it was 5 years ago and the focus has shifted to new technologies and their effects. Perhaps less attention is devoted to the status of women in radio because they are perceived to be a more integral part of the radio workforce. Or, perhaps, more time is being spent researching the "how's" of making the medium more viable, thus ensuring a long and prosperous life for radio. Nevertheless, radio continues to occupy a good deal of our time in our homes, cars, and even in our places of work.

Future research might include the impact of technology and television on the employment trends of women in radio. Studies suggest that women look at the world differently than men (Belenky, Clinchy, Goldberger, & Tarule, 1986; Gilligan, 1982). It might, therefore, be interesting to study the influence women in radio have on women and women's issues and on news coverage in general. In addition, since the last study of the employment trends of women in public radio was done in 1987, an update is needed. Research is needed on female role models in the industry and their impact on the socialization of young women into radio careers; factors that would increase the number of women at the network level; and women who own or manage radio stations. Finally, the small number of minority women in radio news has declined since 1979. This trend and the news/information operations of ethnic stations deserve in-depth study. More than ever, though, much of the success of women in radio will depend on the future of the medium itself.

Notes

1. The survey results did not include the responses of broadcast managers because there were only three women managers in the sample.

2. AWRT continues to operate today, although its membership has dropped from 2,700 members nationwide in 1989 to 1,800 at present.

3. In a telephone interview, Cynthia Smith, a 27-year-old African American who is the executive producer of a talk show on Black radio station WLIB in New York City, said that she believes a major reason for the scarcity of African American women in radio news/talk is the huge demand for African American women to work in television news (personal communication, November 16, 1992).

References

Beasley, Maurine H., & Silver, Sheila. (1977). *Women in media: A documentary source book.* Washington, DC: Women's Institute for Freedom of the Press.

Belenky, Mary F., Clinchy, Blythe M., Goldberger, Nancy R., & Tarule, Jill M. (1986). *Women's ways of knowing: The development of self, voice and mind.* New York: Basic Books.

Butler, Matilda, & Paisley, William. (1980). *Women and the mass media: Sourcebook for research and action.* New York: Human Services Press.

Gilligan, Carol. (1982). *In a different voice: Psychological theory and women's development.* Cambridge, MA: Harvard University Press.

Halper, Donna L. (1987). *RadioActive* (pp. 7-10). Washington, DC: National Association of Broadcasters.

Hosley, David, & Yamada, Gayle. (1987). *Hard news: Women in broadcast journalism.* Westport, CT: Greenwood Press.

Isber, Caroline C., & Cantor, Muriel. (1975). *The report of the task force on women in public broadcasting.* Washington, DC: Corporation for Public Broadcasting.

Marzolf, Marion. (1977). *Up from the footnote: A history of women journalists.* New York: Hastings House.

Smith, Don, & Harwood, Kenneth. (1966). Women in broadcasting. *Journal of Broadcasting, 10*(4), 339-355.

Stone, Vernon A. (1976, October). Surveys show younger women becoming news directors. *RTNDA Communicator,* pp. 10-12.

Stone, Vernon A. (1987, August). Women gain, Black men lose ground in newsrooms. *RTNDA Communicator,* pp. 9-11.

Stone, Vernon A. (1988a, June). News operations at public radio stations surveyed, Part I. *RTNDA Communicator,* pp. 29-34.

Stone, Vernon A. (1988b, August). Minority men shoot ENG, women take advancement tracks. *RTNDA Communicator,* pp. 10-14.

Stone, Vernon A. (1988c, October). Women gaining as news directors. *RTNDA Communicator,* pp. 20-21.

Stone, Vernon A. (1992, August). Little change for minorities and women. *RTNDA Communicator,* pp. 26-27.

Stone, Vernon A. (in press). Women overtake men in radio news director pay. *RTNDA Communicator.*

Stone, Vernon A., & Dell, Barbara. (1972, August). More women in news broadcasting according to RTNDA survey. *RTNDA Communicator,* p. 4.

Women in broadcasting. (1987, March 4). *Variety,* p. 110.

Women in management. (1987, June). *RadioActive,* pp. 7-22.

10a Television
The Face of the Network News Is Male

MARLENE SANDERS

It was 1964 when I became ABC News's second woman correspondent. The other two networks also had one or two women in their correspondents corps of about 50. It wasn't much, but it was a start. By now, nearly 30 years later, one might have expected something resembling parity. Anyone who does lives in a fantasy world.

"The Face of the News Is Male" is the headline of the newest figures, provided by Women, Men and Media, its fourth such survey. Women, Men and Media was founded in 1989 by feminist leader and author, Betty Friedan, a visiting professor at The University of Southern California, along with Nancy Woodhull, then president of the Gannett News Service. The objective was, and still is, to monitor gender issues in the media. This stemmed from a growing awareness of the imbalance and distortion in the coverage and representation of women in film, print, and television.

The news in the latest survey is not reassuring, in fact, it's terrible. And it's not just the television numbers that are poor, but also the report on newspapers.

During February 1992 the three network evening newscasts were judged on the basis of the number of female correspondents reporting and how many people interviewed were women.

In the network survey, men reported 86% of the broadcast news stories, and were sources 79% of the time. The number of women correspondents reporting the news overall dropped from 16% to 14%. The one slight plus is that during the survey period, the number of females interviewed increased from 1 in 10 in 1989 to about 2 in 10 in 1992.

AUTHOR'S NOTE: This chapter is adapted with permission from *Television Quarterly*, 1992, *26*(1), pp. 57-60.

Before discussing the breakdown network by network, a word about newspaper results. In the front-page newspaper study, 20 papers were examined from major and smaller markets during February 1992. The front page and the first page of the local section were measured by bylines (how many women writers) and photos, as well as the op-ed or equivalent page (bylines only). Also counted were the number of women interviewed. Female bylines in the 20 newspapers averaged 34% and women were in photos 32% of the time. Men were interviewed 87% of the time, even being featured in stories about silicone gel breast implants.

The small and medium size newspapers did better than the big dailies like *The Washington Post* and *The New York Times,* both of which came in near the bottom; *The Post* second worst, *The Times,* last. What seems to be happening is that in smaller communities, where newspapers face stiff competition from community papers and local television, editors are recognizing they need female readership to survive.

In the 1960s, the few of us who were female newswriters, producers, or reporters could do very little to change the system. We had to work hard to prove ourselves, as things were, in those almost all male newsrooms. But by the 1970s, the women's movement came along, and women were organizing at the newspapers, news magazines, and at the networks. The network groups were mostly made up of women from other departments, of non-newswomen, since there were so few of us.

Government policy, however, was on our side, and affirmative action was in place. The National Organization for Women challenged the broadcast license of WABC-TV, the ABC owned-and-operated station in New York City. Because all of the networks had their headquarters in New York, the dismal statistics revealed in that challenge made an impression. ABC and CBS began negotiations with their women's groups.

A great deal of progress took place in the ensuing years. NBC though, took an adversarial position, and the women there took to the courts. Years later, the women won, but at a high cost. Most of the leaders of the effort felt they had to leave the network because of their activism. The agreements they reached were monitored for several years, and slippage began immediately afterward.

It was during Lyndon Johnson's presidency that most of the progress for women in the networks took place. In the 1970s, anxious to keep their licenses, local stations reached out to hire women, in some cases, unqualified women, as reporters and anchors. "The class of '72" they were called, and many of them are now stars at the networks. The unqualified drifted away.

Efforts to bring women into the fold slowed as Democratic administrations in Washington gave way to Republican rule. "Quotas" and "affirmative action" became dirty words; deregulation under conservative FCC rules made it possible to remove scrutiny of fair employment practices. Later requirements to monitor public service and news programming were nearly totally eliminated. Instead of being custodians of the public airwaves and serving the public interest, broadcasters were free to program as they chose, and provide their version of the public interest—"what the public is interested in."

And so after the great leap forward of the 1970s, and the marching in step of the 1980s, what we have in the 1990s is a gradual move backward.

Here is what the Women, Men and Media organization found in its 1992 survey.

Females in the News: Television Averages (February 1992)

CBS averaged the highest number of females interviewed, 24%. ABC was again at the low end of the scale with 18%. The major topics for which women were interviewed included: health (25%), legal stories involving mistreatment of or discrimination against women (23%), and economics (19%).

Although U.S. women "brought home the gold" from the Olympics, only one female correspondent reported a sports story during the study period, and only seven females were interviewed about sports. Of these, four were included in a story about eating disorders among women athletes, reported by a male (ABC, 2/10/92).

Out of the 60 news shows aired in February 1992, one had no female correspondents or female interviewees (ABC, 2/3); seven had no female correspondents (ABC, 2/3, 2/7, 2/14, 2/17, 2/26; NBC, 2/6, 2/7); and four had no female interviewees (ABC, 2/3; CBS, 2/25, 2/28; and NBC, 2/12). More females than males were interviewed on only 2 days during the reporting period (CBS, 2/12, 2/13). On only 1 day were there more females than males reporting the news (NBC, 2/28).

On one day (2/3/92) that ABC had no female correspondents or female interviewees, there were 14 stories reported by men, and nine men interviewed. The stories were about politics, environmental pollution, health care costs, education—in short, topics of equal concern to and involving both men and women.

On the 2 days that CBS included no female interviewees, there were 20 stories reported and 45 men interviewed by 16 male and 4 female correspondents. One of the stories, reported by a male, was about a pregnant drug abuser and her dilemma about having an abortion (2/25/92).

Other stories filed that were glaringly low or lacking in female input included one on NBC (2/5/92) about the U.S. Senate lifting the ban on fetal tissue implants. A male reported the story, and three males were interviewed. On the same day and network, a story was carried about shoppers flocking to discount outlets. A male correspondent reported the story; four males and one female were interviewed. Who does most of the shopping in this country?

Also on NBC (2/26/92), a male correspondent reported on the controversy surrounding local health policies for premature babies; only one of the five people interviewed was female. On ABC (2/27/92), a male correspondent reported on the nuclear waste disposal controversy at Nevada's Yucca Mountain. There are many women actively involved in this issue, yet five men were interviewed for the story, not one female. These examples are not the exception; they are, rather, typical of the lack of importance relegated to female commentary and activities.

As in the newspapers, female television correspondents, in general, do not appear to seek out females for commentary any more than their male counterparts. Also, as in the newspapers, there were no days during the study period in which there was a lack of male correspondents or male interviewees.

Before we released the results—still a reporter at heart—I called all three networks to tell them of our findings and to get their views. There was genuine disbelief at their poor showing, after all, a few women anchors are now making the megabucks of their male counterparts, and have reached video stardom. Questions were raised: There were women anchoring (weekends of course), and women co-anchoring in the early morning, and major A.M. broadcasts. Why didn't we count them?

Because only the prime-time newscasts were our focus, that's why. Further, the networks replied, what you are not considering is, for example, the "American Agenda" pieces done by Carole Simpson and several other top women correspondents on ABC. Those pieces take longer to do, so those women cannot be as visible as the breaking news reporters. Yes, but men do some of those long form reports too, and that argument just doesn't sell.

The problem is that women make up only a quarter to a third of the TV correspondent corps. A few women cover the White House and a handful of other visible government departments. Others just don't get on the air often, and their stories are relegated to non-prime-time programming or to syndication.

We found that there has been some progress in the number of women who are executive producers and broadcast producers. The number of bureau chiefs is still small, and at the vice presidential level, if anything there has been slippage. At the height of the progress of the 1970s, CBS News had four; now there are two. ABC has had two news veeps fairly consistently since then, and NBC has two.

There is another problem we don't like to talk about. Not all women in power are our friends. The need to be "one of the boys" does exist. Some women are simply afraid to appear to tilt toward other women, afraid to be labeled feminists. As a result, they therefore fail to make their presence count.

The problem is we women journalists lack power. We are too few in number. We do not hire and fire. We do not make the story assignments unfettered. We do not have the proportion of top jobs that our numbers in the population or the audience justify.

Just as we were so obviously absent from the Senate Judiciary Committee hearings on Clarence Thomas, just as we were barely visible in President Bush's cabinet, just as we are tokens on the boards of corporate America, so we are largely unseen and unheard in the newsrooms of this nation.

Those of us who have fought the good fight, many of us, are no longer there. Outsiders can provide the numbers and make known the problem. And, undeniably, it is tough to agitate for change in a time of recession.

It was never easy. But only the women within news organizations can work for change. Otherwise, the networks and local stations around the country may have to learn the hard lesson that the newspapers in many cities are beginning to understand: that is, if they do not reflect the diverse faces of their audience, Black and white, male and female, young and old, they may lose those viewers to cable and to the increasing presence of the competition. They will have only themselves to blame.

10b Television
The Nature of Sex Discrimination in Local Television News Shops

CONRAD SMITH
ERIC S. FREDIN
CARROLL ANN FERGUSON
NARDONE

This chapter reports results from a national study on the nature and extent of sex discrimination in local, network-affiliated television news operations in the United States. A literature search in December 1992 turned up no indication of new survey work on many of the factors we examined in a 1986 survey, and the studies conducted since 1986 indicate little change in basic conditions.

The proportion of women in local television news has changed little since it reached about 33% in the early 1980s, according to our work and surveys of Stone (1992). Between 1971 and 1982, the proportion of women tripled to 33% (Weaver & Wilhoit, 1986). The surge may have occurred because the Federal Communications Commission in 1971 included women in its equal opportunity guidelines, and, because at about the same time, local TV stations began making profits on local news, hence expanded their news operations. The number of journalists at a typical station grew from 10.5 in 1972 to 19.2 a decade latter (Stone, 1987) but has remained fairly static since (Stone, 1992). In 1986, 14% of the news directors were women, 18% were in 1989, and 16% were in 1990, but the proportion of women news-directors in network affiliates and in larger news organizations has increased (Stone, 1988a, 1988b, 1992).

There is a long tradition of studying sex discrimination in terms of differences in earnings, and we have done so for local television reporters

(Smith, Fredin, & Ferguson, 1988). Sex discrimination can occur in many other ways, of course. In this chapter, we will look at sex discrimination in terms of story assignment, reporter morale, and attitudes toward discrimination, as well as earnings. This study is based upon a nationwide survey of 512 reporters and 131 news directors[1] rather than the specifics of one or two events or stories. We have tried to get behind the unique story to look at the general relationships between individual attributes, such as gender or experience, and workplace conditions, such as earnings or story assignment.

Earnings and Story Assignments

Differences in income presumably reflect far more than just gender. To impose some theoretical order upon this complex issue, we have employed the "human capital" perspective. The human capital perspective emphasizes the importance of individual investment in such qualities as education and experience. Key questions focus upon the "rate of return" for such investments. Thus, is the increase in earnings for each year of experience the same for men and women? This is a pertinent question: In 1986 the median income for male reporters was $470 per week and the median years of experience was 7. For women, the figures are $385 and 5 years. Parcel and Mueller (1983), in a national study of employment in general, found that differences in the rate of return for resources were the principal source of differences in pay between men and women. Compared to men, women generally had a lower rate of return for their resources.

The human capital perspective, however, tends to ignore social processes and social structures over which the individual has little control. Parcel and Mueller (1983), for example, found that the type and extent of discrimination depended partly on the makeup of the local labor market, the type of industry, and the type of occupation. We have attempted to adapt their approach by taking into account pertinent structural factors related to market and news organization.

Our market-level concept is market size. One of our organization-level concepts is the proportion of the reporting staff that is male—one measure of possible tokenism or of slowness in increasing the number of females. The other is the ratings for the late evening local newscasts.

The bulk of differences in reporters' earnings in our sample were accounted for by factors such as market size and experience. Although our analysis indicates there is no systematic, pervasive discrimination of women in terms of earnings, there are indications of discrimination. These explain about 2% of earnings variance, a relatively small but statistically significant amount. For example, women are rewarded less than men as they get older or as market size goes up, or both, suggesting greater age discrimination against women than against men. Women are rewarded more than men for changing news shops often or for moving to larger markets, or both. This suggests that women may be in demand in larger markets more because of their gender than because of their journalistic qualifications.

Another possible indication of tokenism is that, after controlling for market size, all reporters earn more in newsrooms that have a higher proportion of male reporters. In addition, women have a greater earnings advantage than men as the proportion of male reporters in newsrooms increases. Women also receive more financial reward than men for winning news awards. Because news awards are judged predominantly by men, this could mean that women have to be better reporters than men to earn news awards, and that the better paid women who have won awards are being paid for their superior journalistic skills.[2]

Perhaps it is more significant that the earnings of all reporters, in real dollars, have dropped as more and more women pursued successful careers in journalism. The human capital model indicates that, on a macroeconomic scale, discrimination shrinks the pool of available labor. If only men are hired, news organizations may have to pay higher wages to obtain this scarcer human resource. Hiring men and women can therefore help drive down wages. In broadcast and print journalism, the inflation-adjusted median salary declined about $7,000 between 1970 and 1981 as the proportion of women increased by 60%. The decline was greatest in television, where the proportion of women tripled (Weaver & Wilhoit, 1986, pp. 17-22, 82-87).

We also studied story assignments, using the same human capital model. Differences in assignments for 10 types of stories[3] were not statistically significant, except for education. Women covered more education stories than men, but the difference was rather small. We also found that there was no statistically significant difference in the number of newscast-leading stories reported by women and men.[4]

Attitudes About Sexism

Clearly, wages and story assignments can be similar while sexist attitudes still persist. Study of attitudes is difficult because asking people whether they favor sex discrimination can be insulting. Also some answers are more socially acceptable. We tackled this problem in two ways. First, we used data from the reporter survey and from a second survey of the reporters' news directors. This permits some comparisons of each group's perception of the other. Second, we asked both reporters and news directors to respond to a hypothetical incident. This scenario was modeled after Schuman's study of racial attitudes. Schuman (1972) notes that the issue of discrimination often does not emerge by itself; rather, it emerges when values clash in a particular situation. We thought that placing the questions in the context of a decision involving a conflict of values might produce more honest answers. We also thought reporters and news directors would tend to think in terms of stories, that is, in terms of specific incidents rather than abstract concepts, hence the scenario might more accurately reflect the kinds of thought processes generally used on the job. We developed and used the following scenario, which was timely in 1986:

> A news director receives authorization for two out-of-town trips for local interest stories. He decides to send one reporter to Honduras with a local National Guard unit going there on maneuvers. The reporter will also attempt to accompany a contra rebel unit on a border raid into Nicaragua.
>
> One reporter who wants the assignment is a woman. The news director says no, although he considers her one of his best reporters. He says he is concerned about her safety in a contra combat zone. He also feels that as a woman she will have less access to male sources in the National Guard and in Central America. Instead, he offers to send her with the mayor to the National League of Cities convention in Phoenix, which the mayor will chair.

We presented the scenario to reporters and news directors, and then asked how strongly they agreed or disagreed, using a 9-point scale, with the following statements:

1. The news director is justified in not sending the woman because of the danger involved.
2. The news director is justified in not sending the woman because being a woman may compromise her news-gathering ability in Central America.
3. Given that the news director will not send the woman to Honduras, he acted appropriately in offering her the National League of Cities story as an alternative.
4. In general, story assignments should be given without regard to the sex of the reporter.

The first three statements were designed to assess support for equal treatment when this principle might conflict with news-gathering values.

Overall, reporters and news directors said they were strongly egalitarian. About half of news directors and reporters registered the strongest possible disagreement with the statements about danger and compromised news-gathering ability. About one quarter of news directors and reporters indicated the strongest possible disagreement with the consolation assignment, and two thirds of both groups registered the strongest possible agreement with the principle of egalitarianism.

Each respondent was also asked to estimate how most reporters would respond to each statement, and to estimate how most news directors would respond. Thus we could compare reporters' self-reports with how they said most reporters would respond. And we could compare the self-reports of reporters with how news directors said most reporters would respond. The equivalent two comparisons could also be done with news directors.

On almost all measures, both reporters and news directors rated their own peer group as statistically significantly less egalitarian than themselves. One interpretation of these differences is that there is a systematic misperception of one's peers.[5] A second interpretation is that many respondents exaggerate their own egalitarianism, and that something closer to the truth is projected onto their assessments of their peers. We favor the latter interpretation. The reason is that the news directors' perception of reporters tended to agree with the reporters' perception of other reporters. And reporters' perceptions of news directors tended to be similar to or less egalitarian than news directors' perceptions of other news directors (see Table 10b.1).

Based on the perception data from both reporters and news directors, news directors are generally statistically significantly less egalitarian than reporters.

We also looked at the differences between male and female reporters' self-assessments and their perceptions of news directors and other reporters. Differences on self-assessments and perceptions of reporters remained after controlling for the structural factors of market size and organizational factors such as the ratio of men to women in the news organization as well as individual traits such as experience.[6] In terms of self-reports, female reporters are significantly more egalitarian than male reporters on all four statements. But, for the statements concerning danger and news-gathering being compromised, women also perceive "most reporters" as being significantly more egalitarian than men perceive them to be. For the statement on egalitarianism as a general principle, there is no significant difference between men and women on perceptions of news directors or of other reporters.

Morale

One way of getting at the less tangible but still very real aspects of the workplace is to study employee morale. We treated morale as a summary

Table 10b.1 Self-Assessments and Assessments of Peers and Other Group on the Honduras Scenario (1 = Strongly Disagree; 9 = Strongly Agree)

		Assessment of Reporters (Mean, N = 352)		Assessment of News Directors (Mean, N = 131)	
1. Danger justifies not sending the woman reporter to Central America.					
self-assessment		⌐ 2.57	ns	2.68 ⌐	
		***		***	
assessment by respondent's own group	***	3.41	***	4.83	***
		ns		*	
assessment by the other group		⌊ 3.52	***	5.34 ⌊	
2. Compromised news-gathering ability justifies not sending the woman reporter to Central America.					
self-assessment		⌐ 3.09	ns	3.10 ⌐	
		*		***	
assessment by respondent's own group	***	3.45	***	4.29	***
		ns		ns	
assessment by the other group		⌊ 3.56	***	4.63 ⌊	
3. If not sent to Central America, the woman reporter should be given a consolation story.					
self-assessment		⌐ 5.21	***	3.89 ⌐	
		***		***	
assessment by respondent's own group	ns	5.27	ns	5.34	***
		***		ns	
assessment by the other group		⌊ 4.10	***	5.70 ⌊	
4. In general, stories should be assigned without regard to a reporter's gender.					
self-assessment		⌐ 7.89	ns	8.20 ⌐	
		ns		***	
assessment by respondent's own group	***	7.32	***	6.61	***
		ns		***	
assessment by the other group		⌊ 7.62	***	5.37 ⌊	

NOTE: A 5 is neutral on the 1-9 scale. Probabilities of statistically significant differences between pairs of means should be interpreted only as a rough indication, as each pair was tested separately.
* $p < .05$; ** $p < .01$; *** $p < .001$; ns = not significant.

judgment, that is, as an overall evaluation made up of many components, each weighed and balanced against the others. The statement used was: "Reporter morale is good in this shop." Respondents marked their degree of agreement on a 9-point scale. Although the morale question refers to the entire shop, we presume that a good deal of the respondent's own level of morale is being reported.

There is no significant difference between males and females on the morale question. For both sexes morale is quite low: 15% of the reporters marked the lowest possible response to the statement, and half disagreed with it to some extent.

Morale is affected by many things, however, and the theoretical perspective of the human capital model can again be of assistance. Morale can be looked at using the human capital model much as pay was, except that here investment presumably leads to changes in morale. Given low overall morale plus anecdotes of the precariousness of holding a television reporting job, morale may decrease with experience. Further, given differences on egalitarianism between male and female reporters and between reporters and news directors, morale may drop more quickly for women than for men as experience increases. Larger market size might increase morale, particularly if pay is good and ratings are strong, and good pay and ratings may increase morale more for one sex than another.

Awards might increase morale, though if awards do not change the daily routine, then awards may make job problems more salient, hence decrease morale. Further, the decrease could be sharper for females if, for instance, awards lead to a clearer sense of sex discrimination.

Morale could be affected by reporters' attitudes toward day-to-day news decisions. One important decision here would be use of live coverage, which expanded substantially during the time many women were hired.

Attitudes toward other aspects of the job might also affect morale. We looked at attitudes in three important areas: job autonomy, the perceived effectiveness of television as a journalistic medium, and perceived fairness of the workplace.[7] We measured respondents' sense of fairness in several ways. The measures of fairness are based on responses to two statements concerning the Honduras scenario in which differences between men and women appeared. One statement was that the women should not be sent because of the difficulty of dealing with male sources, and the other was that assignments should be made without regard to gender. For each statement, the respondent's own attitude was used as was the respondent's assessment of how most news directors would respond. Also used were measures of the difference between the self-report and the assessment of the news director. The effect of the attitudes upon morale may be different for men and women. Attitudinal differences between sexes has already been found, hence it appears that men and women are coping with somewhat different environments even if they are in the same news shop. Results of the analysis are in Table 10b.2.[8]

Table 10b.2 Hierarchical Regression of Morale on Market-, Shop-, and Individual-Level Variables on Morale for Local Television News Reporters

Variable	B	Standard Error	R^2 Change	F Ratio
Market- and shop-level variables[a]			.051	
market size[b]/news ratings interaction	.030	.0077		14.716***
proportion of reporters that is male	1.540	.7067		4.749*
Individual reporter characteristics			.029	
weekly earnings[c]	−1.489	.8946		2.770 ns
years of TV reporting experience	−.163	.0617		6.976**
news awards (0 = no, 1 = yes)	−2.233	.7810		9.669**
Market size/reporter interactions			.019	
market size/weekly earnings	.342	.1367		6.257*
market size/news awards	.712	.2823		6.362*
Reporter attitudes[d]			.213	
perceived fairness of news shop	.238	.0406		34.272***
autonomy	.304	.0482		39.695***
attitude toward "live" coverage	−.104	.0604		2.987 ns
attitude toward news facts on TV	−.148	.0575		6.588**
value comparison with management	−.108	.0487		4.910*
Market/egalitarian attitude[d] interaction	−.038	.0183	.005	4.285*
Gender	−1.537	.4957	.001	9.610**
Gender-related interactions			.023	
gender/reporting experience	.242	.0711		11.578***
gender/egalitarian management[d]	.109	.0566		3.708*
Constant	4.132	1.7602		5.510*
Adjusted R^2 = .317				

NOTES: a. Blocks of variables entered in order shown. R^2 change is increment in R^2 for that block.
b. Log, thousands of television households.
c. Logged
d. For details on measures, see Smith, Fredin, & Nardone, 1989.
* $p < .05$; ** $p < .01$; *** $p < .001$; ns = not significant (one-tail test).

Attitudes about fairness, autonomy, and the effectiveness of television as a journalistic medium were the strongest predictors of morale. Some effects on morale are gender related, but these results are not straightforward. Further, the gender-related effects sometimes help the morale among women more than the morale among men.

A stronger sense of fairness and autonomy, a stronger sense of the effectiveness of television news, and greater approval of the use of live shots all lead to higher morale, as did greater agreement between self-report and assessment of most news directors on sending a woman to Honduras.

The higher the pay, the lower the morale, but this effect is reduced as market size increases. Receiving awards results in lower morale, but this effect, too, is lessened as market size goes up. Perhaps reporters who win awards have higher standards for themselves, which they less often achieve, and perhaps awards are less likely in small markets to be recognized by peers and managers. The effect of earnings in reducing morale could have a similar explanation. Because other variables are held constant, the measured increase in earnings is not accompanied by any change in other aspects of the job. A pay raise in these circumstances may bring heightened expectations that are not met. (For an example, see Sanders & Rock, 1988).

Perhaps the strongest evidence we found of sex discrimination appeared in an organizational-level variable: Morale for all reporters increases as the ratio of male reporters increases within shops. However, at the individual level, males have lower morale than females, but for females, morale decreases slightly as experience increases. For males, morale increases slightly as experience increases.

In general, market size appears to have an ameliorating effect in that it reduces the negative effect of news awards and pay. This ameliorating effect extends to some assessments from the Central America scenario. We discovered this by looking at the difference between how reporters responded to the idea that a female reporter should not be sent because she would have poorer access to sources, and how reporters predicted news directors would respond. The greater the difference, the more sexist the news director was relative to the respondent. We found that as the gap increased and/or as the market size increased, morale decreased.

The last gender-related result is hard to interpret. For males only, the more news directors are seen as favoring egalitarianism, the higher the morale. No relationship was found for women. Perhaps men are reacting more to the news directors' statements than women, who presumably are more aware of the news directors' actions as well.

Other Needed Research

Our study, based largely on a national survey of local television reporters in network affiliates, found little evidence for tangible sexism of the kind that would be grounds for legal action, but our findings suggest that sexist attitudes do persist. Analysis of responses to a story-assignment scenario indicate that female reporters are more egalitarian than male reporters, but also indicate that female reporters see "most reporters" as more egalitarian than male reporters do. These differences are not related to various structural-, organizational-, and individual-level variables. Further, we found evidence, also based on the Honduras scenario, that news directors are less egalitarian than reporters. However, we did not find major gender differences in story assignment or number of lead stories. We did find some evidence that discrimination is manifested slightly in pay and morale, but other factors were clearly much more important, and some factors worked against men more than women. For example, when other factors were controlled for, men had lower morale than women. Both morale and pay increased for all reporters as the proportion of males in the news shop increased. Women received greater financial rewards than men for awards, and greater financial rewards than men for changing shops often, moving to larger markets, or both. Such results for earnings and morale are not strong, and, though they are plausible, they are not obvious.

Future work should look at the effects of family life on discrimination. For example, in 1990, 90% of all stations had maternity leave policies. However, only 37% provided full pay during the leave, and 21% provided no pay (Stone & Burks, 1991). How has this affected employment of women, or men? Future work should also look at progress of women in reaching the top ranks of management. Further, our findings of attitudinal differences suggest that it is important to study closely both work routines and also the stories produced to determine when and how discrimination may be produced and reproduced in both, as is suggested by the work of Bybee (1990).

Notes

1. The research is based on a 1986 mail survey in which 512 reporters responded to a six-page questionnaire. A separate questionnaire was mailed to each of the 200 news directors. The response rate for each group was 65%. For more details, see Smith, Fredin, and Nardone (1989).

2. Theresa Lukenas, then of WBNS-TV and later of WJBK-TV, suggested this perspective on news awards.

3. The 10 categories, taken from Singleton and Cook (1982), were (1) education, (2) health/medicine/science, (3) consumer news, (4) courts, (5) local/state government, (6) entertainment/culture/arts, (7) minority or women's issues, (8) labor/business/economy, (9) disaster/accident/spot news, and (10) human-interest/people/features.

4. We asked reporters the number of leading stories they had during the 10 days prior to their answering the questionnaire.

5. See O'Gorman with Garry (1976), but see also Fields and Schuman (1976).

6. Details not shown. This analysis was done with hierarchical multiple regression, with sex entered after all other controls except interactions between sex and the other variables.

7. For details on scale construction, see Smith, Fredin, and Nardone (1989).

8. The analysis strategy was parallel to that used for pay. A backward, stepwise multiple regression was run using 48 variables. Interactions between market size and all other variables were tested, since market size can have such diverse results. Also, reporters and anchors have often noted that stations in larger markets are quite different from those in smaller markets. There were 16 significant variables, explaining about 32% of the variation in morale. (For

details, see Smith, Fredin, & Ferguson, 1988; Smith, Fredin, & Nardone, 1989.) These variables were then placed in a hierarchical regression with structural traits entered first, followed by individual traits. Sex-related variables were entered last to make their testing more severe. This is the regression reported in the table.

References

Bybee, Carl R. (1990). Constructing women as authorities: Local journalism and the microphysics of power. *Critical Studies in Mass Communication, 7,* 197-214.

Fields, James M., & Schuman, Howard. (1976). Public beliefs about the beliefs of the public. *Public Opinion Quarterly, 40,* 427-448.

O'Gorman, Hubert J., with Garry, Stephen L. (1976). Pluralistic ignorance: A replication and extension. *Public Opinion Quarterly, 40,* 449-458.

Parcel, Toby L., & Mueller, Charles W. (1983). *Ascription and labor markets: Race and sex differences in earnings.* New York: Academic Press.

Sanders, Marlene, & Rock, Marcia. (1988). *Waiting for primetime: The women of television news.* Urbana: University of Illinois Press.

Schuman, Howard. (1972). Attitudes vs. action vs. attitudes vs. attitudes. *Public Opinion Quarterly, 36,* 347-354.

Singleton, Loy A., & Cook, Stephanie L. (1982). Television network news reporting by female correspondents. *Journal of Broadcasting, 26,* 487-491.

Smith, Conrad, Fredin, Eric S., & Ferguson, Carroll Ann. (1988). Sex discrimination in earnings and story assignments among TV reporters. *Journalism Quarterly, 65,* 3-11, 19.

Smith, Conrad, Fredin, Eric S., & Nardone, Carroll Ann Ferguson. (1989). Television: Sex discrimination in the TV news room—Perception and reality. In Pamela J. Creedon (Ed.), *Women in mass communication: Challenging gender values* (pp. 227-246). Newbury Park, CA: Sage.

Stone, Vernon A. (1987). Changing profiles of news directors of radio and TV stations, 1972-1986. *Journalism Quarterly, 64,* 745-749.

Stone, Vernon A. (1988a, July). *Pipelines and dead ends: Jobs held by minorities and women in broadcast news.* Paper presented at the annual meeting of the Association for Education in Journalism and Mass Communication, Portland, OR.

Stone, Vernon A. (1988b, August). Minority men shoot ENG, women take advancement tracks. *RTNDA Communicator,* pp. 10-14.

Stone, Vernon A. (1992, August). Little change for minorities and women. *RTNDA Communicator,* pp. 26-27.

Stone, Vernon A., & Burks, Kimberly K. (1991, August). Family benefits in TV and radio. *RTNDA Communicator,* pp. 24-25.

Weaver, David H., & Wilhoit, G. Cleveland. (1986). *The American journalist: A portrait of U.S. news people and their work.* Bloomington: Indiana University Press.

11 Re-Visioning Women in Public Relations
Practitioner and Feminist Perspectives

CAROLYN GARRETT CLINE
ELIZABETH L. TOTH

A woman's place is no longer in the home, but in the communication department. Recent census figures estimate that 44% of the workforce is female, but conservative estimates place the percentage of women in public relations at 58.6% (Lukovitz, 1989), although membership in the Public Relations Student Society of America represents a 10-to-1 female majority (Wright, Grunig, Springston, & Toth, 1991).

Professions that have been feminized in the past, such as certain areas of banking, teaching, and nursing, have seen a reduction in salary and status. The fear has surfaced that public relations has already become, in the words of *Business Week,* "the Velvet Ghetto of affirmative action." Will this mean a decrease in salaries and a lowering of status for public relations?

This chapter will review the research that has been conducted on the salaries and status of women in public relations, beginning with early benchmark reports that described practitioner responses to the increasing numbers of women entering public relations. Then, the perspectives of feminist scholars will be presented.

In late 1984, the International Association of Business Communicators (IABC) Research Foundation commissioned a study to examine this trend; the resulting publication, *The Velvet Ghetto* (Cline et al., 1986), was followed in 1989 by an update, *Beyond the Velvet Ghetto* (Toth & Cline, 1989), edited by the authors of this chapter. Both studies looked at existing research on salaries and roles in the profession, and analyzed data from focus groups in the United States and Canada. The first study also conducted nearly 40 in-depth interviews with senior-level practitioners, and analyzed student attitudes and psychographics. The follow-up research included a survey of PRSA (Public Relations Society of America) and IABC members to examine the attitudes of practitioners.

During the 8 years since the first IABC study, research on the status of women in public relations has grown steadily, including theoretical examinations of the nature of feminist theory relative to this area. This chapter will examine some recent findings about the salary and status of women in public relations, attitudes held by practitioners, challenges faced by communicators of both genders, and will provide a look at the issue of "the velvet ghetto" from the feminist perspective.

The Salary Issue

The original *Velvet Ghetto* study looked at the salary surveys conducted by IABC and PRSA, as well as the work of researchers like Broom and Dozier (1986). The conclusion was disheartening: Controlling for such variables as age, education, and experience, the report concluded that it was fair to say that a woman would make between $6,000 and $30,000 a year less than an equally qualified man because of gender. If a woman works for 45 years and loses this $6,000 a year, she will earn—at best— about $300,000 less than the man. At worst, using the $30,000 figure, the bottom line is a penalty of close to $1.5 million for being a woman.

The 1989 study revealed that the most common salary category for the men was more than $65,000—at least $15,000 to $30,000 a year more than the most common category for women. Even with the 7.8-year difference in experience, this is still a major salary difference, but one that is consistent with other salary surveys for the 1980s and 1990s.

The most recent salary studies agree with the findings. A 1991 PRSA study (Wright et al., pp. 13, 25) reported that

> results appear to support the claim that gender discrimination exists in American public relations. . . . Consistent with previous research, a statistically significant degree of salary disparity between men and women appears after the fourth year of employment . . . gender predicts income, roles predict income, managers are paid higher salaries than technicians and women function as public relations technicians more than men.

The 1992 annual salary survey in *PR Journal* provides yet another source of support for the existence of a salary disparity, one that had widened between 1991 and 1992. The median salary in this study was $57,766 for men, 47% more than for women: $39,207. The gender gap was apparent at every level of experience, increasing with the years of experience (Jacobson & Tortorello, 1992, p. 12).

The Situation in 1986

But the numbers did not tell the whole story. We asked top professionals about the impact of feminization on practitioners who want management or upper-management positions. Will the road to top management be closed to communicators if the field is seen as "a woman's profession"? Their answers fell along a continuum. At one end there were those who said things were fine. As one executive explained: "We don't have men and women at this company. We just have people." Others welcomed women into their departments, feeling that they would bring in such feminine skills as empathy and understanding. We found women who fit the definition of a "queen bee" with the attitude of "I made it, so why can't other women?" One highly honored executive had a message for other women in communication: "Don't waste any time or energy thinking about what's different about women in this field. And don't look under the bed at night to see if anybody discriminated against you today. The field is too demanding and challenging and you don't have that time to waste. The women's issue has no role in professional success."

At the other end were those who thought a woman's place was anywhere but in management. "I don't like to hire women managers since they'll take time off when the kids are sick." "They'll only get pregnant and quit." "In the past my clients wouldn't accept a woman executive and I don't want to get them angry."

In between were the worried. One woman explained that the business world still thinks in terms of stereotypes: "You think of nurses as being women. You still think of secondary teachers as being women. There's still that stigma that if a particular profession or career is primarily women, then for whatever reason, it's a less desirable kind of career."

A woman who had served as president of the PRSA worried that feminization might be seen by men as a chance to put public relations down a notch in the corporate hierarchy. "I think it will go back to being seen as a position that you can get rid of. . . . It might be seen as an area that could be done better by someone at the top level or by someone who isn't in our profession . . . maybe someone in the legal, marketing, or finance departments."

We found women and men worried about the impact of feminization. The practitioners discussed their fears that the misunderstanding of the communication role and function by top management threatens the place of public relations and communication in the corporate world. Male and female practitioners alike said they felt ill-equipped for management and were sometimes unsure of where to go for training. They also feared that management bias against communication would make public relations a dead-end job. The president of a major public relations agency advised women, "If you want to get into top management, not just public relations management, get out of public relations all together. Go into some other line or area, such as finance or whatever is the route to the top of that particular organization."

Another concern of the profession was bias, whether blatant or subtle. Women recalled discrimination when they were—or were not—hired. A Texas woman said that, although she thinks things have gotten better since she first started working, she still has vivid memories of bias. "I was told one time I wasn't getting a job because I was married and my husband might move. Another time, I didn't get a job because I didn't have children and it was likely that I would have children. People actually had the nerve to tell me that they were rejecting me for these contradictory reasons."

Communicators reported that women were hired for lower salaries and at lower positions than men. One smaller agency president explained, "New graduates are coming out with public relations degrees, but if they are women, larger agencies start them out as receptionists. They never start a man out as a receptionist. They're always junior executives."

It was almost a no-win situation; when women broke into management they faced the male power structure, the "old boys" network. A woman in Atlanta remembered: "I can really relate to this 'good ol' boy' syndrome. When I was director of communications in my company, I never felt I was taken as seriously as the person who had my job previously. I didn't go out for breakfast with the boys or go out drinking or anything like that, so I wasn't in that inner circle. I always felt kind of excluded and I wonder if that's not the way it is for a lot of women."

Communicators across the country echoed these fears: Women were not taken as seriously as men. They could not be part of the gang, and therefore faced resistance to becoming real members of the management team. According to one woman, "men seem to feel more comfortable having a male report to them and they feel that they speak the same language. Men are singing out of the same page in the hymn book. Females are considered to be in a different denomination, much less the same hymn book."

The 1989 Follow-Up

As part of the later study, *Beyond the Velvet Ghetto,* a survey was sent to members of IABC and PRSA to determine quantitatively what their attitudes were in four areas:

1. attitudes toward the impact of feminization;
2. attitudes toward women as managers;
3. self-perceptions—how helpful did practitioners consider their own demographic characteristics on their careers; and
4. the potential effect of demographic variables on attitudes.

Out of the sample of 1,000 communicators, 443 returned usable surveys. Of these, 38.6% were from men, 61.4% from women, a representative gender sampling given the membership of IABC and PRSA. The typical respondent was a woman between 30 and 34 years old with a college degree. She had been in public relations for 10.1 years, working in a publicly owned corporation. She earned between $25,000 and $43,999 a year and worked with 16.2 people, supervising 3.7. She was a manager or director of either media relations or publications and reported directly to a vice president. She was white, married, with no children under 18 at home.

Her male counterpart was between 40 and 45 years old, with a college degree. He had been in public relations for 17.9 years, also in a corporation. He earned more than $65,000 a year, worked with 43.9 people, supervising 4.6. He was a manager or director of media relations or employee relations and reported directly to the president.

The full results of the survey can be found in the research report or in the Toth and Cline article in *Public Relations Review* (1991), but a brief summary here reveals some disturbing, some reassuring, perceptions about attitudes about women as managers.

- Nearly half the women agreed that the increasing number of women in the field *will* drive down salaries; 41.9% of the men agreed.
- Almost 60% of the women and 50% of the men agreed that it was not likely that opportunities for advancement were the same for men and women.
- Respondents were optimistic about public relations maintaining influence in the organization even with more women in the field.
- More than half of all respondents disagreed with the statement that an increasing number of women would reduce the influence of public relations.
- More than half of the women agreed that it was likely than women could "have it all"—marriage, home, and a public relations career—but only 34.2% of the

Table 11.1   Perceptions of Differences Between Men and Women in Managerial
Abilities and Traits

Trait	Percentage of Men Reporting a Difference	Percentage of Women Reporting a Difference
Negotiating abilities	40.4	49.8
Professionalism	**11.5**	**10.3****
Willingness to sacrifice work over family needs	43.3	49.7
Expression of emotion	67.5	64.0
Ability to play "politics"	38.5	39.7
Networking with the "good ol' boys"	57.4	67.1
Encounters with sex discrimination	**62.3**	**81.3****
Ability to command top salary	**54.0**	**82.1****
Managerial commitment	**19.5**	**16.5****
Managerial motivation	**19.3**	**15.3****
Ability to "get things done"	9.7	15.2

NOTE: ** means for men and women were significantly different at the < .01 level

men agreed. More than 48% of communicators at the vice president level
disagreed.

■ Respondents agreed that there is a double standard at work: 51.8% of the men,
66.4% of the women.

■ Almost half the men reported that men and women make the same sacrifices
to become executives, but nearly two thirds of the women disagreed, some
vehemently.

An additional 11 questions concerned managerial abilities. Respondents
were asked if men and women were different or similar on a 7-point
Likert-type scale.

When asked if they perceived differences in managerial abilities and
traits between men and women, significant differences appeared in "networking with the good ol' boys," "professionalism," "ability to command
top salary," "encounters with sex discrimination," "managerial commitment," and "managerial motivation."

The attributes on the survey and percentages of men and women who
reported that they perceived *differences* between men and women are
detailed in Table 11.1.

Respondents reported on a 7-point scale how helpful age, race, gender,
education, marital status, children, physical appearance, and geographic
locations had been to their careers. For age, there was no significant differ-

ence between men and women. The younger practitioners found their age to be unhelpful. The most helpful age was reported to be 45-59, the generation just before the baby boom.

Because almost all respondents (96.9%) were white, it is surprising that nearly half reported that their race was neither helpful nor unhelpful. More than 80% of the practitioners of color reported that their race had been unhelpful.

Men and women differed significantly on the issue of gender as helpful or unhelpful. Nearly half of the men reported their gender helpful in their careers, compared with only 16.1% of the women. More than twice as many women as men reported that their gender was unhelpful. The age bracket on which feminism had the first major impact—those from 30-44 years—reported the most problems.

Those who finished college programs, both undergraduate and graduate, found their education more helpful than those who had dropped out.

For more than 60% of the respondents, marital status was neither helpful nor unhelpful. Although the difference was not significant, women were more likely to report that marital status was helpful than were men. Those who were single were more than twice as likely to report that their marital status was helpful than were those either married or divorced.

Half of the women with children reported that the children were unhelpful to a career compared with 28.4% of the men. For most of the men with children, the children were neither helpful nor unhelpful. The lack of children, conversely, was not a help, and the overall difference between the genders was not significant.

Men and women alike reported their physical appearance helpful. Aging seemed to impact only those from 45-59 years old, who were less likely to find their appearance helpful than were any other age group. Most found their geographic location to be helpful, with the greatest dissatisfaction reported by respondents under 30 years old.

The survey identified several major areas of concern and targeted topics that require further study and thought. It did provide a few answers: There is concern among a significant number of practitioners that the increasing number of women will have a negative impact on salaries and status; women report that they do face discrimination because of gender; women are the victims of bias—clear patterns of considering men and women to differ in critical areas of managerial attitudes; women earn substantially less than do men in the field. These results supported the anecdotal evidence from focus groups conducted for both *Velvet Ghetto* studies.

The Focus Groups

Focus groups from 1986 and 1989 as well as depth interviews expressed concern with the issue of women as potential managers. Women were perceived of as nurturers, capable of working well with clients, especially in small agencies. Women were seen as caring, sympathetic, understanding. One women in an agency said that she found women drawn to agency work because of "something that I find very natural to the female culture and that is nurturing skills. It's kind of a natural, nurturing capability that women have and it's very important in consulting."

This may also mean that women are viewed as not tough enough for corporate life. One woman said, "Frankly, my blood boils when I read an article by a woman in business who says, 'I think I bring more to the job because I think women are sympathetic and intuitive.' That's the kind of thing that has set women back two decades."

An Atlanta woman agreed, and she discussed her first experience as a manager: "I wanted people who worked with me to be happy. I wanted to identify and sympathize with their problems and give them as much slack as I could in dealing with them. . . . I got walked all over. That was the worst-run office you could imagine." She said she was able to become tougher on her next job because she had been raised in a military family and therefore knew all the "codes" for male behavior.

A second assumption was that women were too emotional. Several men remembered working for a woman as an unpleasant experience because of women's emotional natures. Women agreed with them, as the survey supported. A Dallas woman said that women are harder to work for because they feel less secure in their positions.

Much of this insecurity may relate to the issue of legitimization. In theory, men are comfortable in the corporation because corporations have always been male. Men have always been there and feel they belong. Women entered the workforce by virtue of specific skills, usually clerical or technical in nature. No man took a typing test to enter a management training program. Women had to possess these skills, as they now possess the skills for editing the newsletter, writing the press release, contacting the media. For many women this has legitimatized their role in the company, but as they move into management it often means they must let go of these skills and delegate the tasks. This means casting off the legitimization based on technical competence and relying upon self-esteem and self-worth.

This may be a critical point in a woman's career—letting go of the skills and still feeling part of the management team.

The assumption still exists that children are always a "woman's" problem. Men and women in the focus groups agreed that children are "a bad thing" for a woman in corporate life. A woman spoke of the "threat of children" to her career. Several women reported leaving corporations for agency work because they felt they could not combine a corporate career and children. One man agreed, saying to a woman, "If you're going to lead a normal life, you are simply going to have to take time out of work. You can't concentrate on your career."

A male manager defended paying his female employee less than her male counterpart by saying that she missed work because the kids get sick or they have to go somewhere. For men, children are a reason to ask for a raise; for women they may well mean the end of the climb to management.

There was also the assumption that women cannot "play the game." Women, some argued, have never learned the team spirit—the corporate spirit—that men learn on football teams or in the armed services. Breaking into the management circle and getting onto the fast track are secrets that most women do not learn in male-oriented, male-dominated companies. The women reported that corporations are fraternities all over again and women cannot be accepted. So they are forming small agencies or "old girls networks" to try to emulate, not penetrate, the clubs.

Women in the focus groups reported that because communication is seen as a "soft" career in a corporation, women may have more flexibility than they would in other departments to drop out, raise a family, and then come back. Public relations and business communication can be a rewarding career for the trained specialist. Yet, for some communicators, the route to management is still of critical importance.

It appears that as more women enter the field, many men *are* going elsewhere—into marketing, middle management, and top management. Women may become directors of corporate communication and managers of media relations, but will the higher positions be closed to someone coming from public relations? Already, evidence suggests that there is increasing "incursion" by more male-oriented departments such as marketing into public relations and many of the senior- and mid-level practitioners said that communication would become a dead-end position unless things change.

So what can be done? Is the ghetto inevitable? The rest of this section will deal with two different approaches to the issue of feminization in public relations: some suggestions from successful women and a reexamination of the issue from the viewpoint of feminist theory.

Some Suggestions

At an IABC international convention in Anaheim, CA, senior women communicators joined in a special session to address the status and needs of female managers. The session produced five major recommendations:

1. Accept That the Velvet Ghetto Is Real. Sociology professor David Segal wrote that "much of the problem of inequality is rooted in perceptions that there is no problem" (in Mathews, 1989, p. 1). As Wilma Mathews of AT&T described her work in discussing the original *Velvet Ghetto* results:

> If there is a pattern, that is it: a flat, almost frightening denial that a problem exists. If perception is reality, then the perception of the lack of a problem becomes the reality. What I have found interesting for the almost three years of talking about the situation, is that denial comes most strongly from those people affected by discrimination—the female public relations/communication manager or technician. The second group most loudly denying a problem appears to be students. (p. 1)

This observation may not surprise many educators. A major introductory public relations textbook (Wilcox, Ault, & Agee, 1992, p. 111) tried to explain the impact of salary discrepancy between men and women:

> Optimists believe that equality will be achieved eventually. Pessimists worry that the large number of women in the field will result in a "velvet ghetto" with lower prestige and pay than in fields requiring comparable education and skill. Their arguments tend to overlook the fact that other fields such as law, accounting, and marketing are also seeing large growth in the percentage of female workers without having such a problem.

Study after study, whether funded by IABC, PRSA, or other sources, conducted by researchers throughout the country, have confirmed time and again that salary differences are costing women thousands of dollars each year, impeding their progress, and potentially harming the status of the profession. The Ghetto is real and it is here.

2. Learn How to Play the Game. Team sports teach men some critical lessons, including cooperation. A generation ago, anthropologist Margaret Mead wrote that American women as housewives were the least cooperative women in the world. They couldn't even bear to have someone in their kitchens. On teams, men learn to cooperate and work with people they may not like. As a woman said in Anaheim, "I think you have to learn this for business. You have to learn to integrate the talents and whatnot with these people and it does not matter if you personally like them or not."

Women need to learn the lessons of football: what's the play? Who's quarterbacking the play and how are you supporting him or her? Where's the goal line and what's your job in getting there? If men learn one thing from sports, it's how to lose. One woman explained: "If I say I'm going to get promoted in two years and then I don't I'm not going to slit my throat. I will learn from that experience. Is it possible that women don't set concrete objectives because of their fear of failure? Women don't like to fail. We absolutely do not like to fail, professionally and personally." Yet we all must fail and learn how to profit from that experience.

3. Develop a Career Plan. Too few practitioners have any articulate plan for the future. No plan had guided them to where they were, so rather than figure out where they want to go and what career route would take them there, they seemed to be waiting for some career-altering event to change their lives. One manager pointed out:

> There are very few women who have career paths. Men traditionally can tell you in a company exactly where they plan to be in certain periods of their careers. You absolutely have to have a goal to set it out in very concrete terms, whether it's in a forum like this or in networking, but to get some help in talking it out. So that you say in two years I am going to have that position or I'm going to move to this type of company. But not just that I'm going to get more experience and then move along. That's not a flight plan. That's not a path.
>
> You can talk to most men and they say, I plan to be promoted in the next two years, and they find out how those promotions come about in the political arena in which they work and they achieve it.

4. Define Success. What is success for you? A condo in Vail and a BMW? Three children? A Silver Anvil for pro bono work? Success is a personal matter but a critically important one. One communicator reported a deceptively simple definition for her: to ride in the front of the plane and the back of the limo. As she explained, "I know that for me that connotes a certain financial level, a certain executive level," and she has planned her career accordingly to achieve those levels that spell success for her.

5. Accept Your Limitations. One woman described a book that had affected her greatly, *The E-Type Woman:*

> The E-Type woman is the woman that feels she has to be everything to everybody. That's what we're trained to do and be. The woman who was telling me about

this book is a general manager. . . . What she realized was happening was because we are trained to be everything to everybody. She was given three projects at one time while men were given one because they went and said, when they were given two projects, they couldn't handle them—which has the priority, A or B? And they're told by their bosses, Project A. And in that case, the guy says, I cannot do Project B because I have to concentrate on Project A. We say, "Gosh, we're given three projects to do and we're going to do them real well." And we kill ourselves in the process. And we're not respected because what happens is we keep giving more and more and more. In doing that we focus on us and not where these projects will help lead us.

6. Announce Your Triumphs. Out of a mistaken sense of self-effacement, many women assume news of their successes will quietly spread throughout the organization or that it would be unseemly to brag. Nonsense, according to the top women.

A major theme of the research and meetings has been the issue of control, of individual responsibility for a personal and professional career. The action must be on the individual level first—a reassessment of personal and professional goals of communicators; an in-depth analysis of the workplace and the individual's role in it; a decision to take charge of moving out of the gendered role of a practitioner in "a woman's job."

Then the action must be societal, the networking and cooperation and activities of strong individuals who refuse to accept stereotypes and discrimination as unshakable dogma. Communicators working from a sense of power, a position as valued members of a profession, can bring about change. There is no reason for women to accept the findings of the surveys that we lack the same managerial commitment and motivation as men, but we need organization, power, and planning to change attitudes and realities.

From Feminization to the Promise of Feminism

"From the Feminization of Public Relations to the Promise of Feminism" was proposed by Rakow (1989) as a first effort to examine through a different theoretical lens the increasing numbers of women entering public relations. Rakow and other public relations scholars (see, e.g., Creedon, 1991; Grunig, 1988; Hon, Grunig, & Dozier, 1992; Toth, 1989) have adopted feminist theory perspectives that question the assumptions built into the conclusions drawn thus far in public relations research on gender issues.

One such assumption, attacked by Rakow (1989), was that the increasing numbers of women in public relations will damage the salary and status of the field—the assumption reported in both of the *Velvet Ghetto* studies.

Rakow proposed that the values that have been assigned to white women in this culture (and that are held, not surprisingly, by many white women) such as holding together relationships, families, and communities, should be preferable to organizations desiring to practice excellent public relations. Managers, who determine how public relations will be practiced, optimistically may have defined public relations as a necessarily "feminine" function. Ultimately, Rakow argued for the possibility that "a feminized public relations might alter relations of power between organizations and individuals, providing for communal need rather than organizational greed, and creating a politics of egalitarian participation" (p. 296).

Feminist theory is a label, according to Littlejohn (1992), that represents a group of theories that explore the meaning of gender concepts (p. 239). Considered to be a genre of critical social science, feminist theory involves making value judgments in order to accomplish positive changes. Although feminist scholars do not agree on the types of changes needed in society to ensure women's rights (see Steeves, 1987), their efforts to expose the interpretations of research that continually devalue women in relation to men provide fresh starting places for examining the phenomena of women in public relations.

Three principles of feminist theory that have been useful to examining gender issues in public relations are as follows. First, exposing women's devaluation takes the obligation off women to "fit into a man's world." Earlier research on perceptions of women as "lacking seriousness" in their careers or of women not being "managerial enough" can be reinterpreted if researchers do not expect that women should act like men. Feminists have called such expectations "blaming the victim" for being deficient according to the masculine norms of our society—that is, of "not being aggressive enough," or being "unwilling to take risks," or "being too emotional to get the job done."

Second, feminism has exposed the gendered nature of social science research. Social science research has traditionally been valued for its objectivity. However, built into the assumptions of such research as sex differences has been the use of male behavior as the norm. That is, rather than treat gender as the organizing principle and depict the experiences of men and women equitably, social science has relied upon an underlying comparison of all behavior to that of males.

Feminist scholars have refuted the notion that the male norm should be the point of comparison. Instead, feminists have argued for noncomparative approaches for research that would explain the causes of differences rather than research that merely demonstrated the differences between men and women. For example, Toth and Grunig (in press) argued that reporting on the roles performed in public relations by women and men should be done not as a means of determining how women are somehow deficient, but as a first step in identifying the underlying causes that create any such differences.

Toth and Grunig (in press) found, for example, in a self-reported survey of what activities women and men performed in public relations, that the women reported conducting more activities within the managerial role than did the men. The women also reported conducting both managerial and technical activities within a managerial role. In other words, the women seemed to be "doing it all," while the men were not. These authors then attempted to suggest causes for this difference and encouraged further research to test their conclusions. It may have been, for example, that women started in public relations as technicians and assumed managerial responsibilities without ever giving up the technical tasks. Women may have been encouraged to work harder for managerial rewards and still have been expected to perform the technical tasks. The authors also proposed that the managerial and technical roles be reconceptualized as having taken on connotations of domination and devaluation.

Clearly, feminist theory leads us to ask the more pointed question: "What are the realities that lie beneath the choices of men, women, and organizations when they define what public relations is and who should practice it?" Donato (1990) speculated that employers might prefer women in public relations because this function is viewed to be emotional labor and "women may be more skillful than men in emotional labor" (p. 139). Toth (1989) questioned the "reality" of management work in public relations. She argued that the call for "management" has become an attempt by men to "maintain their personal positions of power" (p. 73). Reskin (1989) proposed that declines in any rewards can prompt men to abandon an occupation to women (p. 260). Because such a term as *managerial* is associated with the masculine, men may well be attempting to preserve their hold on the salary and status of the field by attempting to make it appear more macho.

Third, feminism calls for a transformation and empowerment of women (Grunig, 1988). That is, feminism exposes all research as political in nature. Feminist scholars challenge the status quo. For example, Creedon (1992) called for a re-visioning of systems theory, the most central paradigm used to explain public relations. She objected to systems theory for its "uncritical acceptance of gendered norms," norms that would require women to meet inflexible workplace requirements, to accept sexual harassment as commonplace, to devalue family, and to value male models.

The most recent study of women in public relations (Wright et al., 1991) proposes empowering women because they are the future of the public relations field. "Few women wield influence. Only rarely are they in a position to affect organizational decision making at the highest levels" (p. 33). Although women have an obligation to empower themselves, the study's authors proposed that men and women must work together.

One feminist challenge is to all women and men who desire to work for equity solutions to the disparities in salaries and status in public relations. Ask the following questions: "Does any proposal focus on some deficiency women may possess when compared with men? Or does the recommendation suggest an appreciation for the positive aspects female practitioners bring to public relations and thus hinge on changing the system rather than women?" (Wright et al., 1991, p. 35). It is the latter change in the structures of organization that will permit the many diverse talents of women, of people of color, and any of the many cultures that make up our society to be used for the advancement of public relations.

References

Broom, Glen M., & Dozier, David M. (1986). Advancement for public relations models. *Public Relations Review, 12*(1), 37-56.

Creedon, Pamela J. (1991). Public relations and women's work: Toward a feminist analysis of public relations roles. In L. A. Grunig & J. E. Grunig (Eds.), *Public Relations Research Annual, 3*, 67-84.

Creedon, Pamela J. (1992, August). *Toward a critical feminist analysis of the systems theory paradigm in public relations: Lessons from the gendered infrastructure of sport.* Paper presented at the annual meeting of the International Communication Association, Miami.

Creedon, Pamela J. (in press). Acknowledging the infrasystem: Toward a critical feminist analysis of systems theory. *Public Relations Review.*

Cline, Carolyn G., Toth, Elizabeth L., Turk, Judy V., Walters, Lynne M., Johnson, Nancy, & Smith, Hank. (1986). *The velvet ghetto: The impact of the increasing number of women in public relations and business communication.* San Francisco: IABC Foundation.

Donato, Katharine M. (1990). Keepers of the corporate image: Women in public relations. In Barbara F. Reskin and Patricia A. Roose (Eds.), *Job queues, gender queues: Explaining women's inroads into male occupations* (pp. 129-144). Philadelphia: Temple University Press.

Grunig, Larissa A. (1988). A research agenda for women in public relations. *Public Relations Review, 14*(3), 48-58.

Hon, Linda C., Grunig, Larissa A., & Dozier, David M. (1992). Women in public relations: Problems and opportunities. In J. Grunig (Ed.), *Excellence in public relations and communication management* (pp. 419-438). Hillsdale, NJ: Lawrence Erlbaum.

Jacobson, David Y., & Tortorello, Nicholas J. (1992, September). Salary survey. *Public Relations Journal,* pp. 9-21.

Littlejohn, Stephen W. (1992). *Theories of human communication* (4th ed). Belmont, CA: Wadsworth.

Lukovitz, Karlene. (1989, May). Women practitioners: How far, how fast? *Public Relations Journal,* pp. 14-20, 22.

Mathews, Wilma. (1989). Killing the messenger. In Elizabeth L. Toth & Carolyn G. Cline (Eds.), *Beyond the velvet ghetto* (pp. 1-6). San Francisco: IABC Research Foundation.

Rakow, Lana F. (1989). From the feminization of public relations to the promise of feminism. In Elizabeth L. Toth & Carolyn G. Cline (Eds.), *Beyond the velvet ghetto* (pp. 287-298). San Francisco: IABC Research Foundation.

Reskin, Barbara F. (1989). Occupational resegregation. In S. Rix (Ed.), *The American woman: 1988-1989: A status report* (pp. 258-263). New York: Norton.

Toth, Elizabeth L. (1989). Whose freedom and equity in public relations? The gender balance argument. *Mass Communication Review, 16,* 1, 2, 70-76.

Toth, Elizabeth L., & Cline, Carolyn G. (Eds.). (1989). *Beyond the velvet ghetto.* San Francisco: IABC Research Foundation.

Toth, Elizabeth L., & Cline, Carolyn G. (1991). Public relations practitioner attitudes toward gender issues: A benchmark study. *Public Relations Review, 17*(2), 161-174.

Toth, Elizabeth L., & Grunig, Larissa A. (in press). The missing story of women in public relations. *Journal of Public Relations Research.*

Steeves, H. Leslie. (1987). Feminist theories and media studies. *Critical studies in mass communication, 4,* 95-135.

Wilcox, Dennis L., Ault, Phillip H., & Agee, Warren K. (1992). *Public relations strategies and tactics* (3rd ed.). New York: HarperCollins.

Wright, Donald K., Grunig, Larissa A., Springston, Jeffery K., & Toth, Elizabeth L. (1991). *Under the glass ceiling: An analysis of gender issues in American public relations.* New York: The PRSA Foundation.

12 Women in Advertisements
Sizing Up the Images, Roles, and Functions

LINDA LAZIER
ALICE GAGNARD KENDRICK

Advertising—15- or 30-second broadcast sales blurbs interrupting *Northern Exposure, CNN, The Oprah Winfrey Show,* or *General Hospital;* 7-by-10-inch pretty magazine page messages—brief, innocuous, seemingly simple. No one really takes these concise capitalistic communications seriously, do they?

Not even if the messages are part of a $150-billion-a-year communication industry?

Not even if the average person, every day, is exposed to an average of 1,800 messages?

Not even if these brief blips are "pervasive and persuasive, environmental in nature, persistently encountered and involuntarily experienced" (Pollay, 1986, p. 18)?

Not even if the ubiquitous messages pervade all the media, forming "a vast superstructure with an apparently autonomous existence" (Williamson, 1978, p. 11)?

Not even if the ads make up "the most consistent body of material in the mass media" (Leiss, Kline, & Jhally, 1986, p. 3)?

Not even then?

Advertising: Institution Turned Entity

Critics and commentators from every discipline have grappled with advertising's potential for power. It has been called "the most potent influence in adapting and changing habits and modes of life, affecting what we eat, what we wear and the work and play of the whole nation" (Fox, 1984, p. 97).

It has been compared with "such long-standing institutions as the school and the church in the magnitude of its social influence" because it "dominates the media, it has vast power in the shaping of popular standards, and it is really one of the very limited groups of institutions which exercise social control" (Potter, 1954, p. 167).

McLuhan (1951), who has said that advertising reflects our "collective daydreams," also has commented that "ours is the first age in which many thousands of the best-trained minds have made it a full-time business to get inside the collective public mind . . . to get inside in order to manipulate, exploit and control" (p. v).

Criticisms and concerns have been vented by psychologists, who view advertising as a source of learning or conditioning, with cognitive and affective results; by sociologists, who speak to the role-modeling aspects and advertising's impact on social behaviors; by anthropologists, who examine the rituals, symbols, and cultural meanings involved; by educators, who question the influence on development; and by communications specialists, critics, and commentators, who often address the propagandistic role of advertising and fret over its influence on media content (Pollay, 1986).

The critics concur on one point. Advertising is its own force, an institution turned entity. Society has not put it on a pedestal—indeed, many consumers still scoff, claiming they are unaffected by ads—but the evidence more and more suggests that society has elevated advertising to an invisible podium from which we learn and by which we are influenced.

The Connection to Women

The gender perspective on advertising is dual. A long-standing central concern is that advertising is a shorthand form of communication that must make contact with the consumer immediately, establishing a shared experience of identification—with the best-known method being the use of stereotypical imagery.

A second concern—and the subject of much recent essaying and commentary in the popular press—is advertising's almost blatant centering on a beauty "myth" and an "ideal," exceptionally thin body shape.

These two perspectives, with commentary on their consequences, are the focus for this chapter.

Beyond basic sexism, why are concerns about stereotyping or beauty-typing so disconcerting? A key reason is that the portrayals of women in advertising are not only potentially debilitating and demeaning, but they are also inaccurate. We do not have a demography of demigoddesses. Women today (and during the time frame of many of the research studies) are considerably more than flawless decorative objects, dependent upon or defined by men.

Researchers are not calling for all ads to portray either all working women or older, average, woman-next-door types—indeed, it is a given that advertising's role is to sell solutions, not sociology, and that these social snapshots are not accurate representations of the "real" world—but a consistently biased representation (or nonrepresentation) is damaging to all consumers of these visuals.

Today's advertisements do not reflect the significant strides (both socially and statistically) made by women in the past two decades into the workforce—a phenomenon so socially reshaping it has been dubbed the "third successful revolution in American history" (after the War for Independence and the Industrial Revolution), a revolution that has "reached beyond women's own lives and changed the very way America lives, works, and even thinks" (Hellwig, 1986, p. 129). Ads ignore the booming percentages of women becoming doctors, lawyers, elected politicians, entrepreneurs (women are starting businesses at 3 times the rate of men), corporate executives and board members, business travelers (another third), or as decision makers for major purchases (women buy more new cars than men and consistently make more family financial decisions).

More important, by using outdated stereotypes, ads are simplistically ignoring the complexities of modern women's lives.

Stereotypes

Stereotypes, as we know, are standardized mental pictures that *Webster's* defines as representing an oversimplified opinion or uncritical judgment.

The crux of stereotype "theory" comes compliments of Walter Lippmann (1922) who claims that the abbreviated communiques offer an "economy of effort" because they "substitute order for great blooming, buzzing confusion of reality" (p. 63). As such, they become "the core of our personal tradition, the defenses of our position in society," which give "an ordered, consistent picture of the world to which our habits, tastes, capacities, comforts and hopes have adjusted themselves" (p. 63).

Yes, stereotypes, or "pictures in our heads," can save interpretive effort. But others argue that stereotypes short-circuit or block the capacity for objective and analytic judgment in favor of well-worn, catchall (and possibly outdated) reactions. This could lead to shortchanging. It also leads to the first connection to gender concerns: Advertising to women has consistently been filled with stereotypes.

There is overwhelming evidence that advertisements present traditional, limited, and often demeaning stereotypes of women and men. It is recognized, of course, that stereotypes in advertising can serve a useful function by conveying an image quickly and clearly, and that there is nothing inherently wrong with using characterizations of roles that are easily identifiable. However, when these limited and demeaning stereotypes are as pervasive as those involved in advertising's portrayal of the sexes, it becomes important to question whether those stereotypes might result in negative and undesirable social consequences (Courtney & Whipple, 1983, p. 45).

In print advertising, the results of more than a dozen studies, most conducted in the 1970s and many of them considered benchmark, have shown the messages of advertising to be astonishingly similar: Woman's place is in the home; women are dependent upon men; women do not make independent and important decisions; women are shown in few occupational roles; women view themselves and are viewed by others as sex objects (see Courtney & Whipple, 1985, for citations).

The issues and the findings from television content analyses were similar to (and as debilitating as) those found in the print studies. Taken together, the television studies do two things: (1) point out three prevalent female roles—maternal, housekeeping, and aesthetic; and (2) point out flagrant discrimination—women and girls were seen far less frequently than men, they were shown to have different characteristics from males (less authoritative, active, powerful, rational, and decisive, and more youthful and concerned with attractiveness), they were housewives or in restricted, low-status, subservient occupations (and fewer roles) and they were depicted as less intelligent than males.

The anomalous fact is that although images of women as documented in advertising research hardly changed from study to study throughout the 1970s (and in replications of those studies in the early 1980s), both demography on and attitudes among women changed dramatically (Courtney & Whipple, 1985).

It is imperative not to dismiss the above findings as being outdated. Recent studies have only added to the evidence, documenting the persistence of the previous stereotypical, limiting, or sex object/thin/beauty conventions.

A 1989 study of 353 TV commercials (an extension of the benchmark work of O'Donnell & O'Donnell, 1978) by Lovdal (1989) found men's voices still dominant in voice-overs, women speaking as a subordinate or mostly to those of inferior status, and that men were portrayed in 3 times the variety of occupational roles as were women. These findings confirmed those of Bretl and Cantor (1988) of male characters in higher status occupations and women without occupations and those of Gilly (1988) that men were more likely to be portrayed in independent roles in relation to women who were portrayed in a plethora of stereotyped roles such as wife, mother, bride, waitresses, actress, dancer.

A 1990 study by Ferguson, Kreshel, and Tinkham examined the extent to which *Ms.* magazine adhered to its stated advertising policy of excluding ads for products harmful or insulting to women. The results showed a substantial proportion of advertising promoted products considered harmful (e.g., alcohol, cigarettes) and that although the portrayal of women as subordinate to men or merely as decoration has decreased, *Ms.* advertising has increasingly portrayed women as alluring sex objects.

A 1988 study on role portrayal by Minnigerode was an attempt to update, validate, or exonerate previously documented androcentric bias. After studying 943 ads in eight magazines, Minnigerode concluded that a degree of progress had been made in advertisers' response to previous criticism of female role portrayals, but his central conclusion was that androcentric bias still existed in print advertisements.

A particularly intense reflective analysis by Duffy (1991) of almost all the portrayal studies to date provides a critical review of several of the studies, divides them into methodological types and critiques methodology development of the studies as well as researcher assumptions, and, often, conclusions. Several recent feminist analyses of portrayal research have centered on determining the type of feminist theory as basis of the research, or, as Duffy does, fault the research for using "masculine" methodologies and values. Duffy's work is valuable for its exhaustive review of all previous work and for the interesting challenge she poses that many researchers are remiss for ascribing social effects to advertising or assuming that stereotypical or body-oriented advertising perpetuates patriarchy or inherent cultural chauvinism.

Additional recent studies have examined international advertising's portrayal of women via roles and stereotypes but are not reported here due to the intricacies of both cultural and media organization dissimilarities. (For example, Furnham, 1989; Griffin, Viswanath, & Schwartz, 1992).

Sexism and Stereotypes Replicate Themselves

Three past studies have been considered benchmarks in advertising stereotype/role research: the Consciousness Scale for Sexism study (Pingree, Hawkins, Butler, & Paisley, 1976), Goffman's (1979) "gender advertisements," and Kilbourne's (1987) film on female ad images.

In the late 1980s Lazier-Smith (1988) replicated the three, via content analysis, in what is believed to be the first print replication stereotype study of the 1980s.

In the central study, the Consciousness Scale of Sexism, developed by Butler-Paisley and Paisley-Butler (1974) and elaborated by Pingree et al. (1976) was applied to ads portraying women in *Ms., Playboy, Time,* and *Newsweek,* coding 10 ads in each monthly issue for one year. The "scale" attempts to "measure" sexism by analyzing ad visuals via five levels in one of the first continuums used in content analyses:

Level 1: Put her down (the sex object, dumb blonde, decorative object).

Level 2: Keep her in her place (women shown mostly in traditional womanly roles or struggling with roles "beyond them").

Level 3: Give her two places (women can have an occupation as long as they are still primarily a wife/mother; the career may be something "extra").

Level 4: Acknowledge that she is fully equal (women in multiple roles without reminders that housework and mothering are nonnegotiably woman's work).

Level 5: Non-stereotypic (true individuals, not judged by sex).

In the 1973-1974 study (the real start of the "women's movement"), 75% of all ads were at the two lowest (most sexist) levels—48% at Level 2, considered by researchers to be the status quo, and 27% at Level 1 (sex object).

The second benchmark study was conducted by sociologist Erving Goffman and has been popularized in his book *Gender Advertisements* (1979). In that book, Goffman concludes that women are weakened by advertising portrayals in six categories: relative size (shown smaller or lower, relative to men); feminine touch (women constantly touching themselves); function ranking (occupational); family scenes; ritualization of subordination (proclivity for lying down at inappropriate times, using bashful knee bends, canting postures, puckish, expansive "goofy" smiles); licensed withdrawal (women never quite a part of the scene, usually via blank, far-off gazes).

In essence, Goffman found that ads are highly ritualized versions of the parent-child relationship, with women treated largely as children and that this diminishment is damaging.

The third "study" is a film that uses examples reflecting the findings listed above and that includes examples from Jean Kilbourne's qualitative assessment of advertising. Her first film, released in 1976, was titled *Killing Us Softly.* Her second film, a much-awaited and -demanded update released in late 1987, is titled *Still Killing Us Softly;* the *still* summarizes her assessment of a lack of improvement in imagery toward and about women. Kilbourne's is a provocative collection of examples selected purposefully to show the extent of, and problems with, advertising's sexual imagery and its implication that sexual access to the female is the reward for buying

Table 12.1 Comparison of Female Portrayals in 1973 and 1986

| | Consciousness Scale for Sexism | |
| | 1973 | 1986 |
Level	(N = 447)	(N = 530)
1. Put her down	27%	37%
2. Keep her in her place	48%	35%
3. Give her two places	4%	3%
4. Acknowledge equality	19%	15%
5. Nonstereotypic	2%	11%

many products. Her film illustrates the findings of many of the scientifically drawn samples cited previously.

The 1988 study by Lazier-Smith replicated the method, categories, and procedures of the Consciousness Scale for Sexism and Goffman's sexist categories, coding all ads in the four original magazines from July 1986 to June 1987 (intercoder agreement 94%), with findings from both analyses then applied to Kilbourne's contentions.

The conclusions of the examination of ads some 15 years after women's entry into the workforce and dramatic change in social ways and trends? *No significant change.* The images of women in 1986 ads did not significantly change from the images found in 1973 ads. Portrayals did not "improve" overall to reflect women's increased social status.

And, given the statistical analyses of the data, it can be concluded that not only has sexism *not* improved, but the 1986 ads, in the aggregate, are slightly more sexist than those in the 1973 sample. The median score was Level 2, the traditional sphere. Mode level actually worsened, to Level 1 (sex object/decoration) (see Table 12.1).

It should be noted that though distribution of ads, by level, changed (especially at Levels 1 and 2), the cumulative percentages of ads in the two lowest or most sexist levels improved only marginally—from 75% in 1973 to 72% in 1986.

A current updated replication of the Scale is underway but incomplete; preliminary data indicate that there will be few dramatic changes, especially in Level 1 (sex object/decoration/bimbo) portrayals. One interesting new feature is that many of the elite cosmetic companies are now portraying their products only, without the use of a young, flawless, unobtainable-beauty model.

Goffman traits from the 1988 study did show some improvement, with three categories (relative size, function ranking, and family scenes) appearing so infrequently that they could be considered to no longer apply.

Unfortunately, the largest coded category, ritualization of subordination, could also be considered the most limiting or trivializing.

The findings of these two analyses support the contentions of Kilbourne's film of ongoing and damaging sexist tendencies. The findings indicate we have a case of demigoddesses (mythical beings that seem to approach perfection or the divine) versus demographics—a new "genderation" of sexism.

Conclusions on Stereotypes

These findings are troublesome for several reasons. One is that advertising is supposedly market-driven and the industry is one dedicated to consumer research and monitoring of society, customer reaction, and in message and visual ability to connect to consumers. Why are the new demographics not surfacing in ads? Why are the myths still prevalent over the math?

Second, advertising messagemakers are increasingly female. In 1991, 68% of the advertising students in a national survey of journalism schools were female (L. Becker, personal communication, January 5, 1993). But, while infiltrating advertising agencies and marketing positions (where most messages are created), they are still rare in the upper levels of management or supervision (only 10% of creative directors are female). More important, these females have been fed a steady diet of stereotypical, sexist, thin-and-flawless imagery and seem to be, quite frankly, socialized to it in a "that's the way it is and that's the way we do it" mind set.

(Career opportunities for females in advertising are good because talent, not gender, is the key to advancement. Although the advertising trade publications do annual salary surveys, in an "equality" move, they no longer break salaries into gender categories. The authors agree that "average" cited salaries are generally hugely inflated and therefore inaccurate. Entry-level salaries seem to be equal; discrepancies still exist between male and female salaries at the management level.)

Lastly, it seemed almost shocking to the researcher to see the minuscule "advancement" made in the imagery of women over a decade and a half. We expected to see the new "social reality" reflected in the "modern" ads, a reality markedly different from the reality reflected in academe's first analyses of the early 1970s at the beginning of the women's movement and the entry of women into the workforce.

How can this stereotypical sexism survive given the incredible changes in women's social status? Our only plausible conclusion is that the ads DO reflect our current culture—one of the traditional balance of power (male). The ads reflect the critical components of culture as defined by Dervin and Clark (1988) and Gerbner (cited in Tuchman, Daniels, & Benet, 1978)—its stereotypes, its bigotries, its biases, its dominant values, its tendency toward the status quo, and the ongoingness of the traditional. That is what culture does—it protects itself from change, and, as Gerbner says, manages a social movement either by resistance or by images. That turns the issue of imagery into one of power and explains why "modern" ads reflect the mythical more than the mathematical. The ads also reflect the ongoing confusion in our culture (by both men and women) of what women are—as we grope with what we'll let today's woman *do* or *be,* we at least agree on how she will *look.*

"I've Noticed Non-Stereotypical Ads"

A qualitative comment cogent to the discussion at hand needs to be made: Yes, there HAVE been examples of non-stereotypical or pro-female or feminist-oriented ads recently (*very* recently). The key here is the quantitative amount: "some." The authors, who speak and are interviewed often on whether sexist advertising has decreased, are always given a handful of examples of such "advanced" imagery. The critical thing to remember is that this handful of ads stands out—in the media and in critics' minds—simply because they DO stand out from the continuing barrage of sexist images (traditionally stereotypical, including the new beauty myth and ideal body image) because they are so unusual. But an eyeful does not a visual trend make. What it does is legitimize the ongoing content analyses necessary to actually track imagery changes in the visuals used in all kinds of advertising—magazine and television advertising, yes, but also point of purchase displays, sales promotions, and even promotional items for popular films and music.

Beauty Myth and Ideal Body Image

Much has been written in the popular press recently about the "beauty myth"—from the book of the same name to Camille Paglia's comments to newspaper articles touting the "fashionable" new use of "mature, over-40" models to advertising publications announcing a new "melting pot" of beauty (all colors, all creeds, all ethnicity—and all still young, thin, and flawless). From the bimbo backlash of the lawsuits over the Swedish Bikini Team dropping in on Old Milwaukee drinkers to fretting about a new version of violence and subordination, articles about women and "changing" philosophies of beauty abound.

Clements, in a *New York Times Magazine* (p. 71) article, says

> In the bombardment of the new female images, it has become impossible to hold on to a unified esthetic. This is in part because the role of women has

changed so much in the last several decades that previously undisturbed geological layers of our psyches are being excavated and require expression.

Beauty and body size—especially if they are considered intrinsically unobtainable—are critical to an assessment of images of women in advertising.

Cultivating Images of Thinness: The Role of Advertising

A greatly increased reporting of the incidence of eating disorders among young American women in the 1970s and 1980s prompted some media critics to suggest that unattainable physical ideals portrayed in the media contributed to an eating disorder epidemic (see Smith, 1985; Garner, Garfinkel, Schwartz, & Thompson, 1980; Garfinkel, 1981). Most of the theories of the origin of eating disorders point to the prominent role played by the social environment, so it is no coincidence that advertising and its role in the cultural milieu would feature in such a discussion.

The unfortunate fact of life for many young American females is that the relentless pursuit of thinness does not equate with good health—in fact, because of the devastating physical effects of the eating disorders of bulimia and anorexia, extreme attempts to achieve a thin physique can result in serious illness and even death.

In the first edition of this book, we cited a study of women's magazine ads that pointed to a trend since the 1950s of increased emphasis on models with thin physiques. In this edition we have expanded our look at content studies that point to the prevalence of "thin is in" messages perpetuated by the media by examining both formal quantitative content analyses as well as the qualitative evaluation of selected authors. The net result is increasing evidence that a steady diet of thin images continues to be fed to media consumers—in both programming and editorial matter as well as, and especially in, advertisements.

After our look at content studies, we cite a recent effects study that attempted to assess the impact of repeated exposure to thin images. We conclude with suggestions for a different research approach that may offer some insight into determining the ultimate effect of heavy exposure to images of thinness. Previously applied to such media content/effects areas as violence and sex role stereotypes, the approach known as *cultivation analysis* is presented as a major departure from most media effects studies. However, it could hold great promise for evaluating the "big picture" effects of years of exposure to consonant images in the mass media.

Advertising's Portrayal of the Thin Body

One only need tune in briefly to American television before encountering a commercial message depicting a trim, healthy physique as an ideal. Whether it's Cher as spokesperson for President's Health Clubs or reformed-fatty Tommy Lasorda for SlimFast, the messages are clear. First, thin is in (translation: fat is out) and secondly, thinness is associated with good health and attractiveness. Though much has been made recently over the so-called changing notions of beauty, especially as depicted in the facial features of exotic, multiethnic, and often more mature fashion models (Appelbaum, 1991, p. 18; Foltz, 1992, p. 4F; Teegardin, 1992, p. 1), the fact remains that the bodies of these models, though sometimes decidedly more toned than in the past, are still consistently thin. The studies cited in this section report a trend toward thinness since the 1950s that to date has not been shown to have abated—at least not in women's magazines.

Though time consuming, the task of mapping out the content of media messages is facilitated by what Marcelle Clements has termed the "plentiful visual record" (1991, p. 75) historians have to draw upon from the world of fashion, news, and advertising. Some of the most extensive examinations of the content of advertising with respect to body type were conducted in the mid-1980s. The three chosen to be cited below detail the legacies of both print and broadcast advertising. Numerous other works have had as their focus female body depiction in television programming, editorial material, *Playboy* centerfolds, and even beauty pageants (see, e.g., Garfinkel, 1981; Garner, 1980; Wolf, 1991). But again, our focus here is on advertising.

Two studies reported by Silverstein, Perdue, Peterson, and Kelly (1986) examined some 1,200 ads and articles in both women's and men's magazines as well as photographs of models in selected women's magazines. In the first study *Family Circle, Ladies Home Journal, Redbook,* and *Woman's Day* were chosen for women and *Field and Stream, Playboy, Popular Mechanics,* and *Sports Illustrated* for men. We question somewhat the choices of these men's titles as the editorial environment in most cases does not lend itself readily to food or fashion advertising as is clearly the case with the women's publications. However, we report the results here despite that reservation if for no other reason than the incredibly consonant environment created by the hundreds of body image related ads found in the women's magazines.

For the year 1980, 12 monthly issues of all titles were examined for ads and articles that dealt with body shape and size or with dieting, food, drink or cooking. Results, summarized in Table 12.2 for all magazines studied,

Table 12.2 Ads and Articles in 48 Women's Versus 48 Men's Magazines

		Type of Ad or Article			
	Diet Foods	Body Ads and Articles	Total Food Ads	Food Articles	Alcoholic Beverages
Women's magazines	63	96	1,179	228	19
Men's magazines	1	12	15	10	624

SOURCE: Silverstein, Perdue, Peterson, & Kelly (1986). Used by permission.

supported the authors' hypothesis that women receive more messages about slimness and staying in shape than do men. Again, whether it is appropriate to compare home and fashion magazines directly with sport and fix-it publications is debatable. But the sheer volume of ads and articles involving dieting or body shape is staggering. By adding the "diet foods" and "body ads and articles" categories and dividing by 12 issues, the average number of prominent mentions of body image related messages is more than a dozen per issue.

In the second study, Silverstein et al. (1986) attempted to obtain a measure of the changes in standards of bodily attractiveness for women since the turn of the century. Photographs of bathing suit- or underwear-clad women in *Ladies Home Journal* and *Vogue* were used to collect data on the ratios of bust-to-waist and hip-to-waist. The mean bust-to-waist ratios reported in Figure 12.1 are noteworthy. First, ratios dropped fairly steadily from the beginning of the century to 1925, when they hit a century low. They climbed again until about 1950, after which they exhibited a steady decline until the 1980s. Another general conclusion we draw, though somewhat less obvious, is the consonance of messages in two separate magazines, which indicates relative stability of the messages being presented to women during these time periods.

A third conclusion has to do with the longevity of trends of female body depiction. Since 1965 the combined bust-to-waist ratios of the two magazines has been below 1.3, a trend that continued into the 1980s and that has provided a steady stream of consonant thin-is-in messages to young and middle-aged women of today.

A study by Gagnard (1986), reported in the first edition of this book, examined models in 961 ads from *Ladies Home Journal, Woman's Day,* and *McCall's* for the years 1950, 1960, 1970, and 1984. Data pertaining to models' gender, age, body type, attractiveness, success, and happiness were analyzed, and results supported the following hypotheses:

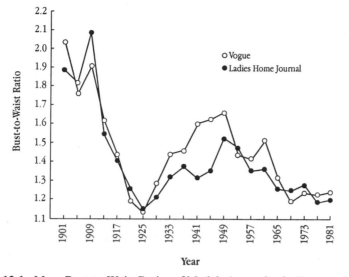

Year

Figure 12.1. Mean Bust-to-Waist Ratios of Models Appearing in *Vogue* and *Ladies Home Journal* at Four-Year Intervals During This Century.

SOURCE: Silverstein, Brett, Perdue, Lauren, Peterson, Barbara, & Kelly, Eileen. (1986). The role of the mass media in promoting a thin standard of bodily attractiveness for women. *Sex Roles, 14*(10), 519-532.

- Models featured in ads in the 1970s and 1980s will be judged thinner than models in ads from the 1950s and 1960s.
- Fewer overweight and obese models will appear in ads for the 1970s and 1980s than in ads from the 1950s and 1960s.
- More overweight and obese males than females will be found in ads for all four decades studied.
- Thin models as a group will be judged more successful than overweight or obese models.
- Thin models as a group will be judged more attractive than overweight or obese models.

Results are summarized in Tables 12.3 and 12.4. Computing of a desirability index, or "Yendex," by the author resulted in thin models receiving the most desirable Yendex rating, followed by average models, overweight models, and obese models.

Effects of Body Image Messages

Although several authors have written about distortion of self-perceived body size in young females and its relationship to development of eating

Table 12.3   Body Types of Models in Magazine Ads

Body Type	1950		1960		Year 1970		1980		Total	
Thin	13	(3%)	15	(5%)	33	(13%)	137	(46%)	198	(15%)
Average	384	(85%)	285	(88%)	191	(76%)	148	(50%)	1,008	(77%)
Overweight	43	(10%)	18	(6%)	24	(10%)	9	(3%)	94	(7%)
Obese	7	(2%)	5	(12%)	3	(1%)	1	(—)	16	(1%)
Total	447	(100%)	323	(100%)	251	(100%)	295	(100%)	1,316	(100%)

disorders, evidence of the extent to which body size distortions are affected by media messages is not available. Indeed the area of research involving marketing practices to women and their short- and long-term effects is just beginning to be tapped.

An experiment by Myers and Biocca (1992) involving a mood test and a body image detection device found that as little as 30 minutes of television programming and commercials affected self-perceived body size estimates and mood of young women. Results supported the notion that an "elastic body image" exists for young women in which their actual body size is in conflict with media messages about ideal body image.

Interestingly, the findings showed that although both body image commercials and body image programming did produce body size overestimations, subjects exposed to body image commercials overestimated to a lesser degree than those who were exposed to neutral image commercials or were in a control setting. Also, depression levels did not increase as hypothesized after exposure to body image commercials. The authors speculated that the surprising results could have been due to a therapeutic value of body image commercials, or that the commercials might have imparted the confidence to be thin by portraying an attainable physical goal.

These befuddling results are not in keeping with the mainstream hypotheses about the deleterious effects of body image messages on women. Is it possible that as researchers we're asking the wrong questions of women in the wrong settings? In the next section of this chapter we suggest that alternative research schemes such as cultivation analysis be applied to assess the widespread, broad-brush effects of exposure to a variety of body image messages.

Semiology and Content Analysis—Combined

In the book *Social Communication in Advertising,* Leiss, Kline and Jhally (1986) propose a research paradigm that draws on the strengths of

Table 12.4 Attractiveness, Success, Happiness, and Yendex* of Models**

Body Type	1950	1960	Year 1970	1980	Total
Thin					
Attractive	1.62	1.87	1.36	1.12	1.25
Successful	2.38	2.13	2.09	1.63	1.89
Happy	2.00	1.73	1.79	1.53	1.62
Yendex	2.00	1.91	1.75	1.43	1.59 (n = 198)
Average					
Attractive	1.60	1.74	1.82	1.69	1.69
Successful	2.32	2.20	2.36	2.18	2.27
Happy	1.79	1.81	1.92	1.63	1.80
Yendex	1.90	1.92	2.03	1.83	1.92 (n = 1,009)
Overweight					
Attractive	2.57	1.94	3.00	2.33	2.54
Successful	2.63	2.83	2.63	2.78	2.68
Happy	2.02	1.35	1.79	1.89	1.83
Yendex	2.41	2.04	2.47	2.33	2.35 (n = 94)
Obese					
Attractive	3.43	3.20	4.30	2.00	3.44
Successful	3.00	2.80	3.33	4.00	3.06
Happy	1.43	1.20	1.67	3.00	1.50
Yendex	2.62	2.40	3.10	3.00	2.67 (n = 16)

SOURCE: "From Feast to Famine: Depiction of Ideal Body Type in Magazine Advertising: 1950-1984," by Alice Gagnard, 1986, *Proceedings of the American Academy of Advertising,* edited by Ernest Larkin.
NOTES: * Yendex represents "desirability factor," computed by averaging scores on the attractiveness, success, and happiness variables.
** Categories were 1 = very attractive, 2 = somewhat attractive, 3 = neutral, 4 = somewhat unattractive, 5 = very unattractive, etc.

two seemingly incompatible methods: semiology and content analysis. We believe that for the purpose of further examining the origin, context, and content of sex role stereotyping in advertising, the unlikely combination of semiology and content analysis could provide a rich and holistic perspective.

Semiology, or semiotics, is a method for examining text that is rooted in linguistics and literary and cultural analysis. The "science of signs" seeks to examine relationships among the parts of a message and to describe the formation of meaning. Semiology uses a qualitative approach, and usually a relatively small number of ads to be analyzed. It relies heavily on the analytical abilities of the highly skilled evaluator, and because it is based on subjective judgments its results are not always replicable between researchers. The latter has proved to be somewhat of a suffering point for the method.

Leiss et al. (1986) observe that the move from the product-centered advertising of yesterday to user-centered advertising so prevalent today has resulted in increasing reliance on the visual text as opposed to lengthy copy to communicate the advertising message. "User-centered advertising draws upon the shared experience, perceptions, and attitudes of the segmented audience." (Leiss et al., 1986, p. 199) How is it that sex role stereotypes are woven into the fabric of modern advertising, and how do they figure in the wider belief systems of consumers? We believe that an examination of how meaning is constructed both by advertisers and consumers would shed light on the issue of sex role stereotyping, and an analysis involving semiology would be appropriate.

Content analysis, which involves counting incidences of the components of the content of a random sample of messages, aims—objectively and numerically—to describe a body of messages by citing trends in the use of words, techniques, visuals, and so forth. The content analyses cited earlier in this chapter described in considerable detail specific characteristics of ads directed toward women and men. As such they are considered to be very objective, but at the same time they do not address the interrelationship of the components of the message, or the message in its entirety—only the manifest content. Also, to the extent that content analyses merely describe media content, they do not offer insight into how it comes into being or how it might be received by the audience.

We agree with Leiss et al. that a combination of semiotics and content analysis, in which carefully constructed "categories" would reflect patterns of images, cultural "lessons," and other cues of shared meanings would make a valuable contribution to the study of media content. And we believe that it would be particularly appropriate for the study of sex role stereotyping.

Cultivation Analysis

A research approach known as cultivation analysis seeks to discover the contributions of mass media, especially television, to the individual's beliefs about social reality. The origin of cultivation analysis was a large-scale media effects research project by George Gerbner begun in the 1960s and labeled Cultural Indicators. Cultivation analysis is the third and final component of Cultural Indicators which seeks to investigate:

1. the institutional processes related to production of media content
2. manifest images in the media
3. relationships between media exposure and audience beliefs and behaviors.

Unlike traditional media "effects" research, which often uses a "one-shot" research design involving attitude measures before and after brief forced exposure to media content in the confines of a laboratory setting, cultivation analysis attempts to describe the long-term cumulative effects of years of media exposure. Cultivation analysis typically involves the study of two groups selected for their degree of media exposure—for example, one group of heavy television viewers, and one group of light television viewers.

> In its simplest form, cultivation analysis tries to ascertain if those who spend more time watching television are more likely to perceive the real world in ways that reflect the most common and repetitive messages and lessons of the television world, compared with people who watch less television but are otherwise comparable in important demographic characteristics. (Signorielli & Morgan, 1990, p. 16)

The Cultural Indicators project grew out of concern in America for the effects of televised violence, and because of that primary focus it examined programming more than advertising. Signorielli and others later used the cultivation analysis paradigm to examine the portrayal and effects of sex role stereotyping in programming, again using groups of heavy and light viewers.

There are several aspects of existing research on cultivation analysis that should hold promise for those who wish to study relationships between media images of thinness and media audiences. First, the suggestion that those heavily exposed to media messages might be somewhat more vulnerable to message effects is a relevant one for young women who suffer from eating disorders. A study by Linda Lazier Smith (1985) in which eating disorder patients were interviewed about their attention to media found them to quite "media conscious." Though this correlation obviously does not ensure that the heavy media consumption was the cause of the eating disorders, the relationship at least bears further investigation.

A second observation is that the almost exclusive emphasis so far on television programming and its effects leaves room for significant contributions in the area of advertising content in television as well as in other media editorial content and/or advertising. One might argue that because of the persuasive nature of most advertising content, that extreme attention to the ad message might pack a stronger punch than programming content. Just as it is possible to ascertain by way of questionnaire items whether a person is a light or heavy viewer of television programming, it is also possible to gather information and classify respondents by their degree of attention to advertising. Research companies routinely collect and sell this information, and similar questions to theirs could be used to categorize respondents.

Using cultivation analysis to determine the effects of body image messages in the media, the research question would come to this: Does a group of females that is heavily exposed to media advertising reflect the version of reality described earlier in this chapter more than a group of females that is only lightly exposed to media advertising? If the answer is yes, then the final hurdle in establishing a cause-effect relationship between conceptions of social reality and advertising messages will involve systematically ruling out the presence of a third or "spurious" variable as a causal explanation. The primary criticism of cultivation analysis results to date has been the inability of some researchers to rule out other social, cultural, or personal factors that themselves differentiate heavy and light viewers and also contribute to their conceptions of social reality. Certainly, this issue would have to be addressed, but despite these potential problems of explanation, cultivation analysis offers a fruitful avenue of inquiry for those who wish to go beyond the content analysis or the single-exposure laboratory experiment.

Roles and Beauty: Not A Black and White Issue

We need to take one last look at the basic and beauty stereotypes and standards—a look beyond the rose-colored glasses of Madison Avenue that sees primarily skinny, flawless, young blondes; we need a clear-eyed look at what we're *really* seeing. The previously cited research has repeatedly monitored problematic portrayals, but it must be noted that these portrayals are predominately WHITE. White women, white beauty standards, white myths.

We have not found any substantial research into stereotypical portrayals or beauty agendas for women of color or women of age. The sexism of the portrayals also comes complete with racism and ageism. Past studies have confirmed that approximately 1% of ads use African-American or older models, regardless of their percentages in the population (12%-16%). And, until recently, national advertisers generally did not devise minority-specific advertising campaigns, although as market research continues to indicate viable target audiences, more product advertisers are developing ethnic/ minority campaigns, usually consigned to specific ethnic publications or neighborhoods.

However, just recently a handful of articles have addressed the White Syndrome. An *Adweek* article (Appelbaum, 1991) in mid-1991 heralded "a melting pot of beauty," noting that "by the end of the decade, beauty barriers had started to crumble," citing a handful of ads using models of color and other-than-U.S. nationalities. (It must be noted that these models are still thin, young, and perfect.)

A "forum" discussion in *Advertising Age* (Brown, 1993) took a different view of the rather new use of women of color, indicating that most black models appearing in ads are so light in color, with the traditional Caucasian features of thinner lips, narrower noses, and straighter hair, that it is often impossible to determine their ethnicity (the article was written by a Black marketer). This would suggest that women of color are being held to "white" standards of beauty. The writer added that beyond the high-fashion inclusion, the diversity of women of color is particularly missing from any of the "standard" depictions of women—housewives or working women.

Although some marketers are including more minorities in ad visuals to more accurately represent America's rapidly shifting demographics, the trend is small, representing ideas out of the "Dark Ages" (without the dark).

Examining role or beauty stereotypes for women of color or age needs to be done, but will be difficult as long as they are so underrepresented in mainstream advertising.

The Black Girls' Coalition, an association of Black models, is working to reeducate marketers and advertising agencies. Their complaints range from "not looking black enough" to not being selected for being too ethnic (Hood, 1993) to the problem that a handful of top models, including Iman, are considered representative.

References

Appelbaum, Cara. (1991, June 3). Beyond the blonde bombshell: America welcomes a new melting pot of beauty. *Adweek's Marketing Week*, pp. 18-20.

Bretl, D. J., & Cantor, J. (1988). The portrayal of men and women in US television commercials: A recent content analysis and trends over 15 years. *Sex Roles, 26*(9/10), 595-609.

Brown, J. Clinton. (1993, February 1). Which Black is beautiful? African-Americans in adland so light it's often hard to tell. *Advertising Age*, p. 19.

Butler-Paisley, Matilda, & Paisley-Butler, William J. (1974, August). *Sexism in the media: Frameworks for research*. Paper presented at the annual meeting of the Association of Education in Journalism, San Diego, CA.

Clements, Marcelle. (1991, September 15). The mirror cracked. *New York Times Magazine*, pp. 70-75.

Courtney, Alice E., & Whipple, Thomas W. (1983). *Sex stereotyping in advertising*. Lexington, MA: Lexington.

Courtney, Alice E., & Whipple, Thomas W. (1985). Female role portrayals in advertising and communication effectiveness: A review. *Journal of Advertising, 14*, 4-8, 17.

Dervin, Brenda, & Clark, Kathleen D. (1988). *Communication as cultural identity: The invention mandate*. Paper presented at the annual meeting of the International Association of Mass Communications Research, Barcelona, Spain.

Duffy, Margaret. (1991, August). *A critical review of studies of portrayals of women in advertising.* Paper presented at the annual meeting of the Association for Education in Journalism and Mass Communications, Boston.

Ferguson, Jill, Kreshel, Peggy, & Tinkham, Spencer. (1990). In the pages of *Ms.:* Sex role portrayals of women in advertising. *Journal of Advertising, 19,* 40-51.

Foltz, Kim. (1992, May 24). The look that sells both girl-next-door and celebrity. *New York Times Sunday Magazine,* p. 4F.

Fox, Stephen. (1984). *The mirror makers.* New York: William Morrow.

Furnham, Adrian. (1989). Gender stereotypes in Italian television advertisements. *Journal of Broadcasting and Electronic Media, 33*(2), 175-185.

Gagnard, Alice. (1986). From feast to famine: Depiction of ideal body type in magazine advertising: 1950-1984. In Ernest F. Larkin (Ed.), *Proceedings of the Nineteen Eighty-Six Conference of the American Academy of Advertising* (pp. R46-R50). Charleston, SC: American Academy of Advertising.

Garfinkel, Paul E. (1981, June). Some recent observations on the pathogenesis of anorexia nervosa. *Canadian Journal of Psychiatry, 26*(4), 218-223.

Garner, David, Garfinkel, Paul, Schwartz, Donald, & Thompson, Michael. (1980). Cultural expectations of thinness in women. *Psychological Reports, 47,* 483-491.

Gerbner, George. (1978). The dynamics of cultural resistance. In Gaye Tuchman, Arlene Kaplan Daniels, & James Benet (Eds.), *Hearth and home: Images of women in the mass media* (pp. 46-50). New York: Oxford University Press.

Gilly, M. C. (1988). Sex roles in advertising: A comparison of television advertisements in Australia, Mexico, and the United States. *Journal of Marketing, 52*(2), 75-85.

Goffman, Erving. (1979). *Gender advertisements.* New York: Colophon.

Griffin, Michael, Viswanath, K., & Schwartz, Dona. (1992). *Gender advertising in the U.S. and India: Exporting cultural stereotypes.* Minneapolis: University of Minnesota School of Journalism and Mass Communication.

Hellwig, Basia. (1986, November). How working women have changed America. *Working Woman,* pp. 129-150.

Hood, Marshall. (1993, February 2). Not a model standard. *The Columbus Dispatch,* pp. B1-2.

Kilbourne, Jean. (Producer & Moderator). (1987). *Still killing us softly: Advertising images of women* [Film]. Cambridge, MA: Cambridge Documentary Films.

Lazier-Smith, Linda. (1988). *The effect of changes in women's social status on images of women in magazine advertising: The Pingree-Hawkins sexism scale reapplied, Goffman reconsidered, Kilbourne revisited.* Unpublished doctoral dissertation, Indiana University.

Leiss, William, Kline, Stephen, & Jhally, Sut. (1986) *Social communication in advertising.* Toronto: Methuen.

Lippmann, Walter. (1922). *Public opinion.* New York: Free Press.

Lovdal, Lynn T. (1989). Sex role messages in television commercials: An update. *Sex Roles, 21,* 715-724.

McLuhan, Marshall. (1951). *The mechanical bride.* Boston: Beacon.

Minnigerode, Wendy. (1988). *Androcentric bias in print advertisements.* Unpublished master's thesis, University of Colorado at Colorado Springs.

Myers, Philip N., Jr., & Biocca, Frank A. (1992). The elastic body image: The effect of television advertising and programming on body image distortions in young women. *Journal of Communication, 42*(3), 108-133.

O'Donnell, William J., & O'Donnell, Karen J. (1978). Update: Sex-role messages in TV commercials. *Journal of Communication, 28,* 156-158.

Pingree, Suzanne, Hawkins, Robert P., Butler, Matilda, & Paisley, William. (1976). A scale of sexism. *Journal of Communication, 26,* 193-200.

Pollay, Richard W. (1986). The distorted mirror: Reflections on the unintended consequences of advertising. *Journal of Marketing, 50,* 18-36.

Potter, David M. (1954). *People of plenty: Economic abundance and the American character.* Chicago: University of Chicago Press.

Signorielli, N., & Morgan, M. (1990). *Cultivation analysis: New directions in media effects research.* Newbury Park, CA: Sage.

Silverstein, Brett, Perdue, Lauren, Peterson, Barbara, & Kelly, Eileen. (1986). The role of mass media in promoting a thin standard of bodily attractiveness for women. *Sex Roles, 14*(9/10), 519-532.

Smith, Linda Lazier. (1985, August). *Media images and ideal body shapes: A perspective on women with emphasis on anorexics.* Paper presented to the Association for Education in Journalism and Mass Communication.

Teegardin, Carol. (1992, November 15). The mature, over-40 woman is becoming fashionable. *Indianapolis Star,* p. H1.

Tuchman, Gaye, Daniels, Arlene Kaplan, & Benet, James. (Eds.). (1978). *Hearth and home: Images of women in the mass media.* New York: Oxford University Press.

Williamson, Judith. (1978). *Decoding advertisements: Ideology and meaning in advertising.* London: Marion Boyars.

Wolf, Naomi. (1991). *The beauty myth: How images of beauty are used against women.* New York: William Morrow.

13 Visual Images and Re-Imaging
A Review of Research in Mass Communication

JOHN R. McCLELLAND

The role of the mass media in presenting and constructing visual images of women was not explored in any detail in the first edition of this book. This chapter is intended to bridge that gap by reviewing some of the current research into such imagery in photography, television, videos and MTV, cinema, and cartoons. In addition, it will discuss some of the theoretical issues involved in audience perception of images and the social and cultural context of these images.

Research into images of women in the mass media tends to concentrate on portrayals and the broad mental images that are presumed to result. Women and minorities have long been portrayed in various mass media in stereotypical roles and in distorted or sexist images. Research on visual imagery—the nature of pictures and how they are presented—has not been a central focus of the effort. Of 101 articles examined for this chapter, only 25 dealt specifically with visual images.

Moreover, much of the research on portrayals concentrates on evaluation of gender differences in content or on a quantitative accounting of female underrepresentation. Critical feminist theory has begun to challenge this research orientation and to shift the discussion toward finding woman-centered meaning from existing media images, or to creating new woman-centered images (Brown, 1990; Rakow, 1992).

AUTHOR'S NOTE: Thanks to William Grisham at Roosevelt University for help with advertising concepts, and to Marilyn Crafton Smith at Appalachian State University for comments on an earlier draft of this chapter.

Ironically, published work on visual portrayals remains predominantly verbal in it presentation. Of 101 sources for this chapter, only 39 had illustrations of any sort except tables of data, while 64 others relied entirely on text and tables. When we exclude books, videos, databases, the popular press, and the industry-or-trade press, the illustrated work drops to 8 in 44 (or 18%) in scholarly journals.

However, no matter what theoretical approach, research method, or form of presentation the authors take, there is agreement on the premise that visual images are powerful means of communication. A single picture can convey impressions quickly, without need for verbalization, and it can convey intended or unintended messages subconsciously. Pictures can carry cultural symbolism.

There is substantial research to indicate that visual images do affect mental images and behavior. This concept is central to Wanta's (1989) study of wire-service and newspaper sports photos, Duncan's (1990) report on newsmagazine and sports magazine photos, the Myers and Biocca (1982) discussion, and others like it, of body imagery and self-perception in TV advertising, and Signorielli's (1989) examination of television portrayals of gender roles.

Growing a Concept

We can find roots of today's concern about the patterns of sexist visual imagery in the women's movement in the 1970s, after rapid social change in the 1960s. Advertising, television drama, cinema, newspaper and magazine editorial content, television news assignments, and more, have all been found to have sexist and ethnic stereotyping in both the verbal and visual content.

Two early works that dealt specifically with woman's image in the mass media were concerned primarily with the overall portrayal and resulting mental image. Tuchman, Daniels, and Benet (1978) and King and Stott (1977) were among many whose work showed the stereotypical and sexist functioning of woman's image in advertising and other media content. These authors/editors and their chapter authors examined portrayals on American and British television in general, in children's television, in magazine advertising and editorial content, and specifically on magazine covers.

Photography in Newspapers and Magazines

Editors and other members of the editorial, art, and photography staffs have a significant influence on the images presented in newspapers and magazines. This section describes studies of how these influences affect the resulting visual images, particularly in terms of sexism and "face-ism."

"The camera never lies" is true only to the extent that lying is an act of choice, because the camera cannot think or choose. The camera, especially if followed by an airbrush or a computer retouching station, certainly can be used in ways that distort its images.

Subject selection is an editorial decision that profoundly affects the nature of the filmed images and thus the choices of which pictures to publish, where and how. Location, camera angle, focus, timing, lighting, and expression all affect the shot. Then cropping, scaling, retouching or highlighting, placement, captioning, and context all affect the picture's final impression.

Editors give informal clues about preferred subject matter, make specific assignments, and decide what pictures to publish and how. Despite efforts by the National Press Photographers Association, *USA Today,* and some others, we find that editors of almost all sorts at newspapers and at most types of magazines still tend to be predominantly male.[1]

Like much sex-role investigation, research in this area tends to concentrate on "image" in the sense of social-role portrayal. But even when simply counting the number of photographs of males and females, these researchers have found quantitative differences that reflect real qualitative differences. They have noted that these differences result both from general social norms and from the publications' editorial processes.

Several studies have focused on women's images in newspaper and magazine news-editorial photographs. For example, men outnumbered women in photos, by ratios of about 3:1, in nearly all sections of several U.S. newspapers examined by Miller (1975), Blackwood (1983), and Luebke (1989).[2] These findings of underrepresentation in newspaper photographs parallel the verbal underrepresentation of women via byline, source reference, or story subject as discussed in Potter's (1985) work on gender-role portrayals in newspapers, and by Greenwald's (1990) study of all kinds of references in newspaper business sections, and by others.

Men outnumbered women, and were shown in less sexist ways, in magazine news photos during the Olympic Games (Duncan, 1990). Duncan (1990) says photographers and editors "are often unaware of the ideological significations of photographs, [but] photos nonetheless serve to shape consensus" (pp. 22-23). Duncan reviewed 1,300 photos in six magazines during two Olympic years and found similarities between some sports photos and the posing of women in soft-core pornography ("cheesecake"). She also reported more posed and sensuous pictures of female athletes, and more vigorous action shots of male athletes; more intrusion on female competitors' privacy (shown crying, or adjusting the crotch of a swimsuit);

and a perception that male-oriented sports magazines used photos that abet men's sense of dominance or erotic fantasies.

Wanta and Leggett (1989) examined wire-service photographs from Wimbledon and newspaper use of these tennis photos. They did not find the concentration on women's bodies and men's faces that Duncan did. They did find the wire service providing more images of emotional men, and the sports editors using more images of women in helpless poses or situations.

Facial prominence is a concept with multiple meanings in photography. Modern media often use the "tight head-shot," nearly filling the picture with the speaker's face. The proportion of a photograph occupied by the face can indicate editorial valuation of brains over body. Thus "face-ism" has been defined as greater facial prominence of men in popular images.[3]

In a decade, facial prominence rose for both sexes, and faster for women, but in most cases women still trailed in this regard in general-circulation magazines' editorial photos (Nigro, Hill, Gelbein, & Clark, 1988, pp. 229-231). These authors contended that even minor differences in scores were both significant statistically and important for understanding, especially in the extreme case of truly big-face pictures. Men appeared in the overwhelming majority of these tightly cropped big-face pictures, those presumed to give maximum valuation to brains over body and to portray the highest sense of authority. Dodd, Harcar, and Foerch (1989) partially replicated the work of Nigro et al., and added a finding that women were more likely to be shown with their mouths open, implying a less serious nature.

Several studies of print media have found rather consistent stereotypical portrayals, with women as homemakers and caregivers, and men in business and leadership. The ones that address pictorial content specifically are Miller (1975), newspaper representation generally; Blackwood (1983), various Eastern newspapers; Nigro et al. (1988), magazine content; Luebke (1989), roles portrayed in newspaper news photos; Johnson and Christ (1988) and Dodd et al. (1989), appearances on newsmagazine covers; Lester (1988), visual elements generally on newspaper front pages; and Duncan (1990), sports photos. These were primarily content analyses that counted appearances and evaluated portrayals of implied gender-based social roles.

Television: News, Entertainment—and MTV

Moving pictures, usually in color and with sound, make this ubiquitous mass medium a powerful tool of sales, persuasion, information, education, entertainment, and socialization. Cablecasting, satellite broadcasting, videocassette sales, and video rentals have multiplied the opportunities for variety of visual presentations on the TV set.

This section discusses women's roles in news and portrayals in entertainment via the video telecommunications medium, and it considers production factors that affect portrayal, such as physical appearance and camera angle.

What sorts of role models do the two sexes see on TV? Several studies found sexist stereotyping in advertising and entertainment content.

Advertising tone has shifted, in some cases to confront issues raised earlier by the women's movement (Ellis, 1990), but women still are portrayed much as they were a decade before (Lovdal, 1989). Signorielli (1989) found little change in the traditional representations of gender roles in prime-time entertainment over a period of 17 years (p. 358). Reep and Dambrot (1988) found that in prime-time drama, an actor's role tended to influence perception more than the actor's sex did.

The advertising chapter of this book by Lazier and Kendrick addresses these issues in detail.

Others found less favorable visibility of women in news. Fung (1988) found women anchors paired with and overshadowed by older men. Sanders (1990, and elsewhere) has discussed the problems inherent in aging and the slow process of moving women into true decision-making roles. Stilson (1990) found little change in the unequal ladders to success in broadcast news, partly because visual appeal mattered more in selection and promotion of women.[4]

Women are poorly represented as makers of news and as sources in broadcast news reporting, and men are interviewed on-camera as news sources (authorities) more often than women are, which reinforces stereotyping (Rakow & Kranich, 1991).

We might also ask more subtle questions about video content, such as what subconscious message viewers receive when taller camera operators (still predominantly men) look downward upon shorter female sources, even when the camera is on an adjustable tripod. Duncan (1990) raised this sort of question about camera angle in still photography. Even casual viewing indicates that some producers are aware of the symbolic potential of relative eye level.

Janet Stilson (1990) is one of several who have summed up two decades of action on women's visibility and influence in television news:

> For all the advances women have made in the TV news business, glamour and sex-appeal still play a primary role in the way female journalists are chosen and utilized at both the national and local level—a surface indication of less

visible disparities that continue to frustrate TV newswomen. . . . Call it the *Cosmo*-girl factor. (p. 24)[5]

Visually, television newswomen bear additional burdens including both youthfulness and aging. Lacking newswomen in the early 1970s, networks and major stations have tended to select attractive-and-talented young women for rapid promotion, ready or not (Fung, 1988, p. 21). Christine Craft sued her station, for example, alleging dismissal because of her age and appearance (Ferri & Keller, 1986; Schoonmaker, 1987). Some TV women want a nest-egg by mid-career, before management sees age lines and drives them off-camera (Foote, 1992, p. 40; Sanders, 1990, p. 24).

Male network anchors tend to be older and grayer than their female colleagues. Foote and Sanders say women haven't been in these jobs long enough to be truly tested by time and wrinkles. They agree with Fung that Barbara Walters, over 60 and still doing prime-time TV in 1993, was rare indeed. She's truly an exception, because for raters of TV magazine show talent generally, "physical attractiveness was the only characteristic judged more important for females" (Serra & Kallan, 1983, p. 537).

In terms of women's images in broadcast news, several questions remain unanswered:

- Will the aging of the baby boomers make older women more acceptable on TV news?
- Will the beauty myth survive on high-definition TV?
- Why, in a fair world, would we have to care?

Women's on-camera roles in news and their portrayals in entertainment have generated extensive discussion, some of which appears in this book's television section by Sanders (Chapter 10a) and by Smith, Fredin, and Ferguson Nardone (Chapter 10b).

Another crucial TV image issue is portrayal of women in entertainment programming. In TV drama, for example, studies have found some changes, and some variation from the predominant stereotyping of women as domestic, emotional, indecisive, unimportant, dependent on men, and so on.

Conventionalisms and the status quo continued to dominate drama programs from the 1960s through the 1980s, despite a few women's roles portraying what the researchers coded as "good," or "modern," or working, or self-sufficient women (Reep & Dambrot, 1987, 1988; Signorielli, 1989). To some, these characteristics reflect movement away from debilitating stereotypes; to others, some of them reflect script writers' disdain for the "family values" that were one issue in the 1992 presidential campaign.

Asked to describe how TV portrays women, members of a public sample split into two camps, one quarter "traditional" and three quarters "contemporary" (Atwood, Zahn, & Webber, 1986).

One approach to gradual change of the images is being attempted in Canada, where government has imposed "voluntary" regulatory guidelines about avoiding sexist stereotyping ("Canadian Broadcasters," 1987; Christopher, 1984).

Music video, especially MTV, bloomed during the 1980s. It added compelling visual imagery to the powerful sound of youth-oriented rock music. Writers disagree about much of the interpretation of images on MTV, but they do not dispute its appeal to its intended audience. Some say female artists of a new kind are using music and visual images to change perceptions and to redefine concepts and roles of women.

Sex and violence on TV have drawn criticism since the 1950s (Kalis & Neuendorf, 1989), and MTV attracted its own critics when it began in 1981. It has provoked organized opposition (Colford, 1985). It has been subjected to content studies of: aggressive cues, by Kalis and Neuendorf (1989); social symbolism, by Lorch (1988); traditional and sexist depiction of gender roles, by Vincent, Davis, and Boruszkowski (1987); sexism in music videos, by Vincent (1989); and social learning via music video, by Christenson and Roberts (1990). MTV and its imagery of women are in books: Kaplan (1987) and Lewis (1990) include elements of the growing debate whether MTV promotes sexism or promotes female self-empowerment; Denisof (1988) is largely historical but addresses the mixed reactions to the question whether MTV content is "Misogyny, Exploitation or Just Fun" (pp. 313-314). And MTV is debated in the popular press: Harrison (1991) and Carlson (1990) explored the actions and images of female rock stars; Sudo (1990) has suggested that these performers are leading a new sort of women's movement; and Herrmann (1992) further documented producers' reliance on "What looks good on the screen."

Several observers said women were portrayed in sexist ways far more often than men were; one study found half of the women dressed provocatively, and many portrayed as sex objects (Sherman & Dominick, 1986, p. 83).

Some feminist researchers, however, have called for a re-visioning of the images of men and women on TV. They contend that MTV and its female stars have been bashing down barriers and making new opportunities and social attitudes for women (Harrison, 1991; Lewis, 1990). Madonna, for example, consciously manufactures such controversies, exploiting a vixen stereotype (Harrison, 1991; Sudo, 1990). Cyndi Lauper, Pat Benatar, and Tina Turner project strength and control, defusing the stereotypes in different ways, some authors assert (Barol, 1985; Harrison, 1991; Lewis,

1990; Sudo, 1990). Some see a constructive role for the nontraditional, sexually provocative performances of Madonna and others, bridging a gap between postmodernist philosophy and feminist ideology (Schwichtenberg, 1992).

Cinema and Cartoons

Research into gender-related imagery in cinema, cinema criticism, and print cartooning is, again, primarily focused on sexist portrayals and quantitative differences in presentation.

Movies and television share the difficulty of separating the strictly visual imagery from the broad mental image of portrayal. And they share the relatively new medium of the home videocassette.

The voluminous published material about cinema images of women deals mostly with the overall portrayal rather than the strictly visual aspects of that portrayal. There is an apparent assumption that filmmakers know how to create visual images consistent with the intended mental images. Thus we find comment upon individual performers' reputations (Kristin, 1989; Rollyson, 1987), the implications of specific, aggressive, female roles (Ellis, 1990), the industry effects of female directors and ageism in casting (Rosenbaum, 1987), sexism and sex-goddess reputation (Kristin, 1989), and even fat-ism (Hersey, 1992).

Women have been commercial artists and publication cartoonists since before the turn of the century, but they often portray women in negative ways, just as their male brethren do.[6] For a while, most of the top-line courtroom artists in the Midwest were women, and bailiffs treated them as "you girls" (Smith, 1981, p. 32).[7] Feminism's public profile after the 1960s evoked a spate of cartoons. In "Gender Inversion Cartoons" from *Playboy* and *Pulling Our Own Strings,* a feminist anthology, Hammond (1991) said cartoonists used visual gimmicks to emphasize physical differences or reverse the sexes' usual social roles. Geraldine Ferraro, the first woman candidate for nationwide elective office, attracted arguably sexist imagery from newspaper editorial cartoonists early in the 1984 campaign, but later got a mixed response (Sena, 1985).

Images of Minorities

Negative portrayals affect not only the female majority of the population but also, and sometimes viciously, groups who are minorities. Race, ethnicity, age, religion, handicap, and sexual preference are a few of the more commonly cited such characteristics. Multiple factors that relate to discrimination can be present in a single person's life or a single media product.

References to minority status were included, generally as a minor aside or a subordinate issue, in approximately one fourth of the U.S.-based works examined primarily for this chapter's study of women's images. As in much imagery work in general, those studies that also deal with minority issues tend to count representations and evaluate the social roles portrayed. But some go beyond, examining the nature of the visual images and its relationship to potential effect on mental images, or examining the potential for stimulating a change in social mores (Brown & Campbell, 1986; Schwichtenberg, 1992).

Canada, with particularly sensitive relationships among its dominant culture, its indigenous peoples, and its recent immigrants, has done several studies of the media images of women and minorities. In a study of 30 years of print media, MacGregor (1989) found minority women to be severely underrepresented and usually portrayed in stereotypical ways.

Perusal of North American and some European works on images of women and minorities leaves these general impressions:

The patterns of insensitivity found in much media content about women is also found for minorities. For all minority groups, this can be severe underrepresentation, and especially for the larger racial-ethnic minorities it can involve derogatory or stereotypical portrayals.

In some media, the implicit messages are distinctly mixed. Brown and Campbell (1986) found MTV perpetuating the status quo, whereas Black Entertainment Television music videos were more likely to portray both minorities and women as helpful or caring individuals. Others, including Lewis (1990, p. 218) have seen MTV as providing a mix of role models that includes increasingly relevant imagery of and for young Blacks or Hispanics—especially males.

Just as both the images of women and the images of minorities deserve continuing research, the imagery of minority women as a distinct category warrants more of its own study.

Advertising's Appeal

Sex sells. That idea is not new, but its use in mainstream mass media advertising has grown immensely.

As mentioned earlier, advertising's treatment of women is explored extensively in Chapter 12, the advertising chapter of this book. Here, let us touch briefly on the visual imagery that advertising uses so powerfully.

This imagery is more than the obvious use of attractive models to catch the potential consumer's attention. It has several characteristics:

1. Objectification. The woman adorns the ad or the product and is perceived as a sex object. ("Heavenly body" strolls past an Eclipse sports car.)
2. Seduction. The woman's role in the ad, and in the male consumer's fantasy life, is sexually suggestive. (The right car or the right beer helps fellas get girls.)
3. Self-Gratification. If the target consumer is female, the woman in the ad is equipping herself to attract or please a man. (Or she may fulfill herself in a socially defined way.)
4. Stereotyping. If sex appeal is absent in an ad, sex-role stereotyping can be present. ("Housewife" actresses sell soap, and male "executive" actors sell investments.)
5. Underrepresentation. Women (and minorities) simply are not seen as much, except in female-oriented material. (Simply being on TV or in print implies importance.)[8]

Advertising uses market research to target the intended audiences. Skilled ad makers of both sexes know about nonverbal coding, symbolism, and the like.

Re-Imaging Visual Issues

Visual images in the media can be seen as symbols of power. Who gets to look at whom, in what ways, is one issue (Gamman & Marshment, 1988/1989).[9]

Recent feminist research has looked at content, image, and representation of gender in the mass media as discourses about power, rather than as issues of equal opportunity or sexist portrayals. Gallagher (1992) has identified two distinct feminist research approaches to media content from the 1980s: film theory and cultural studies.

Feminist film theory is being used to "explore how the media 'construct' definitions of femininity and masculinity (definitions which are often competing and contradictory); and also how these definitions create specific 'subject positions' with which viewers and readers may identify" (Gallagher, 1992, p. 4). This approach rejects the notion that the media mirror reality and places media producers in an active role of constructing meaning, which serves to reproduce patterns of domination and subordination.

Research in this vein explores the notion that images are "re-presentations" because it is impossible to reproduce reality. Several contributions in Lana F. Rakow's (1992) book, *Women Making Meaning: New Feminist Directions in Communication,* suggest that introduction of feminist theory into communication promises to revolutionize research about images of women in media content and how that content is produced.

Cultural studies' contribution to critical feminist theory is the concept that meanings are constructed "as part of a set of social and power relations" (Gallagher, 1992, p. 4). This approach has been used to understand how women construct meaning from forms of popular culture traditionally considered repressive. Mary Ellen Brown (1990) and Lorraine Gamman and Margaret Marshment (1988/1989) have edited two collections of essays that explore the ways in which women negotiate their own meanings and construct visions of empowerment from media content.

The potential contribution of these two research streams to re-image women in the media is largely unrealized. However, the relationship between power and the representation of the female body in media imagery is rapidly becoming clearer. Mary Desjardins, discussing ideas presented by Susan Rubin Suleiman and numerous others, states the case:

> No matter how complex or mediated the relationship, there is a connection between cultural representations of woman/woman's body and not only how political power is distributed among the sexes but also how gender identity is reinforced and perpetuated in that culture. (Desjardins, 1989, p. 67)[10]

That is a strong case for re-presenting the media imagery of the human female for the same reasons this book argues for re-visioning gender values in journalism and mass communication.

Notes

1. Women are few and rarely powerful in newspaper management: Garneau (1988), Rich (1987). The National Press Photographer's Association, the American Society of Newspaper Editors, other professional groups, and some publishers are trying: Williamson (1985), and Editor & Publisher "Equality in Staffing" (1985).

2. This author's calculations, from the researchers' published tabular data. Traditional women's pages were the exception, and sports pages were the extreme, 15:1 male in one case.

3. See Archer, Iritani, Kimes, and Barrios (1983); Dodd, Harcar, and Foerch (1989); Nigro, Hill, Gelbein, and Clark (1988).

4. TV sports sexism: After baseball's Golden Glove Awards, a sportscaster showed video of a female torso wearing two small, shiny, bra-like cups: ". . . and Madonna got . . . two Golden Globes." The co-anchor seemed to glower at him and bite her tongue (WMAQ Chicago, 10:27 p.m., November 5, 1992). Radio journalist Dale Willman saw a similar incident in Boston in October 1992 (private communication).

5. Stilson (1990) refers to *Cosmopolitan* magazine's consistent use of a beautiful young woman's face or face-and-torso in a studio photograph on the cover, and to the emphasis on youthful female beauty in much *Cosmo* content.

6. Sheppard (1984), especially the self-deprecating self-portrait by Peggy Bacon on p. 46. Female comic-strip cartoonists are not so rare as they were a few years ago, and some bring a fresh touch to the genre (Briggs, 1991).

7. This is one of the traces of gritty reality that show through the book's generally rose-colored outlook.

8. The list is distilled from ideas presented by Carolyn Faulder in King and Stott (1977), pp. 37-64; O'Donnell and O'Donnell in Tuchman et al. (1978); Lovdal (1989); MacGregor (1989); Craig (1992); Mazzella, Durkin, Cerini, and Buralli, (1992); and others.

9. Pornography remains a volatile and controversial issue. In some commentary upon media imagery, anger seems to be near the surface. Caputi (1988), for example, is one of those who draws connections between phallic shapes in advertising imagery and a patriarchal society where military rockets get priority over starving people.

10. Desjardins's essay discusses the work of 25 contributors to Suleiman's (1986) anthology, and others.

References

Archer, Dane, Iritani, Bonita, Kimes, Debra D., & Barrios, Michael. (1983). Face-ism: Five studies of sex differences in facial prominence. *Journal of Personality and Social Psychology, 45,* 725-735.

Atwood, Rita A., Zahn, Susan Brown, & Webber, Gale. (1986). Perceptions of the traits of women on television. *Journal of Broadcasting and Electronic Media, 30*(1), 95-101.

Barol, Bill. (1985, March 4). Women in a video cage. *Newsweek, 105,* p. 54.

Blackwood, Roy E. (1983). The content of news photos: Roles portrayed by men and women. *Journalism Quarterly, 60,* 710-714.

Briggs, Pamela. (Producer). (1991). *Four women's voices in the comics* [Video film]. Chicago: Illinois Arts Council and WYCC-TV.

Brown, Mary Ellen. (Ed.). (1990). *Television and women's culture: The politics of the popular.* Newbury Park, CA: Sage.

Brown, Jane D., & Campbell, Kenneth. (1986). Race and gender in music videos: The same beat but a different drummer. *Journal of Communication, 36,* 94-106.

Canadian broadcasters must follow guidelines on sex stereotyping. (1987, January 19). *Broadcasting,* pp. 220, 224.

Caputi, Jane. (1988). Seeing elephants: The myths of phallotechnology. *Feminist Studies, 14*(3), 487-524.

Carlson, Timothy. (1990, September 1-7). Rock's leading ladies [cover story]. *TV Guide, 38,* 2-6.

Christenson, Peter G., & Roberts, Donald F. (1990). *Popular music in early adolescence.* Working paper prepared for the U.S. Congress Office of Technology Assessment, Adolescent Health Project [in ERIC data base #Ed323021].

Christopher, Maurine. (1984, April 23). Canada grapples with sex stereotypes. *Advertising Age, 55,* p. 90.

Colford, Steven W. (1985, August 19). D.C. wives aim at MTV; Ads next? *Advertising Age, 56,* pp. 1, 72.

Craig, R. Stephen. (1992). The effect of television day part on gender portrayals in television commercials: A content analysis. *Sex Roles, 25*(5/6), 197-211.

Denisof, R. Serge. (1988). *Inside MTV.* New Brunswick, NJ: Transaction Books.

Desjardins, Mary. (1989). (Re)Presenting the female body. *Quarterly Review of Film & Video, 11,* 67-73.

Dodd, David K., Foerch, Barbara J., & Anders, H. T. (1989). Content analysis of women and racial minorities as news magazine cover persons. *Journal of Social Behavior and Personality, 3*(3), 231-236.

Dodd, David K., Harcar, Veronica, & Foerch, Barbara J. (1989). Face-ism and facial expressions of women in magazine photos. *Psychological Record, 39,* 325-331.

Duncan, Margaret Carlisle. (1990). Sports photographs and sexual differences: Images of women and men in the 1984 and 1988 Olympic Games. *Sociology of Sport Journal, 7,* 23-43.

Ellis, Kate. (1990). Fatal attraction, or the post-modern Prometheus. *Journal of Sex Research, 27*(1), 111-121.

Equality in staffing—a key element at *USA Today.* (1985, October 26). *Editor & Publisher,* p. 30.

Ferri, Anthony J., & Keller, Jo E. (1986). Perceived career barriers for female television news anchors. *Journalism Quarterly, 63,* 463-467.

Foote, Joe S. (1992). Women correspondents' visibility on the network evening news. *Mass Communication Review, 19*(1/2), 36-40.

Fung, Victoria. (1988, October). Anchor jobs go to young women and experienced men. *Washington Journalism Review,* pp. 20-24.

Gallagher, Margaret. (1992). Women and men in the media. *Communication Research Trends, 12*(1), 1-15.

Gamman, Lorraine, & Marshment, Margaret. (Eds.). (1989). *The female gaze.* Seattle, WA: Real Comet Press. (Originally published by The Women's Press, London, 1988)

Garneau, George. (1988, June 11). Women on the masthead. *Editor & Publisher, 121,* p. 114.

Greenwald, Marilyn S. (1990). Gender representation in newspaper business sections. *Newspaper Research Journal, 11*(1), 68-79.

Hammond, Joyce D. (1991). Gender inversion cartoons and feminism. *Journal of Popular Culture, 24,* 145-160.

Harrison, Barbara Grizzuti. (1991, June). Can Madonna justify Madonna? *Mademoiselle, 97,* p. 80.

Herrmann, Brenda. (1992, May 10). Substance, not sex/Wilson sisters strive to be themselves. *Chicago Tribune,* WomanNews section, p. 2.

Hersey, Brook. (1992, February). Kathy Bates talks about being overweight in Hollywood and how she'd like to see movie images of women change. *Glamour, 90,* pp. 110, 200.

Johnson, Sammye, & Christ, William G. (1988). Women through *Time:* Who gets covered. *Journalism Quarterly, 65*(4), 889-897.

Kalis, Pamela, & Neuendorf, Kimberly A. (1989). Aggressive cue prominence and gender participation in MTV. *Journalism Quarterly, 66,* 148-154.

Kaplan, E. Ann. (1987). *Rocking around the clock: Music television, post modernism, and consumer culture.* New York: Methuen.

King, Josephine, & Stott, Mary. (Eds.). (1977). *Is this your life? Images of women in the media.* London: Virago.

Kristin, Jack. (1989, April). The many faces of Eve/The changing image of the sex goddess. *American Film, 14,* 39-41.

Lester, Paul. (1988). Use of visual elements of newspaper front pages. *Journalism Quarterly, 65,* 760-763.

Lewis, Lisa A. (1990). *Gender politics and MTV: Voicing the difference.* Philadelphia: Temple University Press.

Lorch, Sue. (1988). Metaphor, metaphysics and MTV. *Journal of Popular Culture, 22,* 143-155.

Lovdal, Lynn T. (1989). Sex role messages in television commercials: An update. *Sex Roles, 21*(2), 715-724.

Luebke, Barbara F. (1989). Out of focus: Images of women and men in newspaper photographs. *Sex Roles, 20*(3/4), 121-133.

MacGregor, Robert M. (1989). The distorted mirror: Images of visible minority women in Canadian print advertising. *Atlantis, 15*(1), 137-143.

Mazzella, Carmela, Durkin, Kevin, Cerini, Emma, & Buralli, Paul. (1992). Sex role stereotyping in Australian television advertisements. *Sex Roles, 26*(7/8), 243-259.

Miller, Susan H. (1975). The content of news photos: Women's and men's roles. *Journalism Quarterly, 52,* 70-75.

Myers, Philip N., Jr., & Biocca, Frank A. (1992). The elastic body image: The effect of television advertising and programming on body image distortions in young women. *Journal of Communication, 42*(3), 108-131.

Nigro, Georgia N., Hill, Dina E., Gelbein, Martha E., & Clark, Catherine L. (1988). Changes of facial prominence of women and men over the last decade. *Psychology of Women Quarterly, 12,* 225-235.

Potter, W. James. (1985). Gender representation in elite newspapers. *Journalism Quarterly, 62,* 636-640.

Rakow, Lana F., & Kranich, Kimberlie. (1991). Woman as sign in television news. *Journal of Communication, 41*(1), 8-23.

Rakow, Lana F. (Ed.). (1992). *Women making meaning: New feminist directions in communication.* New York: Routledge & Kegan Paul.

Reep, Diana C., & Dambrot, Faye H. (1987). Television's professional women: Working with men in the 1980s. *Journalism Quarterly, 64,* 376-381.

Reep, Diana C., & Dambrot, Faye H. (1988). In the eye of the beholder/viewer perceptions of TV's male/female working partners. *Communication Research, 15*(1), 51-69.

Rich, Carole. (1987, September 5). A close-up look at women journalists. *Editor & Publisher, 120,* pp. 56, 45.

Rollyson, Carl E., Jr. (1987). More than a popcorn Venus: Contemporary women reshape the myth of Marilyn Monroe. *Journal of American Culture, 10,* 19-25.

Rosenbaum, Byron. (1987, March). The tyranny of the tight butt. *Mademoiselle, 93,* pp. 101, 104.

Sanders, Marlene. (1990, February). The long-term solution: Time/But as solutions go, that isn't good enough. *The Quill, 78,* 23-25.

Schoonmaker, Mary Ellen. (1987, March-April). TV news and the face-lift factor. *Columbia Journalism Review, 25,* 48, 50.

Schwichtenberg, Cathy. (1992). Madonna's postmodern feminism: Bringing the margins to the center. *The Southern Communication Journal, 57*(2), 120.

Sena, John R. (1985). A picture is worth a thousand votes: Geraldine Ferraro and the editorial cartoonists. *Journal of American Culture, 8,* 2-12.

Serra, Michele R., & Kallan, Richard A. (1983). Sexual egalitarianism on TV: An analysis of PM Magazine. *Journalism Quarterly, 60,* 535-538.

Sheppard, Alice. (1984). There were ladies present: American women cartoonists and comic artists in the early twentieth century. *Journal of American Culture, 7,* 38-48.

Sherman, Barry L., & Dominick, Joseph R. (1986). Violence and sex in music videos: TV and rock 'n' roll. *Journal of Communication, 36,* 79-93.

Signorielli, Nancy. (1989). Television and conceptions about sex roles: Maintaining conventionality and the status quo. *Sex Roles, 21*(5/6), 341-360.

Silverstein, Brett, Perdue, Lauren, Peterson, Barbara, & Kelly, Eileen. (1986). The role of the mass media in promoting a thin standard of bodily attractiveness for women. *Sex Roles, 14*(10), 519-532.

Smith, Betsy Covington. (1981). *Breakthrough: Women in television.* New York: Walker & Co.

Stilson, Janet. (1990, September 24). Stuck on the ground floor: Men and women climb different, unequal ladders in TV news; It's likely to stay that way. *Channels, 10,* 20-26.

Suleiman, Susan Rubin. (Ed.). (1986). *The female body in western culture: Contemporary perspectives.* Cambridge, MA: Harvard University Press.

Sudo, Philip. (1990, May 18). Pop music's new women's movement. *Scholastic Update (Teachers' edition), 122,* p. 13.

Trahey, Jane. (1985, August 13). Hey, ladies! Open wide! *Advertising Age, 56,* p. 2.

Tuchman, Gaye, Daniels, Arlene Kaplan, & Benet, James. (Eds.). (1978). *Hearth and home: Images of women in the mass media.* New York: Oxford University Press.

Vincent, Richard C., Davis, Kenneth K., & Boruszkowski, Lilly-Ann. (1987). Sexism on MTV: The portrayal of women in rock videos. *Journalism Quarterly, 64,* 750-755.

Vincent, Richard C. (1989). Clio's consciousness raised? Portrayal of women in rock videos, re-examined. *Journalism Quarterly, 66,* 155-160.

Wanta, Wayne. (1989). The effects of dominant photographs: An agenda-setting experiment. *Journalism Quarterly, 65,* 107-111.

Wanta, Wayne, & Leggett, Dawn. (1989). Gender stereotypes in wire service sports photos. *Newspaper Research Journal, 10*(3), 105-114.

Williamson, Lenora. (1985, August 17). Beyond Tokenism/Women photographers focus on their status and how to achieve managerial roles. *Editor & Publisher, 120,* 17.

PART THREE

Perspectives on the Mass Communication Classroom

14 Women in Mass Communication Education
Progress, Problems, and Prospects

K. VISWANATH
GERALD M. KOSICKI
PAMELA J. CREEDON

The environment in academia has changed radically in recent times in resonance with the changes in other sectors of the society. Principal among the
changes is the infusion of disenfranchised groups, such as women, in relatively large numbers into colleges and universitics. Simply said, women
are entering the ranks of university students and faculty in greater numbers
than ever. The principal objective of this chapter is to examine and report
on some of the conditions in which women faculty work in journalism and
mass communication (J&MC) teaching and research in order to gain a better
understanding of the academic environment in which this transformation
is occurring. This chapter will report on the status of women in mass communication education.[1]

We are interested in three broad groups of questions. First, what are the
socio-demographic characteristics of women faculty members in mass communication education and how are they different from men? We are interested

AUTHORS' NOTE: This research was primarily funded by the Association for Education in Journalism and Mass Communication (AEJMC) and the AEJMC Commission on the Status of Women. Additional essential support was provided by the
Summer Research Opportunity Program administered by The Ohio State University Graduate School and the School of Journalism of The Ohio State University.
Fieldwork was completed by AEJMC headquarters under the supervision of
Jennifer McGill and her assistants. We thank Terry Hynes for her support of the
project, and acknowledge the helpful comments of Pamela J. Shoemaker and
Sue A. Lafky, and the technical assistance of Eunkyung Park and Julius Mayo.

in the distribution of age, education, tenure status, rank, salary, teaching and professional experience.

Second, we explore the institutional milieu in which they work. What are the conditions under which they teach? This includes such things as course loads, research facilities (graduate assistants, and other research support), advising (number of students advised, advising of professional student clubs, etc.), and service (number of committees, professional contacts, among others). Another aspect of institutional milieu is the opportunities and barriers present in the advancement of their academic careers. For example, are there special efforts made by the departments to promote faculty scholarship through such mechanisms as mentoring and other incentives? Do such awards vary among different groups? If so, what are the factors that influence these arrangements?

A third factor that we need to examine includes the career patterns of the faculty. For various reasons, journalism skills teaching and mass media scholarship have come to share the roof in schools and departments of journalism and mass communication (Delia, 1987). Tensions have resulted from departments' attempts to balance skills and conceptual training. This tension may have a profound impact on teaching and research and the rewards associated with each. It is essential therefore to examine how the variable of professional experience affects entry and advancement in academia. A number of studies have documented the barriers and discrimination faced by women within the communication industry (Lafky, 1989; Smith, Fredin, & Nardone, 1989). To what degree does insistence of mass communication departments on professional experience add an additional barrier to the recruitment and advancement of women in the field?

There is yet another issue. According to some scholars (e.g., Betz & Fitzgerald, 1987), the common wisdom was that women had to make two decisions: whether to have a career outside home and if so what career to pursue. They had to weigh their career decisions against traditionally "more important" decisions such as marriage and family (also see Angrist & Almquist, 1975; Betz & Fitzgerald, 1987; Kriger, 1972). Women today also face "role overload": They have to experience multiple roles resulting in role conflicts. In light of these issues, the questions for us involve understanding how these choices, in addition to the ones previously mentioned, affect them. That is, how do multiple roles of spouse, parent, and faculty member, including teacher and researcher, affect their perceptions of their job?

On perception, we will particularly focus on the level of satisfaction with their work. Are women and men equally satisfied or dissatisfied with their jobs? What factors determine job satisfaction? And, do the same factors determine job satisfaction for men and women? In summary, this chapter seeks to understand the environment in which most women journalism and communication faculty operate.

Historical Overview

Interest in the status of women in journalism and mass communication education had its roots in a 1972 study by Rush, Oukrup, and Ernst (1972). The impetus for the study came from a realization that very little was known at the time about female faculty in journalism and communication education. One of its many recommendations was to conduct a more extensive study to examine the perceptions as well as conditions of entry of women into journalism and mass communication education. The present Association for Education in Journalism and Mass Communication's (AEJMC) Commission on the Status of Women in Journalism emerged from one of the recommendations made by the Rush et al. (1972) study.

Subsequently, Sharp, VanSlyke Turk, Einsiedel, Schamber, and Hollenback (1985) conducted a more extensive examination of the working conditions of women faculty and students in journalism and mass communication education. Using multiple methods that included surveys, follow-up interviews, and a content analysis to assess scholarship, the study provided useful data to monitor the progress of women, as well as to articulate some of the major concerns. Schamber (1989) followed up with a more limited examination in 1988. One of the methods in both of these studies included data from Association of Schools of Journalism and Mass Communication, as well as a count of the membership directory of AEJMC. The Sharp et al. (1985) study also included "personal interviews with leaders" in the field.

Finally, Weaver and Wilhoit (1988) conducted a study to report on the number, geographical distribution, demographic profile, and the working conditions including job satisfaction of journalism and mass communication educators. Their methodology was different from the earlier studies: The population for their study included all full-time faculty teaching in journalism and mass communication in 4-year colleges and universities in the United States. The sampling frame was developed from a comprehensive listing obtained from a number of directories. We will cite these earlier findings to contrast with ours as necessary.

Methods

A seven-page, 101-question survey was mailed to all 1,967 active members of AEJMC in spring 1992.[2] Students and members who were retired were not included. Persons who did not respond within several weeks received one postcard follow-up. In all, 1,160 responded, yielding a response rate of 59%.[3]

The study is essentially a census of members, and thus group comparisons reported here are to be interpreted as real differences, as sampling error does not apply. However, we have applied certain statistical tests to the data. This was done not for parameter estimation, but to call attention to differences of significant magnitude. This is in keeping with a general practice in many such studies (e.g., Gray, n.d.).

In the data cleaning stage, several additional cases were removed. This involved persons who were working part time, were completing Ph.D. programs, and teaching part time. We have also eliminated full-time administrators in our analyses of issues (e.g., teaching, mentoring, etc.) that are not likely to be applicable to them. On other issues such as rank distributions, however, they were included. The data reported here are meant to be representative of full-time teaching faculty in the United States who are members of AEJMC. Comparisons with the larger population of journalism educators will be discussed below. Although 59% return of a mail survey is generally considered acceptable, the particular topic under consideration may cause disproportionate responses from parties who feel particularly attuned to the topics. Of course, we have no way to estimate the extent to which this might have happened, and urge readers to keep that caution in mind. Most analyses reported here are based on the full remaining sample of 1,090.

Measures

The questionnaire included items on a number of variables. We will report measures for only those items that have been used in this chapter. The principal contextual variable is gender. The other variables including rank, education, and age were measured by simply asking the respondents for those data.

Overall job satisfaction and satisfaction with individual dimensions: salary, teaching, collegiality, and scholarship were measured by asking the respondents how dissatisfied or satisfied they were with each dimension on a scale of 1 to 10.

Institutional support for research was measured through respondents' ratings on how they perceive the support for research in their unit on a scale of poor (1) to excellent (4). The means of support included graduate assistants, professional travel, library support for journals and books, research funding either within the unit or in the university, and availability of computer support.

Mentoring was measured through respondents rating how often they get advice from their senior faculty on teaching, research, and whether senior faculty collaborate with them on research on a scale of never (1) to frequently (4).

Finally, perceptions and concerns were measured by asking the respondents to rate on a scale no concern (1) to serious concern (4). The issues mentioned included items on child care, conflict between career and family, discrimination, politics in the work place, collegiality, and work load. Some of the items were collapsed to form three new variables: job stress, family concerns, and workplace politics, on the basis of factor analysis.[4]

Analysis

We have presented comparisons throughout the chapter showing the main effects of gender. In cases where main effects appear we have attempted to elaborate them by showing further breakdowns by rank or some other variable. Normally we have used simple *t* tests for this purpose. In the case of job satisfaction we have used hierarchical multiple regression. This permits us to assess the unique contribution of each predictor variable after controlling simultaneously for the others.

We have also simulated a type of cohort analysis to examine the over-time trends in the entry and promotion of women faculty compared to men.[5] Based on the year in which they entered teaching, we divided our sample into six groups (1936-1945, 1946-1955, 1956-1965, 1966-1975, 1976-1985, and 1986-1992). We then examined the percentage of women who entered the field during these cohorts compared to men. We also looked at the proportion of women who were tenured, hold senior (associate and full professor) rank, and the mean number of refereed publications. It has been observed that gender discrimination has been particularly acute in promotion and tenure (e.g., Gray, n.d.). This analysis allowed us to see if such discrimination has in any way abated or intensified. The data on refereed publications will allow us to compare the record of men and women faculty on a variable that is often used as a major criterion in promotion and tenure.

Who Are They?

Our sample shows that about 72% of the respondents in our census are men and about 28% are women. If we were to assume that AEJMC membership is representative of the journalism and mass communication

Table 14.1   Highest Attained Academic Degree, by Gender

	Gender	
Terminal Degree	*Male*	*Female*
Bachelor's degree	2.5%	0.6%
Master's degree	20.1	29.1
All but dissertation	4.4	7.8
Doctorate	65.1	56.3
Doctoral equivalent*	7.8	6.1
	100%	100%
n	791	309

NOTE: * includes Ed.D., J.D., M.D., D.B.A.
phi = .13*
Chi square = 20.16; df = 4
* = $p \leq .01$.

faculty, one may infer that there has been some increase in the number of women who have entered the ranks of academia. In 1972, according to Rush et al., women constituted about 7% to 8% of the J&MC faculty. A subsequent study, by Sharp et al. (1985), reported that by 1983, that proportion had increased to about 17%-19%. Schamber's (1989) follow-up of this latter report indicates that women faculty members made up about 24% of the journalism and communication faculty in 1988. Thus, although women constituted a little more than one sixth of J&MC faculty in 1983, by the time of our survey in 1992, that proportion had inched up to a little less than one-third.

The sample profile shows that women, on average, are younger compared to men. The average age of male faculty members in our sample was about 48 years compared to the average age of about 43 years for female faculty members. In terms of education, our data show that while a smaller proportion of women hold a baccalaureate degree compared to male faculty members, a larger percentage hold terminal master's degrees or are still working on a dissertation while holding a full-time teaching job.

Although a greater proportion of male faculty members have doctoral or equivalent degrees (about 73%), about 62% of women hold a doctorate or an equivalent degree (Table 14.1). This compares well with the numbers reported by AEJMC studies in 1983-1984, where 38% held doctorates (Sharp et al., 1985) and in 1987-1988 when 43% of the female faculty in Schamber's (1989) report held doctorates. Based on this evidence, it appears that the proportion of women holding doctorates has steadily increased in the last few years.

On other acquired characteristics, our data in Table 14.2 show that the male faculty members have about 9 years of professional experience (mean = 9.38, s.d. = 8.78), about a year more compared to the female faculty members (mean = 8.15, s.d., 6.85). Similarly, male faculty members on average have more teaching experience compared to female faculty members. Both these may be explained by the fact that women are relatively younger than men and have entered the ranks relatively more recently. Also, on the former, the barriers faced by women on entry as well as their stay in the industry may also be factors (e.g., Lafky, 1989; Smith et al., 1989).

Institutional Factors

We will now turn our attention to the institutional conditions under which women and men work. We are particularly interested in the relative work load for teaching, advising, and service between men and women. We will also examine the advancement of women in the ranks of academe.

Women and Ranks

In a study of universities in the 1970s, Cole (1981) found that women were less likely to have been promoted within the teaching ranks and if promoted, were promoted rather late. This general situation has not changed much since then. According to data from the National Science Foundation, only 17% of all women faculty are full professors compared to the 44% of men who are full professors (Ehrenberg, 1991). In journalism and mass communication, Sharp et al. (1985) report similar inequities. As of 1983 only 4% of the women in journalism and mass communication were full professors. Our sample, from 1992, shows that about 12.7% (39) of the female faculty are full professors. This compares to 40% (316) of the male faculty who are full professors. So male faculty are 3 times more likely to be full professors compared to female faculty. Although this represents an incremental improvement compared to the previous numbers, the field is still *considerably below* the national average, though the national average may not account for variations among the disciplines.

Both the Sharp et al. (1985) study and ours show that a large number of women entered the field in the past 15 years, but to interpret this we must also know how many of them have advanced in rank, which in an academic setting means promotion and tenure. We also need to consider how we can improve their chances for advancement and what barriers exist to hamper their advancement.

Table 14.2 Mean Differences on Teaching, Research, and Service Workloads by Gender

Dependent Variables	Males Mean	S.D.	Females Mean	S.D.
Ascribed and Acquired Characteristics				
Age*	48.0	8.9	43.4	8.1
Years of professional experience*	9.4	8.8	8.2	6.9
Years of teaching experience*	14.9	9.1	10.5	6.8
Years in rank*	5.1	4.8	3.8	2.8
Assistant professors*	4.4	3.8	3.4	2.3
Associate professors*	5.2	4.1	4.1	3.3
Teaching Conditions				
Number of courses taught	4.8	1.6	4.8	1.6
Number of credits	16.3	8.4	15.8	8.0
Number of students	151.8	118.3	141.3	94.0
New course preparations*	0.9	1.1	1.2	1.2
Assistant professors	1.3	1.3	1.5	1.2
Associate professors	0.9	1.0	0.9	0.9
Full professors	0.6	.9	0.6	0.6
Advising and Student Committees				
Number of undergrads advised*	35.2	41.3	44.2	62.7
Assistant professors	36.1	38.8	35.7	42.3
Associate professors	37.0	35.6	46.5	49.2
Full professors	32.8	45.0	49.1	42.8
Number of grad students advised	6.1	15.2	6.0	16.0
Hours/week spent advising undergrads	4.8	4.8	5.2	5.2
Number of doctoral committees	1.1	2.4	1.0	2.1
Number of master's committees	2.5	3.3	2.6	3.4
Hours/week spent on grad advising	2.3	4.5	2.3	4.1
Number of theses advised	1.5	2.1	1.4	1.9
Number of dissertations advised*	0.5	1.2	0.2	0.8
Assistant professor	0.5	0.4	0.9	0.4
Associate professor	0.4	1.2	0.3	0.8
Full professors	0.8	1.6	0.7	1.4
Service Commitment				
Number of university committees	1.0	1.1	1.0	1.1
Number of college committees	1.0	1.1	1.0	1.1
Number of department committees	1.7	1.2	1.8	1.2
National professional associations	1.6	1.2	1.7	1.2
Local professional associations*	0.5	0.7	0.7	0.8
Assistant professors*	0.5	0.6	0.7	0.7
Associate professors	0.5	0.6	0.7	0.9
Full professors	0.5	0.8	0.6	0.9
Local community organizations	0.7	0.9	0.8	1.0
Student organizations advised*	1.7	0.5	1.6	0.5
Assistant professors	1.6	0.5	1.5	0.5
Associate professors	1.7	0.5	1.6	0.5
Full professors	1.7	0.4	1.6	0.5

*$p \leq .05$.

Table 14.3 Proportion of Women in Various Teaching Ranks

Rank	Sharp et al. (1985)	Weaver & Wilhoit (1988)	Schamber (1988)	OSU/AEJMC (1992)
Instructor	28%	n/a	42%	46% (16)
Lecturer	n/a	43% (40)	n/a	29 (6)
Assistant professor	26	26 (71)	32	41 (145)
Associate professor	14	18 (42)	17	31 (102)
Full professor	4	4 (8)	6	11 (39)
Other	25	n/a	32	n/a

NOTE: Note that cell entries are row percentages and number of cases (*n*), where available from separate studies. Because the entries are row percentages, they do not sum to 100% in any direction. For example, 4% of all full professors in the Sharp et al. study were women, compared to 11% in the OSU/AEJMC study. The Sharp et al. study was based on a count of all 3,076 names listed in the 1983 AEJMC Journalism Directory. Schamber (1988) used a similar methodology based on the 1988 directory and counted 3,080 names. The Weaver and Wilhoit study was based on 893 telephone interviews drawn from a comprehensive population of names meant to be representative of all journalism and mass communication instructors. The OSU/AEJMC study is a census of AEJMC members in spring 1992 with a final, valid number of 783 men and 307 women. Note that in the Sharp et al. and Schamber studies comparable numbers to those presented above were not reported.

Our data show that, while a little more than half of the female faculty in our sample are tenured, they constitute only about 38% of all tenured faculty members in journalism and mass communication. This number is likely to improve as more and more women advance in the ranks.

The distribution of women among different ranks also shows some improvement over the previous years. Table 14.3 compares our data with findings from reports by Sharp et al. (1985), Weaver and Wilhoit (1988), and Schamber (1989).[6] The data show that proportions of women in the top three ranks improved over time. Forty-one percent (145) of the assistant professors, 31% (102) of the associate professors, and 11% (39) of the full professors in our sample are women compared to the previous years, when 26% to 32% were assistant professors, 14% to 18% were associate professors, and 4% to 6% were full professors (Sharp et al., 1985; Weaver & Wilhoit, 1988; Schamber, 1989). The largest improvement is in the rank of full and associate professors where the proportions have almost doubled. The proportion of women among instructors has also increased though only about 5% of the women on mass communication faculties hold that rank. Whether the latter constitutes progress is arguable.

The overall picture suggests a gradual improvement in the entry of female faculty members. It also shows that a greater proportion of the women hold assistant or associate professor ranks compared to men. The question is, will this trend hold and allow for advancement in the ranks, or is it conceivable that the female faculty members have entered and remained in the junior ranks with barriers in their advancement? If the latter is the case, then the inequities seen in our numbers are more likely to continue rather than narrow.

We attempted to answer these questions in two ways. First, we looked at the number of years spent by male and female faculty members in a given rank. Second, at an aggregate level, we looked at the times at which male and female faculty members entered academe.

Years Spent in Rank

One indicator of discrimination in promotion is when women spend more time in a rank compared to men. We asked our respondents (assistant and associate professors only), how long they had been in their present ranks. One possible measure of discrimination would be that women would be found to spend more time in a rank than men.

When we compared our data between men and women for both associate and assistant professors, we found that men reported that they have been in their present rank significantly longer than women (Table 14.2). On average men have been in their present rank for about 5 years compared to about 3.75 years for women. As there has been some concern that women are likely to be held up at the assistant professor level, we did the same tests for both ranks. The differences remained significant and were in the same direction. That is, men were likely to have been holding their present rank longer than women in both ranks.

The proposition that women are likely to remain longer in a lower ranks was not supported at the aggregate level. Of course, this type of aggregate analysis does not imply the absence of individual cases of discrimination.

Some Over-Time Trends

We next examined trends in employment, entry, and advancement of women compared to men, to get an idea when they entered the field and how they fared at each time point.

Our cohort data in Table 14.4 yielded some interesting findings. The data in the first column, "distribution," compares when female and male faculty members teaching today first entered the field. Our data show that 17.5% of women teaching in the field today entered before 1975. This compares to almost 42% of the male faculty entering in this time frame. As a corollary, although more than 80% of the female faculty members in our field joined after 1975, only 58% of the men have done so. A 5-year cohort (data not shown) indicates that 61% of the female faculty joined in the last dozen years. The raw number has also shown a steady rise from

Table 14.4 Cohort Analysis of Faculty and Publications by Gender

	Proportion of Present Faculty		Publications	
Time of Entry into Field	*M*	*F*	*M*	*F*
1936-1945	0.1%	0.3%	30.0	1
			(0.0)	(0)
1946-1955	1.5	0.0	16.0	—
			(19.5)	
1956-1965	10.3	1.6	12.1	5.3
			(15.2)	(2.5)
1966-1975	29.8	15.6	11.7	5.9
			(14.3)	(9.1)
1976-1985	38.6	49.5	6.6	4.8
			(9.3)	(6.1)
1986-1992	19.7	32.9	2.3	1.5
			(3.9)	(2.6)
N	783	307	698	290

NOTE: Cell entries in the first column are column percentages referring to the overall distribution of the sample by cohort. The columns labeled "Publications" refers to the mean (and standard deviation) of peer-reviewed articles by cohort and gender.

31 women who entered between 1971-1975 to 93 women who entered in 1986-1990.

Other relevant trends deserve discussion here. Consider the relationship between time of entry into the teaching profession and current tenure status. For example, 100% of men and women who entered the field in 1936-1945 have been tenured. Almost 96% of the men who entered in 1956-1965 era have been tenured compared to about 75% (3 individuals) of the women who entered at the same time. Similarly, about 89% of the men who entered J&MC teaching in 1966-1975 are tenured, compared to about 81% of the women. On the same lines, about 66% of the male faculty and 59% of the female faculty who entered in 1976-1985 are tenured. The only difference is in the last half-decade, where a slightly higher proportion of women faculty (8.2%) than men (7.5%) are tenured. Whether this is a reversal of a historical trend, or an anomaly, cannot be ascertained unless we can see a sustained trend over a longer time.

Another relationship between cohort and rank deserves some consideration. Is the proportion of women in senior ranks considerably smaller and has there been any change over time? Our data show a narrowing trend. The three male faculty who are teaching today and who entered teaching in 1936-1945 hold senior ranks, compared to the lone female faculty member who entered in the same period but who teaches in a junior position. The trend over time is similar. For example, about 91% of the male faculty who entered in 1956-1965 compared to only 75% of the female faculty who entered around the same time, hold senior ranks. This difference narrows over time. By 1986-1992, about 13% of the male faculty who entered in the last 6 years (1986-1992) compared to about 8% of the female faculty, hold senior ranks. Once again, although the trend is in the right direction, whether this will be sustained over time is an empirical question and will require further follow up.

The last column in Table 14.4 shows the mean number of refereed publications in journals between men and women who entered the field at different times. Refereed journal articles are likely to be highly valued when considering faculty for promotion and tenure, and there are arguments that this criterion has often worked against female faculty, whom it is said are more likely to publish in nontraditional settings and do more collaborative work (Ward & Grant, 1991). Even though we cannot examine the issue of authorship and collaboration in depth, we have data showing the mean refereed journal publications of the faculty entering the field at different times. These data will show if there are differences between men and women and if so, whether they are so overwhelming as to explain the absence of women in the senior ranks. The answer is that they are not. We see a narrowing trend. For example, the male faculty, who entered the field in 1936-1945 had a mean of 30 refereed journal articles compared to one by the lone female faculty member who entered at the same time. This type of disparity is shown to have narrowed. For example, among those who entered in 1956-1965, the male faculty members have on average, about 12 publications compared to about 5 by the female faculty. But the difference narrows to about 7 articles for male faculty and about 5 articles by female faculty among those who entered in 1976-1985. One may infer that, over time, the differences in the number of journal publications between men and women is narrowing, particularly among those who have entered recently. This may be due to two possible reasons: more women and men who are entering recently have doctorates, and thus more of them are socialized to the importance of publishing, for professional advancement as well as satisfaction.

The above cohort discussion clearly shows that there has been some change in the numbers of women entering the ranks, their achievements in terms of tenure and seniority, as well as their record on the traditionally important criterion of refereed publications. It is important to note that much of the change has occurred in the past dozen years. This implies that there is a great potential for the advanced ranks to become more representative (at least, in terms of gender). This point is also supported by recent results reported by Kosicki and Becker (1992) who found a steadily increasing proportion of Ph.D.s being earned in mass communications by women over the period 1989-1991. Over this period, the proportion increased from 38.5% in 1989 to 44.0% in 1990, to 49.3% in 1991. What this also implies is the need for the field to ensure such an advancement free from barriers of discrimination.[7]

The question is what are some of the significant factors that may influence and even impede the promotion and tenure of female faculty members? Two sets of factors are important here. One is work load, particularly if it is disproportionately divided between the male and female faculty members. A second set of factors has to do with the problems and opportunities to engage in scholarship, success in which is vital for promotion and tenure, among other rewards. Next we will examine both factors in greater detail.

Work Load: Teaching

Our data show that the teaching load of women is comparable to men's in terms of number of credits,[8] number of courses and in the number of students taught (Table 14.2). On average, journalism and mass communication faculty members (both male and female) taught about 16 semester credits, five courses, and about 140-150 students in 1992. The variance in the number of students is very high, particularly for male faculty members, reflecting the diversity of institutions in the field.

Women faculty, however, are likely to have significantly more new course preparations (mean = 1.19, s.d. = 1.16) compared to male faculty members (mean = 0.93, s.d. = 1.10). This difference, however, disappears when one controls for the rank of the faculty members. Assistant professors, among both men and women, as expected, are likely to have the highest number of new course preparations compared to associate and full professors. Because a greater proportion of women are assistant professors, the burden is higher on women when compared to men.

Work Load: Advising

Our data in Table 14.2 on advising and serving on student committees also do not show significant differences between men and women on most criteria. There are differences, however, on advising undergraduate students. Women are likely to advise a significantly higher number of undergraduate students than men (mean = 44.2, s.d. = 62.7 vs. mean = 35.2, s.d. = 41.3, $p \leq .05$). Notice the higher standard deviation for the women faculty, indicating greater variance among them. When we controlled this factor for rank, it was interesting to note that among women, the senior faculty are likely to advise a greater number of undergraduate students compared to their male counterparts. Male faculty, however, are more likely to advise on dissertations (mean = 0.50, s.d. = 1.21) than female faculty (mean = 0.24, s.d. = 0.77, $p < .01$). This might be explained in part by the higher percentage of male faculty in senior ranks.

Work Load: Service

There is a widespread feeling that women carry a greater burden on service. It is commonly believed that women are more likely to serve on departmental and other committees, advise student organizations, and engage in other such service chores. If this is true, it is a major barrier in the advancement of women into higher ranks, as few promotion and tenure committees can be expected to place significant value on service.

Our data show no statistically significant differences between men and women on the number of departmental, college, or university committees they serve on, even when we controlled for rank.[9] There were, however, a couple of interesting differences between men and women. Overall, women faculty were more likely to work with local professional associations than men (women: mean = 0.71, s.d. = 0.81, men: mean = 0.54, s.d. = 0.70, $p < .01$). This relationship, however, disappeared when we controlled for rank. Women associate professors are likely to serve on an average of almost two national professional association committees compared to about 1.5 committees by men.

In terms of overall work load it is interesting to call attention to the considerable amounts of time that both male and female members spend on student contact hours, as well as in service on committees. We have so far located no comparative data from other disciplines, but the amount of time spent by the faculty on such matters is itself quite instructive, particularly in light of the recent movements in many state legislatures to make inquiries into faculty teaching and work loads.

Given these findings that the differences between men and women on most dimensions of teaching and service are not statistically significant, but for some exceptions, what then are the likely barriers to the advancement of women?[10] How can we ensure that these barriers are removed to facilitate their promotion and tenure? We focused on two factors that may potentially affect the advancement of the junior faculty: mentoring and institutional support for scholarly productivity. We will examine the two in greater detail in the next two sections.

Table 14.5 Institutional Support for Research by Gender

Types of Institutional Support	Gender	
	Male	Female
Graduate assistants*	1.8	1.7
	(0.9)	(0.8)
Assistant professors	1.7	1.6
	(0.9)	(0.8)
Associate professors	1.8	1.7
	(0.9)	(0.8)
Full professors	1.9	1.9
	(0.9)	(0.9)
Travel to professional meetings	2.3	2.4
	(1.0)	(1.0)
Library books and journals	2.4	2.3
	(0.9)	(0.8)
Research funding within the unit	2.0	1.9
	(0.9)	(0.9)
Funding by the overall university	2.0	2.1
	(0.8)	(0.8)
Computer facilities	2.8	2.7
	(0.9)	(0.9)

NOTE: Cell entries are means and (standard deviations) of types of support available rated on a 4-point scale from poor (1) to excellent (4).
* $p \leq .05$.

Institutional Support for Research

Some ways an institution may promote scholarship are through the provision of funds either within the unit or the college, travel support, and support through graduate research assistants. We asked our respondents to rate their perceptions of support from their institution on some dimensions on a scale from poor (1) to excellent (4). We found the only significant difference between men and women faculty ratings on support of graduate assistants (Table 14.5). Male faculty rated higher (mean = 1.8, s.d. = 0.9) the support for research from their institutions through graduate assistants compared to female faculty (mean = 1.7, s.d. = 0.8, $p < .025$). This may be a small difference but it is significant. Interestingly enough, this kind of support received low ratings from both the male and female faculty. The significant difference disappeared when controlled for rank, which showed that senior faculty are more likely to rate that support higher than junior faculty. Again, in light of the fact that a majority of women are in the assistant professor rank, the long-term implications of this support or the lack of it to junior faculty may affect the advancement of women disproportionately.

There were no differences on other dimensions of support: travel to professional meetings, library books and journals, research support within or outside the unit, and computer facilities.

Mentoring

The academic role itself, as discussed by a number of scholars, is inherently ambiguous (Light, 1974; Locke, Fitzpatrick, & White, 1983). A faculty member is expected to be involved in three areas: teaching, research, and service. Although this is the official policy, what is not explicit is how the three factors are weighted, and what is the best way to achieve a balance in one's academic life. Some learning by junior colleagues about research and teaching expectations and how to cope with them is a result of socialization during graduate school. But a major part of learning, especially in terms of achieving the proper balance among the criteria at a given institution, takes place as a faculty member. A significant source of information on such matters is the senior faculty. They can explain to the juniors the way the system works and how best to succeed in the system. This process of mentoring junior faculty has been recognized by some scholars (e.g., Locke et al., 1984). The mentoring process can be informal or formal. Some institutions formally assign senior faculty as mentors to the junior faculty, while at other institutions, the process is more informal.

The question is to what extent is the mentoring process available in journalism and mass communication departments? How are junior faculty members advised, if at all? Is the advice limited to one area or is it in both teaching and research? Finally, do the senior faculty members formally work with junior faculty members on research projects, success in which is vital for promotion and tenure?[11]

Informal interaction among research collaborators is necessary in a number of disciplines. Women, however, have faced difficulties in such interaction because of sexist attitudes, including not being accepted and not being taken seriously (Brush, 1991). To some extent they may be discouraged from participation in such interactions with other colleagues. This may have the effect of being deprived of opportunities to work on research projects, thus impeding their advancement.

We asked our sample about the frequency with which they received any advice from their senior faculty on teaching and research and frequency of collaboration between senior and junior faculty. The data in Table 14.6 are instructive.[12] There are no significant differences between male and female faculty on the advice they get from the senior faculty on teaching or research. In fact the mentoring of junior faculty by senior faculty rates

Table 14.6 Reported Senior Faculty Mentoring of Junior Faculty by Gender

	Gender	
Mentoring of Junior Faculty by:	*Male*	*Female*
Giving advice on teaching	2.1	2.1
	(0.9)	(0.9)
Giving advice on research	2.1	2.0
	(0.9)	(0.9)
Collaborating on research*	2.0	1.7
	(0.9)	(0.9)

NOTE: *n* varies from 646 to 649 for males, from 282 to 284 for females.
Cell entries are means (and standard deviations). Advice was rated on a scale ranging from never (1) to frequently (4).
* $p \leq 01$.

quite low for both females and males. There is, however, one significant difference in ratings between men and women. Male faculty rated the senior faculty somewhat higher (mean = 2.0, s.d. = 0.9) than female faculty (mean = 1.7, s.d. = 0.9) on research collaboration.

Although the difference is small, it is nonetheless statistically and substantively significant. What are the consequences of this collaboration or the absence of it for promotion and tenure? What is the significance of the finding that male faculty have rated the support of their institutions on graduate assistants higher, though it disappeared after controlling for rank? We will take up these issues in more detail in the discussion section.

Salary

One tangible result of work as a professor is one's salary level. How salaries are determined in the field is highly variable, ranging from unionized environments that do not take an individual's merit into account, to the major research universities, which tend to favor setting salaries by merit, or some combination of across-the-board increases to compensate for inflation, plus merit increases. In institutions where merit pay is awarded, a variety of performance criteria, ranging from success in publishing, teaching, and service, may be involved. Weights attached to these will vary from place to place, as well. Salaries are in part functions of length of service, and rank, as well as tenured status. Still, other variables are known to be related to salary as well, including region of the country, race, type of university and department in which one works, grants obtained, and date of hire.[13] Here, we are primarily interested in reporting only basic descriptive

Table 14.7 Mean Nine-Month Salary Levels by Gender and Rank

Group	9-Month Salary (in dollars)		
	Male	Female	Difference
Overall	42,802	36,200	6,602*
Assistant professor	33,166	32,589	577
Associate professor	40,656	39,073	1,583
Full professor	53,947	48,455	5,492*
n	608	266	

NOTE: Table includes teaching faculty only, excluding administrators.
*p < .05

data related to gender, and will control only for rank, although this is problematic for a variety of reasons.[14]

Our data in Table 14.7 show that overall women earn less than men, a difference of about $6,600, without any controls. Note that our data excludes administrators, while Sharp et al. (1985) and Schamber (1989) included them, thus making the estimates of gender inequity incomparable. When we added rank as a control, the gender gap seemed to diminish at the lower ranks, particularly the rank of assistant professors, where most women are congregated. For assistant professors, the differential, again, without any further controls for other variables known to influence salary, was $577. This was not statistically significant.[15] For associate professors, the differential was $1,583, which was also not statistically significant. The greatest differential, however, was between male and female full professors, $5,492, which was significant.

Job Satisfaction

Another important consideration is one's overall satisfaction with the job. This is generally recognized as an important and complex concept, with a long history of research in industrial and other settings (e.g., Champion, 1975; Worthy, 1950). This literature cannot be directly applied to life in the university. University life has many unique characteristics that can be expected to influence job satisfaction (Field & Giles, 1977). For example, professors work in a professional bureaucracy, which means they have greater autonomy over their core operations (Copur, 1990). In addition, other structures of the universities and their operating principles have a significant impact on the way the members of the professoriate perform their tasks and the satisfaction they may derive from them (Copur, 1990; Davies, 1983; Scott, 1966). These involve such factors as the balance of teaching and research expected, as reflected by the presence of a doctoral program. Individuals will vary in their preparation for life in the university community as measured by their terminal degree. Universities have clearly defined status hierarchies indicated by one's formal rank such as assistant, associate, or full professor, and tenured status. Salary is known to be an important predictor of job satisfaction as it signifies one's level of achievement and provides tangible monetary rewards (e.g., Eckert & Stecklein, 1981). Under conditions of discrimination, however, employees may earn lower salaries than they deserve based on objective indicators and procedures. Individual-level considerations include attitudes toward the workplace, job politics (Chowdhry & Pal, 1957) and possible conflicts of the job (Sullivan & Bhagat, 1992), and family considerations.

Although these concepts have been well studied in different contexts, their influence is somewhat unclear in our field. Further, their influence on job satisfaction, particularly on potential differences between genders, remains to be explored. Our analysis of job satisfaction used one overall measure. This became the dependent variables in a multiple regression equation. The independent variables included two structural variables: whether the respondents teach at a doctoral-granting university and unit. The rationale is that doctoral-granting units expect and promote scholarship, which is key to satisfaction and teaching. On the other hand, these units may also exert pressure to publish, leading to greater stress and dissatisfaction.

As the next block in the regression we also examined whether the terminal degree of the respondent is a master's degree or Ph.D. Three status-related factors: rank (assistant, associate, and full professors), tenure, and salary were entered next. Finally, we included a set of three perception variables: job stress, family concerns, and job politics. All three were formed based on a factor analysis of a number of items measuring the perceptions of the respondents on various issues and how much of a concern the issue was to them personally. All items were entered into a factor analysis equation and three factors emerged.

The first, which we call the job stress factor, included such items as whether the respondents were concerned about working during evening hours, lack of leisure time, a tiring job, and whether it was a stressful job. This factor explained about 35% of the variance. The second factor, family concerns, included items on child care and role conflicts between career and family. It explained about 14% of the variance. The final factor is collegiality, which represents the concerns of the respondents on having

Table 14.8 Predictors of Job Satisfaction by Gender

| | Job Satisfaction | |
Independent Variables	Male	Female
Structural Factors		
Ph.D. granting dept.	.02	.08
Ph.D. granting univ.	.03	−.01
Achieved Factors		
MA terminal degree	.07	.14
Ph.D. terminal degree	.02	−.04
Status Factors		
Assistant professor	−.03	.10
Associate professor	−.10	.20
Full professor	−.09	.13
Tenure	−.04	.02
Salary	.13*	−.05
Faculty Concerns		
Job stress	−.34*	−.35*
Family concerns	−.02	−.15*
Job politics	−.51*	−.50*
Total R^2 for equation	.32*	.31*

NOTE: Cell entries are standardized regression coefficients from the final hierarchical equations.
* $p < .05$

trustworthy colleagues, politics in the job, and whether time required for tenure was too short. This factor explained about 13% of the variance. The three factors together explained about 62% of the total variance. All of the independent variables were entered into the hierarchical regression equation separately for each gender. This way, we were able to see if the patterns were different for each gender or not.

Table 14.8 reports the final betas for each predictor of the dependent variable and gender. Predicting overall job satisfaction, job stress, and job politics emerged as significant predictors for both men and women. In addition, for women, family concerns—conflict between family and career role and child care—has emerged as an additional predictor. This is important, as it highlights and reinforces findings from other studies that found this conflict between the family and career. Further, the issue of child care has been a major concern in recent times, and suggests some possible actions that may be taken to enhance job satisfaction for female faculty. For men, salary emerged as a significant positive predictor, suggesting that the greater the salary, the higher the overall job satisfaction.

Conclusions

The field of journalism and mass communication education, as we have argued in the beginning, is changing rapidly in resonance with changes taking place in other parts of the society. One major change is in the entry of a greater number of women into mass communication education. Our data, when compared with the data from previous studies, show that there has been an increase in the presence of women educators, both in terms of raw numbers as well as in terms of proportion in the past dozen years, though the overall proportion of female faculty remains small compared to that of male faculty. Thus, although the numbers show an increase from previous years, the proportion of women continues to be much smaller when compared to men.

We were interested in four broad groups of questions. First is the demographic profile and background of the journalism educators. Women educators, in our census, were statistically significantly younger than the men. They also have relatively less teaching experience, and somewhat less professional experience than men. This last point needs further elaboration. Given the findings in a number of studies (e.g., Lafky, 1989; Smith et al., 1989) that entry, as well the environment for women in the mass communication industry, has often been hostile and at least less hospitable, what is the effect of using professional experience as a major qualification in hiring women in the mass communication education? By placing a greater emphasis on professional experience, as most journalism schools appear to do, are we placing an additional burden on women? This may become particularly acute when the women, whose advancement in the industry is full of barriers, start competing for academic positions with men from the industry who may hold a higher rank. This requirement and its implications for gender equity among mass communications faculty deserves a reevaluation.

We also found that the educational background of the women academics showed considerable change. Even though a greater proportion of men educators hold doctorates compared to women, the proportion of women holding doctorates has increased considerably. About 62% of the women educators teaching today have doctoral degrees. Given the importance of doctoral training for entry and advancement in mass communication, this figure may suggest that in the future, a greater proportion may enter and advance in the field.

In fact, our cohort analysis (based on year of entry into the field) showed some interesting developments over time. One of the key findings in our study, with potential implications for understanding the prospects of women, is the fact that 8 out of 10 women educators teaching today entered the field in the past dozen years. The very recent increase of women, if continued, will likely lead to a more equitable presence for women in the future.

The other indicators germane to this issue have also shown changes in the direction of equity. Our data show that while there has been an increase in the number of women in higher ranks, the numbers are still significantly less than men's. The differences between men and women, however, in proportion tenured, attainment of senior ranks, as well as record of publications, are decreasing.

Tenure and seniority are of particular importance given our findings that the number of full professors who are women in the field is low by normative standards, despite the upward trend over the past few years. If the trend witnessed in our cohort analysis holds, we may soon see more women in the advanced, tenured ranks. What is unclear is whether the trend will hold up and continue, or if it is just a blip.

The cohort analysis also points out that the differences between men and women faculty in the number of juried publications are decreasing. At most places, publications in scholarly journals are an important criterion in promotion, tenure, and merit pay increases. If the trend holds up, then the prospects for promotion and tenure of women are high *assuming* that there are no other barriers.

We were also interested in examining the institutional milieu, particularly the relative work load on teaching, research, and service between men and women. This is vital to understand because of the perception that teaching and service load may fall disproportionately on women, thus hindering their advancement.

On most indicators of teaching and service, we found no major or significant patterns of difference between men and women. Thus the teaching and service loads between men and women are comparable on most dimensions. But there are one or two areas that may be cause for concern.

We found that women faculty in our census reported more new course preparations compared to men. This difference disappeared when we controlled for rank, where assistant professors of both genders reported similar number of preparations. But when we take into consideration that a greater proportion of women are assistant professors, it becomes an important issue in gender-equity, at least for now. A greater work load through new course preparation may leave less time for scholarship, particularly in institutions where scholarly productivity is a major criterion in promotion and tenure. This becomes a crucial issue when one considers the fact that this is also the stage in the life cycle when the faculty members, particularly women, are likely to start families. Although it can be argued that it is changing to some extent, women in this and many other cultures remain the primary caregivers to young children. Some scholars, taking note of these pressures, have argued that the time required from promotion and tenure should be lengthened as the current requirements may particularly disadvantage women (Brush, 1991). Institutional policies that provide for stopping the tenure clock while on maternity/paternity and family illness leave may go some way in easing the structural barriers, especially if they are flexible enough to recognize and compensate the true child caregiver, whether male or female. These solutions, of course, are unlikely to be helpful in case of covert discrimination. Indeed, some argue that such policies may only prolong the probationary period for parents, but particularly for women. It is not clear, however, what other alternatives exist.

We also found that women advise a greater number of undergraduate students than men. This raises some questions that call for critical examination. It implies that women spend more time with students, which is not always rewarded relative to research. This, at least, is the case in major research universities.

Our research identified two areas that may potentially influence the movement of women in higher ranks. We asked our respondents who are junior faculty to rate their senior faculty on mentoring on teaching, research, and collaboration. We found no differences between men's and women's ratings on teaching and research. But on collaboration, men benefit from the old boys' network. Male faculty rated their seniors higher than female faculty did on collaboration. This small but significant edge appears to be important here. Although the long-term consequence of this difference is unclear, the fact that a majority of female faculty are assistant professors makes it important that their programs of research are well under way.

Another major difference is the rating of institutional support for research. Again, we found no difference between men and women on a number of dimensions, but found on one dimension that male faculty are more likely to be supported through graduate assistants than are female faculty. Coupled with lack of collaboration, this will seriously disadvantage women, most of whom are assistant professors.

In terms of our preliminary salary analysis, we found a substantial gender gap at the highest ranks that colors the overall main effect of gender, but this is shown to decrease at the associate and assistant levels. This result should be viewed cautiously, as it is without the benefit of other controls and will be the subject of further analysis.

Finally, we looked at the determinants of job satisfaction between men and women. One significant factor in both groups was politics in the workplace. If one were to go by the ratings, workplace politics are of particular concern and are a major source of low satisfaction levels for both men and women.

Also, family conflict as a significant predictor emerged only as a concern for women.[16] The problems here are deeper and structural. One way to address this issue is to ensure adequate, affordable child care for the faculty, especially assistant and associate professors, and also to allow for policies to stop the tenure clock in case of a birth or sickness in the family. These two steps by themselves will help minimize structural barriers to advancement. Finally, the consistent negative relationship of workplace politics for both men and women on satisfaction is a telling commentary on the environment in the mass communication field. Whether it is unique to our field or is endemic to higher education, it is absolutely vital to address this issue and aim for its resolution.

Our data and findings, in summary, show that there has been some gradual improvement in the ranks of female faculty and that much of this has occurred very recently. Here is a great potential and an opportunity for the field to rectify its historic wrongs, which if not grasped, is certain to perpetuate the inequities.

Notes

1. Our analysis compares women and men. We do not deal with the issue of minority women separately here, as the numbers become exceedingly small and difficult to analyze. Issues specifically related to minorities in mass communication education will be dealt with in a subsequent report.

2. Many questions were borrowed from studies examining faculty working conditions and attitudes, particularly focusing on women and minorities, at The Ohio State University and the University of Kentucky.

3. Out of 1,160 who responded, we eliminated 39 cases from people not involved in journalism education or who worked part time, including students, yielding a final sample size of 1,121.

4. Factor analysis is a data-reduction technique that replaces a set of input variables with a new set of general factors. The procedure analyzes the patterns of correlations among the original variables, searching for commonalities among the variables. See Kerlinger (1973) or an advanced statistics text for additional details.

5. Normally a formal cohort analysis would involve repeated cross-sectional samples over time. The data are then analyzed by comparing various groups as they mature. Groups, or cohorts, often share some common attribute such as a particular generational experience. We have attempted to use the decade of entry into journalism teaching as a common experience, but have no way to track these groups over time.

6. One must be careful in interpreting the data from different studies as the methods of collection varied among the studies cited here. The Sharp et al. (1985), as well as the Schamber (1989), study are based on counts in the AEJMC directory. The Weaver and Wilhoit (1988) study is based on a carefully drawn sample that was representative of J&MC faculty, while

the present study is a census of AEJMC members, excluding part-time faculty. Despite these differences in methodology, however, the broad patterns in the data are unmistakable and helpful in deciphering change over time, though whether it has been fast enough is a different question.

7. A recent resolution approved by the Association for Education in Journalism and Mass Communication aims at achieving gender parity by the year 2000.

8. This is controlled for differences in the systems: semester versus quarter.

9. Of course, this measure only includes the number of committees and does not consider the amount of work involved in the particular committees nor the amount of attention devoted to them by individuals.

10. Even though we did not find an overall significant difference in service between men and women, one should note that because women are congregated in lower ranks, one would expect the service burden to be lighter.

11. Institutions will vary in the importance they attach to this criterion.

12. The exact wording of the question is as follows: "On a scale of one to four, where one is never and four is frequently, please respond if your senior colleagues: 'advise you on teaching, advise you on research, work with you on research projects.' "

13. Date of hire is associated with the phenomenon of salary compression. This is a circumstance that occurs in a job market in which starting salaries rise faster than the salaries of individuals already in place.

14. These data should be interpreted with extreme caution, as they do not control for many key variables known to influence salary determination. Rank itself is highly problematic, according to some scholars (e.g., Gray, n.d.), because it can be a result of discrimination. In other words, offering rank as an explanation for salary inequities could be seen, under certain circumstances, to be doing little more than explaining one type of discrimination with another. We are preparing a detailed report on this issue as this chapter is being completed.

15. Our data are a census and not a sample, so arguably, any difference might be seen to represent a real difference. However, our respondents do not constitute a full enumeration of the relevant population due to nonresponse bias and other self-report errors. We use statistical significance tests to call attention to certain findings that are unlikely to have occurred due to chance, and because many courts admit such statistical results as evidence (Gray, n.d.).

16. This may change as social attitudes toward child care are redefined as a responsibility of both parents.

References

Angrist, S. S., & Almquist, E. M. (1975). *Careers and contingencies.* New York: Dunellen.

Betz, Nancy E., & Fitzgerald, Louise F. (1987). *The career psychology of women.* Orlando, FL: Academic Press.

Brush, Stephen. (1991, September-October). Women in science and engineering. *American Scientist, 79,* 404-416.

Champion, Dean J. (1975). *The sociology of organizations* (chap. 9). New York: McGraw-Hill.

Chowdhry, Kamala, & Pal, A. K. (1957). Production planning and organizational morale: A case study from India. *Human Organization, 15,* 11-16.

Cole, Jonathan R. (1981). Women in science. *American Scientist, 69,* 385-391.

Copur, Halil. (1990). Academic professionals: A study of conflict and satisfaction in professoriate. *Human Relations, 43*(2), 113-129.

Davies, C. (1983). Professionals in bureaucracies: The conflict thesis revisited. In R. Dingwall & P. Lewis (Eds.), *The sociology of professions.* London: Macmillan.

Delia, Jesse G. (1987). Communication research: A history. In Charles Berger & Steven Chaffee (Eds.), *Handbook of communication science* (pp. 20-98). Newbury Park, CA: Sage.

Eckert, Ruth E., & Stecklein, John E. (1981). *Job motivations and satisfaction of junior college teachers* (O-E-53990, Cooperative Research Monograph 7). Washington, DC: U.S. Department of Health, Education and Welfare.

Ehrenberg, Ronald G. (1991). The annual report on the economic status of the profession 1990-91. *Academe, 77,* 32.

Field, Hubert S., & Giles, William F. (1977). Dimensions of faculty members' sensitivity to job satisfaction items. *Research in Higher Education, 6,* 193-199.

Gray, Mary. (n.d.). *Achieving pay equity on campus.* Unpublished manuscript, The American University, Washington, D.C.

Kerlinger, Fred N. (1973). *Foundations of behavioral research.* New York: Holt, Rinehart & Winston.

Kosicki, Gerald M., & Becker, Lee B. (1992). Annual census and analysis of enrollment and graduation. *Journalism Educator, 47*(3), 61-70.

Kriger, S. F. (1972). Achievement and perceived parental childbearing attitudes of career women and homemakers. *Journal of Vocational Behavior, 2,* 419-432.

Lafky, Sue A. (1989). Economic equity and the journalistic work force. In Pamela J. Creedon (Ed.), *Women in mass communication* (pp. 164-179). Newbury Park, CA: Sage.

Light, Donald. (1974, Winter). Introduction: The structure of the academic professions. *Sociology of Education, 47,* 2-28.

Locke, E. A., Fitzpatrick, W., & White, F. M. (1983). Job satisfaction and role clarity among university and college faculty. *Review of Higher Education, 6,* 343-365.

Rush, Ramona R., Oukrup, Carol E., & Ernst, Sandra W. (1972, August). *More than you ever wanted to know about women and journalism education.* Paper presented at the annual convention of the Association for Education in Journalism and Mass Communication, Carbondale, IL.

Schamber, Linda. (1989). Women in mass communication education: Who is teaching tomorrow's communicators? In Pamela J. Creedon (Ed.), *Women in mass communication* (pp. 148-159). Newbury Park, CA: Sage.

Scott, W. H. (1966). Professionals in bureaucracies: Areas of conflict. In H. M. Vollmer & D. L. Mills (Eds.), *Professionalization.* Englewood Cliffs, NJ: Prentice Hall.

Sharp, Nancy W., Turk, Judy VanSlyke, Einsiedel, Edna F., Schamber, Linda, & Hollenback, Sharon. (1985). *Faculty women in journalism and mass communications: Problems and progress.* Syracuse, NY: Report published with a grant from the Gannett Foundation. (Available from the Association for Education in Journalism and Mass Communication, College of Journalism, 1621 College St., University of South Carolina, Columbia, SC 29208-0251.)

Smith, Conrad, Fredin, Eric S., & Nardone, Carroll Ann Ferguson. (1989). Television: Sex discrimination in the TV newsroom—Perception and reality. In Pamela J. Creedon (Ed.), *Women in mass communication: Challenging gender values* (pp. 227-246). Newbury Park, CA: Sage.

Sullivan, Sherry E., & Bhagat, Rabi S. (1992). Organizational stress, job satisfaction and job performance: Where do we go from here. *Journal of Management, 18*(2), 353-374.

Ward, Kathryn B., & Grant, Linda. (1991). Coauthorship, gender, and publication among sociologists. In Mary Margaret Fonow & Judith A. Cook (Eds.), *Beyond methodology: Feminist scholarship as lived research* (pp. 248-264). Bloomington: Indiana University Press.

Weaver, David, & Wilhoit, G. Cleveland. (1988, Summer). A profile of JMC educators: Traits, attitudes and values. *Journalism Educator, 43,* 4-41.

Worthy, James. (1950). Organizational structure. *American Sociological Review, 15,* 169-179.

15 Exploring New Frontiers
Women of Color in Academia

R. DIANNE BARTLOW
VIRGINIA T. ESCALANTE
OLGA A. VÁSQUEZ

Women of color in journalism and mass communication are underrepresented both in the media industry and academia. Besides the socioeconomic factors and poor educational attainment that tend to characterize much of their life conditions, women of color face many obstacles when they embark on an academic course. They not only encounter the routine struggles customary for any novice, but they also experience difficulty gaining entry to academia; working within the system; and achieving tenure and promotion. Although much of what we discuss applies equally to men of color, here we focus on the particular difficulty ethnic women experience as they join the ranks in academia. We begin by discussing the inequities suffered by professional women of color as they move from the media industry into academia. Then we discuss the dilemmas of identity, discourse, and curriculum these women face as part of the system. Finally, we articulate the final hurdles in the areas of tenure and promotion that ethnic women must leap over in order to endure in the academy.

Women of Color Professionals:
From the Media Industry to Academia

Most persons of color entering academia from the media industry have experienced some degree of discrimination and racism in their field. The obstacles these individuals have encountered form part of a long history of exclusion embodied in unfriendly work environments, selective hiring practices, and exclusive promotion criteria. A recent *Los Angeles Times* cover story, "Hollywood's Family Ties" (Pristen, 1993), for example, refers to the practice of nepotism as one of the foremost barriers to diversity in the workforce. The practice of excluding individuals of color in favor of those who belong to the close social network of relatives and friends is partly responsible for "Hollywood's insularity, narrow perspective and largely homogeneous work force" (Pristen, 1993, p. 8). Wilson and Gutierrez (1985) report the same practice among industry union members of color: who are systematically excluded from "job promotion while young whites who were sons of union journeymen obtained superior status directly out of high school without job experience" (p. 157).

A number of women attending a meeting sponsored by the Women's Steering Committee of the Directors Guild of America in Los Angeles in March 1993 expressed concerns about employment practices in the television and film industry. Erma Elzy-Jones, one of the few African American associate directors and script supervisors in the industry, maintained that industry employers do not look for veteran associate directors or consciously think of hiring women of color. Elodie Keene, a director and supervising producer of *L. A. Law*, has been attempting to hire more women directors on the program, but said that there is a provision in the industry that allows inexperienced young male directors who graduate from film schools, the theater, or surface through familial connections, to be accepted more readily than females. Keene also maintained that these men "are cut much more slack" and given opportunities that women are not. Wilson and Gutierrez note that minority hiring in the film and television industries remained "slow and at minimal levels" (1985, p. 159), while advances in technologies such as cable, pay TV, satellite video transmission, and video recorders made major strides in serving the American public.

As in hiring practices, programs designed to recruit and advance persons of color in the industry are often the first to go amid budgetary crises. For example, the Minority Advancement Program was among the first programs eliminated when the new CEO of CBS Television network, Laurence Tisch, found a need to cut the budget as a result of the growing competition from cable, home videos, and fluctuating advertising revenues (Auletta, 1991). When asked about the impact of his policies on women and minorities in television, Tisch's response was all too revealing of where his priority lay. His answer—"Is there a problem?"—clearly placed the concern on cutting waste rather than on the lack of female and minority personnel in the rank of management.

Representation and pay equity have plagued women of color since long before Sojourner Truth's riveting speech on behalf of those doubly oppressed by race and sex at the 1867 Convention of the American Equal Rights Association. During the Reagan Era affirmative action was feebly enforced to the detriment of all the progress women had made up to that time (Faludi, 1991). By 1980, the networks' two leading female anchors were gone and Charlayne Hunter-Gault, one of the first African American women to anchor a national newscast, was quietly pushed into a slot as a secondary backup anchor at the *MacNeil/Lehrer News Hour*. Recent data compiled by the Office of Women in Higher Education reveal that "in and out of higher education, the wage gap between men and women exists at every level of employment, making it abundantly clear that women get less monetarily from their investment in higher education than their male colleagues" (Touchton & Davis, 1991, p. xi).

In academia, the gross underrepresentation of persons of color and their diminishing presence is also of great concern to policymakers and educational planners. Hope (1992) reports that minorities, that is, Asians, African Americans, Latinos, and Native Americans, comprise less than 5% of the total Ph.D. population. In 1992, the Accrediting Council on Education in Journalism and Mass Communication found that 9% of the faculty of 19 journalism schools accredited in 1991 were minorities, with women comprising about 20% of the faculty ("The Numbers Game," 1992). Less than 400 journalism professors are minority, with the majority of them African American; 41 Asian American; about two dozen Latino; and fewer than a dozen Native American. Ninety-eight percent of full and associate journalism professors are white (De Uriarte, 1992). Although these numbers may indicate a slight increase, proportionately, in comparison to the population, they reveal a decrease. A possible explanation for the decreasing numbers of enrollment and acquired degrees could be attributed directly to national economic and political conditions that have resulted in the dismantling of affirmative action policies and a shift from diversity to "excellence" in the university community (Deskins, 1991). Deskins (1991) and Auletta and Jones (1990) argue that a number of entrenched academics promote a strict adherence to "academic" issues and do not see multicultural issues as relevant. Through such name-calling as "proponents of deconstruction," the members of the "old-guard" in academia hold advocates of multiculturalism accountable to the status quo. The debate will no doubt continue, but the insufficient supply of new minority doctorates remains a key and pressing issue facing academia.

Educators of color point out that in journalism schools there is no academic pipeline to help guide minority students through the doctoral-level work (Mercer, 1991). Other factors contributing to the underrepresentation of a more diverse faculty can be found in research indicating that fewer minority Ph.D. recipients plan academic careers (Vining Brown, 1992).

Industry and government are the major competitors for new minority doctorates, offering them more attractive careers and salaries than those in academia. In addition, minorities with doctoral degrees maintain they cannot find employment in their area of study. Departmental requirements in journalism schools very often are barriers to potential faculty of color. Significant professional experience and a Ph.D. are usually the imposed hiring conditions. Although professional experience can count as much as an advanced degree, scholarship is usually looked at more seriously (Mercer, 1991). This double requirement accounts in part for the shortage of faculty of color, who have been systematically excluded from opportunities to gain the necessary experience and qualifications.

In terms of African American Ph.D.s, Mickelson and Oliver (1991) note the dwindling supply from which schools can easily choose, but argue that a significant number are overlooked and deemed unqualified "if they are not found in the graduate programs of the universities considered to be the best in the field." They maintain "this pattern leads to the faulty perception of a greater shortage of quality African American academics than is actually the case. In reality, the search process itself is to blame for not uncovering highly qualified Black candidates" (pp. 177-178). The researchers contend that the roots of this dilemma can be located historically in a racist ideology that reaches back to examples like those of W. E. B. DuBois, who was unable to obtain a university position after he graduated from Harvard in 1899. Like many academics with degrees from prestigious universities, Dubois was forced to accept work as a research assistant before joining the faculty at a Black college. These universities became the refuge for early African American scholars.

A diverse faculty is a necessary component in any discipline and particularly in journalism schools. These faculty members can help students to expand their worldview to represent a growing multicultural society. In addition, they can mentor students of color who often feel culturally alienated and uncomfortable in university settings where all their professors are Anglo. A diverse faculty can help give students of color the impression that there is something to strive for (Mercer, 1991). African American female students, in particular, have felt an enormous amount of academic pressure on white campuses (Allen & Haniff, 1991). Incidents of faculty insensitivity toward students of color can also be traced historically. Jane Bolin, the first African American woman judge recalls the following event in 1928:

> The sharpest and ugliest memory of Wellesley days occurred in my senior year during a conference, mandatory for seniors, with a guidance counsellor. She exhibited obvious physical shock when told of my plan to study law. She

threw up her hands in disbelief and told me there was little opportunity for women in law and absolutely none for a "colored" one. Surely, I should consider teaching. (Ihle, 1992, p. 148)

More than 60 years later, the negative preconceptions of students of color remain unchanged. One of the authors of this article, a television producer, who is now working on her doctorate, remembers that her undergraduate advisor suggested she change her major because she had experienced difficulty in a particular journalism class. "Years later I saw my advisor while shooting on location in Hawaii. I wanted so much to remind him that he'd discouraged me. I passed, however, because I knew I was fortunate to have had other sources of academic and moral support." Another barrier found by one Chicana doctoral student was the preconception of her ability based on gender and ethnicity. She recalls, "One professor went as far as to admit that at first he didn't think I could complete the program, but I surprised him with my ability to meet the assignments" (Achor & Morales, 1990, p. 279).

Cheng (1990), who argues for a paradigm shift, admonishes that "to be empowered, students need to feel confident about themselves and not feel inhibited" (p. 268). Cheng suggests that we move beyond stereotypical notions such as being "affirmative action charity cases" (Achor & Morales, 1990, p. 279). Cheng explains that "tolerating difference connotes an underlying disregard and indifference" whereas acceptance "connotes approval and support." A diverse faculty of women who adequately reflect the female student population in journalism and communication schools will help alleviate these problems. In addition, a multicultural perspective that includes a more pluralistic curriculum can also provide key and critical components for effecting a much needed change in higher education.

La Malinche's Dialogic: Dilemmas of Working Within the System

Working within the system, women of color confront a variety of common sources of anxiety. Some of these stressors are inherent to the phase of newly initiated: of finding oneself in an unfamiliar, unwelcoming, and oftentimes oppressive culture. Others are the direct result of confronting a system that on the one hand is in dire need of a dramatic reconstruction and on the other holds steadfastly to a threatened power structure based on hegemonic notions of truth, language, and knowledge. Women of color in academia most often rely on the strength of their gender and their ethnicity to endure the realities of their chosen career (Gandara, 1982). This was clearly articulated by all four Chicana participants in a speaker series, "Herstory: Chicanas Confronting the System," sponsored by Chicano/a Fellows Program at Stanford University during the 1988-1989 academic year.[1] When faced with having to defend their rights, all four participants spoke of the heavy reliance on close social networks and on lessons learned in their previous struggles confronting the inequities of the system. A series participant, Sylvia Morales, film critic and producer, pointed out for Chicanas, "We have a tendency to form families when we are away from home."

In academia, issues most often faced by women of color can easily be summed up by that perennial question, "To be or not to be?"—in this case, part of the system? As the newcomer acquires a new language, a new mode of thinking and doing, the nagging thought remains of how to maintain a connection to the "community." The dilemma of women of color in academia is how to create a new dialogue with those in power without compromising the dialogue with those from whose rank she comes. In essence, how does the woman of color lead the conquistador to new realms of understanding without falling prey to the legacy of betrayal that has maligned the 500 year herstory of La Malinche?[2] La Malinche's intelligence, knowledge of several languages and dialects, and her ability to achieve a distinguished place in the new world order of the time is subsumed under a cloak of sexual and political betrayal for her forced association with Cortés.

Today, the identity crisis for the woman academic of color throws into question not only one's own background experience, knowledge, and language, but the institution's as well. Exploring new frontiers of identity, scholarship, and institutional culture, women of color must find solace and strength in the notion of the American public culture as "emergent, multivocal, dialogical, and contested territory" (Mechling, 1990, p. 157) and, in light of La Malinche's fallacy, reclaim their identity as knowers of many truths and many languages. Regrettably, it is not until women of color make up a substantial number of academics that they can challenge the myth of betrayal and as García's (1990) work points out for Chicanas, the cultural and gender inferiority stigma attributed to them.

Secure in the reconstituted social networks of support and in her *ganas* [desires] to take on the challenge of academia, a woman of color faces the hurdle of establishing critical linkages between her background experiences and the academic culture. And nowhere is the task more treacherous and fraught with insecurities than in the area of language. The shift from literary, journalistic, and/or personal everyday written expression to analytic academic language, for example, often produces self-doubt, fear, and anger, emotions formed by previous experiences of exclusion in an educational system that at every turn has discounted or assailed their language, their knowledge base, and their perspective. Though there might be an element of truth in the question of "excellence" of academic form in their writing, women of color could easily relearn the required discourse, if only the system could provide the necessary mechanisms to make the transition. Academic writing is a skill and as a skill can be taught—an instructional component absent in much pedagogy directed at students from diverse backgrounds in the public school system.

As part of the system, women of color face extreme forces to conform to the mind-set of the academy. In their assertions for new lines of thinking in academic circles, they call to the fore new forms of knowledge and new visions of discourse, content, and structure under heavy scrutiny of their intellectual competence and theoretical foundations. They call for an emphasis on the concrete and experiential as a basis for theoretical deliberations, the inclusion of community forms of communication as valid areas of study, and a curricular focus on multicultural perspectives based on local cultures in the United States rather than on a strict adherence to a foreign focus. The right to exercise the choice to complement their assigned readings with the work of local, regional, or Third World luminaries, in many campuses across the country, did not come without heated debate and, in some cases, extreme personal and professional sacrifice (Rosaldo, 1989). Although this strategy puts women academics of color at odds with conventional notions of knowledge and truth, scholars have suggested that to ignore outsiders' perspectives "artificially restricts and stultifies the scholarly imagination" (Matsuda, 1988, p. 3). According to Matsuda, minority scholars have contributed to "eradicating apartheid," in the case of legal knowledge, by buying, citing, discussing, and teaching outsiders' scholarship.

Exercising a new course of action and reflection in the curriculum is not without obstacles (Freire, 1981). Colleagues and the students themselves are not accustomed to the responsibility that accompanies a multicultural curriculum. Without such guideposts as the "correct answer," the "one truth," and the authority of the teacher to mark their path of exploration, students experience anxiety, confusion, and a lack of structure. Becoming comfortable with anxiety, uncertainty, and even fear, as Mechling (1990) suggests, involves a radical departure from the standard norm of compliance, reliance, and anonymity common in most American classrooms. Most students are not ready to give up the security of invisibility in favor of being held accountable for their role in the creation of knowledge. Although most students would agree that they find the multicultural approach open to their opinions, nonthreatening, and at times enlightening, they nevertheless question its credibility, faddishness, and its marginal status. Conventional notions of the transmission and acquisition of knowledge as theoretically and historically based are not easily displaced. In particular, students find difficulty in co-constructing knowledge—of believing that they and others apart from the teacher are valid sources of knowledge.

Walking the Tenuous Tenure Line

Faced with overwhelming odds, women of color in academia are on a "tenuous" track to tenure. Along the way, they must confront life decisions about their cultural identity vis-à-vis the ethnocentric bounds of academia, finding refuge in another institution when one does not work out, about fighting back in order to pave the way for others, and about dropping out when the task of changing the system becomes an insurmountable task (Reyes & Halcon, 1988). Balancing both their obligations to their profession and their community, women of color in academia must walk a tightrope on their way to tenure. As numerous studies over the past two decades have repeatedly indicated, the road to tenure is strewn with various obstacles they must overcome (Blum, 1988). It is not uncommon for nonminority peers to question and label the work of minority scholars as inappropriate, self-serving, limited, narrow in scope, and lacking in objectivity (Blum, 1988; Nieves-Squires, 1991; Reyes & Halcon, 1988).

As pioneers in higher education, ethnic female scholars encounter greater pressures, heavier stress, and an increased possibility of failure or "push out" arising from intractable and arbitrary standards. Their research focus on diverse communities is often devalued and, according to Garza (1992), has helped to keep them in the role of second class citizens. Their teaching and service to their students, institution, and community are often discounted as peripheral in performance evaluations. Although their effort serves as an undeniable resource to the university, it draws away from their scholarship and publication: the measuring stick of excellence in academia.

In paving the way for themselves and subsequent generations, women of color often bear the burden of being the "only one"—if not the first— member of their group to be hired in their respective departments. They enter an arena where stereotypes prevail and are frequently greeted with resentment or blatant hostility. It is not uncommon for female scholars to feel they must toil doubly hard to keep abreast of the research and theoretical lines of thought prominent in their department while maintaining a focus on their chosen line of inquiry. Feeling misunderstood and alienated and without the benefit of support or mentors, women of color in academia suffer incredible isolation. Often alone, their only recourse is to maintain, at a high cost of telephone bills, a strong connection with other scholars of color who are spread across the country.

According to Reyes and Halcon (1988) institutions of higher education are reluctant to hire minorities or more than one person of color per department because of deeply ingrained beliefs that minority scholars are not as qualified as nonminorities and because higher numbers of faculty of color reduces the calibre of the faculty already on board. Thus minority men and women "continue to be plagued with the assumption that we are tokens and have been hired without the appropriate credentials, experience, or qualifications" (p. 303). Women of color continually find themselves trying to prove that they are as intellectually competent as their Anglo counterparts. Latinas, for example, receive an unmistakable message that they are seen as Mother Earth sorts, as women who are "powerless, pathological, prayerful, and dutiful family members (Nieves-Squires, 1991, p. 4).

Despite their efforts, women of color find that their contributions are overlooked, discounted, or devalued. They are beleaguered by work conditions that cripple their efforts and compromise their success in academia. Clearly, they are subjected to professional judgment or evaluation greater than that experienced by their Anglo peers and such criteria as tenure rules are often selectively reinforced against their favor (Reyes & Halcon, 1988). These cases range from undue pressure to publish to a willful disregard of research, teaching, and service at peer review time. In what Reyes and Halcon have characterized as "hair-splitting decisions," academics of color are subjected to subjective judgment that prevents them from being hired or promoted. In one case that is being challenged at the university level, a department chairperson refused to grant maternity leave to a Latina and explicitly cautioned her that to ask about stopping the tenure clock would be looked upon unfavorably during tenure review.

Although these types of arbitrary decisions present stumbling blocks, the toughest fight for women of color is the validation of their research. In many instances, women of color have chosen to conduct research that addresses the economic, educational, and political problems in their communities. They experience a double bind of being devalued not only because they are women but also because they are minority (Nieves-Squires, 1991). In the words of Reyes and Halcon, women of color "want to speak for ourselves, to define, label, describe, and interpret our condition from the 'inside out' " (1988, p. 7) instead of reading it in the social science literature written by nonminorities.

The heavy service loads resulting from mentoring more than their share of students, including nonminority students seeking a female with whom they can identify, also jeopardize the chances of achieving tenure. Nieves-Squires asserts that the high demands of advisement and committee assignments allocated to women of color limits their time for research and publishing. Yet, when performance evaluations are conducted, this service is rated negatively and accorded little or no weight. A Stanford report, for example, found that minority professors work on two sites—the campus and the community—yet their work is usually not seen as service to other staff, faculty, and students, but rather as a personal matter (Nieves-Squires, 1991). Thus, integration in the inner sanctum of academia can come only if more than a handful of academicians come from underrepresented groups.

Recommendations for the Future

The issues that address inequities in higher education of women of all ethnicities are complex and tied to a variety of factors connected to larger social, economic, and historical conditions too vast to be explored here. However, the problem remains that ethnic scholars—and in particular women in academia—are severely underrepresented. A review of the pertinent literature focusing on ways of improving the plight for women and persons of color in academia offer several recommendations. Below, we provide a synthesis of these recommendations:

- Improve the rate of enrollment and degree completion through a functional change in higher education that validates previous professional experience at the same time that it institutes mechanisms to facilitate the transition.
- Obtain a commitment by the institution and graduate departments in written policies to increase access of minorities.
- Enforce the Accrediting Council on Education in Journalism and Mass Communications (ACEJMC) Standard 12 to realize the goal of greater representation of individuals from diverse backgrounds.
- Promote curriculum revisions that help prepare students to understand, cover, communicate with, and relate to a multicultural, multiethnic, multiracial, and otherwise diverse society.[3]
- Make financial aid adequate and accessible for those pursuing a Ph.D.
- Recognize the historical contributions of ethnic women scholars.
- Encourage scholarship generated by women and scholars of color.
- Establish guidelines that decrease differentials in salaries for men and women with the same training and experience.
- Provide an environment free of discriminating practices that promotes comfortable levels for both students and faculty of color.

Notes

1. Presentors included Demetria Martinez, Sister Rosa Maria Zarate, Dolores Huerta, and Silvia Morales, November 1, 1988 to February 16, 1989.

2. La Malinche, the Indian interpreter given to Cortés by the Indians of Potonchan in Tasbasco is known to have been a valuable member of the invading force (MacLachlan & Rodríguez O., 1980). She spoke both Nahautl and Maya and later became the conqueror's mistress and trusted advisor. For this role, La Malinche, known as Dona Maria by the Spaniards, became a symbol of sexual and political betrayal of indigenous Mexico (Limón, 1990). Unfortunately, the symbolism of La Malinche has also been subverted by patriarchal culture to mean women who use their sexuality to deceive men.

See also José Limón's essay on "La Llorona, The Third Legend of Greater Mexico: Cultural Symbols, Women, and the Political Unconscious," for a discussion on the use of the symbol of La Malinche as "a scapegoat for the ills and misfortunes" of Mexican society (p. 406).

3. The Accrediting Council on Education in Journalism and Mass Communication mandated universities to adopt the Standard 12 provisions, which promote minority and female representation at the student and faculty levels. Multicultural, multiracial, and multiethnic curriculums must also be representative.

References

Achor, Shirley, & Morales, Aida. (1990). Chicanas holding doctoral degrees: Social reproduction and cultural ecological approaches. *Anthropology Education Quarterly, 21*(3), 269-287.

Allen, W., Walter, R., Haniff, E. R., & Haniff, Nesha Z. (1991). Race, gender, and academic performance in U.S. higher education. In W. Allen, R. Walter, E. G. Epps, Edgar R. Haniff, & Nesha Z. Haniff (Eds.), *Colleges in black and white* (pp. 105-106). Albany: SUNY Press.

Auletta, Gales S., & Jones, Terry. (1990). Reconstituting the inner circle. *American Behavioral Scientist, 34*(2), 137-152.

Auletta, Ken. (1991). *Three blind mice: How the networks lost their way.* New York: Random House.

Blum, Debra E. (1988, June 22). To get ahead in research, some minority scholars choose to "play the game." *Chronicle of Higher Education,* p. A.22.

Cheng, Li-Rong Lilly. (1990). Recognizing diversity: A need for a paradigm shift. *American Behavioral Scientist, 34*(2), 263-278.

Deskins, Donald R. (1991). A regional assessment of minority enrollment and earned degrees in U.S. colleges and universities. In W. Allen, R. Walter, E. G. Epps, Edgar R. Haniff, & Nesha Z. Haniff (Eds.), Colleges in black and white (pp. 36-37). Albany: SUNY Press.

De Uriarte, Mercedes L. (1992, October/November). On multiculturalism, academy trails media industry. *EXTRA!,* p. 25.

Faludi, Susan. (1991). *Backlash: The undeclared war against American women.* New York: Crown Publishers.

Freire, Pablo. (1981). *Pedagogy of the oppressed.* New York: Continuum.

Gandara, Patricia. (1982). Passing through the eye of the needle: High-achieving Chicanas. *Hispanic Journal of Behavioral Sciences, 4,* 167-179.

García, A. (1990). The development of Chicana feminist discourse, 1970-1980. In C. Dubois & V. L. Ruiz (Eds.), *A multicultural reader in United States women's history* (pp. 413-418). New York: Routledge & Kegan Paul.

Garza, Hisauro. (1992). Dilemmas of Chicano and Latino professors in U.S. universities. *The Journal of the Association of Mexican American Educators,* pp. 6-22.

Hope, Richard R. (1992). Minorities in the graduate education pipeline: An introduction. In J. M. Jones, M. E. Goertz, & C. V. Kuh (Eds.), *Minorities in graduate education: Pipeline, policy and practice* (pp. 17-18). Princeton, NJ: Educational Testing Service.

Ihle, Elizabeth L. (1992). *Black women in higher education: An anthology of essays, studies, and documents.* New York: Garland Publishing.

Limón, José. (1990). La Llorona, the third legend of greater Mexico: Cultural symbols, women, and the political unconscious. In A. R. Del Castillo (Ed.), *Between borders: Essays on Mexicana/Chicana history* (pp. 399-432). Encino, CA: Floricanto Press.

MacLachlan, Colin M., Rodríguez O., & Jaime E. (1980). *The forging of the cosmic race: A reinterpretation of colonial Mexico.* Berkeley: University of California Press.

Matsuda, M. (1988). Affirmative action and legal knowledge: Planting seeds in plowed-up ground. *Harvard Women's Law Journal, 11,* 1-17.

Mechling, Jay. (1990). Theory and the other; Or, is this session the text? *American Behavioral Scientist, 34*(2), 153-165.

Mercer, Joyce. (1991, June 6). Who's in the classroom? *Black Issues in Higher Education,* p. 10.

Mickelson, Roslyn A., & Oliver, Melvin L. (1991). The demographic fallacy of the Black academic: Does quality rise to the top? In W. Allen, R. Walter, E. G. Epps, Edgar R. Haniff, & Nesha Z. Haniff (Eds.), *Colleges in black and white* (pp. 177-178). Albany: SUNY Press.

Nieves-Squires, Sarah. (1991). Hispanic women: Making their presence on campus less tenuous. *Project on the status and education of women* (pp. 1-14). Washington, DC: American Association of American Colleges.

Pristen, Terry. (1993, January 31). Hollywood's family ties. *Los Angeles Times,* Calendar Section, p. 8.

Rosaldo, Renato. (1989). *Culture & truth: The remaking of social analysis.* Boston: Beacon.

Reyes de la Luz, María, & Halcon, John J. (1988, August). Racism in academia. *Harvard Educational Review,* pp. 299-313.

The numbers game. (1992, April). *Quill,* p. 14.

Touchton, Judith G., & Davis, Lynne. (1991). *Fact book on women in higher education.* New York: Macmillan.

Vining Brown, Shirley. (1992). Minorities in the graduate education pipeline: An update. In J. M. Jones, M. E. Goertz, & C. V. Kuh (Eds.), *Minorities in graduate education: Pipeline, policy and practice* (pp. 26-27). Princeton, NJ: Educational Testing Service.

Wilson, Clint, Jr., & Gutiérrez, Felix. (1985). *Minorities and media: Diversity and the end of mass communication.* Beverly Hills, CA: Sage.

16 The "Glass Ceiling" Effect on Mass Communication Students

LARISSA A. GRUNIG

More than a century ago the revered Cuban poet Jose Martí made an impassioned plea for educational opportunities for women,

> something which will secure their happiness, because enhancing their minds through solid studies, they will live on a par with men as comrades, not at their feet like beautiful toys, and because of her self-sufficiency, a woman will not feel hurried to attach herself—as a reed to a wall—to the first passerby, but instead, she will ponder and decide, leaving aside the rogues and liars and choosing the industrious and sincere.[1]

Women faculty members, too, deserve to live "on a par" with their male colleagues. However, women who teach journalism often encounter a "glass ceiling" that limits the likelihood of their advancement. That is, they can envision a career track that would lead to the prestige and job security inherent in becoming tenured, but their chances of actual promotion are less than those of their male counterparts.

This disparate treatment in tenure and promotion because of gender has been documented in several recent studies.[2] It has led columnist Colman McCarthy (1991) to call female professors "academia's stoop laborers." He considered the treatment of women in academia "a deliberate debasement of the values professors . . . are called on to preserve" (p. A27). And, he challenged "the senior, tenured faculty and mostly male professors who gather in faculty lounges and respond with nothing more than tut-tuts" to rally to the defense of "their nontenured, underpaid and mostly female colleagues" (p. A27).

What has been largely missing from such discussions of the glass ceiling for faculty women is the impact this barrier may have on their students. As one expert on the campus climate for women—faculty and students alike— explained, federal policies such as Title IX have gone a long way toward abolishing the rules that once allowed male and female students (and their professors) to be treated differently (Sandler, 1984). However, increasing awareness of sex discrimination has not solved all problems of unequal treatment and opportunity. As the president of the American Association of University Women (AAUW) put it, "The bias that exists in how girls are taught is no longer blatant, but they experience it on a daily basis" (Sharon Schuster, cited in Jordan, 1992, p. A1). In other words, we agree with the conclusion of a report released by the AAUW: More has been said than done to improve schooling for girls despite 20 years of research and reform efforts aimed at ensuring gender equity in education (American Association of University Women [AAUW], 1992).

A senior associate of the Center for Women Policy Studies explained that "there are tremendous similarities between the slew of reports we're seeing today and the slew of reports we saw in the 70's" (cited in Blum, 1991, p. A1). As Pat Reuss, a lobbyist at the National Organization for Women's legal defense fund put it, "All we got was a few little crumbs" (cited in Nasar, 1992, p. G3). And at some universities, even the crumbs may have been taken away from female students and professors alike. A report released in 1991 by Case Western, for example, determined that in some respects the situation for women students, staff, and faculty actually had deteriorated since a 1973 gender study done there.

Today's undergraduate is tomorrow's practitioner; today's graduate student is tomorrow's professor.[3] Thus focusing attention on the ramifications of sex discrimination in academia seems doubly appropriate: If the glass ceiling can be shattered, then both the communication professions and future generations of students stand to benefit.

If, on the other hand, academia retains its disparate reward structure for men and women, we send a forceful and negative message to female students. As McElrath (1992) explained, we also may hinder the recruitment of faculty women from among the ranks of female graduate students who observe that their female professors hold less powerful positions than do men.

This chapter begins with a brief examination of the discriminatory patterns and practices many academic women face. It goes on to explore the effects such discrimination may have on students. It concludes with strategies for change, with the hope of enhancing both women's chances to be promoted and the future success of their graduates.

These recommendations have special significance for three groups of students: ethnic and racial minorities, returning students, and women. These "nontraditional students" represent the increasing pluralism of the academy and, in fact, of American society. A physicist at the State University of New York recently spelled out the challenge that this diversity presents the campus: "If our student body is changing so quickly, either we accommodate or we won't exist" (cited in Staff, 1992, p. A7).

At least one campus compiled its own report of discouraging statistics related to the status of African Americans on campus. At the University of Maryland, graduation rates of these undergraduate students are "distressingly low" and getting worse; fewer African Americans are hired and tenured now than 5 years ago; doctoral enrollments declined during the past decade; and the proportion of professional and executive staff increased insignificantly during that same period (Clague, 1992). Perhaps most discouraging is that the university's Committee on Excellence Through Diversity found that its statistics were not significantly different from the country as a whole.

With women undergraduates outnumbering men, Gillespie (1987) said, "One might wonder why a faculty member would persist in the use of the pronoun 'he' when over 50% of the students are now likely to be women." Since the mid-1980s, women have been awarded more bachelor's (53%) and master's degrees (52%) than men (Nasar, 1992). The growing percentage of female students is especially evident in programs of journalism and mass communication. Undergraduate enrollments, in particular, are polarized by gender.

Women's educational excellence begins in high school. A massive study conducted by the U.S. Department of Education's Office of Research recently determined that women's high school class rank exceeds that of men by at least 10 points; that women outranked men in math, science, and foreign languages; that women were more likely to win scholarships to college and that once there, they earned their degrees faster; that women's grade point average in each major exceeds men's in college (including the GPA of women in engineering, science, math, and business); and that women who go on to graduate school are considered more qualified (Adelman, 1991). Despite women's educational capital, this 20-year study comparing men's and women's achievement found that 13 years out of high school women (even those without children) earned 31.9% less than do men. The author of the report attributed this disparity to residual bias (Adelman, 1991).

Further, more than 40% of today's students are over age 25. At the master's degree level, 53% are older than 30 (and two thirds of them attend school part time) (Rudavsky, 1992). Two out of every three students over age 34 are women (Staff, 1986). Like minorities and all female undergraduates, these older, nontraditional students—overwhelmingly female—need new ideas and programs to meet their special situation.

A feminist perspective will be brought to bear on the problems facing these three types of students. That is, the chapter is written from a woman's perspective and it is transformative in nature—seeking to empower students (and faculty) regardless of their age, race, or gender. It emphasizes an inclusive feminist consciousness rather than the exclusivity that characterized feminism earlier in this century, when the woman's movement was marked by class, race, and political orientation (Schneir, 1972).

Just as feminist literature is not uniform in its analysis of inequality or in its recommendations for overcoming sexual oppression (Currie & Kazi, 1987), the recommendations that make up the final section of this chapter vary widely. These strategies should not be perceived as a monolithic solution for the barriers facing any single group of afflicted students. In fact, the relevant issues for any one group may be quite different from—if not in actual conflict with—the issues of another group. In the same way, what stands to benefit faculty women may not always be in the best interests of all of their students at all times. The challenge of this chapter lies in finding the junctures wherein injustices can be fought and equality won for significant numbers of women and people of color without sacrificing respect for the individualism that has characterized women's progress in academia to date.

Developing a lengthy list of alternative recommendations seems the best way to accommodate the differing work patterns between women and men and even among women (Bernard, 1964). As the director of women's studies at Duke (O'Barr, cited in O'Shea, 1988) put it:

> We've got to remember that there's no homogeneity among women. We can't discuss "what women want" as if biology predetermines needs. As we focus more on women's issues, we are coming to grips with the fact that there are many different types of women. There is no one thing women, as a group, want; there are many things. (p. 41)

Problems Faculty Women Face

Findings of an extensive case study of women on a journalism faculty of a large eastern university showed little direct evidence of sex discrimination on promotion and tenure (Grunig, 1989). However, in this case—substantiated by the experiences of women on a dozen other campuses—all women interviewed spoke of the subtle pattern of bias, misunderstanding, and insensitivity they believe contributes directly and indirectly to limiting their chances for success in higher education.

The main sources of inequality seemed to be the small numbers and powerlessness of women on the typical faculty. In the department studied, for instance, women constituted less than one quarter of the 21-person faculty (contrasted with a student body that was about two-thirds female). Only one of the department's 13 tenured professors was a woman. Related problems included tokenism; a heavier advising load for women; lack of role models in academia; and few opportunities for sharing resources and information, mentoring, networking, and coalition-building.

Causes of these problems included men's perceptions that women "didn't fit in," women's own feeling that they lack power, their ineptness in negotiation, their real lack of influence and support (from home as well as from the university), the realization on the part of decision makers that women are almost "captives" of a geographical region, the burden of home responsibility that women continue to accept, the "imposter syndrome" that causes women to downplay or dismiss their accomplishments, and women's insistence on working independently.

Other traditional causes of discrimination against women include sex-role stereotyping, male-female interaction, and social norms. Still another problem is the conflict typically experienced by young, female professors of low academic rank. Locke (1992) found that these women were more teaching oriented than men and that they had significantly better teaching ratings. However, they were torn between teaching—which they liked—and research, which was required for promotion.

This kind of frustration and discrimination can affect the careers of all women in academia—not just the untenured, relatively powerless ones. For one dramatic example, consider Carolyn G. Heilbrun. This prominent literary critic recently quit her job of 32 years with Columbia University in disgust over what she considered the university's male establishment. Heilbrun felt downtrodden, isolated, and powerless to fight the sexist policies she encountered at Columbia. Her case became famous when more than 500 feminist scholars met at a conference called "Out of the Academy and Into the World with Carolyn Heilbrun." Their purpose was to honor Dr. Heilbrun, trade information, and plan for the future (Leatherman, 1992).

The study cited earlier in this chapter concluded with recommendations for enhancing the promotion and tenure picture for women—suggestions that may well have emanated from the Heilbrun conference as well. Crashing the glass ceiling that keeps faculty women from being advanced or tenured depends on hiring more women to teach, sensitizing their male colleagues about difficulties peculiar to women, fostering women's risk-taking behavior, building supportive structures for women on campus and across campuses, and team-building between genders within departments of journalism.

Although each of these factors—problems, causes, and solutions—warrants an extensive examination in itself, the more pressing concern of this chapter is to look at the impact upon students, male and female alike. How does having few faculty women affect undergraduates, for example? And what is the consequence for graduate students who are advised by women faculty in junior roles? The next section of this chapter extrapolates from extensive literature to explore the effects of problems such as the small number of faculty women and their relative lack of power on their classes.

Problems Students Face

The relatively small number of women who teach in the typical journalism or mass communication department represents an imbalance between female faculty and female students. The Sharp report (Sharp, Turk, Einsiedel, Schamber, & Hollenback, 1985) found that both male and female students are attracted to female teachers for advising because they:

automatically think that the women are going to be more sympathetic and more understanding of them and should spend more time with them than male faculty members. They are more willing to presume upon a woman's time and take up more of a woman's energy with problems than they might with a male. (p. 51)

Advising is one of three kinds of university work considered "feminine" and thus frequently devalued. In fact, according to Knefelkamp (1987), advising—along with teaching and involvement with student activities (such as health services, resident life, and student organizations)—may be denigrated by male professors. In her view, these aspects of faculty work, often considered "hand-holding" for students, spark the need for a revolution to reassess promotion criteria. She argued that although the denigration or devaluation of advising is most often the case at large universities, the evaluation of such care-taking work tends to be more a result of socialization than situation. In other words, men in all type of universities value research, for example, more than they do the relational work involved in student advising. With the growing majority of women undergraduates in journalism, and the preference of both male and female students to seek female advisers, demands for such advising on female faculty without hope of reward or recognition represents a double burden.

Although this imbalance in numbers can be counterproductive for women professors, their students suffer as well. Female undergraduates, in particular, seek out nonparental adults for support and guidance on campus. A recent study at the University of Maryland (Taub, 1991) found that contrary to typical expectations that collegians would be quite independent, most students continue to consider relationships both with adults and with peers extremely important.

Despite the importance of significant one-on-one relationships, then, women students encounter too few same-sex role models and find few mentors—especially female senior professors who are powerful and well connected. Thus the question of power, more than numbers alone, informs this discussion of women in academia. For faculty women to gain voice, they need to ascend to positions of power.[4]

Only when women are promoted to top administrative positions or tenured faculty slots can they be truly effective as advisers, as mentors, as role models, as determinants of the classroom climate, and as shapers of the curriculum studied by male and female students alike. The following sections of this chapter deal with each of these five problem areas—*advising, mentoring, role modeling, affecting the classroom climate,* and *transforming the curriculum.*

Advising

As mentioned above, women faculty members are perceived to be more accessible than men to students in need of advice (Sharp et al., 1985). Additional literature dealing with female role behavior also suggests that women are expected to be more humanitarian and compassionate than men (White & Crino, 1981). One noted scientist argued, also, that faculty women—whom she considered more intuitive than men—make superior advisers because "they answer students' questions even before they know what to ask" (Wise, 1988). These perceptions may lead to demands that diminish the time remaining for research activities that ultimately lead to promotion and tenure (Grunig, 1988).

Along the way, of course, the overburdened female adviser may not be able to devote the appropriate energy or time to all of the students requesting her help.[5] She also may find that her heavy advising load and personalized interaction with students may adversely affect her own program of research; we know that even highly research-oriented female professors have been socialized to accept the role of nurturer and giver to students (Simeone, 1987).

Male professors cannot be expected to "take up the slack," especially with female students. Despite the fact that women in graduate school consistently make better grades than do men,[6] male faculty members tend to encourage same-sex students and to consider female students as less capable and less professionally committed than their male colleagues.[7] This, of course, is a serious perceptual problem for women in professional programs such as journalism. When male professors perceive their female students (especially those who are older and with children)[8] to have less potential and less commitment to the field, they hesitate to invest time and energy in advising them.[9] Finally, graduate students whose dissertations are advised by someone of the same sex show greater productivity (Menges & Exum, 1983).

Women and minority faculty members at The Ohio State University recently recalled their own experiences as students—commenting that their most valued advisers were those who counteracted the prevailing message that discouraged other women and minorities from pursuing professional goals. Students fortunate enough to have such advisers considered themselves better prepared for their role as professors. Others, however, complained of graduate advisers who did not respect them because of their gender or race and still others who did not consider female students as valuable future colleagues (Bourguignon et al., 1987, p. 29).

Mentoring

Closely related to the issue of advising—whether it be curricular, dissertation/thesis, or professional—is mentoring. The trusted counselor or guide, from the beginning of our understanding of the term, was an advantage for male students. (The original Mentor, friend of Odysseus, was entrusted with the education of Odysseus' son Telemachus.) Having a mentor also can be an advantage for junior faculty members. However, a recent study of women who teach public relations found that almost 80% of the respondents do not have a mentor. At the same time, most said they are trying to play this role for their students (Zoch & Russell, 1991).

Just as the study of the journalism department described above showed that faculty women find too few mentors, so the literature suggests that their students find too few academicians willing or able to serve as special tutors in the ways of academia or the professions for which they prepare.[10] As Lewis (1975) explained, "The vast majority of academics who survive graduate school, credentialing and publishing are either men or women who have been and continue to be selected and trained by men" (p. 33). Wise (1988) agreed, urging female students to be especially clear on what they want to achieve "because men won't help you; they're too busy grooming other men."

Because advancement in academia is a more current concern than is initial access (whether "access" means being hired for an entry-level teaching position or admitted to an undergraduate or graduate program),[11] mentoring has become central to the discussion of equality for women students and professors alike. However, without enough faculty women—and especially powerful female professors—the need for academic mentors is likely to go unmet. But why is this special attention so important for students in particular?

Direct benefits for the protégé include recognition and encouragement, honest criticism and feedback, advice on balancing responsibilities and priorities, knowledge of the informal rules for success, information on how to act in a variety of settings (both academic and professional), learning how to make contact with authorities in a discipline or leaders in the field, skills for showcasing one's work, and a perspective on long-range academic or career planning (Hall & Sandler, 1983). Graduate students, in particular, consider a close mentoring relationship with their adviser as a key determinant in feeling prepared for what they would encounter as faculty members themselves.[12]

Benefits accrue to the mentor as well.[13] In addition to the satisfaction inherent in helping develop a junior person's abilities and simply in informal work with students (Zoch & Russell, 1991), two major advantages for the sponsor include ideas for and feedback about his or her own projects, and a network of former mentees at other universities or in the professions—people likely to increase the mentor's power and visibility (Hall & Sandler, 1983, p. 3). Thus developing the skills of female faculty members as mentors for female, minority, and older students also enhances the likelihood of advancement for the faculty. One noted feminist scientist recently argued for the creation of a formal reward system for faculty mentors (Colwell, 1988).

Unfortunately, the "who you know" being as important as the "what you know" creates problems for female champions and for their would-be protégés. Because introduction to the authorities within a department of the university or a corporation capable of hiring and promoting the graduate is one critical aspect of mentoring, the most powerful and well-connected people make the most effective mentors. Women, held to the lower ranks in academia, rarely have those connections.

Men, who tend to be more highly placed on the academic hierarchy, still may not serve female students well as advocates. Just as they tend to invest less time and energy advising women than men, they are less willing to serve as mentors for female novices. The literature shows that men tend to affirm students of their own sex (Hochschild, 1975; Tidball, 1976) and to avoid mentoring relationships with women students, in part because they fear the accusation of sexual harassment (Hall & Sandler, 1983, p. 4).

Minority students find even fewer mentors than do females. The irony is that minority students, who drop out at a higher rate than do majority students and more often for nonacademic reasons, have the greatest need for informal interaction with senior professors and are least likely to experience it (Duncan, 1976; also see Chitaytat, cited in Hall & Sandler, 1983, p. 7). Taub (1991) found that African American women report significantly more social isolation from both peers and adults than do white women on a predominantly white campus.

Reasons for the difficulty minorities—especially female students of color —have in securing mentors include the following (Hall & Sandler, 1983):

> Senior professors, who tend to be white males, are uncomfortable working closely with students so unlike themselves. Senior professors who may be women or minorities are so overloaded with committee and other responsibilities they hesitate to take on proteges. These students have research interests that fall outside the mainstream of the discipline and thus are considered "risky" by senior faculty. (p. 7)

Finally, the many older women who enter or return to the campus have special needs for mentoring that also often go unmet. They must learn of changes in the academic system since they left school, discover ways to balance family and scholarly demands, and be encouraged to venture into the new domain for which they are preparing. Barriers to these women finding mentors include the faculty's doubt about their commitment to education (because of their tendency to enroll on a part-time basis), concern that their future accomplishments will be limited by age (thus making them poor candidates for an investment of time and energy), and the threatening aspect of their being of equal adult status (and perhaps greater life experience) (Hall & Sandler, 1983, p. 7).

Role Modeling

Advising involves the dedication of time and energy to one's students. Mentoring goes one step further, to encompass a personal relationship based on trust, encouragement, and the passing along of inside information to a favored novice. Both of these important avenues for academic and professional success involve one-on-one interaction between student and faculty member. As a result, the few women in the typical department of journalism or mass communication find themselves spread too thinly among the many female students, in particular, who stand to gain from this personal attention from another woman. Also, because powerful professors make the most effective advisers and mentors, the relative lack of influence most women enjoy in academia further limits their usefulness to students.

Thus we turn our attention to a more impersonal yet effective mechanism that can encourage female undergraduates and graduates to stay in school, to get their degrees, and to achieve professionally—role modeling. Role modeling depends less on power than do the previous two processes, so it shows great promise as a way to enhance students' scholarly and journalistic achievement. Still, role modeling for female, minority, and older students does require the visibility of professors like themselves in terms of sex, race, and age.

Role modeling can accomplish two main goals for students: showcasing a person worthy of imitation and dispelling any misperceptions a student may have about the determinants of his or her own success. Aspiring to accomplish what the role model has achieved can be a step forward in terms of goal-setting. Without taking classes from female professors who have managed to get hired in predominantly male university faculties, female graduate students may not believe that such entrée to what has been called a "bastion of male clubbiness" (Rohter, 1987) is possible—at least for the ordinary student. According to Bird (1968), without adequate numbers of role models, we are destroying talent. The price of occupational success is made so high for women that barring exceptional luck only the unusually talented or frankly neurotic can afford to succeed. Girls size up the bargain early and turn it down.

On the other hand, understanding the barriers that many entry-level women, Blacks, and older people in academia or the workforce face adds a critical dose of reality. Otherwise, students may take for granted the achievements of faculty or professional women. A former vice president for academic affairs counseled female students to "be prepared for rebuffs, exclusion, criticism and rejection; it never lets up" (Colwell, 1988). Bernice Sandler, former director of the Project on the Status and Education of Women sponsored by the Association of American Colleges, explained, "What I worry about is that many [students] think it will be easy to have a full-time career and a full-time family" (cited in Greene, 1986, p. 33).

Thus one key suggestion of the "velvet ghetto" study (Cline et al., 1986), a major research project funded by the International Association of Business Communicators to explore the influx of women into the study and practice of public relations, involved the development of career-path models. This would be accomplished largely through exposing students, men and women alike, to practitioners who had chosen different approaches to their personal and work lives.

Professors themselves, of course, can serve as role models—especially for graduate students intending to teach. Role modeling is most effective, according to the director of women's studies at the University of Maryland, when it is accomplished at least in part through self-disclosure. Beck (1983) argued: "It is vital to tell students who I am. Women need role models and visible support. The more students know about me, the more effective I can be as a feminist teacher" (p. 160). Thus she humanizes herself and personalizes the teaching process early on in her courses by sketching her intellectual history and the facts of her life that she considers relevant to the class.

Affecting the Classroom Climate

"Wide Gender Gap Found in Schools: Girls Said to Face Bias in Tests, Textbooks and Teaching Methods" headlined a recent article in *The Washington Post* (Jordan, 1992, p. A1). The article went on to describe a series of studies that showed boys favored over girls by both peers and teachers in the typical classroom.

"Classroom climate" can be defined broadly enough to encompass the situation for girls and women throughout their school experience—whether it be in class, in meetings with academic advisers, or socializing with peers. In these diverse settings, women throughout the country find themselves being treated differently from men (Sandler & Hall, 1986). Such discriminatory treatment may be unconscious. As the first female chemistry teacher at the University of Maryland (and current department chair there) explained, her colleagues need to be sensitized on the importance of providing an equitable setting for their female students. Sandra Greer explained: "We weren't educated this way. We didn't learn it because it wasn't there" (cited in Greene, 1988, p. 10). Creating a fair classroom environment is important, in turn, Greer said, because the way women are treated in the classroom has tremendous impact on their future careers.

Even in the short run, however, students thrive in a climate that helps them move through a hierarchy of cognitive complexity. As undergraduates progress beyond the simple memorization that characterizes tasks during their first couple of years on campus, they need what Knefelkamp (1987) called "an environment of psychological safety" in the classroom. She equated "classroom climate" with "classroom as a community," emphasizing several key variables that help make "climate" a viable concept:

- empathy
- support
- dialogues among peers and between students and professor
- mutual responsibilities
- self-discovery, but guided by the professor, who sets the tone for the overall classroom climate

Contrast these characteristics with what too many women encounter with their male professors. Devaluing women in the classroom ranges from the severity of sexual harassment to the seemingly trivial: frequent interruptions (including interruptions by male students), failure to be called on in the first place, lack of eye contact, forgetting women's names, using generic male language, and focus on appearance rather than accomplishments. The latter behaviors, often considered minor annoyances or called "micro-inequities," may be so commonplace and so subtle that the classroom situation is considered "normal." As Sandler and Hall (1986) put it, "Frequently, neither women nor those who treat them differently are aware of what has occurred; indeed, the possible lack of awareness by both parties is what makes the behavior and its impact so insidious" (p. 2).

Hall and Sandler (1982) were careful to point out that women themselves may create a chilly climate for other women. They further noted that minorities and older students often experience a similar lack of attention and devaluation. They termed minority women on campus "an endangered species," doubly likely to be neglected in the classroom (1986, pp. 12-13). And, graduate students are particularly apt to suffer from what Hall and Sandler called the "male climate," where male professors are even more predominant and women students are fewer.

The crux of the classroom climate problem, in Sandler and Hall's expert opinion, comes down to a few women faculty and an abundance of insensitive men. As Atkins (1983) put it:

The combination of invisibility symbolized by the "Faculty Locker Room" [male] and the high visibility of THE WOMAN adds up to an environment that makes growth slow and difficult. If women are set apart we are deprived of the warmth and acceptance that encourages full human growth. When we exist as outsiders and are forced to justify our existence or defend our presence in the University, we cannot perform to our fullest. (p. 9)

Transforming the Curriculum

An ethnocentric curriculum is one that focuses on the perspectives of a single cultural group. Just as the culture of the United States is becoming increasingly heterogeneous, so too is the typical campus. That diversity comes from racial and ethnic groups as well as an increasing proportion of female students. However, early in this country's most recent women's movement, Friedan (1963) lamented:

> That we have not made any respectable attempt to meet the special educational needs of women in the past is the clearest possible evidence of the fact that our educational objectives have been geared exclusively to the vocational patterns of men. (chap. 13)

Now that women are the majority in journalism classes and in some aspects of the field itself, such as public relations, gearing the educational experience to their interests seems especially important. Appropriately, then, the newest standard of the Accrediting Council for Education in Journalism and Mass Communication calls for attention to the concerns of women and minorities—both students and faculty. However, 30 years later— Title IX, affirmative action, and the EEOC notwithstanding—Friedan's challenge has not been met.

Nothing short of a "transformation of the curriculum" seems adequate. This buzz phrase enjoys more lip service than realization, however.[14] Although the expression refers to integrating scholarship by and about women throughout the disciplines, few students actually are exposed. The president of Lincoln University expressed outrage at the situation: "In a world where demographic shifts have already stood the concepts of majority and minority on their heads, it is no longer intellectually defensible to presume to discuss human endeavor and human interaction from the perspective of only one group" (Sudarkasa, 1987, p. 42). An art historian called women in academia "the forgotten half" of the record (Ferris Olin, cited in McMillen, 1987).

Depriving women of their history, in Schneir's (1972) view, deprives them of their group identity. The president of Wellesley College suggested courses informed by scholarship on women and minorities to help these previously excluded groups identify with their history and culture. Otherwise, she predicted they would come to academia as "something entirely without reference to them and their own lives" (Keohane, 1986, p. 88). Another expert on college curricula agreed that equal representation of women in college texts and programs of research would increase educational excellence (Elizabeth Minnich, cited in Kaplan, 1987, p. 3).

Transforming the curriculum depends on changing the approach to teaching courses as well as their content (Grunig, 1990). However, the proliferation of departments of women's studies during the past decade cannot be expected to counteract the patriarchal view that predominates on the typical campus. Women's studies has been considered a "continuing ghetto-ization of women's interests" (Kolodny, 1981; also see Dudovitz, Russo, Duvall, & Cramer, 1983).[15] The ghetto actually may be more like a posh suburb, however, for privileged, white, middle-class women. According to two teams of feminist scholars, women's studies is in danger of becoming an elitist enterprise (Bowles & Klein, 1983; Stanley & Wise, 1983). This hegemony of discourse does not encourage alternative models to meet the diverse needs of minority and older students, in particular.

A further problem inherent in relying on women's studies to eradicate the "blind spots" in students' education is that the courses reach too few students. Their audience tends to be small and homogeneous, rather than large and diverse. Instead of concentrating what knowledge exists about women and people of color into special, separate departments, then, this information should be an integral part of all fields. Challenging the monistic canon requires hiring more Blacks and women to teach. As Sudarkasa (1987) put it, "Their influence in fields in which they have been active shows why it is important to recruit such scholars in disciplines where they are few or nonexistent" (p. 42).

Conclusions

Hoffman (1986) summarized the challenges facing educators when she described what she called the difficulty of "applying theory to practice" in academia:

> The transformative potential in integrating the recent scholarship on women into the curriculum; of increasing the numbers, status, and authority of women staff and faculty on college campuses; and of challenging the bureaucratic forms of domination and subordination through organized resistance to central-ized authority and depersonalized control remains a vision of what could be. (p. 118)

Looking at the case of the large eastern university and its discriminatory practices against the women who teach journalism there, and extrapolating from the literature to explore the effect of such discrimination on students, has yielded a similarly bleak picture. Too many students are victims of social, intellectual, and economic inequality. However, this study has produced little evidence that students, including women, are consciously trying to change their situations on campus—much less challenging such a powerful institution as the university.

Given the devalued position in which so many women, minorities, and returning students find themselves, the logical question is, Why do they acquiesce? Unlike some brave and independent faculty women, most students seem to subscribe to the myth of equality. Also, it seems likely that, course by course, semester by semester, many students are finding it all they can do simply to try to complete their degrees.

The educational process, though, happens in myriad circumstances—many of which happen to be stacked against people of color, women, and older students. This chapter should establish that injustice strikes women who teach and women who study alike.

The diversity represented by women, minorities, and returning students on campus adds richness to the faculty who teach, advise, and encourage them—but it also creates the need for almost individual solutions that impedes progress on any large-scale, institutional basis. Many educational experts would argue, in fact, that reform must take place at the national—rather than institutional or individual—level (AAUW, 1992). However, attacking the problems of sexism, racism, and ageism at that societal level is beyond the scope of this chapter.

The following recommendations represent an effort to balance idiosyncratic solutions with practical remedies affecting enough students to make real progress toward equity for all. This approach is consistent with the goal articulated by McIntosh (1983) a decade ago: that we refuse to define women as a problem and instead begin to think about women as varied human beings.

Recommendations

Putting these recommendations into practice will require the cooperation of men as well as the commitment of women. White men hold the doors of power; they may choose to open them or to keep them closed to older students, people of color, and women. Further, history has shown that no revolution succeeds if only a small group with special needs is emotionally involved. Instead, men in higher education must come to realize that what happens to their female colleagues in a sense happens to them. In other words, it is in the self-interest of men not to waste women's resources. A national study of girls and self-esteem concluded that to shortchange girls is to shortchange America (AAUW, 1992). As geneticist and women's advocate Estelle Ramey (1988) said in a keynote address: "You can't ignore half the population—or you do so at your own peril."

Increased attention to the problems of female students and faculty members undoubtedly will cost men some comfort in the short run. However, the problems described above will not go away if we ignore them. Hoping this inequitable situation will evaporate on its own only leads to missed opportunities, thwarted ambitions, high levels of stress on the part of both men and women, and poor performance of the academic unit.

All of this is not to say that programs of journalism and mass communication are fundamentally flawed, or "rotten to the core." Rather, it is to suggest that academe must be altered fundamentally to become inclusive. The following map of the academic terrain shows the areas in which reform seems most possible. These places are situated along the same dimensions as the problem areas identified earlier: advising, mentoring, role modeling, affecting the classroom climate, and transforming the curriculum.

Advising

■ Create a mechanism for rewarding advising and other, related responsibilities now considered "feminine."

■ Develop counseling programs and referral services for nontraditional students.

■ Encourage female and minority graduate students to pursue areas of the discipline in which there are relatively few women and people of color now.

Mentoring

■ Increase awareness among both faculty and students of the potential benefits of mentoring.

■ Enhance the faculty's skill in mentoring, perhaps through publications that inform "how to" and "how not to." For examples, see the Association of American Colleges' pamphlet on academic mentoring (Hall & Sandler, 1983, p. 15).

■ Create a mechanism for rewarding mentoring.

■ Encourage communication professionals to become mentors—working through educators and advisers of student chapters of professional organizations who would, in turn, increase their base for networking among powerful professionals.

■ Require students to seek mentors in their sequence areas, perhaps by making mentoring a component of every internship or volunteer activity.

■ Increase students' awareness of the discrimination they may face. As a male sociology professor said, "Much of the problem of inequality is rooted in perceptions that there is not a problem" (Segal, 1988). Educators cited in a magazine article emphasized the importance of young women considering the issue of discrimination while they are still in college and have "lifestyle choices" (O'Shea, 1988, p. 70).

Role Modeling

- Make the life stories of communication professionals available to students. Stories should include the problems as well as the rewards inherent in their careers. This might be accomplished, as the "velvet ghetto" study (Cline et al., 1986) suggested, through student chapters of professional associations such as the IABC, the Public Relations Society of America, Women in Communication, the National Association of Black Journalists, or the Society of Professional Journalists. Look for women or people of color who preside over these professional organizations as well as city editors, news anchors, magazine publishers, heads of public relations or advertising firms, and corporate vice presidents in charge of communication.

- Include examples in textbooks of women and minorities in top managerial positions.

- Women and minority faculty members should "tell it like it is" when recounting their experiences. However, during self-disclosure they must take care not to pass along their own anger, suspicions, and fears (feeling victimized is disempowering). Students, as well, should feel free to self-disclose during class. Although the expression of emotional reactions seems to be more common in courses specifically dealing with sex and gender (Adler, 1984), faculty should be prepared to deal with such discussion in any class.

Affecting the Classroom Climate

- Adopt at least 14 of the 15 strategies proposed in the American Council on Education's "New Agenda of Women for Higher Education."[16] In addition to the explicit suggestion to provide a supportive climate in the classroom and elsewhere on campus, recommendations included seeking commitment from campus leadership to understand and address the concerns of women students, faculty and administrators; considering how campus policies and planning affect men and women alike; establishing effective policies to contend with sexual harassment; auditing and reporting on the status of women on campus; developing policies that support children and families; appreciating diversity; creating a senior position as advocate for women; and fostering women's leadership, including minority women.

■ Following general policy recommendations emanating from the landmark "chilly climate" study (Sandler & Hall, 1986), develop a policy advocating nonsexist language; educate all members of the academic community about climate issues (primarily through workshops, informal discussions, and written materials); ensure that grievance procedures for students, faculty, and staff accommodate subtle as well as overt differential treatment; recognize women's[17] accomplishments; include women in informal professional and social activities; support formal and informal networks of women; avoid asking women to fulfill stereotypically "feminine" roles; provide women with ongoing feedback (both positive and negative) about their work; and make equitable treatment for all students and faculty part of the formal reward structure.

Transforming the Curriculum

■ Following the recommendations in an article that argued for a feminist research agenda in journalism and mass communication (Grunig, 1988), more research should be done about women—and women should be able to be promoted doing this kind of work.

■ Transform the curriculum to provide students with knowledge about all of the cultures that make up American society in general and the journalistic enterprises in particular.

■ Examine the experiences of each culture or gender from its own perspective.

■ As advocated by the team assessing the status of junior faculty at Ohio State (Bourguignon et al., 1987, p. 63), consider reducing the teaching load for all untenured professors to help them get their research program started. The team's report urged the enhancement of research support funds and opportunities specifically for women and minority junior faculty. Several respondents indicated that they "perceived a diminishment of the worth of their research if it was focused on either women or minorities" (Bourguignon et al., 1987, p. 64).

■ Regularly gather demographic data by sex, race, and age. Information should be both statistical and anecdotal and should pertain both to students and to faculty, full and part time.

■ Following the plan in operation at American University (Knefelkamp, 1987), approve no new courses in the general education curriculum without consideration of gender, race, class, and age.

■ Develop courses especially for women who want to study the topic of women or multicultural diversity and journalism or mass communication. Provide male students the chance to study with and about females who are interested in this area.

Finally, an overriding concern that permeates all other considerations should be discussed: the need to recruit, hire, and promote more women and minorities. This understanding reinforces the importance of the recommendations listed in the initial case study of sex discrimination in promotion and tenure (Grunig, 1989). In addition, search committees should facilitate the hiring of more women and minorities mainly by (1) recognizing that these candidates may not have such detailed curriculum vitae as would men their age because they have faced different obstacles and enjoyed different opportunities; (2) becoming sensitive to the makeup of the committee, being careful at the same time not to overburden the small number of women constantly asked to serve on these draining groups; and (3) interviewing minority and female candidates who are not hired to find out whether they believe they have been treated equitably throughout the application process.

Other suggestions, borrowed from a treatise on recruiting minority professors, include (1) supporting aspiring professors who are A B D to finish their dissertations; and (2) becoming willing to hire one's own doctoral students. As one university official (cited in Heller, 1988) put it, "After all, if a student is good enough to get a Ph.D. at your school, why isn't she good enough to teach there?" (p. A17).

Consider also the legal aspects of hiring women. What are the responsibilities of deans interviewing, hiring, evaluating, and firing women? What are the accompanying dictates of the human relations movement of the 1980s? Bring legal experts in personnel and civil liberties to campus to meet with those in a position to assess letters of application, to offer conditions of employment and promotion, and to dismiss faculty members. Cases of discrimination in hiring, promoting, or tenuring female employees or of sexual harassment (be it on the job, in an internship, or between professor and student) would be a logical starting point. Continue by developing a code of standard practice not so much legally as humanistically dictated.

In conclusion, recognize that the foregoing list of strategies culled from extensive literature, personal experience, and anecdotal information is deliberately incomplete. That is, it includes *only recommendations that stand to enhance the development of both faculty women and their students.*

Notes

1. From the April 11, 1882, article "Women's Education," *La Opinion Nacional* (Caracas newspaper).
2. See, for example, Adams (1983), Sharp et al. (1985), Bourguignon et al. (1987), Gillespie (1987), Grunig (1989), Zoch and Russell (1991), and Blum (1991).
3. One additional ramification: Because graduate assistants administer so many large, core courses, they have the potential to influence an immense undergraduate population. Thus the students already teach the students (Dudovitz, Russo, Duvall, & Cramer, 1983).
4. For a counterargument, see Moglen (1983, p. 131). Moglen questioned whether feminists should accept and use power within any "mainstream hierarchical structures that support relationships of domination and inequity."
5. Other impingements on faculty women's time include their assignment to a disproportionately large share of large, unprestigious undergraduate classes (Astin & Bayer, 1973) and governance activities (Turk, 1981). Service, in particular, presents a double whammy. According to junior faculty members at The Ohio State University (Bourguignon et al., 1987, p. 53), service may not count at all. On the other hand, too much service may count against one—showing an inappropriate emphasis on this one of the three traditional criteria for promotion (at the expense of teaching and, particularly, research).
6. Gillespie (1987) explained that this phenomenon occurs despite the prediction that GRE scores consistently rank women lower as a group than men.
7. For enlightenment on the problem of these attitudinal barriers, see, for example, Tidball (1976) and Speizer (1981) citing Heyman (1977).
8. The pamphlet *Women Winners* (Hall & Sandler, 1982) argues that marriage and children tend to be advantages for male students, who are then perceived as mature and stable.
9. A related problem is the university's unwillingness to support married women students financially, assuming that their husbands would support them (Bourguignon et al., 1987, pp. 58-59).
10. See, for example, Bourguignon et al., 1987.
11. As the director of women's studies at Duke University observed:
Historically, the women's movement has been an attempt to change women's status, to gain access to male institutions. Now, we've moved beyond that. We've determined that the institutions themselves—the content, organization, and structure of law, business, academia—have to be changed. We're here, and we don't like what we see. (O'Barr, cited in O'Shea, 1988, p. 70)
12. Bourguignon et al., 1987, pp. 30-31. See also Adler, 1976.
13. Even the university benefits from mentoring, especially in terms of increased productivity of junior faculty and commitment of students, decreased attrition of graduate students and faculty (especially women and minorities), and increased likelihood that students or faculty who do leave will continue to support the institution rather than criticizing it (Hall & Sandler, 1983, p. 3.).
14. *Transforming* is the preferred term over other, seemingly synonymous, words. *Mainstreaming* or *integrating,* for example, are considered too narrow. As a member of Wellesley College's Center for Research on Women explained, the concept of a "transformed curriculum"

prompts scholars to change how they approach their scholarly materials almost as second nature (Peggy McIntosh, cited in McMillen, 1987).

15. Volume 10, number 1, of *Women's Studies Quarterly* (1982) is devoted to this concern.

16. For a synopsis of this report, see McMillen, 1988. Copies are available for $2 from ACE's Publications Dept., One Dupont Circle, Washington, D.C., 20036-1193.

17. The "chilly climate" report (Sandler & Hall, 1986, p. 18) emphasizes the need to recognize the special concerns of *minority* women.

References

Adams, Harriet Farwell. (1983). Work in the interstices: Women in academe. In Resa L. Dudovitz (Guest Ed.), *Women's Studies International Forum special issue: Women in academe*, pp. 135-141. Oxford: Pergamon.

Adelman, Clifford. (1991). *Women at thirtysomething: Paradoxes of attainment.* Washington, DC: U.S. Department of Education.

Adler, Emily Stier. (1984). "It happened to me": How faculty handle student reactions to class material. *Feminist Teacher, 3*(1), 22-26.

Adler, Nancy E. (1976). Women students. In Joseph Katz & Rodney T. Hartnett (Eds.), *Scholars in the making: The development of graduate and professional schools* (pp. 202-203). Cambridge, MA: Ballinger.

American Association of University Women. (1992, June). *Creating a gender-fair multicultural curriculum.* Washington, DC: AAUW.

Astin, Helen S., & Bayer, Alan E. (1973). Sex discrimination in academe. In Alice S. Rossi & Ann Calderwood (Eds.), *Academic women on the move* (pp. 333-356). New York: Russell Sage.

Atkins, Annette. (1983, Winter). The camels are coming, the camels are coming. *St. John's Magazine,* p. 9.

Beck, Evelyn Torton. (1983). Self-disclosure and the commitment to social change. In Resa L. Dudovitz (Guest Ed.), *Women's Studies International Forum special issue: Women in academe*, pp. 159-163. Oxford: Pergamon.

Bernard, Jessie. (1964). *Academic women.* University Park: Pennsylvania University Press.

Bird, Caroline. (1968). Foreword. *Born female.* New York: David McKay.

Blum, Debra E. (1991, October 9). Environment still hostile to women in academe, new evidence indicates. *Chronicle of Higher Education,* pp. A1, A20.

Bourguignon, Erika, Blanshan, Sue A., Chiteji, Lisa, MacLean, Kathleen J., Meckling, Sally J., Sagaria, Mary Ann, Shuman, Amy E., & Taris, Marie T. (1987, November). *Junior faculty life at Ohio State: Insights on gender and race.* Columbus: OSU Affirmative Action Grant Program, Office of Human Relations and University Senate Committee on Women and Minorities.

Bowles, Gloria, & Duelli-Klein, Renate. (Eds.). (1983). *Theories of women's studies.* London: Routledge & Kegan Paul.

Clague, Monique W. (1992, December). Are we headed toward racial strife? *The Faculty Voice* (University of Maryland independent faculty newspaper), p. 1.

Cline, Carolyn G., Toth, Elizabeth L., Turk, Judy VanSlyke, Walters, Lynne M., Johnson, Nancy, & Smith, Hank. (1986). *The velvet ghetto: The impact of the increasing number of women in public relations and business communication.* San Francisco: IABC Foundation.

Colwell, Rita R. (1988, April 13). Panelist at the mini-symposium on "Women and the sciences: Expectations, reality, hope." College Park, MD.

Currie, Dawn, & Kazi, Hamida. (1987, March). Academic feminism and the process of de-radicalization: Re-examining the issues. *Feminist Review, 25,* 77-98.

Dudovitz, Resa L., Russo, Ann, Duvall, John, & Cramer, Patricia. (1983). Survival in the "master's house": The role of graduate teaching assistants in effecting curriculum change. In Resa L. Dudovitz (Guest Ed.), *Women's Studies International Forum special issue: Women in academe* (pp. 149-157). Oxford: Pergamon.

Duncan, Birt L. (1976). Minority students. In Joseph Katz & Rodney T. Hartnett (Eds.), *Scholars in the making: The development of graduate and professional schools* (pp. 233-241). Cambridge, MA: Ballinger.

Friedan, Betty. (1963). *The feminine mystique* (chap. 13). New York: Norton.

Gillespie, Patti P. (1987, November). *Campus stories, or the cat beyond the canvas.* Presidential address to the Speech Communication Association, Boston.

Greene, Elizabeth. (1986, April 23). Feminism on campuses draws support and scorn; Many students in the middle. *Chronicle of Higher Education,* pp. 31-33.

Greene, Jon. (1988, May 10). Report criticizes gender-bias here: Plan offers women opportunities. *Diamondback,* p. 1.

Grunig, Larissa A. (1988). A research agenda for women in public relations. *Public Relations Review, 14*(3), 48-57.

Grunig, Larissa A. (1989). Sex discrimination in promotion and tenure in journalism education. *Journalism Quarterly, 66*(1), 93-100, 229.

Grunig, Larissa A. (1990, August). *Seminars: The intersection of pedagogy and content in transforming public relations education.* Paper presented to the Public Relations Division, Association for Education in Journalism and Mass Communication, Minneapolis.

Hall, Roberta M., & Sandler, Bernice Resnick. (1982, August). *Women winners.* Washington, DC: Association of American Colleges, Project on the Status and Education of Women.

Hall, Roberta M., & Sandler, Bernice R. (1983). *Academic mentoring for women students and faculty: A new look at an old way to get ahead.* Washington, DC: Association of American Colleges, Project on the Status and Education of Women.

Heller, Scott. (1988, February 10). Recruiting minority professors: Some techniques that work. *Chronicle of Higher Education,* p. A17.

Heyman, I. M. (1977, June). Women students at Berkeley: Views and data on possible sex discrimination in academic programs, cited in Speizer, Jeanne J. (1981, Summer). Role models, mentors and sponsors: The elusive concepts. *Signs: Journal of Women in Culture and Society, 6*(4), 698.

Hochschild, Arlie Russell. (1975). Inside the clockwork of male careers. In Florence Howe (Ed.), *Women and the power to change* (pp. 47-80). New York: McGraw-Hill.

Hoffman, Frances L. (1986, May). Sexual harassment in academia: Feminist theory and institutional practice. *Harvard Educational Review, 56,* 105-121.

Jordan, Mary. (1992, February 12). Wide gender gap found in schools. *The Washington Post,* pp. A1, A8.

Kaplan, Peter. (1987, March 26). Female researchers face discrimination, visiting expert says. *Diamondback,* p. 3.

Keohane, Nannerl O. (1986, April 2). Our mission should not be merely to "reclaim" a legacy of scholarship—We must expand on it. *Chronicle of Higher Education,* p. 88.

Knefelkamp, Lee. (1987). Women's moral development: On Carol Gilligan's work. *Feminism and structures of knowledge.* Graduate Polyseminar, University of Maryland, College Park.

Kolodny, Annette. (1981). Dancing through the minefield: Some observations on the theory, practice and politics of a feminist literary criticism. In Dale Spender (Ed.), *Men's studies modified: The impact of feminism on the academic disciplines* (pp. 23-42). Oxford: Pergamon.

Leatherman, Courtney. (1992, November 11). "Isolation" of pioneering feminist scholar stirs reappraisal of women's status in academe. *Chronicle of Higher Education,* pp. A17-A18.

Lewis, Lionel S. (1975). *Scaling the ivory tower: Merit and its limits in academic careers.* Baltimore, MD: Johns Hopkins University Press.

Locke, Edwin A. (1992, January). Survey finds junior female faculty suffer research anxiety. *The Faculty Voice* (University of Maryland independent faculty newspaper), p. 6.

McCarthy, Colman. (1991, September 28). Academia's stoop laborers. *The Washington Post,* p. A27.

McElrath, Karen. (1992). Gender, career disruption, and academic rewards. *Journal of Higher Education, 63*(3), 269-281.

McIntosh, Peggy. (1983). *Interactive phases of curricular re-vision: A feminist perspective.* Working Paper No. 124. Wellesley, MA: Wellesley College Center for Research on Women.

McMillen, Liz. (1987, September 9). More colleges and more disciplines incorporating scholarship on women into the classroom. *Chronicle of Higher Education,* pp. A15-A17.

McMillen, Liz. (1988, January 27). Council asks colleges to adopt "new agenda" on women's issues. *Chronicle of Higher Education,* pp. A17-A18.

Menges, Robert J., & Exum, William H. (1983, March/April). Barriers to the progress of women and minority faculty. *The Journal of Higher Education, 54*(2), 123-144.

Moglen, Helene. (1983). Power and empowerment. In Resa L. Dudovitz (Guest Ed.), *Women's Studies International Forum special issue: Women in academe,* pp. 131-134. Oxford: Pergamon.

Nasar, Sylvia. (1992, October 22). Women move closer to pay equality with men: Research shows major gains in '80s. *Atlanta Journal/Atlanta Constitution,* pp. G1, G3.

O'Shea, Catherine. (1988, August). Success and the southern belle. *Southern Magazine,* pp. 39-41, 43, 67-70.

Ramey, Estelle R. (1988, April 13). Mini-symposium on "Women and the sciences: Expectations, reality, hope." College Park, MD.

Rohter, Larry. (1987, January 4). Women gain degrees, but not tenure. *The New York Times,* p. E9.

Rudavsky, Shari. (1992, July 6). Master's degrees quadrupled in past 3 decades. *The Washington Post,* p. A9.

Sandler, Bernice R. (1984, February 29). The quiet revolution on campus: How sex discrimination has changed. *Chronicle of Higher Education,* p. 72.

Sandler, Bernice R., & Hall, Roberta M. (1986). *The campus climate revisited: Chilly for women faculty, administrators, and graduate students.* Washington, DC: Association of American Colleges, Project on the Status and Education of Women.

Schneir, Miriam. (1972). Introduction. In Miriam Schneir (Ed.), *Feminism: The essential historical writings* (pp. xi-xxi). New York: Vintage.

Segal, David R. (1988, April 4). [Letter to the editor]. *Outlook* (University of Maryland faculty publication).

Sharp, Nancy W., Turk, Judy VanSlyke, Einsiedel, Edna F., Schamber, Linda, & Hollenback, Sharon. (1985). *Faculty women in journalism and mass communications: Problems and progress.* Syracuse, NY: Report published with a grant from the Gannett Foundation. (Available from the Association for Education in Journalism and Mass Communication,

College of Journalism, 1621 College St., University of South Carolina, Columbia, SC 29208-0251.)

Simeone, Angela. (1987). *Academic women: Working towards equality*. South Hadley, MA: Bergin & Garvey.

Speizer, Jeanne J. (1981). Role models, mentors and sponsors: The elusive concepts. *Signs: Journal of Women in Culture and Society, 6*(4), 698.

Staff. (1986, April 23). Small but active feminist groups work to meet campus women's basic needs. *Chronicle of Higher Education*, pp. 31-32.

Staff. (1992, June 24). Historians and sociologists are not the only ones who notice that demographic changes in American society are altering the face of college campuses. *Chronicle of Higher Education*, p. A7.

Stanley, Liz, & Wise, Sue. (1983). *Breaking out: Feminist consciousness and feminist research*. London: Routledge & Kegan Paul.

Sudarkasa, Niara. (1987, February 25). Radical and cultural diversity is a key part of the pursuit of excellence in the university. *Chronicle of Higher Education*, p. 42.

Taub, Deborah J. (1991). *Autonomy and mature interpersonal relationships in African-American and white undergraduate women*. Unpublished master's thesis, University of Maryland, College Park.

Tidball, M. Elizabeth. (1976). Of men and research: The dominant themes in American higher education include neither teaching nor women. *Journal of Higher Education, 47*(4), 373-389.

Turk, T. G. (1981). Women faculty in higher education: Academic administration and governance in a state university system. *Pacific Sociological Review, 24*, 212-236.

White, Michael C., & Crino, Michael D. (1981, Summer). A critical review of female performance, performance training and organizational initiatives designed to aid women in the work-role environment. *Personnel Psychology, 34*, 227-245.

Wise, Phyllis M. (1988, April 13). Panelist at the mini-symposium on "Women and the sciences: Expectations, reality, hope." College Park, MD.

Zoch, Lynn M., & Russell, Maria P. (1991). Women in PR education: An academic "velvet ghetto"? *Journalism Educator, 46*(3), 25-35.

17 Body Language
Gender in Journalism Textbooks

LINDA STEINER

If education is important—and we must believe it is—then textbooks are important. They articulate and celebrate a discipline's paradigms and procedures, not only describing what that discipline is and what it does but also prescribing, albeit often in ways that accommodate existing distributions of authority and power, how that discipline ought to be practiced.

Newswriting textbooks have a particularly significant, if understudied, role. Whether they are former practitioners with little training in pedagogy or scholars with little interest in skills courses, newswriting instructors typically assign textbooks—usually one. Journalism textbooks document what has been described and prescribed to students not only about what is news or newsworthy and how to report news, but also who can or should report the news and what personal attributes reporters need. Understanding these textbooks helps explain newsroom practices, since, given both the impact of the authors' professional experiences and their explicit commitment to "realism," they are committed to defining and enforcing standard newsroom procedures, demographics, and dynamics. More to the point, they tell us how writers, editors, and publishers have been educated, having thus some predictive, explanatory power for not only their newsroom judgments but also behavior toward colleagues. These textbooks are clearly important in the academic training of future reporters, especially now that most college graduates getting hired by newspapers majored in journalism (*Journalism Career and Scholarship Guide,* 1991, p. 31). Furthermore,

AUTHOR'S NOTE: A more detailed study of 150 American and British journalism textbooks was published in *Journalism Monographs* No. 135 (October 1992). Portions are included here by permission of AEJMC.

students of advertising, public relations, and other media professions often start with the same basic journalism courses, therefore study the same textbooks. Media students, then, are well socialized into particular professional norms and values well before they find jobs.

Given these assumptions about how textbooks define a field and limit who can successfully enter it, textbooks' presentation of women and racial and ethnic minorities has been a particular concern for more than 20 years. The examination here of how college-level news reporting textbooks published in the United States between 1890 and 1990 have treated gender gives evidence of evolution, although revolution is too strong a word. The history of displacements in reporting textbooks published in multiple editions and across different textbooks suggests changes, particularly in notions of how women practice journalism. Indeed, the controversy, such as it is, over gender and over the connection of social identity to news reporting has inspired remarkable discontinuities in journalism textbooks, which otherwise are marked by relative stability.

Oppositional readings of these textbooks are possible. On the other hand, opportunities are relatively limited for multiple interpretations of textbooks, even in journalism, where students are presumably discouraged from ingesting information uncritically. The fact that many of the authors have been senior professors, deans, well-known journalists, or editors at major newspapers presumably confers some credibility and authority beyond that which is inherently granted teachers and their tools.

One way to study emerging conceptions of whether or how gender makes a difference to journalists is by studying those textbooks that appeared in multiple editions. Despite their fundamental conservatism and commitment to conventional practices, textbooks are rewritten in the aftermath of paradigmatic revolutions. Assigned only the ninth edition of Curtis MacDougall's *Interpretative Journalism* (1987), for example, students learn new understandings and new ways of doing things without realizing that anything had been changed from the first one, published in 1938. Such insertions and deletions, in the interests of textual economy and simplicity, are also starkly dramatized in John Hohenberg's *Professional Journalist,* whose first edition noted that women reporters proved their professional competence during World War II; Hohenberg then commented, "If home and motherhood had not proved stronger attractions, many of them would be there yet" (1960, p. 7). But Hohenberg's 1978 edition conceded that the women who kept newspapers afloat during the war "had great difficulty in maintaining their foothold once peace came" (p. 19). The 1983 edition eliminated the "ghetto-ized" discussion of women reporters.

This chapter examines what a broad range of introductory newswriting textbooks say about how or whether gender makes a difference. After offering a brief account of its method and a highly collapsed overview of journalism education in the United States, the chapter proceeds more or less chronologically, beginning with some pamphlets published in the 1890s. The chapter ultimately turns to feminist theorizing for suggestions on how journalism education can be further transformed.

As a qualitative analysis of 130 college-level books, the first issue is what they say explicitly about who can be a (successful) journalist. Nearly every newswriting and reporting textbook published over the past hundred years begins by declaring that journalism skills are not innate; authors promise that any smart, industrious person can become a reporter. But at the same time, many denied that women can acquire those skills. One of many editor-scholar pairs to collaborate on a textbook explained:

> Newspaper work is so demanding physically that many women who can teach or do ordinary office work cannot stand up under it. Its general tempo—with the deadline-fighting element always present—is such as to bar many women because of nervous temperament. Although there are exceptions, of course, most women are incapable of covering police and court news. (Porter & Luxon, 1935, p. 8)

Language is also at issue, because whether the language of newspaper "men" applies to women is often not clear. Few textbooks defined their audience as clearly as George Knapp's *Boys' Book of Journalism* (1939). Until the 1970s, authors routinely used masculine nouns and pronouns to describe the "newsman" and "his" qualifications. Some may not have intended to exclude women, although even so, actual students, especially women, may not have interpreted references to "man" as including woman. Grant Hyde's 1921 handbook stipulated that masculine pronouns must be used whenever gender is irrelevant; Hyde ruled "Every student will select his or her own course" stylistically "faulty" (Hyde, 1921, p. 16).

More important, the regularity with which textbooks first broadly discuss "reporters," then specify precisely what women can and cannot do, calls into question whether authors' intentions were generic. For example, William Maulsby began: "Really, if a man has the right stuff in him it makes no difference where he starts. The good reporter gets to the top in a reasonably short time no matter where he begins. . . . Age, influential relatives, and luck play almost no part" (1925, p. 67). No mention of gender here. But discussing society news 200 pages later, Maulsby said women gladly serve as vacation correspondents to "make a little pin money."

Third, the treatment and status of readers is relevant, because textbooks long equated, entirely on the basis of gender, readers' and reporters' interests. The founding dean of the first university journalism school stated this formula succinctly: "Since [society] news largely concerns women and women's affairs, the position is generally held by a woman" (Williams & Martin, 1911, p. 253). Regardless, the conception of womanhood is universalized. Textbooks not only conflate "female" and "feminine" but also erase potential differences among women on the basis of class, ethnicity, education, physical abilities, occupation, or sexual preference. Indeed, pre-1970s reporting textbooks ignored race and ethnicity except with reference to the race of subjects. But whether or not they try to prevent women's intrusion into reporters' semantic space by using masculine nouns generically, textbooks treat the female as violating male physical, economic, cultural, and social space. Maleness is taken for granted. Women are "the other." A few early textbooks acknowledged the stereotype—or reality—of reporters as hard drinkers, as disheveled, as Bohemian; maleness has its faults. But usually a disembodied sort of masculinity is implicit and unproblemmatic, while a highly embodied feminity looms as the dangerous exception.

Early Journalism Education

The apprentice approach to journalism training held sway late into the 19th century, despite some disparate calls for formal education. From 1886 to 1900 Martha Louise Rayne, a poet, novelist, song-writer, reporter, and editor, ran a journalism school in Detroit for women; it emphasized being accurate, bright, and newsy. Rayne's 1893 *What Can a Woman Do* included a chapter on journalism, which called for professional journalism training and promoted journalism as "agreeable, wide-awake work, with no more drudgery than there is in other occupations, and with many compensations" (1893/1974, p. 44). The resistance to journalism schools and to newsroom employment of college graduates was otherwise expressed in gendered rhetoric; book-learning was disdained as effete, impractical, and "womanish" for a profession praised as lusty, vigorous, "masculine." Influential journalists supported journalism education only once they saw advantages for enhancing their status and sense of professionalism. This coincided with increasing pressure on universities to begin teaching practical subjects and with growth in the news industry itself.

The University of Pennsylvania offered a sequence of five journalism courses in 1893-1894. The University of Illinois launched a 4-year curriculum in 1904; the University of Missouri, having intermittently offered courses in journalism since 1878, opened the first full-fledged school in 1908. Columbia's journalism school finally opened in 1912. By 1920 some 28 schools in the United States offered a journalism major and 131 schools provided journalism courses; by 1928 about 300 colleges offered courses and 56 had separate schools or departments. Now about 325 colleges and universities offer majors.

In 1903 a long-time literary editor mused, "Why any woman who can get $800 a year for teaching should wish to take up the harder work of newspaper reporting is difficult to understand" (Shuman, 1903, p. 157). Hard life that it entailed, reporters earned more money, status, and glamour than did nurses and school teachers. Despite discouraging words from textbooks and teachers, women applied to journalism schools, especially at the co-educational land grant schools. These schools often admitted women if only because they had not anticipated the need to exclude them. Women now represent two thirds of the journalism enrollments.

The First Generation of Textbooks

The primary instructional resources for would-be journalists before 1900 were short manuals; not until journalism was incorporated into university curricula was there a strong demand for textbooks. Having often bemoaned the scarcity of reporting textbooks, in the 1880s and 1890s *The Journalist,* "A Weekly Publication Devoted to Newspaper Men and Publishers," published several "how-to" serials. Reprinted as booklets, these "Text Books" generally referred only to men—and gentlemen. In contrast, Nevada Hitchcock's *What a Reporter Must Be* (1900) addressed young women and young men, "since sex makes practically no difference in the requirements of a reporter." She told reporters, "Be gentlemanly. . . . Be womanly," explaining, "By womanly is not meant womanish" (p. 21).

By the 1890s, the same trends toward specialization and hierarchical organization that had transformed other business enterprises were introduced into newspapers. Furthermore, department stores and newspapers were becoming intensely mutually dependent. The new consumer dreamworlds needed buyers, especially women, and newspapers relied on department store advertising revenue. The resulting demand for women as readers, and as writers for them, came to be acknowledged in textbooks; although a dozen textbooks published before 1920 never referred to women, others mentioned them in the context of society news. Edwin L. Shuman provided an extensive, if negative, assessment of the "ambitious feminine army" encroaching on journalism. In *The Art and Practice of Journalism* (1899), Shuman said articles "from a woman's standpoint" are "naturally superficial and frothy" and insufficiently virile, although women's brains are as good as men's. He advised women determined to find jobs despite the hazards to write for the children's or society pages, or to concentrate on stories, sketches, and verse. "[T]he literary way is beset with fewer rocks and precipices for the feminine traveler" (p. 156). According to

Shuman, however, newspaper work was defeminizing: "[Women] will swiftly lose many of their high ideals and sweet and tender ways, as inevitably as if they had been run through a machine for the purpose. And what is the use?" (p. 156). Shuman's often-cited *Practical Journalism* (1903) conceded that "acrobatic" (yellow) journalism employed more women and paid well; but it was difficult, risky, and unpleasant, if not despicable. Shuman maintained: "The work of news-gathering, as a rule, is too rude and exacting for them. . . . Local reporting work deals too exclusively with men and the affairs of men to give women a fair chance in it" (p. 148-149).

Otherwise repeating Shuman, Charles Olin explained that when women publish humorous sidebars, "Her story is not supposed to add anything of importance to the report of her brother journalists, its whole value lying in the fact that it is written from a wholly feminine standpoint, in a bright feminine manner, with little touches of feminine sympathy, pathos and sentiment" (1906, p. 51).

Women's Textbooks

Gender-differentiation in the newsroom prompted debate over whether women should take the same courses as men. Complaining about journalism schools "overflowing" with co-eds, especially because women "almost invariably get married and quit about the time they have had enough experience to be of some real use around the office," one 1935 textbook encouraged women to take a few electives (Porter & Luxon, 1935, p. 9). These courses tracked (or rather, derailed) women in ways acceptable to men, indeed, in ways that mirrored the public/private distinction marking the larger social order, that is, away from the high status public arenas that men took to be their exclusive territory, and toward domestic, consumption roles that remained lower status, despite women's attempts to glamorize them. By 1940 a dozen universities offered courses on writing for women, which were seldom taken by male students but often required for female majors (Beasley & Theus, 1988, pp. 22-23).

Men no more wanted to teach these electives or develop textbooks for them, however, than they wanted to write news for women. Stepping into the breech, women instructors took full responsibility for steering women toward areas demanding "distinctly feminine background and experience," taking pains as well to legitimize this as a serious mission requiring high ideals and expertise, if not a college degree. Of the handful of journalism textbooks single-authored over the century by women, the majority directly address women and were published between 1926 and 1936, when courses specifically for women emerged.

Genevieve Jackson Boughner, who taught the first course on feature-writing for women at Wisconsin and later at Minnesota, set the trend with her 348 page tome. *Women in Journalism* firmly directed women toward specializations where "they may capitalize on their tastes and instincts rather than oppose them, as they are called upon to do in many lines of newspaper writing in which they duplicate men's work" (1926, p. viii). Boughner diligently ennobled each specialization associated with women. For example, an advice column "brings into play the protective, mother side of her nature"; she compared the advice columnist to a priest or minister (p. 176). Even beauty experts need both a "feminine love of beauty and daintiness" and scientific knowledge of physiology and hygiene.

Ethel Colson Brazelton's *Writing and Editing for Women* (1927) offered analogous topics, vocational counseling, and classroom exercises. Brazelton, who taught journalism for women at Medill, insisted:

> The fact of sex, the "woman's angle," is the woman writer's tool, but it must never be her weapon. No self-respecting woman writer would exploit sex in writing any more than she would in personal living. She will not, as a writer, think about being a woman. But being a woman, she is possessed of a real advantage in the business of doing, recording, interpreting women's interests, ways and work. (p. 8)

Like Boughner, Brazelton vigorously celebrated women's beats as requiring college preparation and technical skills. For example, covering clubs required the entire range of journalism skills, plus knowledge of sociology, philosophy, economics, art, hygiene, drama, music, homemaking, civics, and politics. Like Boughner, Brazelton also promoted careers outside reporting, especially public relations; neither mentioned college-level teaching.

For all their agreement about women's inbred talents, women authors notably left nothing to chance or "nature." They even discussed physical appearance, "almost as important as the good manners and pleasing personality without which a feminine newspaper career is decidedly handicapped" (Brazelton, 1927, p. 190). Ironically, men interrupted their discourse on how successful "reporters" should dress (suit brushed, etc.) to say: "Women reporters may ignore the foregoing. They know all about its importance by instinct" (Bond, 1933, p. 150).

The women only reluctantly and indirectly admitted the economic handicap of women's "specialness." Brazelton downplayed gender prejudice on the part of editors, insisting that "common sense, courtesy, persistence, courage and quiet cheerful determination make mightily for success" in both finding and keeping jobs. Forced to acknowledge inequalities in pay, she speculated that women earn at least a third less than men for similar work because of "continual turn-over due to feminine restlessness" and marriage (1927, p. 207).

The exception proving the rule, Nancy Mavity oriented her 1930 reporting textbook for a comprehensive course (i.e., including men) and integrated models of and for women reporters. An *Oakland Tribune* writer, Mavity not only connected gender differences to child-rearing practices but also admitted that certain acquired differences—like emotionalism—handicap women. She decried the notion that personal charm was women's route to success, although she knew this had long been taught.

The Status of Society Editors and the Feminine Mystique

Several textbooks published after the 1920 Constitutional Amendment enfranchising women said nothing about women reporters. But as the economic stakes and competition increased, textbooks grew more insistent that woman's news was society news; as the director of the Medill School put it, women writers enjoy a "peculiar fitness" for features, club news, and certain forms of criticism (Harrington & Frankenberg, 1924). But even though a couple of men claimed society departments deserved respect, social news did not consistently command high status. Robert Neal (1939) ferociously attacked society editors as creating misery for the copy desk. Probably the only female on the staff, the pretty little society editor may rationalize that rules need not worry her. Her only other possible defense, Neal speculated, is that society news is "unbelievably monotonous" (p. 360).

Textbooks of the postwar period dealt with the awkward problem of removing women from responsible newsroom positions in various ways, sometimes by applauding women's unique instincts for covering domestic life and more often punishing women for having a domestic life. The widely used *Exploring Journalism* (Wolseley & Campbell, 1943) said realistic young women will see the fourth estate as a man's world: "Their prospective employers are men and prefer to hire men. Moreover, many of them are convinced that journalism is a man's profession and that the woman who doesn't believe her place to be in the home should choose an occupation sheltered from the ugly realities that journalists encounter" (p. 52). It somewhat awkwardly cautioned students against expecting too much from wartime opportunities: wartime jobs were temporary "because it was recognized that after service in the conscript forces men would have some claim upon their old positions" (p. 95). Instead, women were put on the advertising, publicity, and "segregated" editorial tracks in which they excel, that is, dealing with domestic and social life.

Grant Hyde's 1952 offering called the society desk not only "almost universally the first job for women" but also their last. "What holds them there is the pleasure they gain from acquaintance and cooperation with the most active and interesting women in the community" (Hyde, 1952, p. 358). He somewhat lamely described the society desk as "a pleasant position, of which many male newspaper workers may well be envious" (p. 358).

Carl Warren's *Modern News Reporting* (1951) asserted that reporting "can be mastered by any young man or woman with average brain capacity plus initiative, study, practice and experience" (p. 1). But Warren confidently reinforced notions about women's psychology: "Perhaps the most important point of all in writing for women is that, much more than men, they desire personalized and humanized news. You cannot hold a woman's interest long with abstractions, logic, inanimate things and processes" (p. 360). "The average feminine reader" is uninterested even in the activities of women in (masculine) fields like politics and business. He encouraged women reporters to capitalize on their "natural inquisitiveness and ability to talk information out of men" and women's need for glamour (p. 8).

Warren agreed with Hyde and other male authors of the time that editors' reluctance to hire women was justified: "A good many young women treat a job as a stopgap between school and marriage . . . whereas marriage and its economic responsibilities rivet a man more closely to his job. Some women who continue working after marriage often are absent because of illness at home, confinement periods or just for shopping" (1951, p. 8). The 1959 edition added that editors hesitate to assign women stories "when there is an element of danger" (p. 10).

The 1960s brought minimal change. Theoretically, Siegfried Mandel's 1962 book offered women the choice to compete with men or enter one of the domains "specialized to her sex." On the other hand, he said, while marriage and parenthood stabilize men, making them better employees, these same events—"the natural fulfillment of any girl"—make women a greater employment risk (pp. 275-276). Therefore, Mandel's conclusion was euphemistic and conditional: "Due to the fact that there are certain interests in which woman admittedly excels, the woman journalist of real ability, with favorable environmental conditions, looks toward future horizons that are both broad and bright" (p. 270). Eventually women students were explicitly steered away from general reporting toward women's pages, where maturity (i.e., delays resulting from motherhood) is less problematic. Despite women's "natural advantage" in "distaff writing," they apparently need to be taught its basics; Mandel, Curtis MacDougall, and several other authors continued to provide highly detailed instructions for covering weddings and other social events.

Paradigm Changes in the 1970s

Lobbying for various significant changes in mass media, feminists reasoned that the same logic justifying creation of the minority affairs beat defined by race should also apply to ethnicity, sexual orientation, and gender. The second wave of the women's movement particularly critiqued ways that sexist language symbolized and reinforced contempt for women.

Retooling in news media and in textbooks over the past two decades has been neither quick nor complete. The most consistent shift of the 1970s was the deletion of society news; newspapers' erasure of women's sections justified their wholesale elimination in textbooks. But long after the major wire services adopted stylebooks that condemned sexist language and that called for equal treatment of genders in all areas of coverage, several textbooks aggressively protested linguistic change, defending use of the masculine generic as merely a graceful, convenient space- and time-saver. Although language is always symbolically loaded, the resistance betrays an underlying current of fear that concessions will appear to cede authority to feminism. William Metz (1977/1991) debates feminists at length, particularly on language issues. His chapter on sexism in the news mocks feminists for getting "teed off" on silly issues, such as the term *women's lib.*

Many authors are open to linguistic change despite its symbolic implications for newsroom dynamics; they adopt gender-neutral language and insert examples or photographs of women reporters or even append guides to nondiscriminatory communication. Others avoid gendered pronouns but hedge their bets. Having conceded that replacing masculinist words was reasonably easy, for example, one book quotes the *Washington Post Deskbook* on eliminating sexist language with its apology intact: "But some words and forms are so historically and culturally embedded they defy efforts to eradicate them. Moreover, awkward and self-conscious new forms can interfere with readers' comprehension" (Garrison, 1990, p. 169).

Often the very commitment to gender-blind language seems to inhibit authors from addressing whether a reporter's gender matters to sources or readers. Fred Fedler (1989) has come to emphasize avoiding sexual and other stereotyping, at least as long the effort to eliminate male bias (i.e., by the "he/she") did not distract readers. He now extensively addresses the need to recruit minority reporters, especially blacks, as a matter of both social justice and economics. But although he says that reporters who cannot speak Spanish cannot obtain stories from Spanish-speaking sources, he does not ask whether gender makes a difference.

In 1930 Mavity had asked students to consider what women reporters should do if male sources were flirtatious or vulgar. Threaten to call the police? Give a lecture on chivalry? Leave? Ken Metzler's 1986 book proposes answers. Metzler advises women not to date sources, to dress conservatively, and to ignore off-color remarks. After all, "social and business mores don't change overnight" (p. 295). Meanwhile, he encourages women to use feminine wiles and to exploit men's "natural propensity" to trust women with personal details.

A half-dozen textbooks offer more ambitious analyses of the potential impact of gender and race on journalism practice. Ohio University's Ralph Izard (1982) critiques coverage skewed by prejudice on the basis of race, sex, age, as well as physical ability. A certain amount of resistance to change does not upset Izard, who opts for practicality: "Reporters cannot please everyone. The language cannot be restructured every time someone gets a new idea" (p. 334). But because "unconscious neglect" causes much of the distortion, Izard encourages individuals and institutions to rethink their own socialization and the limits of their knowledge. Izard rejects the claim that one must be a member of a group to cover it adequately; such identification may present an actual or apparent conflict of interest. Izard concludes, "The ideal must be functional integration of a news organization's staff, with reporters assigned to coverage areas in which they have expertise and interest" (p. 339).

Gary Atkins and William Rivers (1987) draw parallels between women and minorities of race, ethnicity, and sexual orientation. Arguing against the "assimilation bias," Atkins and Rivers defend minority beats, because newsrooms until recently were bastions for white males. Their presentation of women's issues emphasizes content, however, not those producing the content; and they imply that sincere, sensitive reporters of any race or culture can cover any other culture.

Shifting Perspectives on Gender

Textbooks have shifted from telling students that gender is everything (thereby nearly disqualifying women from reporting) to gender counting for nothing. The one constant over time is that gender is a problem for women—all women. Neither authors' newspaper or university affiliations nor geography seem to be variables affecting textbook content. Women are figures at the margin, intruders. Except for the brief mention in the 1910-1930 period of newsmen's rough talk and rough ways, men's only handicap is their inability to write about clothes or fashion. Several authors openly admit that men are simply not interested in women and children and do not want to write for or about them. Otherwise, no textbook seriously considers what male-ness means for journalism practice.

To the extent the "female" question is confronted, two possibilities have been proposed. First, female-ness, equated with femininity, is very meaningful; it dictates what, how, and for whom women may write in ways that globally distinguish femaleness from masculinity. Conversely, modern textbooks construe it as identical with normative masculinity. Their integration of women with men (seemingly casual but probably calculated on the statistical realities of both newsroom and classroom) implies that neither men nor women have bodies or embodied experience. Therefore everyone should and can cover all topics identically, presumably objectively. Recent textbooks both profess sensitivity and respect for multiculturalism and emphasize shared humanity. But they also warn reporters to transcend race, culture, and gender—to distance themselves from the cultural-social settings and life experiences in which all other humans are grounded.

Training for the Newspaper Trade (Seitz, 1916) shows the slippery language used to negotiate the still-tricky woman "problem":

> To be a woman reporter is not especially agreeable. . . . But the fashion writer, the society reporter and the producer of special articles is [sic] well employed. The woman is man's equal on a newspaper and is paid what she earns. . . . The typewriting machine has led to the hiring of many young women in clerical departments at good pay and under easy working conditions. They fill these minor positions, from which promotion is slow, to better advantage than men. The men on the small jobs who cannot advance, grow less useful and become discontented as their years and needs increase. The girls get married and so give way to others. (pp. 36-37)

Thus women were essentially limited to a couple of specialties men reject and to low-pay, low-status "feminized" positions.

Pre-World War II textbooks delivered contradictory reasons for women's unfitness. Newsroom behavior was too crude for the feminine sensibility or the work was too exacting. Women lacked necessary knowledge and expertise or male sources would not trust them. They were defeminized by contact with men or they wasted their training by marrying. They had no sense of humor or they did not take work seriously. More important, those who bemoaned the slush and gush of society pages failed to acknowledge how journalists and journalism educators were re-producing it. Newspapers needed "pleasant" copy that would not only attract women readers but more specifically reproduce those readers as eager consumers of the domestic goods and services sold by department stores and other advertisers. One author rather cryptically warned those who dislike society writing not to do it "if it can be avoided" (Byerly, 1961, p. 133). Women often had no choice.

Until recently textbooks took for granted a connection between reporters' interests and their gendered abilities, the association of women with children the most pronounced. Even *Herald-Tribune* reporter India Mc-Intosh, whose chapter in *Late City Edition* (Herzberg, 1947) off-handedly dismissed complaints of a women's ghetto, advised "girls" to exploit their femininity and make the most of stories about women and babies that the city desk believes are "naturally" their province. Thomas Berry declared that just as women can best teach early elementary grades, "so are the best articles for this age group usually done by women writers" (1958, pp. 377-378). Many postwar textbooks drew on the increasingly popular interest in psychology to buttress their claim that women constitute a different species. Although the definition of women as unable to be abstract, logical, or impersonal was intended to explain readership, it was more or less explicitly applied to women reporters as well.

Nearly all textbooks on the market now are scrupulous about gender-neutrality. A few authors cannot follow their own advice. Two experienced journalists and teachers violate their own admonitions about stereotyping in describing a police reporter, Ruth Lockwood, apparently a 36-year-old mother of two boys: "With her large frame and her brown hair swept haphazardly into a bun, Lockwood looks more like a fifth-grade music teacher than someone whose job is to chase fire engines and ambulances" (Porter & Ferris, 1988, p. 44). But otherwise women are now carefully integrated. "Women" is no longer an entry in the index. The women's pages are remembered, if at all, as a minor historical artifact.

When textbooks now characterize women's professional status, it is to deny that women are disadvantaged. Several textbooks published over the past 10 years confidently dismiss gender as any continuing problem, saying "feminine" journalists who complain about promotions should realize promotions are slow for men, too. A long-time reporter and department chairman at New York University begins his discussion of women and minorities: "Regarding women, there's almost no need for this section" (Stein, 1985, p. 5). Not only are women—white and black—working in every newspaper department, including sports, they are also editors and publishers.

Women faculty members, many of whom edited feature and women's pages, taught courses in these areas, and wrote textbooks for those courses, have been no less pragmatic than male colleagues. They also wanted their students to get jobs, wherever they might be, and to protect their legitimacy. So they taught women to write "as" women. Conversely, that the couple of textbooks recently written by women disregard gender as an issue is no surprise when the profession now insists on erasing gender in the interest of objectivity.

Directions for Change

Textbooks do not stand apart from university life. Speculation about gender(ed) practices in the unofficial curriculum—lectures, classroom discussion, homework assignments, mentoring, and career counseling as well as extra-curricular student life—is outside the scope of this chapter. But the possibility that educators who continue to condemn gender neutrality because it results in "stilted presentation" in writing also prefer "virile presentation" in the classroom presents a serious concern.

The emphasis here on university life is also not meant to discount the impact of larger social ideologies. Female reporters are certainly not the only women who face the allegation that they can produce babies but not knowledge, while men produce pure impersonal truth that transcends their social identities. Male journalists and teachers imported rather than invented the variety of ways for devaluing and limiting women writers and women's writings. Likewise borrowed is the "solution" to the problem of women writers: women must either stake out an entirely new territory (always taking the risk that men might later claim it) or move to a low-status, low-rent district that men do not want.

All this is by way of saying that, at some level, further transformations in textbooks also require changes in journalistic practices, in mass communication pedagogy, in education generally, in all arenas of social life. "Schools cannot teach what society does not know" (Spender, 1982, p. 3). But it is also worth noting that feminist theory offers distinct possibilities for a re-ordered, "re-visioned" understanding of gender and gendered politics and values that may be encouraged and dramatized in mass communications and mass media education, including its textbooks. In suggesting that "standpoints" emerge not in biology (not all women are feminists and some men are) but in the complex, layered experiences of historical agents, feminists have theorized the epistemological consequences of identity politics in ways that address some of the issues plaguing reporting textbooks. Feminist standpoint theorists argue that the structure and content of people's thoughts are always tied to material conditions of their lives; it matters that people have different bodies, different sexual preferences, different physical abilities, and different experiences of race and class (Harding, 1986, 1991). Gender does not account for everything; some individuals treat their gendered experience as tangential. On the other hand, intersections of already interstructured identity factors will generally enter into human experience, thus values and perceptions.

Textbooks' explanations of the connections between social identity and professional behavior will become more useful when they attend to the various ways that complex interactions of race and gender and class and so forth can enter people's experiences, "even" those of journalists. Textbooks need to help students take seriously ways in which personal experiences affect their judgments about whose problems are considered newsworthy and their decisions about how (or what) news is obtained, organized, and written. MacDougall's recent editions, for example, complain that feminists' objections even to restructured women's pages leave editors without a formula for attracting women readers. But the objection is precisely to that formulaic commodification ("objectification") of readers to suit publishers' commercial purposes.

More sophisticated understandings of gender and social identity pave the way for more authentic, liberating communications, ones that give voice to those least heard and most in need of being heard. Students need to learn not how to persuade "Woman," defined as white, middle class, and heterosexual, to read department store advertising but how to serve the different communication and news needs of all kinds of women. In this light, textbooks must question a pedagogy that assumes that students want or should all want to work for mainstream masculinist organizations, that blindly insists on value-free rules, and accepts conventional dichotomies of private/public, female/male, and subjective/objective. Among other things, feminist ethnomethodology offers models for re-thinking the otherwise hierarchical and potentially exploitive relationship between reporter and source. Additional transformations in the definition of news, in newsroom structure, and in journalistic practices, including how we recruit and train students and reporters, will emerge concomitant with continuing changes in journalism education.

References

Atkins, Gary, & Rivers, William. (1987). *Reporting with understanding.* Ames: The Iowa State University Press.

Beasley, Maurine H., & Theus, Kathryn. (1988). *The new majority.* Lanham, MD: University Press of America.

Berry, Thomas Elliott. (1958). *Journalism today.* Philadelphia: Chilton.

Bond, F. Fraser. (1933). *Breaking into print: Modern newspaper techniques for writers.* New York: McGraw-Hill.

Boughner, Genevieve Jackson. (1926). *Women in journalism.* New York: D. Appleton.

Brazelton, Ethel M. Colson. (1927). *Writing and editing for women.* New York: Funk & Wagnalls.

Byerly, Kenneth. (1961). *Community journalism.* Philadelphia: Chilton.
Fedler, Fred. (1989). *Reporting for the print media.* New York: Harcourt Brace Jovanovich. (Previous edition published 1984)
Garrison, Bruce. (1990). *Professional news writing.* Hillsdale, NJ: Lawrence Erlbaum.
Harding, Sandra. (1986). *The science question in feminism.* Ithaca, NY: Cornell University Press.
Harding, Sandra. (1991). *Whose science? Whose knowledge? Thinking from women's lives.* Ithaca, NY: Cornell University Press.
Harrington, H. F., & Frankenberg, T. T. (1924). *Essentials in journalism.* Boston: Ginn & Company.
Herzberg, Joseph. (1947). *Late city edition.* New York: Henry Holt.
Hitchcock, Nevada Davis. (1900). *What a reporter must be.* Cleveland, OH: Ralph Hitchcock.
Hohenberg, John. (1978). *The professional journalist.* Chicago: Holt, Rinehart & Winston. (Other editions published 1960, 1973, 1983)
Hyde, Grant Milnor. (1921). *Handbook for newspaper workers.* New York: D. Appleton. (Later edition published 1925)
Hyde, Grant Milnor. (1952). *Newspaper reporting.* Englewood Cliffs, NJ: Prentice Hall.
Izard, Ralph. (1982). *Reporting the citizens' news.* New York: Holt, Rinehart & Winston.
Journalism Career and Scholarship Guide. (1991). Princeton, NJ: Dow Jones Newspaper Fund.
Knapp, George F. (1939). *The boys' book of journalism.* New York: Dodd, Mead.
MacDougall, Curtis M. (1987). *Interpretative reporting.* New York: Macmillan. (Previous editions published 1938, 1948, 1957, 1963, 1968, 1972, 1982)
Mandel, Siegfried. (Ed.). (1962). *Modern journalism.* New York: Pitman.
Maulsby, William. (1925). *Getting the news.* New York: Harcourt, Brace.
Mavity, Nancy. (1930). *The modern newspaper.* New York: Henry Holt.
Metz, William. (1991). *Newswriting.* Englewood Cliffs, NJ: Prentice Hall. (Previous edition published 1977)
Metzler, Ken. (1986). *Newsgathering.* Englewood Cliffs, NJ: Prentice Hall.
Neal, Robert M. (1939). *Editing the small city daily.* Englewood Cliffs, NJ: Prentice Hall.
Olin, Charles H. (1906). *Journalism.* Philadelphia: Penn Publishing.
Porter, Bruce, & Ferris, Timothy. (1988). *The practice of journalism.* Englewood Cliffs, NJ: Prentice Hall.
Porter, Philip W., & Luxon, Norval Neil. (1935). *The reporter and the news.* New York: D. Appleton-Century.
Rayne, Mrs. Martha. (1974). *What a woman can do.* Salem, NH: Arno Press. (Originally published 1893 by Eagle Publishing Company, Peterburgh, NY)
Seitz, Don C. (1916). *Training for the newspaper trade.* Philadelphia: J. B. Lippincott.
Shuman, Edwin L. (1899). *The art and practice of journalism.* Chicago: Stevens & Handy.
Shuman, Edwin L. (1903). *Practical journalism.* New York: D. Appleton.
Spender, Dale. (1982). *Invisible women.* London: Writers and Readers Publishing Cooperative.
Stein, M. L. (1985). *Getting and writing the news.* New York: Longman.
Warren, Carl. (1951). *Modern news reporting.* New York: Harper & Brothers. (Other editions published 1929, 1959)
Williams, Walter, & Martin, Frank L. (1911). *The practice of journalism.* Columbia, MO: E. W. Stephens.
Wolseley, R. E., & Campbell, Laurence. (1943). *Exploring journalism.* Englewood Cliffs, NJ: Prentice Hall. (Other editions published 1949, 1957)

18 Listening to Women's Stories
Or Media Law as if Women Mattered

CAROLYN STEWART DYER

What if women could incorporate their experiences into the law that governs speech and press? Would they consider freedom of expression[1] the most vital liberty? What values would be central to feminist conceptions of the law? Would feminists make different decisions from those the courts have made, or write different laws?

These are questions posed in a tentative essay on a feminist vision of media law in the first edition of this book. The intent was to open debate about media law as if women had a say. Back in 1989, most of media law, with the exception of the law of obscenity, had gone unexamined by feminist legal scholars. Although feminist legal scholarship has flourished in law schools and law journals in the interim, few of the ideas or concerns of these scholars have found their way across campus to journalism and communication programs and communication journals. Little has changed in the study of media law; the debate has not been joined as yet, and it's time to revise the essay.

The objectives this time are to describe media law as it is relative to gender and to analyze parts of media law from feminist perspectives and to examine this time why it has resisted and escaped feminist analysis. The central questions are: How do women's stories of their experiences in this society relate to communication law, and how would the law need to change to accommodate women's experiences? To get to that point, however, we must consider how all law is made and interpreted and introduce the major premises of First Amendment law and feminist legal studies. Communication law encompasses a broad range of topics, but this chapter will focus a feminist light on only some of them: freedom of speech and press, libel, privacy, and obscenity.

317

Legal Process and Principles

The law as we know it is whatever a majority of the U.S. Supreme Court says it is, what a coalition of interests in a legislative body think it should be, what members of a jury can agree it is. It is the construction of reality as decision makers see it. Although both men and women play roles in each of these legal arenas today, the processes were established to serve the needs and protect or advance the interests of the property-holding white male establishment when the Constitution and Bill of Rights were ratified in the 18th century.

The U.S. Supreme Court and the highest courts in the states have been central to development of communication law. To resolve controversies, the courts rely on principles and practices biased in favor of doing things the way the judges believe they have always been done. In this process, judges look to the decisions made in the past to determine what the precedents, or previous rules of law, were and apply them to what they consider the important facts of the current case.

The law changes over time as judges sometimes decide that the situation in the present case is different in some way from precedent and so modify old principles. When judges modify the law, they attempt to determine what traditional, accepted, everyday practice—known as the common law— is and use it to establish a new rule of law (Levi, 1949, pp. 1-2). Often, there are conflicting legal interests or rights in a case, each with its own precedent. To decide such cases judges attempt to balance the interests to reach a compromise or middle-ground resolution.

This process of making law is backward-looking and conservative of existing relationships among and between people and institutions. The law depends on the judges' interpretation of what facts are relevant, what the precedent is, what the common law or traditional practice has been, what conflicting rights and interests are, and how statutes and the Constitution apply (Levi, 1949, pp. 2-8). In this interpretation, predominantly male judges rely on their experiences and vision (Fund for Modern Courts, 1985).[2] To the extent that their experiences differ in relevant respects from those of women, judge-made law is likely to fail to recognize and meet the needs of women.

American law rests on liberal principles of individual autonomy and freedom and the assumption that equally rational individuals exercise free will under conditions of limited government. The system recognizes a set of natural or fundamental human rights that provide freedom of action in some spheres and that limit action to provide security in others. These rights are presumably available to all people (R. Dworkin, 1985, pp. 182-204). The liberal legal system favors empirical and objective methods for gathering evidence. Rationality and logic are preeminent modes of thought in the law. In deciding cases, judges seek to neutrally apply abstract, generalizable, universal laws and, if not eternal, at least well-seasoned truths (Wechsler, 1959).

Theories of Freedom of Speech and Press

In communication law, the courts test governmental actions and laws against the First Amendment to the Constitution, which provides for freedom of speech and press as part of the fundamental American rights and liberties. The traditional, liberal reading of these rights provides that expression should be shielded from prepublication or prior restraint by government and subject to penalties after communication in very limited circumstances. Although the Supreme Court makes some exceptions to absolute, unconditional protection for speech and press, such as those for obscenity and threats to national security, the American media and most communication law scholars tend to believe that freedom of expression should be legally unlimited. Legal scholar Frederick Schauer (1992) has called this belief the ideology or orthodoxy of the First Amendment.[3] The press clause of the First Amendment has been interpreted as providing special protection for the organized press, the commercial and noncommercial print and broadcast media, making them the only businesses specifically protected by the Constitution (Stewart, 1975).

The right to freedom of speech and press is usually understood as negative freedom, that is, freedom *from* government interference. Some believe these rights are empty, especially for those who do not have easy access to the mass media through which to speak. As a remedy, legal scholar Jerome Barron (1967) has argued that the government should take a positive role and provide freedom *for* speech and press through a court-enforced right of access to the media.

For many theorists and most judges, freedom of expression is more important than other rights guaranteed in the Constitution. Central to many theories of the First Amendment is the belief that it protects a *system* of freedom of expression such that if one entity's freedom is abridged, the freedom of all others in society is diminished (Emerson, 1970).

Legal Rights of Women

The Constitution that protects the mass media as institutions and freedom of expression as an abstraction does not yet contain a provision protecting

any fundamental rights of women other than the right to vote.[4] Specific
rights of women have been developed one by one in state and federal legislation and by the courts' interpretation of the equal protection clause of
the 14th Amendment, which was adopted in 1869 to bar the states from
denying the newly freed slaves the rights provided white men in the Constitution.[5] The Supreme Court first ruled in 1971 that discrimination on the
basis of sex violated the equal protection clause (*Reed v. Reed*, 1971).[6] The
Supreme Court first balanced freedom of the press against prohibitions on
sex discrimination in 1973 when it ruled in *Pittsburgh Press v. Pittsburgh
Commission on Human Relations* (1973) that a newspaper could not
publish sex-segregated want ads.

Women and the Media

Women own and manage relatively few mass media institutions and
generally lack the economic resources to establish their own. Even where
women fill many lower ranking positions in which they create the messages that are printed or broadcast, the media remain male institutions with
male definitions of what news is and what is entertaining. Women also fill
few newsmaking roles in society, making it difficult to get their messages
into the media from the outside. Both these factors cause the activities and
interests of women to be ignored or segregated out of the mainstream of
the news and entertainment and women to be represented in the media as
men see them (Tuchman, 1978; "Women Writing More," 1988). Lacking
substantive equality with men in the law, media, and society, women have
less access to media to tell the truths of their experiences in effective and
meaningful ways.

Feminist Jurisprudence
and Feminist Methods

Feminist jurisprudence is the study of the relationship between law and
society from the points of view of women. It is a rich, rapidly developing,
critical approach to legal analysis. Feminist methods begin by asking "the
woman question" to examine whether the law takes into account women's
experiences and whether existing legal standards disadvantage women
(Bartlett, 1990, p. 837). To bring women's experiences into interpretation
of the law, feminist scholars look at the law in the context of the real-life
practicalities of women's lives rather than at man-made abstractions and

generalizations (Bartlett, 1990, p. 849-863). In studying legal cases, this can mean reviewing women's courtroom testimony in addition to the judges' categorized summary of it to find significant but previously overlooked specifics. Through the process of consciousness-raising,[7] feminist legal scholars also draw on women's narrative stories about their lives in this patriarchal society as a basis of knowledge about common experiences (Abrams, 1991; Bartlett, 1990, pp. 863-867; Lahey, 1991; Matsuda, 1989a; Scheppele, 1989). Feminist scholars strive to listen to and believe what women say and take it seriously (Cain, 1990, p. 845; MacKinnon, 1987, pp. 110-113; West, 1987, pp. 81-89) as they propose transformations of the law.

Most early feminist scholarship reflected a bias of its own, relying on the experiences of its largely privileged white women authors as the basis for generalizations about all women (Cain, 1990, p. 846; Spelman, 1990). Being called to account for failing to recognize the additional disadvantages women experience based on race and class in particular, feminist scholars have begun to address more fundamental questions such as: Whose viewpoint does the law and its mechanisms reflect and what are the consequences? How might other biases be taken into account and offset (Bartlett, 1990, p. 848)? This broadened approach has recognized the contributions of Black feminist theorists and male and female Critical Race Theorists to an understanding of the law (Delgado & Stefancic, 1992; Matsuda, 1989a; P. Williams, 1990).[8] Some scholars have joined the insights of feminist and critical race scholars to view law from the perspective of "outsiders,"[9] generally (Matsuda, 1989a, p. 2323). Feminist legal scholars have found and argued that the law embodies white male standards as universal (Cain, 1990, p. 806; Williams, 1982). Although it claims to be neutral, to value "point-of-viewlessness," and to rely on objective judgment, the law, at best, is neutral and objective from the viewpoint of men (MacKinnon, 1982, p. 539, and 1987, pp. 210-211; Scales, 1986, pp. 1376-1380).

Much of the feminist critique of existing law has focused on the harms women suffer and how they have been inadequately addressed by or entirely ignored in the law (A. Dworkin, 1985; MacKinnon, 1987; West, 1987, 1988). One of the central projects of feminists in the past 20 years has been to make known the harms they experience as a consequence of rape, incest, domestic violence, sexual harassment, and pornography and to seek legal redress. A central problem for feminists has been communicating subjectively experienced personal harms in a male legal system that demands objectivity and abstraction (West, 1987, p. 85, 1988, pp. 64-66). The task has been difficult, first, because until recently women have only told each other about their pain (MacKinnon, 1982; West, 1987, p. 96),[10] and second, "women often find painful the same objective event or condition that men find pleasurable" (West, 1987, p. 81).[11] And finally, the law that privileges speech offers little incentive or encouragement for listening to what outsiders say (Cain, 1990, p. 844).

Perspectives on the meaning and importance of difference and equality tend to distinguish the various strains of feminist jurisprudence (Cain, 1990; Dalton, 1987-1988; Littleton, 1987; Minow, 1987). At issue are questions whether women are the same as or different from men in legally relevant respects; whether differences, if they exist, should be recognized in law; and how equality should be defined or by what standard similarities and differences are measured. These positions distinguish varieties of feminist thought, but the distinctions are imprecise and fluid.

Liberal Feminist Approaches

Feminists who take a liberal approach in their critiques of the law argue that women are rationally and politically the same as or similarly situated legally to men and therefore are entitled to share equally in all legal rights and privileges (Cain, 1990, p. 819; MacKinnon, 1983, p. 640; West, 1987, pp. 83, 91). They seek integration of women into a reformed legal system. The focus of liberal legal feminists, as it is for classical liberals, is individual autonomy, the opportunity for everyone to exercise free will and share in decision making. The failed Equal Rights Amendment to the Constitution was a liberal mechanism that would have established as fundamental law women's equal rights with men. Both legislation and litigation against sex discrimination in employment and education and for women's rights seek reforms based on liberal conceptions of women's legal status. Liberal feminists recently have challenged the legal measures of equality and the definitions of what it means to be a woman that are derived from male experiences (Cain, 1990, pp. 829, 832).

Many feminist legal theorists argue, however, that there are differences between men and women that should be recognized in strategies to reform the law and society and in differences in the law as well. The range of views on difference is considerable. At one end are liberals who seek substantive equality in the law and limit their view of difference to the strictly biological argument that only women become pregnant and bear children. For them employment policies, practices, and benefits should recognize this fact so that women are not legally and occupationally disadvantaged (Krieger & Cooney, 1983). Others focus on social, cultural, and psychological differences resulting from different roles men and women have traditionally filled in a patriarchal society.

Cultural Feminist Jurisprudence

Cultural feminists *embrace* the differences they see between men and women. Often drawing on the work of psychologist Carol Gilligan (1982), they argue that women by nature offer a different approach to the law and relationships that emphasizes care and consideration (Cain, 1990; Sherry, 1986). For example, legal scholar Christine A. Littleton proposes an "equality of acceptance" that requires that "social institutions react to gender differences . . . in such a way as to create equality between complementary male and female persons, skills, attributes and life styles" (1987, p. 193). The test of equality would be whether women and men are equally capable of exercising a right under the resulting law (Littleton, 1987, p. 198). Critics of cultural feminism argue that to accept the premise that men and women have different natural qualities, values, or characteristics is to risk the perpetuation of stereotypes that have been used to the disadvantage of women (Dalton, 1987-1988, p. 5; Scales, 1986, p. 1381).

Radical Feminist Jurisprudence

Radical feminists see differences between men and women as representing the patriarchal system of inequality characterized by male supremacy and dominance of women in law and society, and both are in need of revision, not mere reform.[12] These feminists view gender as a male construction of the inferior nature and subordinate place of women in society, a construct that is internalized by women (MacKinnon, 1982, pp. 529, 533; Scales, 1986, p. 1393). Radical feminists seek major social change resulting in women's having equal power with men. They believe that winning formal equality with men in a male-defined system is inadequate. Among the goals articulated for radical legal feminists are an equality that ends dominance and disadvantage altogether. They do not want to be equally powerful with privileged men and together dominate some other group. The legal system as envisioned by radical feminists would be fair with reference to "real human predicaments" (Scales, 1986, p. 1380) rather than to abstract principles. Both cultural and radical feminism have been challenged as being "essentialist," as claiming there is a female essence that is biologically or culturally based and for deriving their characterizations and definitions of women's nature from the experiences of privileged white women and failing to recognize the many differences among women (Harris, 1990; Spelman, 1988; J. Williams, 1991).

Postmodern Feminist Approaches

Joining other critical legal scholars, some feminists who take a post-modernist approach challenge the existence of objective reality and the viability of objectivity as a method in the law (Chamallas, 1992; Scales, 1986, p. 1378).[13] Instead they regard all knowledge and categories of analysis, such as gender or class, as social constructs (Cain, 1990, p. 838). In this view, all individuals are different from each other. As a consequence, the current task for feminists who accept this critique, then, is to see that multiple perspectives are brought to bear in the law (Bartlett, 1990; Chamallas, 1992; Matsuda, 1989b).

Feminist Perspectives on Freedom of Expression

From the liberal feminist perspective, freedom of expression is one of the fundamental liberties that women have at least nominally enjoyed for a considerable period of time. It may reasonably be argued that the government has met its obligation with regard to women's negative freedom of expression; it has not generally prevented women, on the basis of their sex, from speaking and writing. Through exercise of this right women have carried out the debate about women's inferior role in society, and many feminists agree with legal scholar Robin West's conclusion that "First Amendment principles further more than they hinder feminist goals" (1987, p. 138). The courts have not used gender as an explicit criterion in determining whether First Amendment rights to speak or publish should be upheld or limited. Indeed, some of the principals in landmark First Amendment cases have been women, including Elizabeth Baer, one of the defendants in *Schenck v. U.S.* (1919), the first such case decided by the Supreme Court.

The presence of feminist content or content of particular importance to women, however, has been the basis for limiting distribution or circulation of books and magazines to library patrons and school children. A variety of women's publications has been among the material removed from public and school libraries (*Newsletter on Intellectual Freedom* [NIF], 1979-1988).[14] *Ms.*, the mainstream feminist magazine, has been targeted several times, although a federal court ordered a New Hampshire school board to return it to the shelves (NIF, July 1979, p. 1; March 1982, p. 44; May 1982, p. 83). To the extent that their feminist content is the basis for the censorship of publications, the enforcement of the First Amendment is failing to meet the liberal notion of equal application of the law.

Cultural, radical, and postmodern feminists all ask more, if not more important, questions than simply whether freedom of expression has been enforced in a gender-neutral manner. Do women have substantive equality with men to exercise this freedom? Are women's needs and interests negatively affected by the system's preference for freedom of expression over other rights and values? Is freedom of expression as it has been defined of equal value to all men and women? Is there need for an interpretation that acknowledges differences between and among men and women? Have women been equally able to use the courts to affirm these rights when they are abridged?

As do other fundamental liberal rights guaranteed by the Constitution, freedom of expression rests on the premise that all people are equal. In a system in which that is not true, the radical view is, women do not have equal access to the benefits of this right (MacKinnon, 1987, pp. 129, 208). Catharine MacKinnon, one of the authors of the feminist antipornography ordinance for Minneapolis, has been an outspoken critic of the liberal position that freedom of expression must be absolutely protected from government interference (1985; 1987, pp. 206-213). MacKinnon points out that the courts have never accepted an absolutist interpretation of the First Amendment, but it has become "the implicit standard from which all deviations must be justified" (MacKinnon, 1987, p. 208).[15]

Court decisions, MacKinnon argues, "have justified exceptions to First Amendment guarantees when something that matters is seen to be directly at stake." (1985, p. 28). The problem for women and other outsiders is that their harm has not mattered. For those whose gender, race, or class effectively precludes them from exercising free speech, MacKinnon argues, negative freedom from government restraint does not provide useful protection or an opportunity to speak. This freedom is more likely to be used by those who have it to harm women and other outsiders (MacKinnon, 1987, pp. 208-209).[16] In her view, freedom of speech is the liberal flag in which those who have it wrap themselves while denying it to others (MacKinnon, 1987, p. 208). The radical feminists' goal is to change the legal system so that women and their harm matters when balanced with freedom of expression.

To make the First Amendment meaningful to women, MacKinnon argues, the state must also take an affirmative approach, providing a right of access that would guarantee women the opportunity to speak (1987, pp. 207-208).[17] She says it would work like affirmative action in employment: "Some people's access has to be restricted in the interest of providing access to all" (MacKinnon, 1987, pp. 208). Less specifically, legal scholar Patricia Cain calls for the development of feminist legal theories that protect speech and encourage listening, "a listening that privileges (temporarily) the previously silenced" (Cain, 1990, p. 844).

Feminist Perspectives on Libel and Privacy

The torts of libel and invasion of privacy are intended to provide the legal means for people who have been harmed by the publication of statements about them to seek redress and damages from the publishers. The Supreme Court has ruled that the First Amendment limits the circumstances under which damages may be awarded so that the media are not unduly harmed by huge damage awards or frivolous suits that sap their time, energy and resources.

To oversimplify a bit, a libelous statement or image is untrue, and it harms the subject's reputation. Whether the subject can find legal redress, however, depends on how the publisher came to circulate the libel and whether the subject is a public or private person. To protect the system of freedom of expression, the Supreme Court bars plaintiffs from winning libel cases unless the publisher was at fault. This balance between harm to the system of freedom of expression and harm to a person as a consequence of libel was struck in favor of the First Amendment in the 1964 Supreme Court libel decision in *New York Times v. Sullivan*. As a consequence, the primary focus in most libel cases is not on the falsity of the statement or the harm the subject suffered, but whether the publisher was at fault, whether he or she knowingly lied, was reckless in publishing potentially damaging information, or was negligent about the reliability of the information published (Bezanson, Cranberg, & Soloski, 1987, pp. 104-107).[18] Privacy law involves four different torts or wrongs: (a) publication of information that puts the individual in a false light, (b) public disclosure of private information, (c) appropriation or use of a person's name or image for commercial purposes without consent, and (d) intrusion into an individual's personal space (Prosser & Keeton, 1985, p. 851).

Women have not played a substantial role in the development of the torts of libel and privacy.[19] Relatively few plaintiffs in libel and privacy cases are women, and libel has not been a central focus of the feminist critique of the law.[20] Because libel and privacy are the torts intended to provide means of redress for individuals harmed by publications, there is reason to question how this area of the law relates to women's experiences and how it has addressed injuries or harms women have claimed.[21] Nevertheless, the promise of the law of libel and privacy to right wrongs by the media is rather empty. One study found that only 11% of libel plaintiffs and 17% of privacy plaintiffs won their suits against media defendants (Bezanson et al., 1987, p. 116).[22]

Whether libel and privacy law works from the liberal feminist perspective depends on whether women have equal opportunity with men to use the law and whether women's cases are treated the same as similar cases involving men. The available data on libel and false light privacy litigation do not answer these questions directly. They do show that only 11% of libel plaintiffs in one study were women and that more than 60% of the libel cases involved plaintiffs who were considered public, as opposed to private, persons (Bezanson et al., 1987, pp. 7, 10).[23] The researchers argue that the small proportion of women among libel plaintiffs is explained by the fact that women are underrepresented among public figures and officials who initiate most libel cases (Bezanson et al., 1987, p. 7).[24] Despite women's relative absence from public positions that would make them the primary actors in hard news stories, they do appear in the media as minor actors, subjects, and victims in hard news stories; as subjects of feature stories and pictures; as participants in reported social and cultural events; and in various roles in ads, cartoons, and entertainment content and programming.

Women may be no less and perhaps more vulnerable to false reports and invasions of privacy in those contexts in which they are identified in the media (Allen & Mack, 1990, p. 472-473).[25] To the degree that women suffer different kinds or different degrees of harm from the harm men experience as a consequence of false statements about them or invasions of their privacy the law is likely to fail to serve women more than men. Feminist legal critiques suggest that rather than failing to exist, women's injuries from libel and invasion of privacy may have been unspoken because of inferior social status and lack of experience in using the legal system to seek redress.[26]

As sex objects in this society, women are especially vulnerable to reputational harm from portrayals of a sexual nature. Some women have filed libel suits when falsely identified as participants in sexual activity or false light privacy cases when the publication of images created the false impression that they consented to being publicly portrayed in the nude or as participants in sexual activity.[27] Other cases have been filed as appropriation, or private facts cases. A survey of a variety of such cases involving sexual portrayals found that the plaintiffs rarely won (Colker, 1986, p. 41).

Seen in a feminist light, these cases often involve contradictions between conflicting social expectations of women: they are expected to be modest and virginal but available for men to use at will; and once women have breached modesty or lost their virginity they are less worthy of compassion and legal protection. Black legal scholar Regina Austin (1992) has argued that a Black woman who appeared to be identified as a prostitute in a network television documentary could only argue her case by adopting a white male middle-class perspective and engaging in a put-down of other Black women who are prostitutes (*Clark v. ABC,* 1983).

A Feminist Reading of *Pring v. Penthouse*

How sexual portrayal cases are handled in court demonstrates the point that when women suffer harm, the law ignores their injuries and society trivializes their claims. In *Pring v. Penthouse* (1982) an award-winning baton twirler and former Miss Wyoming sued *Penthouse* for libel and false light invasion of privacy because it published a fictional story about a baton-twirling Miss Wyoming who could cause men to levitate by performing fellatio on them, which she did during the Miss America pageant.[28] As a consequence of the story, Pring testified, she was subjected to street harassment, obscene phone calls, and lewd propositions so distressing that she left college. She also said that parents withdrew their daughters from her baton-twirling classes. She continued to be identified, and sometimes harassed and shunned, long after the case was completed (Spence, 1986, pp. 305-308, 457-458; UPI, July 6, 1986).

In overturning the jury decision in Pring's favor, the Court of Appeals said that the *Penthouse* story could not be "reasonably understood" as presenting facts about Pring (*Pring v. Penthouse,* 1982, p. 442).[29] By using the "reasonable person"[30] standard the court failed to give credence to Pring's story and did not address either the type of harm a woman such as Pring might suffer or the irrational but real behavior of those who harassed and demeaned Pring as the object of a dirty joke. This joke continues in legal discussion and literature, as the case is frequently trivialized.[31] The contrast between the appellate court's decision and Pring's claims exemplifies the point that what many women would find painful, many men may experience as pleasurable, sexual fantasy.

The Consent Defense in Privacy Cases

A substantial number of privacy cases involving sexual portrayals revolve around the question whether the subject gave consent for publication.[32] A typical case involves pictures for which an aspiring model or entertainer agrees to pose. Often there is no payment; the woman and the photographer each get copies of pictures for their portfolios. The subject may sign forms giving the photographer broad, unspecified authorization to use the pictures (*Douglas v. Hustler,* 1985). Sometimes pictures are taken for a specific purpose to which the woman agrees and they are used later for another purpose to which the subject would not have consented (e.g., *Ann-Margaret v. High Society Magazine,* 1980; *Douglas v. Hustler,* 1985). After the pictures are published, causing the woman harm, she turns to the law to seek redress through an appropriation suit. If it can be demonstrated that the woman gave broad enough permission to cover publication of the pictures or gave implied consent by her actions or failure to withhold consent, she does not win, regardless of the harm she suffers; that is, the harm does not matter. At a minimum, the subject is likely to suffer harm because of the false impression created that she consented to public distribution of the sexual portrayal and she may suffer additional harm, including embarrassment, loss of reputation, and economic losses.[33]

The concept of consent used in the law of privacy rests on the liberal presumption that free and equal people, acting in their own self-interest, voluntarily consent to diminish their liberty for other objectives, such as money. From the radical feminist perspective that women are not free and equal but rather are subordinate to men, we cannot assume that women give consent freely or that they act in their best interests if they do consent, nor can we reasonably assume that women who do grant consent are not harmed anyway (Colker, 1983, pp. 214-222; MacKinnon, 1987, pp. 100, 180-183).

As the cases and other women's experiences reveal, some women pose nude or engage in sexual acts for money—on camera or off—because they feel they have no economic alternatives. In some instances, women's consent has been coerced through sexist flattery, deception, threats of physical or psychological harm, or actual injury (MacKinnon, 1987, pp. 180-183).[34] Finally, as illustrated in some of the sexual portrayal cases, and more frequently noted with regard to other sexual abuses of women, when women just say "no" or grant limited consent, they are often ignored or not taken seriously, and when they report the offenses or sue for damages, they are not believed (Chamallas, 1988; Colker, 1983, p. 216; MacKinnon, 1985, p. 4).[35]

Drawing on her feminist critique of how the Supreme Court has handled a variety of cases involving women and other outsiders, feminist legal scholar Martha Minow argues that courts perpetuate systematic discrimination if they base decisions on "apparent choices made by plaintiffs, victims, or members of minority groups as a justification for holding against them. The Court may presume incorrectly that the choices are free and uncoerced, or the Court may wrongly attribute certain meanings to a choice" (Minow, 1987, p. 84). As a corrective to passive reliance on the liberal assumptions of the law, she suggests that judges consider the human consequences of their decisions rather than "insulating themselves in abstractions" (Minow, 1987, p. 89). Minow's critique also suggests that judges should actively question whether consent was voluntarily made by a person who understood the possible consequences and who was in a truly equal position to grant informed consent.

The Public Interest and Public Significance Standards

In privacy cases involving public disclosure of arguably private facts, the primary defense is that the information was of legitimate public interest and that the disclosure would not offend a reasonable person (Prosser & Keeton, 1985, p. 851) or it involved a matter of public significance (*Florida Star v. B J F,* 1989). The courts have, with a few exceptions, accepted a circular argument as a definition for "public interest" with regard to privacy law. The argument is: the media are intended to appeal to the public; the public read, watch, and listen to the media; therefore what's in the media is of public interest. In effect then the public interest is what the media say it is; indeed, from 1974 to 1984, the media lost less that 3% of the private facts cases that reached appeals courts (Bezanson et al., 1987, p. 116). Matters of "public significance" are not well defined either, but they do include the commission and investigation of violent crime and under some circumstances include the name of the victim of the crime (*Florida Star v. B J F,* p. 2611).

From a feminist perspective, the problem with the public interest standard for public disclosure of private facts cases is that the media are male institutions and conduct business with male definitions of the actual public interest in news and entertainment. By using these standards for privacy cases the courts have license to discount women's experience of harm.[36] The points made about the reasonable person standard's use in the Pring case apply here as well. If published information is uniquely or particularly offensive or harmful to women or other outsiders, the courts may say, in effect, they are supersensitive because reasonable people—privileged white men—would not be offended.[37]

Another specific case can illustrate how the public significance standard ignores the harm women suffer. In *Florida Star v. B.J.F.* (1989), B.J.F., a woman who was raped in a public place, sued the *Florida Star* for publishing her name in a report on the assault. Her name was published in violation of a Florida law prohibiting publication of the identity of a rape victim after police accidentally placed her name in a publicly available record and a reporter-trainee copied and used it in violation of both the law and newspaper policy. During the trial, B.J.F. testified that her name and address were published in the phone book and therefore calls were received at her house from a man who threatened to rape her again. As a consequence of her identification in the newspaper, she testified that the fear she experienced led her to seek police protection, change her phone number, and ultimately to move, and she required counseling as a result of the emotional distress she suffered.

In overturning the jury decision in B.J.F.'s favor, the court said it acknowledged the "highly significant" interests of a rape victim in privacy and physical safety. Nevertheless it found the interests of freedom of the press in reporting lawfully obtained information about matters of public significance higher. Twice in the decision, the court mentioned as justification for its ruling that a ruling against the newspaper *might* lead to self-censorship by the media with regard to other information released by the government. That is, the court weighed the speculative, hypothetical harm to freedom of the press more heavily than the actual harm a real woman experienced.[38]

Regardless of the theory of gender difference one considers, it seems likely that if women held equal power—not merely equal numbers—in the legal system and in the media, women's conception of harm would be incorporated into the definition of the generalized public interest or public significance and their harm would be taken into consideration in privacy cases and balanced against the media's interests in publicizing what people consider private facts.[39]

Feminist Approaches to Obscenity and Pornography

To date, the only area of media law to receive a considerable feminist analysis is the law of obscenity. The attention grew out of women's recognition that although women and children are usually the subjects in pornography, the law of obscenity had never considered pornography a women's issue. Under existing law, material that meets the Supreme Court's definition of obscenity is not protected by the First Amendment and may be regulated. The Supreme Court's definition of obscenity is that which

> the average person, applying contemporary community standards, would find that, taken as a whole, appeals to the prurient interest; that which depicts and describes in a patently offensive way sexual conduct as described by state law; and that which, taken as a whole, lacks serious literary, artistic, political or scientific value. (*Miller v. California,* 1973)

The definition of obscenity addresses sexually explicit material as a gender-neutral offense against community morality and sensibilities (Henkin, 1963), but it contains the "average person" standard similar to the reasonable person standard in privacy law, which represents the male view. Many feminists regard pornography as harmful to women, not simply offensive to them. According to MacKinnon and Andrea Dworkin, the best known of the advocates of this position, pornography that shows women in positions of subordination says, in effect, that the social role of woman is to be violated and dominated and further that women want to be treated that way (A. Dworkin, 1985; MacKinnon, 1985, pp. 206-213). In their view, pornography eroticizes the subordination of women to men. Because of the threat that pornography poses to women of being abused, MacKinnon and Dworkin also argue, pornography has the effect of silencing many women's speech against it or making their speech wholly ineffectual (A. Dworkin, 1985, pp. 17-20; MacKinnon, 1985, pp. 56-68). From this perspective, pornography, like sexual harassment in employment and education, discriminates against women on the basis of sex and should be treated as sex discrimination in the law.[40]

As MacKinnon had done in articulating sexual harassment law, Dworkin and MacKinnon drew on the testimony of women at public hearings in Minneapolis, who described experiencing a wide range of specific physical harms because of pornography, to draft an ordinance for that city. The ordinance treated pornography as sex discrimination in violation of women's civil rights.[41] The ordinance defined pornography as "the graphic sexually explicit subordination of women through pictures or words that also includes" one or more of nine specific characteristics, such as "women are presented as sexual objects who enjoy pain or humiliation" (Dworkin & MacKinnon, 1988, pp. 99-105).[42] If material met the definition, the ordinance empowered women to file complaints with the civil rights commission or civil suits in court to seek damages from those who created or used pornography and injunctions against further engaging in the discrimination. Women would have had a legitimate claim when: They were coerced into participating in the production of pornography; it was forced on them; they were assaulted on account of specific pornography; or they were subordinated because of the trafficking in, or availability of, pornography.

In ruling on a similar Indianapolis ordinance, the Court of Appeals found that pornography does have the effects the ordinance outlined, but it found the ordinance in violation of the First Amendment (*American Booksellers v. Hudnut*, 1985). In a relatively unusual action, the U.S. Supreme Court decided the case against the ordinance without entertaining substantive arguments from either side, in effect declining to listen to women's speech (*American Booksellers v. Hudnut*, 1986).[43] A bill with somewhat similar provisions, The Pornography Victims' Compensation Act of 1991, was introduced in the U.S. Senate. MacKinnon continues to argue that the courts could balance the First Amendment right of pornographers against the right of women to be free from harm, and they could uphold similar legislation if they would decide that harm to women matters (1987, ch. 16; 1991).[44]

Although the civil rights ordinance is the most familiar feminist approach to pornography, it is not universally supported by feminists (Berger, Searles, & Cottle, 1991; Burstyn, 1985; Kaminer, 1992). Perhaps the most common reaction among feminists is to agree with the Dworkin-MacKinnon critique of pornography, but to question the wisdom of their reliance on the patriarchal state, through civil rights commissions and the courts, for enforcement.[45] This reaction rests on the liberal belief that freedom of expression has done feminists more good than harm. Some fear passage of such an ordinance will trigger a backlash against women that will result in suppression of sexually explicit feminist material, such as feminist exposés of violence against women and feminist works on women's health and sexuality, particularly lesbian sex (Colker, 1984-1985, pp. 698-699, notes 70-74).[46] Some argue that the MacKinnon-Dworkin ordinance reflects only one view of sexually explicit material, which disregards the fact that some women, even feminists, regard images of sexual domination and submission as erotic (Snitow, Stansell, & Thompson, 1983; West, 1987, pp. 116-117).

The fact that antipornography civil rights ordinances have been adopted with the enthusiastic support of politically conservative, fundamentalist religious groups—which are antifeminist on most women's issues—is of particular concern to some critics of the Dworkin-MacKinnon approach. Because of the nature of the coalition, these critics argue, feminist issues are vulnerable to being overshadowed, co-opted, or ignored in the enforcement of the law (Burstyn, 1985; Kaminer, 1992).

Media Law as if Women Mattered

Media law, it turns out on examination, is not much different from other law from the perspective of women. The First Amendment, for the most part, does protect women's voice from legal constraints. As a result women can advocate reform necessary to create a society that may better value women's contributions. Individual women with the necessary resources have at least some access to an audience for their messages as a consequence of the First Amendment; for these women the barriers are social, political, and economic rather than legal. The First Amendment, which has so far never been interpreted authoritatively to deny protection for feminist speech, does provide a solid base from which to launch legal challenges to censorship and to punishment of sexually explicit or politically radical feminist expression. To the extent that existing First Amendment law is applied in a gender-neutral manner, it nearly meets liberal feminist visions of law in an egalitarian future.

But is that enough? Like most liberal elements of the law, the First Amendment does nothing to ensure that those who lack social and political power and economic resources can actually exercise the liberty it promises or be free of harm from its exercise by the powerful causes. In short, the First Amendment provides formal equality rather than substantive equality for the exercise of free expression. It does more to protect the abstract idea of freedom of expression than it does to see that people can actually speak, and it does nothing to guarantee listening.

The analysis of the law of libel, privacy, and obscenity reveals that the First Amendment has also served as a barrier to the relatively powerless who seek redress for injuries suffered as a consequence of other people's exercise of freedom of expression. The tests the courts have adopted and the manner of their application to the facts of specific cases have militated against the courts' truly hearing the accounts women have told of their injuries, particularly those to which women and other outsiders are most vulnerable; they perpetuate the harm of sexual objectification of women. Indeed media law lags behind other areas of the law, such as sexual harassment and employment discrimination law, which have begun to recognize the fact that women's and other outsiders' experiences are different from those of privileged white men in this patriarchal society and the differences are often harmful to women and other outsiders.

The cases and some of the criticism of the antipornography ordinances in particular reveal that resistance to a feminist analysis of media law as opposed to feminist analysis of other areas of the law lies in the ideology of the First Amendment that regards the absolutist interpretation as the only approach. While championing the marketplace of ideas, advocates of the absolutist view do not value the listening implied in that metaphor and do not tolerate suggestions that any other interests be balanced against freedom of the press.

The feminist challenge to media law is to find a means of protecting expression that values all expression and that treats women and other outsiders as if they matter as much as abstract principles do. Feminist legal analysis needs to re-vision the law to address the harm communication causes individuals and groups in society. It may be that a balance should be struck, as Patricia Cain (1990, p. 844) suggests, to temporarily privilege the speech of those who have been silenced and ignored.

Notes

1. The terms *freedom of speech* and *freedom of the press* are used interchangeably with the more expansive term *freedom of expression* to refer to the same concepts and law deriving from the First Amendment to the U.S. Constitution. This body of law is referred to as *media law, communication law,* or *First Amendment law,* again, interchangeably.

2. About 93% of state and federal judges are men.

3. He says this ideology holds sway in law, journalism, library, and art schools and among practicing journalists, librarians, and creative and performing artists.

4. The Equal Rights Amendment (H.R.J. Res 208, 92nd Cong., 1st Sess., 1971) that failed to win ratification provided: "Equality of rights under the law shall not be denied or abridged by the United States or by any state on account of sex."

5. It provides in relevant part: "No state shall . . . deny to any person within its jurisdiction the equal protection of the laws."

6. In the case, the Supreme Court ruled that an Idaho law that gave preference to men over women as administrators of the estates of the deceased violated the equal protection clause.

7. Consciousness-raising has been defined as women listening to each other as they tell personal stories, often stories silenced by dominant discourse (Cain, 1990, p. 843).

8. Among the topics addressed by Critical Race Theorists has been hate speech, a topic of significance to communication law scholars. See, for example, Delgado (1982) and Matsuda (1989a).

9. *Outsider jurisprudence* is a term coined by Mari Matsuda to refer to the work of feminists and scholars of color (also identified as Critical Race Theory) to address the social and political relationship of women and so-called racial and ethnic minorities to mainstream jurisprudence. See Matsuda, 1989a, p. 2323, note 15 and J. Williams, 1991, p. 298, note 10. See also Stefancic and Delgado, 1991.

10. This has occurred in women's consciousness-raising discussions, which explore the personal and value subjective truth (MacKinnon, 1982, pp. 519-520, 535-536).

11. For example, the office pass may be sex and pleasurable for men, sexual harassment and painful for women.

12. MacKinnon (1987, p. 176) refers to this group as simply "feminists," unmodified by a traditional political label that, she argues, detracts from the emphasis of feminism on women as a group.

13. Both the critical legal studies movement and those who engage in a postmodernist critique of the law challenge the notion of objectivity.

14. Among the most frequently removed or threatened books is *Our Bodies, Our Selves* (NIF, July 1977, p. 100; July 1981, p. 92; July 1975, p. 105; September 1975, p. 138; July 1981, p. 92; May 1982, p. 100, 101; March 1983, p. 29; May 1986, p. 78; November 1987, p. 223; January 1988, p. 3). Other feminist books that have been removed from libraries are *Fear of Flying* (NIF, May, 1982, 87), and *The Women's Room* (Doyle, 1983, p. 3).

15. Her view is echoed by Schauer's "ideology of the First Amendment."

16. For example, MacKinnon argues, Blacks are harmed by the protected speech of the Ku Klux Klan; Jews are harmed when Nazis are protected in their hateful demonstrations through Jewish neighborhoods; women are harmed by the protected self-expression of pornographers.

17. MacKinnon's right of access is similar to Jerome Barron's (1967); his right of access, however, would occur primarily in response to expression already carried in the media.

18. The Iowa Libel Research Project found that 87% of media libel cases decided by appellate courts between 1974 and 1984 focused mainly on the issue of fault (Bezanson et al., 1987, p. 106).

19. Allen and Mack (1990) have written that the history of the privacy tort "bears the unmistakable mark of an era of male hegemony" and that the sex of the plaintiff has mattered in many privacy cases but that the courts have relied on patriarchal views of female modesty in deciding cases (pp. 442, 470-471).

20. Only 11% of the plaintiffs in libel cases covered in the Bezanson et al. (1987, p. 7) study were women. On feminist analyses, see Colker (1983, 1984-1985, 1986) and Allen and Mack (1990). Defense attorney Gerry Spence (1986), a man, has published an essentially feminist critique of a libel case. Bender (1990) has written a feminist analysis of some aspects of tort law.

21. "Existing categories of privacy torts potentially have one of their most worthwhile applications as aids to female victims of gender-related privacy invasions" (Allen & Mack, 1990, p. 443).

22. For cases that reached appellate courts between 1974 and 1984, the success rates varied widely among the privacy torts: false light, 11.5%; private facts, 2.8%; appropriation, 33.3%; intrusion, 37.5%.

23. Public persons in libel law are those who hold or run for public office or who thrust themselves into the public eye. They are people who have high visibility in the media, either locally or nationally.

24. Colker argues that when women file libel actions, they are frequently ruled to be public figures even though they do not seem to meet the legal definition of public figures (1983, p. 213). Public figures have a heavier burden of proof in libel cases.

25. Allen and Mack suggest the assumptions that women are "limited by their obligations" permits rationalization of prying into their affairs and the social expectations of higher moral conduct by women encourages surveillance and exposure, both of which would be invasions of privacy (1990, pp. 472-473).

26. Women socialized in this society may regard their libel and privacy injuries as private and unimportant or believe that the legal system will regard them as trivial, especially if they observe how the legal system has treated other wrongs against women, such as rape and domestic violence. Hoyman and Stallworth (1986, pp. 79-80) found that even in the area of sex discrimination law, less than half of those filing suit in a sample of workers were women.

27. Colker lists all such cases she could identify. Some of the plaintiffs were men (1986, pp. 41-3, note 7). A considerable number of women's libel and privacy cases do involve their portrayals as sexual objects.

28. *Pring v. Penthouse,* 695 F.2d 438 (10th Cir. 1982), *cert. denied,* 462 U.S. 1132 (1983). The story, "Miss Wyoming Saves the World," by Philip Cioffari was published in the August 1979 issue of *Penthouse.* Kimerli Pring held the Miss Wyoming title in the summer of 1979. Cioffari attended the Miss America pageant in which Pring competed. A jury awarded Pring the largest amount of damages in a libel case up to that time, but the Court of Appeals overturned the verdict and the Supreme Court declined to hear the case.

29. See also, Colker (1983, pp. 225-226).

30. See Bender, 1990, p. 25. Chamallas discusses the use of a "reasonable victim" standard as a means of seeing sexual harassment from the perspective of its usually female victims (1988, pp. 806-809). A similar approach would have been appropriate here.

31. The case is often cited in discussions of large damage awards. See, for example, Smolla (1986, pp. 162-164) who says Pring was worried that readers would assume "where there's smoke there's fire" (p. 164). See also Spence (1986, pp. 307, 458).

32. Consent is the primary defense in appropriation cases and it may be a relevant defense in some private facts cases. Colker (1986) also considers the implication of consent, when none was given for a sexual portrayal, as the *injury* in some false light cases.

33. Colker argues that the woman is harmed in part because her sex-based civil rights are violated; she is "only portrayed sexually because she is a woman" (1986, p. 46, note 31). Vanessa Williams, Miss America 1984, was forced to resign after pictures taken in a scenario similar to that described were published in *Penthouse* (Colker, 1984-1985, p. 687; Smolla, 1986, pp. 160-162).

34. The most well-known presentation of this point involves Linda Marchiano who was hypnotized, imprisoned, beaten, and threatened by her agent-husband to consent to participation as Linda Lovelace in the movie *Deep Throat* (Colker, 1983, p. 216; Lovelace, 1980; MacKinnon, 1985, pp. 32-38).

35. On sexual harassment, see, for example, MacKinnon (1979, pp. 161-162, and 1987, pp. 110-113; Chamallas, 1988, pp. 801-810). On rape see, for example, Estrich (1987, pp. 42-56). See also Chamallas (1988, pp. 797-800).

36. West argues that men's "conception of pain—of what it is—is derived from a set of experiences which *excludes* women's experience" (1987, pp. 144, 227).

37. Colker argues that the reasonableness standard harms women by defining sensitivity from a male point of view (1983, p. 227).

38. In a dissent, Justice White, joined by the Chief Justice and the court's only woman, Justice O'Connor, said "The Court's concern for a free press is appropriate, but such concerns should be balanced against rival interests in a civilized and humane society. An absolutist view of the former leads to insensitivity to the latter."

39. Not all feminists agree that rape victims' names should be withheld from publication or that failure to withhold should be punished. For example Geneva Overholser, editor of the *Des Moines Register,* believes women should volunteer to be identified (see Overholser, 1990).

40. MacKinnon was prominent in the development of the legal argument that sexual harassment was sex discrimination (MacKinnon, 1979), a view the Supreme Court accepted in *Meritor Savings Bank v. Vinson* (1986). MacKinnon says: "It became possible to do something legal about sexual harassment because some women took women's experience of violation seriously enough to design a law around it, *as if what happens to women matters"* [emphasis added] (1987, p. 103).

41. The Minneapolis ordinance was vetoed by the mayor in 1984. A similar ordinance adopted in Indianapolis was found unconstitutional by a federal Court of Appeals, and the Supreme Court affirmed that decision without substantial review (*American Booksellers v. Hudnut,* 1986).

42. Listening to women's stories is unusual in the fields of pornography research and legislation (Lahey, 1991). Feminist Wendy Kaminer, who opposes antipornography legislation, is contemptuous of women's testimony. "Like a TV talk show, the (Massachusetts) Attorney General's commission presented testimony from pornography's alleged victims, which may or may not have been true. It's difficult to cross-examine a sobbing self-proclaimed victim; you either take her testimony at face value or you don't" (1992).

43. Justice Sandra Day O'Connor, the only woman on the Supreme Court, had voted to give the case a full review.

44. The court has found that harm to children featured in pornography matters (*New York v. Ferber,* 1982).

45. Several writers suggest that the courts do not have a good record with regard to female sexuality in general. They have trouble distinguishing among stranger, acquaintance, and marital rape, and consensual sex; they fail to see abortion as an issue about a woman's control over the use of her body; they have been unpredictable in deciding on pregnancy benefits and

related reproductive issues. See Allen (1988), Chamallas (1988), Estrich (1987), and Tong (1984).

46. For example, see discussion above about censorship, particularly about *Our Bodies, Ourselves.*

References

Abrams, Kathryn. (1991). Hearing the call of stories. *California Law Review, 79,* 971-1052.

Allen, Anita L. (1988). *Uneasy access.* Totowa, NJ: Rowman & Littlefield.

Allen, Anita L., & Mack, Erin. (1990). How privacy got its gender. *Northern Illinois Law Review, 10,* 441-479.

American Booksellers v. Hudnut, 771 F.2d 323 (7th Cir. 1985), *affirmed* 475 U.S. 1001 (1986).

Ann-Margaret v. High Society Magazine, 498 F. Supp. 401 (S.D.N.Y. 1980).

Austin, Regina. (1992). Black women, sisterhood, and the difference/deviance divide. *New England Law Review, 26,* 877-887.

Barron, Jerome A. (1967). Access to the press—A new First Amendment right. *Harvard Law Review, 80,* 1641-1678.

Bartlett, Katharine T. (1990). Feminist legal methods. *Harvard Law Review, 103,* 829-888.

Bender, Leslie. (1990). Feminist (re)torts: Thoughts on the liability crisis, mass torts, power and responsibilities. *Duke Law Journal, 1990,* 848-912.

Berger, Ronald J., Searles, Patricia, & Cottle, Charles. (1991). *Pornography and feminism.* New York: Praeger.

Bezanson, Randall P., Cranberg, Gilbert, & Soloski, John. (1987). *Libel law and the press.* New York: Free Press.

Burstyn, Varda. (Ed.). (1985). *Women against censorship.* Vancouver, BC: Douglas & McIntyre.

Cain, Patricia A. (1990). Feminism and the limits of equality. *Georgia Law Review, 24,* 803-847.

Chamallas, Martha. (1988). Consent, equality, and the legal control of sexual conduct. *Southern California Law Review, 61,* pp. 777-862.

Chamallas, Martha. (1992). Feminist constructions of objectivity: Multiple perspectives in sexual and racial harassment litigation. *Texas Journal of Women and the Law, 1,* 95-142.

Clark v. ABC, 684 F.2d 1208 (6th cir., 1983).

Colker, Ruth. (1983). Pornography and privacy: Towards the development of a group based theory for sex based intrusions of privacy. *Journal of Law and Inequality, 1,* 191-237.

Colker, Ruth. (1984-1985). Legislative remedies for unauthorized sexual portrayals: A proposal. *New England Law Review, 20,* 687-720.

Colker, Ruth. (1986). Published consentless sexual portrayals: A proposed framework for analysis. *Buffalo Law Review, 35,* 39-83.

Dalton, Clare. (1987-1988). Where we stand: Observations on the situation of feminist legal thought. *Berkeley Women's Law Journal, 3,* 1-13.

Delgado, Richard. (1982). Words that wound: A tort action for racial insults, epithets, and name-calling. *Harvard Civil Rights/Civil Liberties Law Review, 17,* 133-181.

Delgado, Richard, & Stefancic, Jean. (1992). Images of the outsider in American law and culture: Can free expression remedy systemic social ills? *Cornell Law Review, 77,* 1258-1297.

Douglas v. Hustler, 769 F.2d 1128 (7th Cir. 1985).

Doyle, Robert P. (1983). *List of books some people consider dangerous.* Chicago: American Library Association.

Dworkin, Andrea. (1985). Against the male flood: Censorship, pornography and equality. *Harvard Women's Law Journal, 8,* 1-29.

Dworkin, Andrea, & MacKinnon, Catharine A. (1988). *Pornography and civil rights: A new day for women's equality.* Minneapolis: Organizing Against Pornography.

Dworkin, Ronald. (1985). *A matter of principle.* Cambridge, MA: Harvard University Press.

Emerson, Thomas I. (1970). *The system of freedom of expression.* New York: Random House.

Equal Rights Amendment, H.R.J. Res. 208, 92nd Cong., 1st Session, 1971.

Estrich, Susan. (1987). *Real rape.* Cambridge, MA: Harvard University Press.

Florida Star v. B.J.F. (1989).

Fund for Modern Courts. (1985). *The success of women and minorities in achieving judicial office: The selection process.* New York: Author.

Gilligan, Carol. (1982). *In a different voice: Psychological theory and women's development.* Cambridge, MA: Harvard University Press.

Harris, Angela. (1990). Race and essentialism in feminist legal theory. *Stanford Law Review, 42,* 581-616.

Henkin, Louis. (1963). Morality and the Constitution: The sin of obscenity. *Columbia Law Review, 63,* 391-414.

Hoyman, Michele, & Stallworth, Lamont. (1986). Suit filing by women: An empirical analysis. *Notre Dame Law Review, 62,* 61-82.

Kaminer, Wendy. (1992, November). Feminists against the First Amendment. *Atlantic Monthly,* pp. 110-118.

Krieger, Linda J., & Cooney, Patricia N. (1983). The Miller-Wohl controversy: Equal treatment, positive action and the meaning of women's equality. *Golden Gate University Law Review, 13,* 513-572.

Lahey, Kathleen A. (1991). Pornography and harm—Learning to listen to women. *International Journal of Law and Psychiatry, 14,* 117-131.

Levi, Edward H. (1949). *An introduction to legal reasoning.* Chicago: University of Chicago Press.

Littleton, Christine A. (1987). Equality across difference: A place for rights discourse. *Wisconsin Women's Law Journal, 3,* 189-212.

Lovelace, Linda. (1980). *Ordeal.* New York: Bell Publishing.

MacKinnon, Catharine A. (1979). *Sexual harassment of working women.* New Haven, CT: Yale University Press.

MacKinnon, Catharine A. (1982). Feminism, Marxism, method and the state: An agenda for theory. *Signs: Journal of Women in Culture and Society, 7,* 515-544.

MacKinnon, Catharine A. (1983). Feminism, Marxism, method and the state: Toward feminist jurisprudence. *Signs: Journal of Women in Culture and Society, 8,* 635-658.

MacKinnon, Catharine A. (1985). Pornography, civil rights, and speech. *Harvard Civil Rights/Civil Liberties Law Review, 20,* 1-70.

MacKinnon, Catharine A. (1987). *Feminism unmodified.* Cambridge, MA: Harvard University Press.

Matsuda, Mari J. (1989a). Public response to racist speech: Considering the victim's story. *Michigan Law Review, 87,* 2320-2381.

Matsuda, Mari J. (1989b). When the first quail calls: Multiple consciousness as jurisprudential method. *Women's Rights Law Reporter, 11,* 7-10.

Meritor Savings Bank v. Vinson, 477 U.S. 57 (1986).

Miller v. California, 413 U.S. 15 (1973).

Minow, Martha. (1987). The supreme court 1986 term—Foreword: Justice engendered. *Harvard Law Review, 101*, 10-95.

New York v. Ferber, 458 U.S. 747 (1982).

New York Times v. Sullivan, 376 U.S. 254 (1964).

Newsletter on Intellectual Freedom, 1979-1988.

Overholser, Geneva. (1990, October). Covering rape: A time of transition. *ASNE Bulletin*, pp. 14, 16-17.

Pittsburgh Press v. Pittsburgh Commission on Human Relations, 413 U.S. 376 (1983).

Pornography Victims' Compensation Act of 1991. S. 1521, 102nd Cong., 1st Session, 1991.

Pring v. Penthouse, 695 F.2d 438 (10th Cir. 1982), *cert. denied*, 462 U.S. 1132 (1983).

Prosser, William, & Keeton, W. Page. (1985). *Prosser and Keeton on law of torts* (5th ed.). St. Paul: West.

Reed v. Reed, 404 U.S. 71 (1971).

Scales, Ann C. (1986). The emergence of feminist jurisprudence: An essay. *Yale Law Journal, 95*, 1373-1403.

Schauer, Frederick. (1992). The First Amendment as ideology. *William and Mary Law Review, 33*, 853-869.

Schenck v. U.S., 249 U.S. (1919).

Scheppele, Kim Lane. (1989). Foreword: Telling stories. *Michigan Law Review, 87*, 2073-2098.

Sherry, Susanna. (1986). Civic virtue and feminine voice in constitutional adjudication. *Virginia Law Review, 72*, 543-616.

Snitow, Ann, Stansell, Christine, & Thompson, Sharon. (Eds.). (1983). *Powers of desire*. New York: Monthly Review Press.

Smolla, Rodney A. (1986). *Suing the press*. New York: Oxford University Press.

Spelman, Elizabeth V. (1988). *Inessential woman: The problems of exclusion in feminist thought*. Boston: Beacon.

Spence, Gerry. (1986). *Trial by fire*. New York: William Morrow.

Stefancic, Jean, & Delgado, Richard. (1991). Outsider jurisprudence and the electronic revolution: Will technology help or hinder the cause of law reform? *Ohio State Law Journal, 52*, 847-858.

Stewart, Potter. (1975). "Or of the press." *Hastings Law Journal, 26*, 631-637.

Tong, Rosemarie. (1984). *Women, sex, and the law*. Totowa, NJ: Rowman & Allenheld.

Tuchman, Gaye. (1978). *Making news*. New York: Free Press.

U.S. Constitution, Amendment I, XIV.

Wechsler, Herbert. (1959). Toward neutral principles of constitutional law. *Harvard Law Review, 73*, 1-35.

West, Robin L. (1987). The difference in women's hedonic lives: A phenomenological critique of feminist legal theory. *Wisconsin Women's Law Journal, 3*, 81-145.

West, Robin L. (1988). Jurisprudence and gender. *University of Chicago Law Review, 55*, 1-72.

Williams, Joan C. (1991). Dissolving the sameness/difference debate: A post-modern path beyond essentialism in feminist and critical race theory. *Duke Law Journal, 1991*, 296-323.

Williams, Patricia. (1990). *The alchemy of race and rights*. Cambridge, MA: Harvard University Press.

Williams, Wendy W. (1982). The equality crisis: Some reflections on culture, courts and feminism. *Women's Rights Law Reporter, 7*, 175-200.

Women writing more front-page news, but not making it, study says. (March/April 1988). *Media Report to Women*, p. 7.

19 Changing Media History Through Women's History

SUSAN HENRY

Women's participation in American journalism is as old as the field itself. We know, for example, that the first press in the American colonies (established in Cambridge, MA, in 1638) was owned by a woman, and that at least 17 women worked as printers in colonial America before the ratification of the Constitution in 1788. Still more women labored in print shops as compositors, binders, writers, and press workers during this period.[1]

Yet, although the work of American women journalists can be traced as far back as the field's origins, the historical study of women journalists, of women's images in the mass media, and of their presence as members of mass media audiences has a much shorter lineage. Women began to move up "from the footnotes" of journalism history texts only about a dozen years ago, and substantial research by journalism historians on topics related to women began less than a decade before that.[2]

In this brief time, however, such research has progressed rapidly. The new stories of more than 100 women journalists have been told, many historical studies of media consumed primarily by women have been carried out, women's media images during different periods have been studied, and the roles played by the mass media in advancing or retarding social, political, and economic developments of particular importance to women increasingly have been examined.

As a result, unlike historians studying women and journalism only a decade ago, today's researchers have a substantial body of scholarly literature on which to draw. These scholars no doubt will be influenced by the methods and subjects chosen as well as by the conclusions drawn in these earlier works. Thus this is an appropriate time to begin an evaluation of the state of this literature, to examine the effects this research has had on the larger field of journalism history, and to suggest directions that future research might take.

New Research, New Integration

Certainly one of the most striking aspects of the historical research on women and American journalism is its quantity. The field has attracted a large number of productive, imaginative scholars. One indication of the quantity of published articles on women is found in the first 10-year index (covering 1974-1983) of *Journalism History,* the oldest journal in the field. Here "women," with 26 entries, is the third largest topic category, preceded only by the large, miscellaneous categories labeled "general" and "biographies." In addition, 12 of the 35 entries listed under "biographies" refer to studies of women ("Cumulative Index, Vols. 1-10, 1974-1983," 1983).

Similar evidence of the proliferation of this research is found in an article by Donald Shaw and Sylvia Zack (1987) analyzing the previous decade of historical articles published in *Journalism Quarterly,* the main professional journal for research in mass communication, and in *Journalism History.*

Citing work that has, in their opinion, contributed "new evidence and perspective" to the field, Shaw and Zack single out 108 individual articles. Of these, 26—almost a quarter of the total—are on topics related to women. The authors make no attempt to count or categorize all articles appearing in these two journals during this time, yet the fact that they cite such a large number about women is an indication of the amount of strong published work available.

Recent articles on women in journalism history are notable for more than just their quantity; they also are varied in the subjects covered. A substantial amount of this research is devoted to "retrieving" previously unrecognized women journalists and placing them within the historical record, but, in addition, excellent studies have been done on topics such as suffrage and birth control publications, the effects women journalists' "marginal" professional status has had on their journalism and their careers, how women and particular women's issues have been covered by both specialized and mainstream media, and methodological and conceptual issues growing out of the study of women.

In contrast, most books on women and journalism history published in the 1970s and 1980s have been biographies of individual women rather than studies of wider trends and issues. Still, many of these in-depth studies constitute significant contributions to the literature, particularly in light of the many hundreds of biographies and autobiographies of male journalists crowding library shelves. It also should be noted that these books have taken as their subjects a range of women and types of journalism. For example, recent well-received biographies include studies of Freda Kirchwey, owner, editor, and publisher of *The Nation* (Alpern, 1987); of suffragist editor and activist Abigail Scott Duniway (Moynihan, 1983); of Dorothy Day, publisher of the radical *Catholic Worker* (Roberts, 1984); and of *Life* magazine's renowned photographer, Margaret Bourke-White (Goldberg, 1986). At the same time, recent group biographies have examined in less depth, still more women journalists' lives.[3]

In addition to their progress in studying the individuals, publications, and issues previously unknown or unrecognized within journalism history, historians of women have begun to succeed in another important area: the integration of their research into the overall picture of American journalism history, especially as it is being taught in colleges and universities. A rough indication of their success can be found by examining the table of contents of the dominant text in the field,[4] Edwin Emery and Michael Emery's *The Press and America*. The third edition, published in 1972, and the sixth edition, published in 1988, are very different in their inclusion of material related to women. These differences are evident beginning with the first sentence of each edition's foreword—which announced in 1972, "Journalism history is the story of man's long struggle to communicate freely with his fellow man" (Emery, 1972, p. iii) and was revised in 1988 to read, "Journalism history is the story of humanity's long struggle to communicate" (Emery & Emery, 1988, p. v). They continue to the last page of each index, where the heading "women in journalism" references a total of 5 pages in 1972 and 103 pages in 1988. These additional pages primarily reflect the legions of women's names now included in the sixth edition's voluminous lists of printers, reporters, editors, publishers, broadcasters, photographers, and advertising and public relations practitioners. A dozen and a half illustrations showing women journalists also have been added during the 16 years, and the expanded 1988 annotated bibliographies accompanying each chapter contain many new sources on women and journalism history.

Reasons for the New Research

It is now possible, then, to identify a substantial and varied body of published work on women and journalism history, and to note a systematic integration of material about women into the key journalism history text. What accounts for this progress? The most obvious answer is that the number of scholars doing historical research on women in journalism has increased markedly.

Although there is no reliable way to determine how many journalism historians have studied topics related to women during any period (and whether good work was produced that was not accepted for publication it certainly is notable that since the early 1970s the journalism faculties of American colleges and universities have included growing numbers of the professors most likely to study women—that is, women. Just as many more women have become professional journalists in the last decade and a half, so have many more become journalism professors.

The most recent study to bring together detailed data on journalism educators found that in 1991 women made up 28% of higher education journalism faculties, compared with only 7%-8% in 1972 (see Viswanath, Kosicki, & Creedon, Chapter 14, this volume). Although this still shows a serious imbalance between men and women (and the imbalance is compounded by significant rank and salary differences), it more than doubles the percentage of a decade earlier. A related earlier study examined the authorship of full-length *Journalism Quarterly* articles by women, noting an increase from 7% during the 1960-1971 period to more than 16% for 1979-1983 (Sharp, Turk, Einsiedel, Schamber, & Hollenback, 1985, p. 3).

Certainly not all women teaching journalism are also doing research on women, and only a minority of those are historians. But there is little doubt that the increase in the number of female journalism professors has coincided with a marked increase in the amount of scholarly work on women in journalism history—much of it authored by women—being published. And, as more work has been published, additional researchers have been drawn to the study of women and journalism history.

Yet this small influx of women journalism historians cannot by itself explain the progress made in research on women, for few historians would risk studying women in journalism if they thought there was little chance their work would be accepted or valued by others in the field. Professors just beginning their careers—as was the case with many female scholars researching women during the 1970s—need to be particularly sensitive to the publishing potential of their research.

Understanding their success thus also requires recognizing what I believe is another important factor: the interest in and openness to research on women shown by a number of important male journalism historians. For more than a decade, some of the field's most respected men have given particular encouragement to scholars studying women in journalism history. Their personal enthusiasm for—and public recognition of—this research has meant that those who pursue it generally have not had to fight the kinds of hard battles to establish the value of their work that, for example, many well-known American historians studying women face even today.[5]

Evidence of such support has been noted above. It includes the increasing references to women in *The Press and America,* the many articles related to women singled out in an article on important research in journalism history coauthored by Donald Shaw, for several years Journalism *Quarterly's* associate editor for history, and the three dozen articles of women published during *Journalism History's* first decade, when it was edited by Tom Reilly. By calling attention to research on women in these varied ways, male journalism historians have helped to legitimate this work and to encourage its production.

Admittedly, scholars studying women in journalism history do face serious problems, such as a scarcity of both primary data and useful analytical models. As a rule, however, they have not had to overcome opposition to their work by established, influential male journalism historians and journal editors; indeed, the support of such people likely has provided important encouragement for these research efforts. Many things help account for their support, including the high quality of a great deal of this published work and the very capable scholars responsible for much of it. But I believe two less obvious factors also are important in explaining why major male journalism historians have encouraged research on women. These factors particularly deserve consideration because, to my mind, they bear directly on the future of historical research on women in journalism.

The first factor arises from the status of journalism history within the larger field of mass communication research. Simply put, the larger field exhibits a marked social science bias—which favors methods utilizing quantification—as well as a preference for research that examines current media issues.[6] Because most journalism history does not use social science research methods (although these methods have been applied, with very revealing results), and history, by definition, examines the past, this work tends to have a kind of undeserved secondary status as mass communication research. Thus journalism historians seldom are included as part of university communication research centers, just as their work usually is less well funded than that of social science mass communication researchers. Similarly, *Journalism Quarterly* prints far more articles utilizing social science research methods than traditional historical methods.[7]

Yet, ironically, this situation may well have made established male journalism historians more receptive to research on women than would have been the case if history were seen as more central to mass communication research overall. These historians can recognize the benefits of encouraging all scholars who are producing good history, no matter what its subject, since this will further strengthen a field that sometimes is unfairly viewed as peripheral. Indeed, new researchers as a whole tend to be encouraged, since they can help revitalize the field, both with their numbers and with their scholarship. This same secondary status seems to have made journalism historians less rigid than journalism social scientists in defining "acceptable" research subjects. As a result, new historians may be discouraged from exploring nontraditional research areas less frequently than are their social scientist colleagues.

A second factor also helps explain the support given journalism historians studying topics related to women. It is important to note, I think, that most of this research is substantially conservative: Research on women and journalism history has seldom challenged accepted ideas about such matters as how individuals should be studied or what criteria should be used in determining the significance of different media or journalists. Thus the specific topics examined in this research—for example, women journalists or the media coverage of women at different times—are new, but the scholars carrying out this research generally have studied their subjects within the accepted, male-developed framework of journalism history. As a result, their findings can easily be integrated into the field's existing literature, further strengthening the established framework because it is applied to women as well as to men.

This is not to say these scholars purposely have avoided developing radically different ways of thinking about their subjects, or that resistance necessarily would arise if they did. It is much more likely that, in the struggle to locate and analyze data needed for research on women, assumptions about journalism history simply have not been questioned. Similarly, solving the many practical problems often involved in studying women may have left researchers with little energy to pursue some of the more interesting implications of their studies, or to take advantage of useful literature outside of the field that might lead them to quite different subjects and analytical frameworks.

New Directions for Research on Women and Journalism History

As understandable as this conservatism is, it must be overcome, and alternative approaches to the study of women in journalism history must be developed. A logical starting point for this development is with the comments of those who have thought about this field and its future. Although no full-fledged critique of the existing research has yet been published, several scholars have made important points that can be utilized in finding new approaches.

The first point has been suggested independently by two well-known journalism historians. Mary Ann Yodelis Smith (1982) advises that historical studies of women "media processors" must be better developed so that they move beyond the traditional narratives that have dominated the literature. She stresses the need to analyze the lives of women journalists rigorously, and especially to provide sociocultural context for them (pp. 149-150). Similarly, Zena Beth McGlashan (1985) warns against the "positivist trap of creating but not critiquing heroes." Rather, she explains, the work done by women journalists must be critically examined, and differences between women should be carefully noted (p. 59).

Second is the observation by communication theorist H. Leslie Steeves (1987) that most research on women and journalism history rests on "liberal feminist" assumptions that do not question the established mainstream American media system, instead studying—and applauding—the "notable" women who were able to succeed within that system. Steeves also notes that these studies seldom examine how such factors as class, race, and sexual orientation have affected the work done by these women (p. 103).

Third is feminist communication scholar Lana F. Rakow's (1986) recommendation of a "recovery and reappraisal approach" to the study of contemporary popular culture produced by and for women. She explains that this approach "calls not for adding women artists to a literary or artistic canon but for a re-evaluation of the criteria that establish canons and determine the artistic and social merit of creative expressions." Although she does not apply this concept to journalism history, Rakow praises historical studies of popular culture—especially of popular novels written by women for women readers—that avoid the kind of analysis usually applied to male-oriented popular culture and instead explore, within a true female context, the reasons such works were created and the functions they performed (pp. 28-32).

Social scientist Brenda Dervin (1987), like Lana Rakow, does not specifically address the study of journalism history, but she takes Rakow's advocacy of a female point of view in research on popular culture a step further when she explains that the "essential mandate" of all feminist communication research is to "invent approaches that allow us to hear the meanings of women on their own terms, including their observations of the structures that constrain them." We must, in short, focus on "giving women voice so that we may hear their reality" (p. 12).

A final useful observation comes from journalism historian Catherine Covert (1981). In an extremely perceptive article identifying and questioning the assumptions that male journalism historians have imposed on their field, she describes the male assumption that "history is about autonomy":

Journalism history has classically celebrated independence and individual autonomy rather than subordination and dependence. The actions of strikingly autonomous individuals have been chronicled. "Freedom" has been valued as an existential state. (p. 4)

As a result of this assumption, she says, historians have paid little attention to the influences of family, friends, and professional networks on
journalists' careers. Similarly, the histories of small-town newspapers and
other media that do not fit the "conflict" model of journalism and government—media that were devoted more to building community than to
maintaining an adversary relationship with the power structure—seldom
have been carefully studied (pp. 4-5).

The observations of these six writers are both complementary and
cumulative; taken together, they form a kind of general outline for future
research on women and journalism history. This research, they suggest,
should be analytical and critical, moving beyond description to an understanding of why things happened and what they meant at the time to the
women involved in them as media creators or audiences. This process may
well require challenging and revising previously accepted precepts of
journalism history that are not applicable to women. And it surely will lead
to the discovery of new research subjects, as well as new ways of looking
at old ones.

Using Five Concepts From Women's History

Valuable ideas for carrying out the recommendations made by these
communication scholars can be found in a large body of work that has
received little attention from most journalism historians: the literature of
women's history. The observations of women's historians can be particularly useful, for, far more than journalism historians studying women,
they have noted the limitations of so-called contribution history, in which
"man becomes the measure of significance" by which women's lives are
judged and women are added to the existing historical scholarship only if
they meet the male standard—as has been the case in much of the work
done on women in journalism history. Contribution history is a first step
in building women's history, these scholars say, but it should be only a
transitional development on the road to new ways of studying women, new
criteria for choosing subjects of study, and new questions being asked.[8]

Many different techniques for moving forward have been suggested by
women's historians,[9] but one approach seems especially useful in directing
future research on women and journalism history, for it helps solidify the
six scholars' ideas briefly described in the previous section. This approach
calls for replacing male-defined research with scholarship in which, in the
words of historian Carroll Smith-Rosenberg (1980), "the events and processes central to women's experience assume historical centrality, and women
are recognized as active agents" (p. 57). Joan Wallach Scott (1983) calls

this an effort to "construct women as historical subjects," and she explains that it goes "far beyond the naive search for heroic ancestors of the contemporary women's movement to a re-evaluation of established standards of historical significance" (p. 145).

Just as women's historians have perceptively analyzed the problems of contribution history, so have they produced an extensive body of analytical research that is applicable to journalism history. Yet little of this research has yet been taken advantage of by historians of women and journalism, and I believe this is one reason the work most of these historians have produced remains largely descriptive and unquestioning of traditional, male-defined standards of journalism history.

As a first step toward utilizing this research, I have identified five concepts developed by women's historians that I believe can be used to help create new kinds of research on women and journalism history. These concepts are discussed, in turn, below. I also have utilized research conducted by women's historians to describe specific topic areas deserving of study that do not fit within conventional journalism history standards of significance, and thus may lead to a redefinition of these standards. In the process, I hope to show how historical research on women and journalism can change along the lines recommended by the communication scholars cited earlier.

Women's Culture

One area in which women's historians have contributed substantial useful research is that of the study of 19th-century American women's culture —the separate, self-created culture apparently shared by many middle-class women in which concerns of domesticity and morality were able to redefine and take control of the "separate sphere" into which they developed shared, female-identified values, rituals, relationships, and modes of communication that were sources of satisfaction and strength. Although historians disagree about some of the details of this culture and about the extent to which it tended to be either confining or liberating, they do generally agree that it was an important, sustaining part of the lives of many bourgeois women of the period (Berkin, 1985, pp. 209-210; Scott, 1983, pp. 148-149).[10]

Research on women's culture provides a valuable context for studying particular forms of 19th-century journalism that have previously received little attention. Such a study might begin with an examination of the journalism produced by the women who lived and believed most fervently in the values of this culture. One excellent example of this journalism is

The Advocate of Moral Reform, the weekly newspaper produced by the American Female Moral Reform Society.

Carroll Smith-Rosenberg (1985) describes her first attempts to understand the Society:

> It was so self-consciously female, so militantly antimale that it resisted all my efforts to subordinate it to a male schema. The rhetoric and programs of the American Female Moral Reform Society forced me to recognize it as a uniquely female institution, radically different from male philanthropies and reforms. (p. 20)

Her surprise is understandable, for the Society, formed in 1834, zealously attacked two problems that could barely be discussed in polite society of the time: prostitution and the sexual double standard that permitted middle-class males free sexual license. Its tactics included stationing members in front of brothels, where they would pray and sing hymns, and legislative lobbying campaigns, but its most important and effective work took place in the pages of *The Advocate* (Smith-Rosenberg, 1985, pp. 109-118).

Through *The Advocate,* the Society was able to carry its message beyond New York City, where it was founded, throughout the East Coast. By 1838 *The Advocate* claimed 16,500 subscribers, making it one of the country's most widely read evangelical newspapers, and in rural areas—where it circulated extensively—it may well have been the only newspaper a family received. Indeed, *The Advocate* was full of letters from rural readers describing their feelings of frustration over their confined lives and their gratitude for the connections they felt with other women through involvement in this moral reform effort. These letters often detailed the sins of male seducers and adulterers, as did the paper's editorials; lists of names of accused sinners also were printed. And one solution was proposed over and over: Women must control society's moral standards and behavior, and thus male licentiousness (Smith-Rosenberg, 1985, pp. 115-122).

One other aspect of *The Advocate* is particularly interesting: By 1843, all positions on the paper were held by women. The two women hired as editors in 1836 were among the first female weekly newspaper editors in 19th-century America, and in 1835 a female subscription agent was hired, in 1841 a female bookkeeper replaced the male financial agent, and two years later all the typesetters were women. All of this was part of a conscious campaign by the Society to show that women could work successfully in traditionally male fields (Smith-Rosenberg, 1985, pp. 122-123).

The Advocate is waiting to be studied by a journalism historian who can analyze it within the context of women's culture of the period. In addition, research should be carried out on other media related to 19th-century women's culture, and especially on groups of these publications, because this would make it possible to see trends and draw broad conclusions. We know, for example, that between 1784 and 1860 close to 100 magazines dealing with women's interests were published (Degler, 1980, p. 377). Most of them have not been studied.[11] Both the advertising and editorial contents of these publications deserve analysis, because advertising aimed at women may well have been particularly powerful in reinforcing the boundaries of their separate sphere, and thus keeping women within it.[12]

We also know that during the same period the American Female Moral Reform Society was most active, another reform movement—abolition—was attracting still more middle-class women and bringing them further outside their domestic worlds, even as it drew on the values developed within those worlds. The important—and still largely unstudied—work done by abolitionist women included much of the writing published in antislavery newspapers (Degler, 1980, p. 303; Lerner, 1979, p. 153). A full understanding of the women's culture underlying this journalism might well lead to a valuable reevaluation of it.

These three kinds of studies might combine in particularly significant ways, for they would provide examples of journalism fervently produced within the confines of women's culture to bring its ideals to a wider world, journalism produced primarily by those outside the culture who helped to solidify it, and journalism produced by women formed by the culture but applying their values to a different, although related, cause. Research in all three areas could result in new conclusions about the cultural roles journalism can play. And these in turn might lead to new criteria for determining media influence and historical significance.

Women as Community-Builders

Women's historians also have carried out valuable research on women's previously unrecognized work as community-builders. They point out that this work often began with women's recognition of immediate community needs that were first addressed in practical, informal ways, then became larger efforts to raise funds and create formal institutions—libraries, orphanages, and kindergartens, for example. Once these institutions became fully established and licensed, men usually took them over. And on an individual level, women have historically supplied continuity to their communities by maintaining and passing on to their children important family, religious, and social values (Lerner, 1979, pp. 165, 179).

Traditional historians generally have ignored this kind of work by women, although they have recorded the histories of many of these institutions once they were run by men (Lerner, 1979, p. 179). Recently, however, women's historians have begun to study these activities, and much excellent research has been done on the post-Civil War work of the "social feminists" who, building on many of the values of women's culture, became activists in such social reforms as the temperance, settlement, and child-welfare movements (Degler, 1980, pp. 326-327; Smith-Rosenberg, 1985, pp. 167-175).

Included in this literature is valuable information on Black women's institution-building and reform work. Because for decades following the Civil War many Southern communities lacked any kind of social welfare organization—or did not permit Black access to those organizations that did exist—Black women were particularly active in founding and sustaining such institutions as schools, orphanages, and old people's homes. In the cities, they organized settlement houses, child-care facilities, health clinics, and community improvement campaigns (Lerner, 1979, pp. 83-93). Similar work by urban immigrant women in the late 19th and early 20th centuries also has been documented by women's historians.[13]

This varied scholarship on women as community-builders can be utilized by journalism historians in understanding the extensive work done by women in the medium that has most consistently welcomed their involvement: community journalism.[14] If this journalism were studied with a better recognition of women's roles in it, and better analyzed within the context of the historical literature on women's community-building, a new evaluation of its place in journalism history might result. And it should be kept in mind that community journalism includes many minority newspapers, where women no doubt also played important roles.[15] Indeed, one of the country's leading Black social reformers, Ida B. Wells, also edited or worked as a reporter for a number of Southern Black community newspapers (Lerner, 1979, p. 85; Scott, 1984, p. 347).[16]

Women's Formal and Informal Connections

Studies of women's culture and women's work as community-builders in the 19th-century United States have resulted in much new information about the close relationships these women often had with each other. Women historians have shown that, beginning around 1800, women increasingly bonded together in formal, single-sex clubs and associations that were particularly popular in the last 30 years of the century, when millions of women joined (Degler, 1980, pp. 315-327; Scott, 1984, pp. 279-294). Among the members of these organizations were society's "new women," who, starting in the 1870s, began to move beyond conventional female roles to enter such previously male worlds as higher education, business, medicine, and the arts. Sometimes unmarried, these women found personal female support networks especially important (Smith-Rosenberg, 1985, pp. 176-177, 247-256).[17]

Historians studying women in American journalism should look for evidence of these kinds of formal and informal relationships in their subjects' lives and use the literature from women's history to help understand the importance of these connections. Knowledge of organizational memberships might well be particularly useful in studying women journalists of the last quarter of the 19th century, when such organizations proliferated and mainstream journalism initially was opened to women. Still, the total numbers of full-time female journalists in this period were small; according to U.S. census figures, they were 288 out of 12,308 full-time journalists in 1880 and had grown to 2,193 out of 30,098 in 1900 (Beasley & Silver, 1977, p. 38). As both distinct minorities in the profession and often "firsts" at their particular periodicals, these women must have needed the support of other women, and the connections made in the process may have influenced their work.[18]

I found that an understanding of these kinds of informal and organizational ties was key to my study of a late 19th-century American journalist, Helen Campbell. Campbell was a member of many organizations for professional women, including Sorosis, the first New York City women's club (which was founded by journalist Jane Cunningham Croly), and was an activist in the new home economics movement. Thus she spent much time with other women journalists and with women in business, the arts, and the professions. Divorced after 10 years of marriage, she also had an extensive friendship network composed of other women reformers, the most notable being feminist writer Charlotte Perkins Gilman. I have argued that these connections both influenced the contents of her writing—which often focused on the need for urban reforms—and helped provide her personal support for her work as a journalist (Henry, 1984).

Strong connections to other women no doubt have been important for 20th-century women journalists as well, so they too need to be examined. And, because the early 20th century saw the establishment of many new professional organizations for women (Degler, 1980, p. 324), historians studying women journalists of this later period often may find that their subjects were members of women's press clubs with surviving archival records and publications that can provide useful insights about the professional networks of individual women.[19] Through such materials we may learn a great deal about how women journalists have been able to succeed in a predominantly male world.

Journalism historians who are able to collect data on these kinds of relations will find that these data also aid them in establishing valuable cultural contexts for their studies. At the same time, they may find that such information challenges the high value put on journalistic autonomy that Catherine Covert identified as underlying so much of our published journalism history. As a result, this kind of research may lead to a systematic questioning of that value and to new studies of the importance of supportive personal relationships for both female and male journalists.

Women's Work

Just as they have found new ways of interpreting and understanding the personal lives of women, so have women's historians redefined the very concept of work. These historians began by defining work the same way male economists—and most other historians—did: as paid labor. They soon discovered, however, that this excluded most of the work done by women in the past, including carrying out extensive household, child-care, and voluntary community tasks. Now, work is understood to include both paid and unpaid labor done both outside and inside the home (Lerner, 1979, pp. 178-179; Norton, 1986, p. 40).

Because so much of journalism history is the study of men and women at work, this redefinition has a direct bearing on the field. This is particularly the case, I believe, when the new definition is combined with other observations about the unrecognized work of women. Among these observations is one made by a historian reviewing the biographies of the 1,359 women included in the three volumes of *Notable American Women,* who was struck by the fact that numerous women had let men take credit for their work. These women, she said, seem to have made themselves "purposely invisible" (Scott, 1984, p. 156). Similarly, a noted women's psychologist has observed that married women's work often includes helping their husbands do their work. Women may take great satisfaction in this, she explains, because "women, more easily than men, can believe that any activity is more satisfying when it takes place in the context of relationships to other human beings—and even more so when it leads to the enhancement of others." Yet, because "most of this activity has not been done in direct and open pursuit of their own goals—therefore it is not activity in the male definition of it" (Miller, 1986, p. 54).

Journalism historians who understand these different concepts of work will begin to discover new examples of women's work in journalism. My own research, for example, has resulted in the identification of a cohort of American women in the 1920s and 1930s who worked with their better known husbands to produce journalism for which they received little public credit. The list so far includes Ruth Hale, wife of famed newspaper columnist Heywood Brown; Jane Grant, wife of *New Yorker* founder

Harold Ross; Katherine White, wife of *New Yorker* writer E. B. White; and Clare Boothe Luce, who developed the initial plan for Henry Luce's *Life* magazine. But to me the most interesting couple in this cohort is composed of Doris E. Fleischman and Edward L. Bernays, who together formed the firm of Edward L. Bernays, Counsel of Public Relations, and who were wholly equal partners in the business from the time of their marriage in 1922 until Doris Fleischman's death in 1980 (Henry, 1988). No doubt other cohorts of journalists' wives who did similar work in their husbands' names can be found.

I also have been studying the work done by three generations of women in one newspaper publishing family, the Otis-Chandler *Los Angeles Times* dynasty. As I chart the largely unpaid and unrecognized work of publishers' wives, sisters, and daughters over more than three quarters of a century, I am noticing both patterns and differences that establish a wide range of women's roles (Henry, 1987). Studies of women family members in many of the country's other publishing dynasties would allow similar opportunities to compare women's work over time and under changing social, political, and economic circumstances.

Uncovering women's contributions that have been hidden behind male accomplishments does more than add another dimension to our knowledge of the work done by women in journalism. It also calls into question the tendency of journalism historians to pay little attention to journalists who worked behind the scenes or lacked official titles. Equally important, it illustrates the importance of better recognizing the collaborative effort—some of it between husbands and wives—that may well have been behind a substantial amount of our journalism. And such recognition once again challenges the underlying value of autonomy in journalism history.

Women Media Audiences

Finally, I suggest that journalism historians can learn from one additional area in which women's historians have reexamined published American history. They have questioned the ways traditional historians have characterized particular historical periods or developments, pointing out that often these characterizations apply only to the men of a society. Indeed, they have shown that the events that have socially, intellectually, economically, or politically benefited men frequently have worked in opposite ways for women. For example, the Renaissance, which opened up many new opportunities for men, resulted in new restrictions upon women (Lerner, 1979, p. 175).

In the United States, the Jacksonian period has been reevaluated in a similar way. Women's historians have found that although for white men the 1830s and 1840s were a time of greatly expanded economic, social, and political opportunities, during that time women's positions deteriorated in many ways. They were, for example, no longer permitted to enter most of the business and professional occupations that had previously been open to them. Similarly, the "lady"—with all the restrictions on personal behavior that implied—became the feminine ideal. And in comparison with white males—large groups of whom gained voting rights during the Jacksonian period—women's political disenfranchisement seemed all the more extreme (Lerner, 1979, p. 18).

This new way of looking at one period in American history should be instructive to journalism historians, for it suggests that the label and characterizations we have given media trends and developments also should be reexamined in light of women's experiences. The journalism of the Jacksonian era is a good place to start this reexamination, for this is the time of what is usually thought to be a seminal advancement in American journalism history: the beginning of the penny press. Emery and Emery (1988) label this inexpensive, readable, and entertaining form of journalism "the newspaper for the masses" and "the press of the common people" (pp. 115-119). Michael Schudson (1978), who has carefully studied the penny papers, explains that not only were they "spokesmen [sic] for egalitarian ideals in politics, economic life, and social life" (p. 60), but they "created a genre which acknowledged, and so enhanced, the importance of everyday life" (p. 26).

But were women among the "common people" to whom the penny press was meant to appeal? Was the "everyday life" of women recognized in these papers? These are questions that have not been asked of the penny press,[20] even though it has been characterized as journalism that served the masses and in Schudson's words, "expressed and built the culture of a democratic market society" (p. 60).

Journalism historians do credit Horace Greeley's *New York Tribune* with advocating educational, legal, employment, and marriage reforms for women (although Schudson does not mention any of this). But such contents seldom are interpreted as adding to the democratic base of the penny press in any key way. Thus a systematic examination of the *Tribune* and other penny papers in terms of women readers still is needed.

The literature of women's history makes it possible to identify many of women's common concerns during this time (and research on women's culture is applicable here), just as it also makes it clear that most women had sufficient literacy skills to read the penny press (Degler, 1980, p. 306). Urban areas attracted women who were interested in access to jobs and independent lives.[21] And, because married women of the period were responsible for their families' domestic well-being, the advertisers who financed penny newspapers would have benefited from appealing to women consumers. Clearly, then, although women were excluded from many areas of Jacksonian life, there is no reason they should have been excluded as penny press readers. If they were, then our accepted characterization of this journalism is inaccurate.

A systematic historical reexamination in terms of women readers would be useful for all American journalism that has been strongly characterized in terms of the size and composition of its audience. Certainly the metropolitan daily newspapers of the 1880s and 1890s, which have been heralded as the country's first truly mass-circulation press, deserve such analysis. Significantly, historians have noted that, for the first time, large, urban Sunday papers of the period began to carry special women's pages, with articles on such topics as fashion and family life, that were thought to appeal to middle-class women (Emery & Emery, 1988, p. 231; Schudson, 1978, p. 100). It may be that such articles were far more important in increasing circulation than has been thought.

But other questions about these papers also must be asked. For example, we are told they attracted large numbers of working-class readers, but what in their contents would have appealed to working-class women? How popular with them were the women's pages that were considered such an innovation? And what kinds of coverage did these papers give the more substantial concerns of many urban women related to such topics as health, education, religion, and employment?

Because male journalism historians have studied most journalism primarily in terms of male audiences, these kinds of questions about the extent to which media audiences included or excluded women seldom have been asked. Thus we do not know their answers, or whether or not those answers will change our characterizations of different media at different times. The point is that until attempts are made to answer key questions about women audiences, such characterizations cannot be accepted uncritically.

Conclusions

There is no guarantee that any of the five concepts discussed above, taken from women's history and applied here to journalism history, will lead to a radical revision of that history. But it is clear that the development of these concepts by women's historians has not simply added new information to American history; it also has made it necessary to rethink previously accepted interpretations and information. Because of this, and because these concepts have such clear relevance to the history of journalism, their application is highly recommended.

There is little doubt that further research in these areas would expand our knowledge of women and journalism through the identification of new research subjects and the utilization of new analytical techniques. Indeed, one final lesson from this exercise is that the published scholarship of women's history offers journalism historians innumerable new research topics and approaches.

The solid base of the existing research on women and journalism history has placed the field in an excellent position to begin moving more rapidly out of its transitional stage. Scholars should be ready increasingly to bring to their work the kind of analysis, contextual interpretation, and questioning of assumptions that critics have said is needed. The rich literature of women's history provides a good starting point for that development, providing ideas that will sometimes challenge the field and often broaden and deepen it.

Notes

1. Much of my early journalism research focused on colonial women printers. For published examples of this research, see Henry (1976, 1979, 1980, 1985).

2. Marion Marzolf published the first comprehensive history of women journalists and the media's treatment of women in 1977 (Marzolf, 1977). In the acknowledgment section of her book, Marzolf notes that when she began her research in 1972 she found women "Mentioned mostly in the footnotes in standard journalism history texts" (p. ix). But, she explains, "I resolved to search for them and recover their lost history." An earlier book containing valuable information of women in journalism history in Ishbel Ross's *Ladies of the Press* (1936). Although Ross's work contains valuable information on some 19th-century women journalists, its emphasis is on her own contemporaries during the first third of the 20th century. This makes it a valuable source for today's journalism historians studying women of this period.

3. The range of women journalists studied in recent group biographies is impressive, as indicated by the titles of three important histories: *Viewfinders: Black Women Photographers* (Moutoussamy-Ashe, 1986), *Brilliant Bylines: A Biographical Anthology of Notable Newspaperwomen in America* (Belford, 1986), and *Women of the World: The Great Foreign Correspondents* (Edwards, 1988).

4. A 1977 survey of journalism departments found that three-fourths used *The Press and America* as the text in their history courses (see Endres, 1978, p. 31).

5. For recent references to this problem by four well-known women's historians, see Joan W. Scott (1987, p. 1055), Mary Beth Norton (1986, p. 41), Carol Berkin (1985, p. 209), and Ann Firor Scott (1984, p. 366).

6. This bias is tellingly illustrated by a recent article in which the author reports a purported study of the "article productivity" of this country's journalism professors. He does this by collecting all research articles published in nine journals, then ranking schools and individual researchers according to the total number of articles produced. The nine journals include both general publications such as *Journalism Quarterly* and *Journal of Communication* and those covering narrower media topics such as *Journal of Advertising, Journal of*

Broadcasting, and *Public Relations Review.* But no journal that carries a high proportion of historical research is included in the study, and as a result much of the journalism history being published in journals is excluded. In addition, no recognition of this inattention is given in the article; apparently it simply did not occur to the author that this key area of journalism research should be taken into consideration in his ranking of schools and individual scholars (see Schweitzer, 1988).

7. See "Special Supplement: Cumulative Index Volume 51-60 (1974-1983)" (1984). The introduction to the index notes that 84 articles on "history and biography" were published in *Journalism Quarterly* between 1974 and 1983 (p. iii). By my rough estimate (attempting to count articles only once, even when they are listed in more than one topic category), approximately 1,000 articles were published in the journal during the period covered by the index. Thus less than 10% of the total were histories.

8. See, for example, Gerda Lerner (1979, p. 146) and Joan Wallach Scott (1983, p. 147). For an interesting argument advocating the continued production of contribution history, see Hilda L. Smith (1984).

9. For an excellent summary of ideas from the recent literature, see Joan W. Scott (1987). The best compilation of critical writing on women's history during the previous decade probably is a book edited by Berenice Carroll, *Liberating Women's History* (1976).

10. For a good overview of the debate among women's historians over the form, dimensions, and implications of 19th-century women's culture, see the combination of articles collectively titled *"Politics and Culture in Women's History"* in the spring 1980 issue of *Feminist Studies.* For suggestions on how future research might best address the combined oppressive/liberating elements of separate spheres and women's culture, see Kerber (1988).

11. One historian who has made good use of some of this material is Ann Douglas; see her *The Feminization of American Culture* (1977).

12. Kerber (1988) notes that American advertising during the 1920s was used to help "redefine the housewife" and in the 1950s "to sustain that definition" (p. 28). Informed by an understanding of women's culture and separate spheres, journalism historians might well find it worthwhile to examine this advertising anew. Such an examination would be a significant addition to the field of women's history, particularly in light of Kerber's argument that more research needs to be done on women's separate sphere during the 20th century (p. 18).

13. See, for example, Baum, Hyman, and Michel (1976, pp. 165-185).

14. Two good sources detailing women's participation in community journalism are Ross (1936, pp. 458-464) and Karolevitz (1985, pp. 125-131).

15. Some useful references to women's work in U.S. minority media are to be found in *The Ethnic Press in the United States: A Historical Analysis and Handbook,* an excellent collection edited by Sally M. Miller (1987).

16. Also see, in Penn (1891/1969), the chapter titled "Afro-American Women in Journalism" (pp. 367-427), which contains effusive profiles of 19 Black women journalists (including Ida B. Wells) working in the last half of the 19th century. Many of them were involved in social causes, especially temperance.

17. For a description of specific early 20th-century support and friendship networks, see Cook (1979).

18. Many educated Black women—who were "double minorities" in their professions— had an important support network in Delta Sigma Theta, a sorority founded in 1913 and now thought to be the country's largest Black women's group (see Giddings, 1988).

19. The Women's National Press Club in Washington, D.C., for example, has excellent archives that could be well utilized to chart relationships among journalists in that area of the country. For one study drawing on these materials, see Beasley (1988).

20. The other major scholar of the penny press, Dan Schiller, should be credited for commenting in a footnote: "The sex-biased character of the penny press deserves more study" (Schiller, 1981, p. 16). This is, however, the extent of Schiller's comments on women and the penny press in his book—a not unexpected situation because even the major critiques of Schiller and Schudson's work do not note the lack of attention given to women as penny press subjects or audiences. See, for example, Eason (1984) and Nerone (1987); also, see the responses to Nerone's article by Schudson, Schiller, Donald L. Shaw, and John J. Pauly in the same issue of *Critical Studies in Mass Communication* (pp. 405-415).

21. One of the first historians to point out the advantages of urban life for women was David M. Potter in his classic 1962 essay, "American Women and American Character" (see Potter, 1973).

References

Alpern, Sara. (1987). *Freda Kirchwey: A woman of the Nation.* Cambridge, MA: Harvard University Press.

Baum, Charlotte, Hyman, Paula, & Michel, Sonya. (1976). *The Jewish woman in America.* New York: New American Library.

Beasley, Maurine H. (1988). The Women's National Press Club: Case study of professional aspirations. *Journalism History, 15,* 112-121.

Beasley, Maurine H., & Silver, Sheila. (1977). *Women in media: A documentary source book.* Washington, DC: Women's Institute for Freedom of the Press.

Belford, Barbara. (1986). *Brilliant bylines: A biographical anthology of notable newspaper-women in America.* New York: Columbia University Press.

Berkin, Carol. (1985). Clio in search of her daughters/women in search of their past. *Liberal Education, 71,* 205-215.

Carroll, Berenice. (Ed). (1976). *Liberating women's history.* Urbana: University of Illinois Press.

Cook, Blanche Weisen. (1979). Female support networks: Lillian Wald, Crystal Eastman, Emma Goldman. In Nancy E. Cott & Elizabeth H. Pleck (Eds.), *A heritage of her own: Toward a new social history of America of women* (pp. 412-444). New York: Simon & Schuster.

Covert, Catherine L. (1981). Journalism history and women's experience: A problem in conceptual change. *Journalism History, 8,* 2-6.

Cumulative index, vols. 1-10, 1974-1983. (1983). *Journalism History, 20,* 73-83.

Degler, Carl. (1980). *At odds: Women and the family in America from the revolution to the present.* New York: Oxford University Press.

Dervin, Brenda. (1987). The potential contribution of feminist scholarship to the field of communication. *Journal of Communication, 37,* 107-120.

Douglas, Ann. (1977). *The feminization of American culture.* New York: Knopf.

Eason, David L. (1984). The new social history of the newspaper. *Communication Research, 11,* 141-151.

Edwards, Julia. (1988). *Women of the world: The great foreign correspondents.* Boston: Houghton Mifflin.

Emery, Edwin. (1972). *The press and America: An interpretative history of the mass media* (4th ed.). Englewood Cliffs, NJ: Prentice Hall.

Emery, Michael, & Emery, Edwin. (1988). *The press and America: An interpretative history of the mass media* (6th ed.). Englewood Cliffs, NJ: Prentice Hall.

Endres, Fred F. (1978). Philosophies, practices and problems in teaching journalism history. *Journalism History, 5*(1), 1-3, 30-31.

Giddings, Paula. (1988). *In search of sisterhood: Delta Sigma Theta and the challenge of the Black sorority movement.* New York: William Morrow.

Goldberg, Vicki. (1986). *Margaret Bourke-White: A biography.* New York: Harper & Row.

Henry, Susan. (1976). Colonial woman printer as prototype: Toward a model for the study of minorities. *Journalism History, 3,* 20-24.

Henry, Susan. (1979). Private lives: An added dimension for understanding journalism history. *Journalism History, 6,* 98-102.

Henry, Susan. (1980). Sarah Goddard: Gentlewoman printer. *Journalism Quarterly, 57,* 23-30.

Henry, Susan. (1984). Reporting "deeply and at first hand": Helen Campbell in the 19th-century slums. *Journalism History, 11,* 18-25.

Henry, Susan. (1985). An exception to the female model: Colonial printer Mary Crouch. *Journalism Quarterly, 62,* 725-733, 749.

Henry, Susan. (1987). "Dear companion, ever-ready co-worker": A woman's role in a media dynasty. *Journalism Quarterly, 64,* 301-312.

Henry, Susan. (1988, July). *In her own name? Public relations pioneer Doris Fleischman Bernays.* Paper presented at the annual conference of the Association for Education in Journalism and Mass Communication, Portland, OR.

Karolevitz, Robert F. (1985). *From quill to computer: The story of America's community newspapers.* National Newspaper Foundation.

Kerber, Linda. (1988). Separate spheres, female worlds, woman's place: The rhetoric of women's history. *Journal of American History, 75,* 9-39.

Lerner, Gerda. (1979). *The majority finds its past: Placing women in history.* New York: Oxford University Press.

Marzolf, Marion. (1977). *Up from the footnote: A history of women journalists.* New York: Hastings House.

McGlashan, Zena Beth. (1985). Women witness the Russian Revolution: Analyzing ways of seeing. *Journalism History, 12,* 54-61.

Miller, Jean Baker. (1986). *Toward a new psychology of women* (2nd ed.). Boston: Beacon.

Miller, Sally M. (Ed.). (1987). *The ethnic press in the United States: A historical analysis and handbook.* Westport, CT: Greenwood Press.

Moutoussamy-Ashe, Jeanne. (1986). *Viewfinders: Black women photographers.* New York: Dodd, Mead.

Moynihan, Ruth Barnes. (1983). *Rebel for rights, Abigail Scott Duniway.* New Haven, CT: Yale University Press.

Nerone, John C. (1987). The mythology of the penny press. *Critical Studies in Mass Communication, 4,* 376-404.

Norton, Mary Beth. (1986, April 13). Is Clio a feminist? *New York Times Book Review,* pp. 1, 40-41.

Penn, I. Garland. (1969). *The Afro-American press and its editors.* New York: Arno. (Original work published 1891)

Potter, David M. (1973). American women and American character. In Don E. Fehrenbacher (Ed.), *History and American society: Essays of David M. Potter* (pp. 278-303). New York: Oxford University Press.

Rakow, Lana F. (1986). Feminist approaches to popular culture: Giving patriarchy its due. *Communication, 9,* 19-41.

Roberts, Nancy L. (1984). *Dorothy Day and the Catholic worker.* Albany: SUNY Press.

Ross, Ishbel. (1936). *Ladies of the press.* New York: Harper & Brothers.

Schiller, Dan. (1981). *Objectivity and the news: The public and the rise of commercial journalism.* Philadelphia: University of Pennsylvania Press.

Schudson, Michael. (1978). *Discovering the news: A social history of American newspapers.* New York: Basic Books.

Schweitzer, John C. (1988). Research article productivity by mass communication scholars. *Journalism Quarterly, 65,* 479-484.

Scott, Ann Firor. (1984). *Making the invisible woman visible.* Urbana: University of Illinois Press.

Scott, Joan W. (1987). Gender: A useful category of historical analysis. *American Historical Review, 91,* 1053-1075.

Scott, Joan Wallach. (1983). Women in history: The modern period. *Past and Present, 101,* 141-157.

Sharp, Nancy V., Turk, Judy VanSlyke, Einsiedel, Edna F., Schamber, Linda, & Hollenback, Sharon. (1985). *Faculty women in journalism and mass communications: Problems and progress.* Syracuse, NY: Report published with a grant from the Gannett Foundation. (Available from the Association for Education in Journalism and Mass Communication, College of Journalism, 1621 College St., University of South Carolina, Columbia, SC 29208-0251.)

Shaw, Donald Lewis, & Zack, Sylvia L. (1987). Rethinking journalism history: How some recent studies support one approach. *Journalism History, 14,* 111-117.

Smith, Hilda L. (1984, November). Women's history and social history: An untimely alliance. *Organization of American Historians Newsletter,* pp. 4-6.

Smith-Rosenberg, Carroll. (1980). Politics and culture in women's history. *Feminist Studies, 6,* 55-64.

Smith-Rosenberg, Carroll. (1985). *Disorderly conduct: Visions of gender in Victorian America.* New York: Knopf.

Special supplement: Cumulative index to volumes 51-60 (1974-1983). (1984). *Journalism Quarterly, 61.*

Steeves, H. Leslie. (1987). Feminist theories and media studies. *Critical Studies in Mass Communication, 4,* 95-135.

Yodelis Smith, Mary Ann. (1982). Research retrospective: Feminism and the media. *Communication Research, 9,* 145-160.

20 A Bridge to the Future
How to Get There From Here Through Curriculum Reform

LANA F. RAKOW

Earlier in the century, Sigmund Freud was provoked into asking, "What do these women want?" Decades later, academics, perhaps equally exasperated, are asking, "What do these feminists want?" At first pacifying women's complaints might have seemed like a fairly simply proposition. Give women a little affirmative action here, a little equal pay there, and a little nod in their direction when teaching history. Yet feminists have not gone away, and the complaints have intensified.

Those who have read this far in this book should have a better idea of what problems women face as students, faculty members, readers and audiences, and professionals in mass communication careers. The causes of these problems run deep, so deep that the solutions attempted by even the most well-intentioned have produced very little change. Some contributors to this book suggest how feminist theory helps us see the deeper taken-for-granted patterns that keep an oppressive gender system in place. Some contributors suggest strategies for alleviating specific problems. Now I would like to take what they have started a step further. First, let me fill in some of the historical and theoretical dimensions that help us understand our contemporary social world of gender. Then, I will talk about the different kinds of futures that different kinds of feminists are working toward. Finally, I will sketch out the bridge I think we need to build to get us to

AUTHOR'S NOTE: I am grateful to Pamela J. Creedon, Cheris Kramarae, Karlene Ferrante, and Kathryn Cirksena for their comments on the first version of this chapter. I want to thank the faculty of the Communication Department for their work producing the curriculum described in this chapter; however, the interpretation given here to the curriculum is my own and may not represent the interpretation of all faculty in the department.

what I see as the best future scenario. That bridge takes the shape of curriculum reform, intended ultimately to change the media industries for which our graduates work. Perhaps then we will have an answer to that question, "What do these feminists want?" and some insight as to how to get it.

Understanding the Present

Why is gender a problem? Underlying our society is a structure and set of values that emphasize individualism, competition, the transcendence of property rights over other rights, hierarchy, the separation of public and private activities and moralities, and a reliance upon science for problem solving. Our gender system—of two distinct and hierarchically ordered groups of people—is not incidental to these ideas; in fact, the two are inseparably entwined.[1] The classical liberal ideas of the Enlightenment, mixing with 19th-century American notions of industrial capitalism and social evolution, produced a vision of society consisting of individuals (and eventually organizations, in the 20th-century version known as pluralism) competing with each other for limited resources or rewards. The "best," of course, would win.[2] These individuals were assumed to be white and male, not surprisingly.

As industrialism was allowed to shape the structure of our economic and political system, these competing individuals came to be seen as occupiers of a public world of business and government. White women and women and men of color were excluded from the public sphere, with white women specifically consigned—in a "complementary" manner to the men in their lives—to the "private sphere," of the family, of nurturance, of caregiving.[3] People of color were relegated to a separate class upon whose backs the public and the private rested (in their roles as seasonal workers, maintenance workers, housekeepers, and nursemaids, for example). The split in values between the public and private spheres, then, came to define what being a woman or a man meant and still means, defined according to white standards. *Man* came to stand for rationality, competition, aggression, individualism. *Woman* came to stand for emotionality, nurturance, cooperation, community. Of course, none of this was or is biologically determined. In fact, at different times in Western history, *man* and *woman* have meant very different things.

Nonetheless, these values have been assigned to two different groups of people who occupy two different—and unequally valued and unequally powerful—regions of activity in society. As long as white women and people of color were denied the status of either "human" or "citizen," they could continue to be excluded from the public world of the "individual," or "normal" human. But people of color and white women have fought long and historic battles challenging those definitions, often, however, on the very principles of the system that has been oppressive to them. These are such principles as "equal opportunity." Despite the appeal of the phrase, it rests on the assumption of a society of individuals free to compete in a hierarchically ordered contest of winners and losers. Some white women may achieve some success at entering the white male domain of ownership, management, and leadership, or it might be some Black men. Regardless of which group makes some headway, the system remains much the same, and *most* white women and people of color will be losers.

Visions of the Future

Can our gender system by changed? If it were changed, what would the world look like? Imagining future scenarios is a good exercise. It allows us to build a bridge between what we are fighting for today and what we want tomorrow to be. It shows us a possible outcome of the changes we are advocating. It makes clear the assumptions that underlie our present thinking. It helps us set our strategies and our priorities for bringing about a different world.

Few of us would choose as our ideal future one that included poverty, homelessness, militarism, physical abuse and assault, and environmental disaster. Yet the very principles of competition, individualism, aggression, and hierarchy lend themselves to the perpetuation of these problems. Unfortunately many people do not see a connection between these masculine-identified values and the crucial social problems that we face. Indeed, liberal feminists, as Pamela Creedon points out in the first chapter, have been among those to accept the system as a given. Radical feminists, on the other hand, recognize the need for fundamental change. It is small wonder that they see their cause as so urgent and so profound. Nothing less than the health and well-being of all of us and the planet are at stake.

Rather than a future marked by more of the same life-threatening problems, can we envision a future based on those values historically relegated to the private sphere—cooperation and nurturance?[4] Here is the possibility for building a new world community with broad-based political participation and decision making, justice and fair treatment, dignity and purpose. And it is here that radical feminism has the most to offer, for radical feminism recognizes, not that women have special virtues because of biology (women can be aggressive and competitive as well as men, they are just less likely to be because of prescriptions against it) but that the values relegated to women have been the values that are to be avoided, even ridiculed, by men because of their association with women (and, of course, men can be cooperative and nurturant as well as women, they are just less likely to have the training and incentive).[5]

Building a Bridge

How will we be able to accomplish such a profound social change? The usual remedies suggested for changing women's status—providing women more opportunities in the workplace, treating them like their male counterparts when it comes to hiring and promotion, showing women in more diverse and less sexual ways in media content—will not bring them about. However, there is another more effective approach that those of us engaged with the practice and examination of mass communication can take. In fact, we are in an excellent position to lead the way for making broad social change in our gender relations. Communication, especially mass communication, is both a culprit and a solution to our gender problems and, ultimately, our general social problems.

The approach I am advocating is the bridge to take us from the world we now must live in to the world in which we would like to live. That bridge comes in the shape of curricular reform (primarily undergraduate). Reforming the curriculum would have the ultimate effect of changing our systems of communication and eventually, society.

Why is curricular reform so important to changing women's status and making deep changes in our social system of values? First, our current curricula in journalism and mass communication overwhelmingly support and sustain the status quo. Because media industries and large corporations are such significant financial contributors to our programs and employers of our graduates, the industry tail has been wagging the dog of communication studies for a long time. Our undergraduate curricula are designed, by-and-large, to serve these industry interests. Perhaps this would be a justifiable arrangement if our system of mass media was all that it could be. But it is no news to any of us that mass communication is currently comprised of large, wealthy organizations controlling technologies for the overriding purpose of making a profit. Although journalists, advertisers, and public relations specialists justify their trades in terms of the social and economic good of society, a convincing case has been made by more than one media scholar that the justification of these practices provides a useful political foil for the real business of media business.

Even if making a profit is seen as a harmless by-product of performing social useful functions of providing news and entertainment, should we be satisfied with our current media arrangement? A few industries, a few producers, a few editors, a few spokespeople, speaking to and at the rest of us? Both the structure and content of our media systems preserve an undemocratic process whereby some get to define the world for everyone else. It is here that definitions of *woman, man, Black, Asian, Hispanic* get constructed and displayed in particular ways.[6] It is here that public policy struggles over child care, welfare, pornography, poverty, and unemployment, get played out. We must look to the content of our media systems, not only to see how few women are used as characters in prime-time television or how objectified women are in advertising or pornography, but also to see how our identities and our experiences are defined for us. The solution to oppressive media content cannot simply be "more women characters" or "less exploitation of women's sexuality" or more hard news about women. In fact, we have seen that media industries can take these demands and produce characters, visual images, and news that is no more flattering, useful, unexploitive, or meaningful than it was before, but done in the name of the "new" and "modern" American woman. That is because the basic structure and purpose of the media industries have not changed, and women are not *freely* telling their own stories and experiences with complete access to the media as citizens and not as employees subject to professional and/or employer controls.

Our communication systems *could* provide us forums for discussion and debate, for genuine dialogue rather than monologue, for the sharing of values and rituals originating *from* us, not directed *at* us. They could provide us with a commonly achieved culture and a commonly-arrived-at society. They could provide those of us long without "voice"—that is, the presence and weight of our participation in public discussion—the opportunity to have it. Here I share the sentiments of the Women's Institute for Freedom of the Press Associates' Statement (Allen, 1988, p. 68) that a means of communication must be available to all who need and want it and that changes in our structure of mass communication must come to include the voices of all those who are left out. Our critique, then, of the role of women *in* media industries *must also include* a critique of the media industries themselves.

Do our current curricula place an analysis and critique of the media at its foundation? The answer, if we are honest, is that most do not. We should not be content primarily to be in the business of sending our students— women as well as men—out to continue a system of communication that is undemocratic. We should not be content to encourage our women students to make their way within the industries as the industries currently exist in order to get their individual piece of the career success pie. Why not, instead, encourage them to *transform* the industries for which they work?

The transformation of our media system by means of the curriculum will not be an easy task, but it may have been made easier by the presence of so many women as students of our programs. Since 1977 (white) women have been the majority of students in journalism education, a fact that has been viewed with considerable concern by some. Men faculty and administrators seem most concerned that the status and salaries of journalists and public relations practitioners will decline, given the historic pattern of other occupations associated with women. In fact, it would seem that those concerned about the entrance of a majority of women into our programs and then into media industries are ultimately concerned about what the *presence* of women signals—those values of cooperation and community, for example, that have been so little appreciated and that represent an antithesis to the values of competition and rationality that are deemed essential for good employees and good business. If indeed women represent these values (whether they all actually possess them or not), we can take advantage of this historic turn of events to move toward fundamental social change. Rather than socializing out of our students the feminine values they may bring to our programs, why not give them the tools to put those values to work for a larger social purpose?

I recognize how startling the proposal to make fundamental changes in our curricula is to those—women and men—who are communication professionals and educators. I anticipate objections about making journalism education political in such a way. But why? *Journalism education is already political.* It is already a collection of social practices, politics, and economics that trains certain people into taking up a particular vision of the world (whether they are trained as reporters, advertising media buyers, or public relations practitioners) that enables them to sell their services to large, powerful organizations that exist primarily to make a profit (despite how good individuals and professions may feel about the value of what they do). As a consequence, certain interests are served by our present system of journalism education and our present system of communication. Why not serve other interests? Why not teach our students to serve *all* our interests? Why shouldn't women be the group to show us that our communication systems need major changes? To accept the industries as they are, and in fact to bolster them with the work and talent of our graduates, is already a profoundly political act.

What would this new curriculum look like, a curriculum that took the possibility of social change as seriously as the status quo; a curriculum that was grounded in the values of democracy, cooperation, and community; a curriculum that located any professional skills within a critical and theoretical framework? Would we need a course in copyediting or newspaper management? Advertising copywriting? Public relations campaigns? Or would we decide that media industries ought to train their own employees? That universities should not abdicate their responsibilities for theoretical and critical analysis in exchange for meeting the career demands of their students? The objections that will rise up from industries and administrators at the suggestion of removing such courses would be embarrassing evidence of just how political the curriculum already is.

As a step toward designing a new curriculum, let me describe what I see as essential characteristics of a new curriculum:

1. Ethical

Although most journalism and mass communication programs are committed to the principle of freedom of the press or of speech, I propose that position be abandoned in favor of a new principle, the *right to communicate*. Unlike the principle of freedom of speech, which has been interpreted to mean freedom from *government* restrictions on speech, the principle of the right to communicate is based on the premise that everyone has the right to free and equal *voice*, that is, the presence and weight of our participation in public discussion. Consider whose voices have been protected by the application of the principle of freedom of speech. Now consider whose voices would be unsilenced if the principle of the right to communicate were applied.

Evidence that those with the most power in our society—whites, males, and those with more education and income—gain from a free speech principle while those with the least power—people of color, women, and those with less education and income—would gain from a right to communicate principle can be found in a recent survey conducted for the American Society of Newspaper Editors (Wyatt, 1991). The survey demonstrated that women and African Americans are more fearful of speaking out than men and whites. They are also more likely to favor restrictions on free speech. I would suggest that the "free speech" of people with less power is routinely suppressed by the free speech of those with power through intimidation, violence, lack of opportunity to participate, and the other political and economic restrictions that keep subordinate groups in their places.

It is time for journalism and mass communication programs to take seriously the ethical obligation to support the speaking rights of those whose speech has long been suppressed or ignored.

2. Independent

Many journalism and mass communication programs owe their financial and political existence to special interest groups—media industries, influential politicians and alumni, private and public funding institutions and agencies, and university administrators who are pleased by large enrollments and successful graduates. The effect of these external constituents on the curriculum is overwhelming.

Can we find ways to finance our programs without selling our curricula to the highest bidders? Can we find ways to make our programs attractive to students, administrators, and external constituents without sacrificing our responsibility to be unabashedly and unfearfully theoretical and critical? I think we can. Although we all are familiar with the high student demand for professional communication programs, we have underestimated the extent to which students will be interested in a broader, theoretical context within which skills can be learned as a by-product, not a goal, of the program. As for our university administrators, most of us are familiar with the low status our professional programs enjoy, even if administrators may support our programs because of high student and constituent demand. If we can demonstrate intellectual integrity and rigor in addition to student demand and constituent satisfaction, we will have improved our position in the academy. To satisfy constituents, I suggest we identify our many other constituents besides media industries to whom we should be accountable.

3. Holistic

To construct this new curriculum, we should reconsider how we have conceptualized the study of communication. We have divided up the world into speech, interpersonal, organizational, and mass communication, and further into studies of radio, magazine, television, advertising, and public relations. Is this how people experience the world? Do any of these areas exist in isolation from each other? Instead, let us think about the world from the perspective of people and groups (especially women and other subjugated groups, whose standpoints are usually disregarded) and see what the world of communication looks like.

Understanding how people think about the world and relate to each other is fundamental to understanding how our systems of communication do and could work for us. The study of journalism and mass communication is narrow and incomplete when it tries to isolate itself from the range of human communication activities. Our students need to see the mass media within the larger context of human ritual and human interaction, as part of all human interpretive and political activity. Although we have been correct in grounding our programs in the study of liberal arts in general, we need to work toward the consolidation of our programs with such programs as speech communication, rhetorical studies, telecommunication, and film studies. Then we must design a curriculum to blend these areas into a student's course of study.

4. Inclusive

Any curriculum—but especially one dealing with human communication —ought to study the broadest possible range of people, including women and men of color, white women, and people from other cultures and countries. This will mean more than simply adding a section on women's newspapers and African American newspapers to a mass media history course. Contributions in this book such as those by Susan Henry, Carolyn Stewart Dyer, H. Leslie Steeves, Jane Rhodes, and Marilyn Crafton Smith suggest how we will need to reconsider our frameworks and assumptions to make the curriculum inclusive. While working to transform current courses to accommodate these new points of view, we still will need to offer separate courses, courses on women and communication and African Americans and communication, for example, until we have achieved a totally integrated curriculum and until racism and sexism have been eradicated.

What would a transformed course look like? Imagine just one course, a mass media history course, that gave equal weight to Native Americans, Hispanics, African Americans, and Asian Americans, as well as European Americans; to women of each group as well as men. Imagine the topics that might be covered. What media systems have each group used? For what purposes? What have been the underlying philosophies and goals behind them? How do the media of subordinate groups differ from those of dominate groups? Have women of each group been active participants in creating media for their group or have they had to find alternate forms of communication themselves? How have media been used to exercise or assert the power of a group or change its status? How has the content and the audiences of dominant media affected relations among these groups? These topics barely scratch the surface.

To those who teach media history who may complain there is no time in a semester to teach this material because there is too much to cover already, I would ask them to reconsider the significance of what they are teaching. Alongside the history of media for these many groups, and considered in relation to the media of these groups, the media history of one group, European American men, assumes its proper perspective.[7]

5. Visionary

It has become a cliché to advocate this or that aspect of the curriculum in the name of "preparing students for the 21st century." The disturbing assumption behind this phrase is that the 21st century is somehow waiting in the wings for us, already shaped and predetermined. While we are preparing our students for the 21st century, who is preparing the 21st century? When did universities abdicate their responsibility to provide a critique of the present and a vision for the future? Let's not prepare students to live in the 21st century; let's prepare them to create it.

What would our students need to study about communication if we were looking ahead at the possibilities of the future rather than trying to live up to a standard of the past? They would first need to understand how humans make meaningful worlds to live in, how this has been done in the past, how problems are produced through our definitions and interpretations, how conflicts are produced through our conflicting definitions and interpretations, how humans interact with each and the role of technology in changing those patterns of interaction. They would need to study knowledge and information, what it is, who is believed to have it, and how we believe people come by it. They would need to examine what and how the members of a society need to know, and by whom and how that knowing should be accomplished. After all, that is really what the study and practice of journalism is all about and that is really what our media systems are all about. Ultimately, our subject matter is ontology (the study of how we are) and epistemology (the study of how we know).

Perhaps the features of this new curriculum I have been describing sound impractical if not outrageous. I know from firsthand experience that they are not. The curriculum of the Communication Department at the University of Wisconsin-Parkside embodies most of these characteristics. The curriculum is independent of the financial strings of media industries and funding agencies. It is both holistic and inclusive. Students take a general course of study that includes what others consider speech and interpersonal, organizational, rhetorical, and media studies rather than a specialization. The faculty has agreed that courses should incorporate the theories and experiences of white women, people of color, and other cultures and countries. This integrative approach complements our separate courses on communication and gender, communication and ethnicity (an umbrella course for studying a specific group each time the course is offered), and intercultural communication. One theme of the program is understanding that our conflicts arrive from differing interpretations of reality; that we must look at the power that different groups, cultures, and countries have to force their interpretations on others; that an ethic of dialogue and community is necessary for solving our human problems. Our students learn what can be considered professional communication skills of research and message design and production (verbal, written, and technological) as part of the pedagogical design of these theoretical courses (e.g., through group projects and assignments) with only a select few separate skills courses. They graduate from our program to go into a wide range of jobs, for nonprofit organizations as well as for-profit ones, for alternative media as well as dominant media. Our department enjoys a very good reputation on our campus among students, faculty, and administration as an exciting and intellectually challenging program.

Ours is not the only approach that will produce a curriculum for the future, but it demonstrates that curriculum change can be both possible and practical. If we want to bring about a new world, one built upon those feminine-associated values of community and cooperation rather than the masculine-associated values of individualism and competition, one where women and other subordinated groups have acquired equal consideration and equal voice, we can start in our own programs. When the question is posed, "What do these feminists want?" we will have an answer. We want a bridge in the shape of curriculum reform that will take us and our students from the world we must live in today to the world we want to live in tomorrow.

Notes

1. For more discussion of our gender system, see Lana F. Rakow (1986).

2. This is a simplistic version of a complicated historical process, obviously. Those unfamiliar with this version of our past might wish to refer to Richard Hofstadter (1955a, 1955b), Daniel Boorstin (1974), and Robert Wiebe (1980).

3. There has been a great deal of attention to this historical and contemporary phenomenon by feminist historians and sociologists. See Ann Douglas (1977), Barbara Welter (1976), Rosalind Rosenberg (1975), and Eva Gamarnikow and colleagues (Gamarnikow, Morgan, Purvis, & Taylorson, 1983).

4. I don't mean to romanticize the private sphere, however. Kathy Cirksena has wisely reminded me to point out the pathology of the private sphere that can be obscured by focusing on the positive values with which it is mythologically endowed. The pathology takes such forms as the economic and emotional dependence of women on men, the high incidence of domestic violence, and the expectation that a woman should subordinate her own needs to those of others.

5. This treatment of the subject bears my own, radical feminist, interpretation; other feminist interpretations will vary. For an introduction to one classification system describing different feminist political and philosophical differences, see Jaggar and Rothenberg (1984), though I disagree with their characterization of radical feminism. Jaggar and Rothenberg classify feminists into liberals, radicals, socialists, and women of color.

6. There has been little research on this phenomenon as it relates to people of color, with such interesting exceptions as Tom Nakayama's (1988) work on Asian Americans as model minorities and James Olive Horton's (1986) work on antebellum Black men's construction in newspapers of the ideal Black woman.

7. I have designed and taught such a course as I have described. I would be happy to share my syllabus with anyone who has an interest.

References

Allen, Martha Leslie. (Ed.). (1988). *1988 directory of women's media.* Washington, DC: Women's Institute for Freedom of the Press.
Boorstin, Daniel J. (1974). *The Americans: The democratic experience.* New York: Vintage.
Douglas, Ann. (1977). *The feminization of American culture.* New York: Knopf.
Gamarnikow, Eva, Morgan, David, Purvis, June, & Taylorson, Daphne. (Eds.). (1983). *The public and the private.* London: Heinemann.
Hofstadter, Richard. (1955a). *The age of reform: From Bryan to F.D.R.* New York: Knopf.
Hofstadter, Richard. (1955b). *Social Darwinism in American thought.* Boston: Beacon.
Horton, James Oliver. (1986). Freedom's yoke: Gender conventions among antebellum free Blacks. *Feminist Studies, 12*(1), 51-76.
Jaggar, Alison M., & Rothenberg, Paula S. (1984). *Feminist frameworks: Alternative theoretical accounts of the relations between women and men* (2nd ed.). New York: McGraw-Hill.
Nakayama, Tom. (1988, July). *Foucault, race and contemporary communication studies.* Paper presented to the annual convention of the Association for Education in Journalism and Mass Communication, Portland, OR.
Rakow, Lana F. (1986). Rethinking gender research in communication. *Journal of Communication, 36*(4), 11-26.
Rosenberg, Rosalind. (1975). In search of woman's nature, 1850-1920. *Feminist Studies, 4*(1/2), 141-154.
Welter, Barbara. (1976). *Dimity convictions: The American woman in the nineteenth century.* Athens: Ohio University Press.
Wiebe, Robert H. *The Search for order, 1877-1920.* Westport, CT: Greenwood Press.
Wyatt, Robert O. (1991). *Free expression and the American public.* Murfreesboro: American Society of Newspaper Editors and The Chair of Excellence in First Amendment Studies, Middle Tennessee State University.

Author Index

Editor's Note: I compiled my first index in the 1950s in order to earn my Girl Scout Museum Merit Badge. The document was a private manuscript held by the library of President James A. Garfield in Mentor, Ohio. I was told exactly what to do: index the names of people and the capitalized words. No decisions. No hassles. No consciousness. Today, the politics of indexing are becoming as important to feminists as the politics of language. Dale Spender (1982) wrestled with the ways that "women's ways of classifying and analysing the world have been repeatedly erased" (p. 787) in her index to *Women of Ideas*. Catharine Herr Van Nostrand took a stab at putting together "locator" topics of relevance to women in her index to *Gender-Responsible Leadership*.

We didn't have an index in the first edition of this volume because of space limitations, and I hadn't done an index since my Girl Scout experience. I decided to attempt a collaborative index for this volume that would allow individual authors to have some voice in the way in which their chapters would be indexed. I asked them to generate index entries that they felt were appropriate to their chapters. Most chose to become involved, and several spent considerable time thinking through the appropriate terms and categories for their entries. My job was to compile these varied responses, categorize them to some extent, and to generate a separate author index. (Chapter notes and reference lists were not included in either the Author or Subject Index.)

Subject Index

About the Contributors

R. Dianne Bartlow is currently pursuing a doctorate in communication at the University of California at San Diego. Previously, she was a producer for the KCBS Television 2 *On The Town* program. Her work has been honored by the Academy of Television Arts and Sciences and the NAACP. She is a former faculty member of the Department of Mass Communication at California State University at Hayward.

Maurine H. Beasley, elected president of the Association for Education in Journalism and Mass Communication for 1993-1994, is a Professor of Journalism at the University of Maryland-College Park, where she has been a full-time faculty member since 1975. She is the author/coauthor or editor of seven books, including *Taking Their Place: A Documentary History of Women and Journalism* (1993) with Sheila J. Gibbons. She holds bachelor's degrees in journalism and history from the University of Missouri-Columbia, a master's degree in journalism from Columbia University, and a Ph.D. in American civilization from George Washington University. Her professional experience includes about 13 years of newspaper reporting.

Carolyn Garrett Cline is a Visiting Professor of Journalism at the University of Southern California in Los Angeles where she specializes in public relations and research. One of the original authors of the *Velvet Ghetto* study as well as *Beyond the Velvet Ghetto,* her research interests concern both women's issues and psychological theories. She is currently exploring Jungian psychology as it relates to women in management, specifically applying the Myers-Briggs Type Indicator as a tool to resolve conflict in public relations and business communication management. She practiced public relations for agencies, not-for-profit organizations, and corporations in Boston, Chicago, and Los Angeles. She earned her Ph.D. in Mass Communication from Indiana University, where she also earned an M.A. in Journalism. She holds a B.S. from Boston University.

Judith A. Cramer, Assistant Professor of Communication Arts at Long Island University, Southampton, earned her M.A. in Communication Arts from the University of Hartford in Connecticut. Her B.S. is in Sports Information/Journalism from Keene State College in New Hampshire. She has worked as a news and sports reporter, news director, and talk show host and producer in commercial and public radio in New England and Ohio. She has written several journal articles and is the author of a chapter on women sports journalists in *Women, Media and Sport: Challenging Gender Values,* also published by Sage.

Pamela J. Creedon is an Associate Professor of Journalism at The Ohio State University where she is also a member of the graduate faculty of the Center for Women's Studies at Ohio State. An Accredited Business Communicator since 1988, she earned her M.A. in journalism from the University of Oregon and her B.A. in English from Mount Union College. She joined the OSU faculty in 1984 after a 14-year career in public relations, both in the corporate and non-profit sectors. She is currently editing *Women, Media and Sport: Challenging Gender Values,* also by Sage.

Carolyn Stewart Dyer is an Associate Professor in the School of Journalism and Mass Communication at the University of Iowa where she has also held the positions of head of undergraduate studies and associate director. She earned her Ph.D. in Mass Communication and M.A. in journalism from the University of Wisconsin-Madison and her B.A. in government from Beloit College. She does research on media law and history. In law, she addresses the interaction between the media and legal processes with regard to women's concerns. In history, she focuses on the business of publishing frontier newspapers before the Civil War. She has been involved in the feminist and antirape movement for more than a decade.

Virginia T. Escalante is on leave from the University of Arizona where she is an Assistant Professor of Journalism. She is the instructor for a bilingual community newspaper produced by journalism students, and her work focuses on training future journalists to cover minority communities. Previously, she was a reporter for the *Los Angeles Times* where she was a member of a 1984 Pulitzer Prize-winning team. She is currently pursuing a doctorate in communication at the University of California at San Diego.

Eric S. Fredin is an Associate Professor of Journalism at The Ohio State University. He earned his Ph.D. from the University of Michigan in Mass Communication and his B.A. in English from Oberlin College. He worked as a newspaper reporter in Michigan for several years. His recent research has focused on newspaper story organization and the value of quotations and background information, the knowledge gap, and the role of media images in election coverage.

Marilyn E. Gist, Associate Professor of Management and Organization in the School of Business Administration at the University of Washington, earned her M.B.A. and Ph.D. from the University of Maryland in Business Administration, both with concentrations in organizational behavior and research methodology. She is a widely published scholar in psychology and management journals, and her research interests center on the study of self-regulatory factors in training and performance. Her background includes several years' experience as a manager in both the public and private sectors. In addition, she has served as a consultant or trainer in the areas of performance motivation, career development, managing cultural diversity, and organizational assessment and development.

Larissa A. Grunig, Associate Professor in the College of Journalism at the University of Maryland, College Park, received her doctorate also from UMCP in Public Communication. Her research interests center on development communication, public relations, communication theory, gender issues in journalism, organizational response to activism, organizational power and structure, and scientific and technical writing. Her professional experience includes newspaper reporting and editing in Colorado and more than 20 years of public relations consulting throughout the country. She has written more than 100 articles, book chapters, monographs, reviews, and conference papers. She is coeditor of the new *Journal of Public Relations Research.*

Susan Henry is a Professor of Journalism at California State University at Northridge. She earned her Ph.D. in Communications from Syracuse University. She completed her M.S. in journalism from the University of Illinois and her bachelor's degree from the University of Connecticut. She has published widely in the area of women's history, and edited *Journalism History* from 1985 to 1991. She also coordinated the work of the Task Force on Sexual Harassment at Northridge that published numerous first-of-a-kind materials and brochures on sexual harassment.

Sammye Johnson is a Professor in the Communication Department at Trinity University in San Antonio. She worked for 10 years as a magazine editor and writer in San Antonio and Chicago, earning 16 national, regional, and local awards for writing, editing, and design. She earned her B.S. and M.S. degrees in magazine journalism from Northwestern University's Medill School of Journalism. She continues to be an active free-lance writer and editor, publishing more than 200 articles since 1980. She also conducts research in magazine content and history, which has been published in various communication journals.

Alice Gagnard Kendrick is an Associate Professor in Advertising at the Center for Communication Arts, Southern Methodist University. She holds a Ph.D. degree in Communications from the University of Tennessee and a B.A. and M.A. degree in journalism from Louisiana State University.

Gerald M. Kosicki, an Associate Professor of Journalism at The Ohio State University, earned his Ph.D. in Mass Communications from the University of Wisconsin-Madison. He earned his M.A. in journalism from Ohio State and his bachelor's degree in communication from John Carroll. He worked for five years as a daily newspaper reporter and assistant city editor. He has authored numerous journal articles and book chapters on political communication and media effects. He is co-director of the Ohio state annual national surveys of journalism enrollments and journalism graduates.

Sue A. Lafky is an Assistant Professor in the School of Journalism and Mass Communication at the University of Iowa. She earned her bachelor's degree at the University of Oregon and her master's degree and Ph.D. from Indiana University. She has worked at newspapers in Oregon and Indiana, is a founding member of the Feminist Teacher Editorial Collective, and previously taught at Temple University. She served as chair of the Commission on the Status of Women for the Association for Education in Journalism and Mass Communication in 1992-1993.

Linda Lazier is an independent marketing communications consultant in Indianapolis. A former advertising faculty member at The Ohio State and Indiana universities, she earned her Ph.D. in Mass Communication with a minor in Women's Studies from Indiana University. Her M.A. and B.A., both in journalism, are from Ball State University. She teaches part time for Indiana University/Indianapolis and for Ball State's Indianapolis graduate communications program.

John R. McClelland is an Associate Professor of Journalism at Roosevelt University in Chicago. He has worked as a photographer, reporter, political writer, copy editor, feature editor, city editor, and managing editor of weekly and medium-sized daily newspapers in Illinois, Arkansas, and Tennessee. He earned his M.A. in journalism from The Ohio State University and his bachelor's degree in communication at the University of Illinois in Urbana. He has also taught at Miami University of Ohio.

Carroll Ann Ferguson Nardone completed her master's degree in journalism from The Ohio State University and then joined the mass communication faculty at El Paso Community College in Texas.

Lana F. Rakow is Associate Vice Chancellor for Undergraduate Studies and Associate Professor of Communication at the University of Wisconsin-Parkside. Prior to her current administrative position, she was chair of the Communication Department at UW-Parkside. She is a feminist scholar interested in issues concerning women's and men's talk, theories of gender, and the construction of gender in and through technology. Her books include the *Revolution in Words: Writing Women 1868-1871* (edited with Cheris Kramarae), *Gender on the Line: Women, the Telephone, and Community Life,* and *Women Making Meaning: New Feminist Directions in Communication Research* (an edited volume). As an administrator, she is also interested in curricular reform and organizational change.

Jane Rhodes is an Assistant Professor in the School of Journalism at Indiana University. Her doctorate, from the University of North Carolina at Chapel Hill, is an historical study of Mary Ann Shadd Cary, the first African American woman newspaper editor and publisher in North America. She earned her M.A. and B.S. degrees from Syracuse University and has written extensively on African American woman as communicators and media subjects.

Marlene Sanders is a Visiting Professor of Journalism at New York University, and program director of "Women, Men & Media," founded by Betty Friedan. The first woman to anchor an evening network newscast, the first newswoman to cover the Vietnam War, and the first woman to be named a network news vice president, she worked in television news for more than 35 years. Until 1991, she hosted a weekly public affairs program at WNET TV in New York City. Prior to that she was a news correspondent and award-winning documentary producer for CBS News for 10 years and ABC News for 12 years.

Conrad Smith is an Associate Professor at The Ohio State University. He is the author of *Media & Apocalypse,* a book about journalists' professional values as reflected in disaster reporting. He received his bachelor's degree in physics and his master's degree in photography and cinema from Ohio State. He received his doctorate from Temple University.

Marilyn Crafton Smith is an Associate Professor in the Department of Art at Appalachian State University where she teaches graphic design, visual communication, and feminist and multicultural perspectives in art and media criticism. She has a Ph.D. in Mass Communication from the University of Iowa. Her dissertation examined discourses of conservatism and feminism in relation to contested meanings of family on prime-time television. In addition to feminist media, her research interests include feminist theory and critical approaches to visual culture and mass communication.

H. Leslie Steeves is an Associate Professor in the School of Journalism and Communication at the University of Oregon. She has published many articles related to gender and communication. Her present work examines international, development communication theories and strategies from a feminist perspective. She is most interested in the context of Africa. In 1991 she lived in Kenya and taught at the University of Nairobi on a Fulbright grant. Her master's degree in agricultural journalism and doctorate in mass communication are from the University of Wisconsin-Madison. She has a bachelor's degree in forestry from the University of Vermont.

Linda Steiner is an Assistant Professor in the Department of Journalism and Mass Media at Rutgers University. Her major research interests are the feminist mass media, especially the American women's suffrage newspapers of the 19th and 20th centuries; and the applications of feminist theorizing to the development of a critique of journalism institutions, journalism conventions, and journalism ethics. She has published articles in a number of communication journals and has authored several book chapters, as well as a *Journalism Monograph*. Her Ph.D. is from the University of Illinois at Urbana.

Elizabeth L. Toth is an Associate Professor and Chair of the Public Relations Department at Syracuse University's S. I. Newhouse School of Public Communications. She has authored more than 25 articles and papers, and is coauthor of *The Velvet Ghetto* and *Beyond the Velvet Ghetto,* benchmark research reports on the impact of the increasing percentage of women entering public relations. She co-edited an award-winning book, *Rhetorical and Critical Approaches to Communication*. Her master's degree and Ph.D. in Communication are from Purdue University. She has a B.S. in speech from Northwestern University and spent 9 years in government public relations in North Carolina.

Olga A. Vásquez is an Assistant Professor in the Department of Communication at the University of California at San Diego. As an anthropologist of education, her areas of research are literacy, language, and culture with a special emphasis on minority populations. Her published works include a coauthored manuscript, *Pushing Boundaries: Language in a Mexicano Community,* "Language as a Resource: Lessons from 'La Clase Magica,' " in the *92nd Yearbook of the National Society for the Study of Education,* and a short biography of Mari Luci Jaramillo, to be featured in *50 Women in American Education.*

K. Viswanath, an Assistant Professor of Journalism at The Ohio State University, earned his Ph.D. and M.A. in Mass Communication from the University of Minnesota. He also hold master's and bachelor's degrees in communication and journalism from Osmania University in Hyderabad, India, and a honor's degree in science (chemisty and biochemistry) from New Science College in Hyderabad. His research interests include macro-social aproaches to the study of mass communication, and mass media and social change.